Feed-Forward

Feed-Forward: On the Future of Twenty-First-Century Media

Mark B. N. Hansen

The University of Chicago Press :: Chicago and London

Mark B. N. Hansen is professor of literature and media arts and sciences at
Duke University.

The University of Chicago Press, Chicago 60637
The University of Chicago Press, Ltd., London

24 23 22 21 20 19 18 17 16 15   1 2 3 4 5

ISBN-13: 978-0-226-19969-6 (cloth)
ISBN-13: 978-0-226-19972-6 (paper)
ISBN-13: 978-0-226-19986-3 (e-book)
DOI: 10.7208/chicago/9780226199863.001.0001

Library of Congress Cataloging-in-Publication Data

Hansen, Mark B. N. (Mark Boris Nicola), 1965– author.
 Feed-forward: on the future of twenty-first-century media / Mark B. N.
Hansen.
     pages cm
 Includes bibliographical references and index.
 ISBN 978-0-226-19969-6 (cloth: alkaline paper) — ISBN 978-0-226-19972-6
(paperback: alkaline paper) — ISBN 978-0-226-19986-3 (e-book) 1. Digital
media—Philosophy. 2. Technology—Philosophy. 3. Experience. 4. Whitehead,
Alfred North, 1861–1947. I. Title.
 B54.H36 2015
 302.23′10112—dc23   2014025657

To Mimi

Contents

Preface

This book has been a long time in the making and is the result of a process of intellectual development that has taken me from the study of the legacy of phenomenology, and specifically the endgame of Edmund Husserl's late manuscripts on time and time-consciousness, to the philosophy of organism of British philosopher Alfred North Whitehead. A large part of my effort in *Feed-Forward* is precisely to effectuate a certain coming-together of Whitehead's speculative empiricism with late Husserlian phenomenology, including its exciting extensions in the work of Eugen Fink and Jan Patočka. If this means that I seek to develop a speculative phenomenology on the basis of Whitehead's genuinely strange conviction that the metaphysical structure of reality has to remain de jure inaccessible to direct experience, my work here owes a great deal to the generosity Whitehead accords entities following his conception of the solidarity of the actual universe at every given moment in its ongoing process. For Whitehead, experiential entities, or what he calls "societies," are composed of assemblages of other entities that they do not so much subsume as "host."

As a result of my five years of wrestling with Whitehead, I have come to appreciate how his categorical separation of the speculative from the experiential goes hand in hand with the refreshing, if peculiar, *environmental* status he accords evental agency. Speculative actual entities are available for participation in multiple experiential entities precisely because their genesis remains autonomous from their experiential power. We could say that Whitehead's segregation of concrescing actualities holds the key to understanding how societies or events can cohere while remaining composed of elements they do not synthesize or otherwise assimilate into some narrowly construed subjectivity proper to them.

This motif of the subject as host for the "superjective" operation of "alien" elements informs Whitehead's own self-inscription within the history of Western philosophy. In *Science and the Modern World*, Whitehead positions his precursor William James as the inaugurator of a new period in philosophy. And in his own reckoning with James's startling claim that "consciousness doesn't exist," Whitehead positions himself as James's successor, the one who can make good on James's insight. For if James "does not unambiguously explain what he means by the notion of an entity" and cannot for that reason account for the distinction between consciousness as "entity" and as "function," no such shortcoming afflicts Whitehead's philosophy.[1] Indeed, Whitehead's entire speculative scheme is predicated precisely on the notion that consciousness *is* the function of hosting, that consciousness itself is nothing other than the hosting of other entities that act through it:

> But that part of the bodily event, in respect to which the cognitive mentality is associated, is for itself the unit psychological field. Its ingredients are not referent to the event itself; they are aspects of what lies beyond the event. Thus the self-knowledge inherent in the bodily event is the knowledge of itself as a complex unity, whose ingredients involve all reality beyond itself, restricted under the limitation of its pattern of aspects. Thus we know ourselves as a function of unification of a plurality of things *which are other than ourselves.* Cognition discloses an event as being an activity, organising a real togetherness *of alien things.*[2]

Whitehead can then agree with James that consciousness is a function, while also retaining the category of entity now understood not as a substance but as that alien, "superjective" power operating *through* the "subject": "Accordingly," Whitehead continues the above passage, "consciousness will be a function of knowing," here following James to the letter. "But," he then abruptly interjects, "what is known is already a prehension of aspects of the one real universe. These aspects are aspects *of other events as mutually modifying*, each the others."[3]

Whitehead's frankness about the operation of alien elements in consciousness helps us to understand the curious informality and openness of his at first glance forebodingly formal metaphysical scheme. And it also offers a model of intellectual exchange that occupies the opposite pole from the kinds of critical appropriation that continue to reign supreme in much knowledge production in the humanities, especially in areas where theory occupies center stage. In his readings of philosophers from the tradition, James but also Descartes, Locke, Hume, and even Kant, Whitehead is never interested in criticism for its own sake. Rather when he does criticize, he does so almost exclusively as a way of strengthening their positions, of showing how they inaugurated modes of thinking that they themselves lacked the perspective to follow to their culmination.

Though I do not think I can lay claim to any similar generosity with the scholars I host in *Feed-Forward*, I do attribute to the spirit of this generosity some of what it took to find a meeting ground between the late phenomenological project of Husserl and Whitehead's radically environmental account of agency. Despite their stark opposition from a methodological perspective, phenomenology and speculative empiricism converge in their interest in how the force of the settled world itself gives rise to process, continuously and mundanely, and in how this same force furnishes the source for the creativity and intensity of experience at all levels. I don't think I could have come to this conclusion without some capacity to let these two intellectual archives simply resonate through one another beyond the terms of any imaginable synthesis.

At a more local, though certainly no less fundamental, level, I hope that some similar generosity and openness is at play in the manifold intellectual exchanges I have had—with colleagues, audiences, students, collaborators, reviewers, artists, and others—over the years of gestation of my project. More than anything else, it is these exchanges, in person and in writing, that have spoken through me during the writing of the book and that, I sincerely hope, now shine through what I have written.

Though I didn't start to read Whitehead in earnest until 2008 or 2009, I had followed with avid interest the attention paid to him at the annual Society for Literature and Science (now Society for Literature, Science, and the Arts) conferences, which for a series of years featured panel streams devoted to the philosopher. I owe a debt to all of the participants in these events and especially to the organizer of many of them, Steven Meyer. When I did finally get around to reading Whitehead, I did so in the context of my interest in the phenomenological problem of protention on which I had focused while doing research as a Fulbright Research Scholar in Beijing, China, from 2006 to 2007. This produced the very first iteration of my book, a lecture I delivered at ForArt: Institute for Research Within International Contemporary Art, at Oslo University. I want to thank audiences there, as well as my host Ina Blom, for the opportunity to share my work in its earliest, still quite inchoate form.

This initial presentation was followed by a series of lectures at various venues, including the Clark Art Institute in Williamstown, Massachusetts; the Columbia University Faculty Workshop on Media Studies; the transmediale festival in Berlin, Germany; the Center for Advanced Media Studies at Johns Hopkins University; the Program in Arts and Technology at the University of Dallas; the Department of Media Studies at the University of Copenhagen; the Faculty of Aesthetics at Aarhus University in Denmark; the Henkle Memorial Lecture for the Department of Modern Culture and Media at Brown University; the Center for 21st Century Studies at the University of Wisconsin–Milwaukee; the Department of American Studies at Leibniz University of Hannover, Germany; the Camden Philosophical Society in Camden, Maine; the School of Film and TV at Shanghai University; the School of Architecture at Syracuse University; the Department of Media Studies at Ruhr University of Bochum, Germany; the University of Maryland; the University of the Arts in Cologne, Germany; the Department of American Studies at the Goethe University of Frankfurt, Germany; the Internationale Kolleg für Kulturtechnikforschung und Medienphilosophie (IKKM) at the Bauhaus University, Weimar, Germany; the John Fekete Inaugural Lecture at Trent University, Canada; the Interdisciplinary Graduate Program at Princeton University; Hexagram at Concordia University; and the Hebrew University of Jerusalem.

I wish to thank everyone in attendance at these events and especially my hosts: Stephan Andriopoulos, Brian Larkin, Bernadette Wegenstein, Charissa Terranova, Ulrik Ekman, Lotte Philipsen, Mette-Marie Sørenson, Morten Kyndrup, Mary-Ann Doane, Richard Grusin, Shane Denson, Shaoyi Sun, Mark Lindner, Erich Hörl, Marie-Luise Angerer, Bernd Herzogenrath, Lorenz Engell, Bernhard Siegert, Victoria Dezwaan, John Fekete, Jeff Dolven, Chris Salter, and Hava Aldouby. I also wish to thank the Fulbright Commission for supporting my year in China as well as a short-term visit to Hannover, Germany, and the IKKM for supporting my stay in Weimar, Germany.

Beyond these more formal occasions for hosting the thought of others, I have had innumerable exchanges with colleagues and friends, all of which have influenced the development of my thinking in ways I can't even begin to understand: Bruno Clarke, Cary Wolfe, Wu Hung, Miao Xiao Chun, Wu Wenguang, Jussi Parikka, Wolfgang Ernst, Antoine Hennione, Christa Blümlinger, Michael Cuntz, Astrid Deuber-Mankowsky, Tom Mitchell, Tom

Gunning, Bill Connolly, David Rodowick, Bill Brown, Jim Chandler, Lauren Berlant, Beth Helsinger, Debbie Nelson, Didier Debaise, Steven Shaviro, Brian Massumi, Erin Manning, Luciana Parisi, Ian Bogost, Tim Morton, Judith Jones, Ralph Pred, Patricia Clough, Brigid Doherty, Tom Levin, Eduardo Cadava, Noam Elcott, Scott Richmond, Sam Weber, Bernard Stiegler, Warren Neidich, Lone Koefoed Hansen, Rafael Lozano-Hemmer, Vittorio Gallese, Ludovica Lumer, Joshua Kates, Daniel Stout, Jason Potts, Lynn Kirby, Malcolm Legrice, and Ori Gerscht. I wish to remember my former colleague Miriam Hansen, who showed me the bar for critical rigor.

I also owe a considerable, if less easily identifiable and more diffuse, debt to those closer at hand, my colleagues at Duke, especially Kate Hayles, Tim Lenoir, Barbara Herrnstein Smith, Michael Hardt, Rey Chow, Fred Jameson, Susan Willis, Anne Garetta, Toril Moi, Owen Flanagan, Mark Olson, Nancy Armstrong, Rob Mitchell, Scott Lindroth, Bill Seaman, Hans von Miegroet, Ian Baucom, and Srinivas Aravamudan. I can't imagine a more hospitable and energizing place to work, teach, and think.

I want especially to thank all of my students whose considerable influence on me is complicated—though only in good ways—by their own development and the becoming-superjective to which it subjects my thinking. Thanks to the members of *s-1: Speculative Lab*: Zach Blas, Pinar Yoldas, Michael Tauschinger-Dempsey, Yair Rubenstein, Amanda Starling Gould, Patrick Lemieux, Nicholas Pilarski, Luke Caldwell, Max Symuleski, Libi Striegl, and David Rambo (plus my fantastic colleague Mark Olson); and thanks to all the students in my seminars at Duke, especially (in addition to the above) Jung Choi, Marie-Pier Boucher, China Medel, Jessica Jones, Clarissa Lee, Nyuol Tong, Alex Monea, Melody Jue, Bobo Bose-Kolanu, Jenny Rhee, and Abe Geil; as well as to students from before: Michelle Menzies, Shane Denson, Bernie Geoghegan, and Jim Hodge. You all are the future.

I want to thank Jussi Parikka and Steven Shaviro for their truly Whiteheadian generosity as readers of a manuscript with which I know (and I hope) they are eager to argue. Let me also thank my editor, Alan Thomas, for all of his encouragement over the years, as well as my copy editor, Jennifer Rappaport, and the entire team at the University of Chicago Press.

I wish to thank Ulrik Ekman and Erich Hörl for the many conversations that have challenged my assumptions and more than once helped me overcome my own doubts. Let me also thank Kate Hayles and Tim Lenoir for their quiet support and constant influx of new ideas. And let me extend a special note of gratitude to Tom Mitchell, whose encouraging skepticism continues to keep me in line, even from a distance.

Finally let me thank those whose influence is most dispersed and atomic as well as most pronounced: my parents, Yvonne and Howard Hansen; my sister, Natalie Hansen; my children, Wilson, Michael, and Sophie; and my wife, Mimi Lukens.

Mimi, I dedicate this exploration to you.

Introduction: Whitehead as Media Theorist?

Philosophy is the self-correction by consciousness of its own initial excess of subjectivity. Each actual occasion contributes to the circumstances of its origin additional formative elements deepening its own peculiar individuality. Consciousness is only the last and greatest of such elements by which the selective character of the individual obscures the external totality from which it originates and which it embodies. An actual individual, of such a higher grade, has truck with the totality of things by reason of its sheer actuality; but it has attained its individual depth of being by a selective emphasis limited to its own purposes. The task of philosophy is to recover the totality obscured by this selection. It replaces in rational experience what has been submerged in the higher sensitive experience and has been sunk yet deeper by the initial operations of consciousness itself.　　**Alfred North Whitehead, *Process and Reality***

The Elemental

In their effort to shift the focus of media theory to the figure of the network, Alex Galloway and Eugene Thacker coin a new term: the "elemental." Networks, they say,

> are elemental, in the sense that their dynamics operate at levels "above" and "below" that of the human subject. The elemental is this ambient aspect of networks, this environmental aspect— all the things that we as individuated human subjects or groups do not directly control or manipulate. The elemental is not "the natural," however (a concept that we do not understand). The elemental concerns the variables and variability of scaling, from

the micro level to the macro, the ways in which a network phenomenon can suddenly contract, with the most local action becoming a
global pattern, and vice versa. The elemental requires us to elabo-
rate an entire climatology of thought.[1]

Appearing on the final page of *The Exploit*, this call for a climatology of
thought and, more generally, for an "elemental" approach to media, perfectly summarizes the contribution of Galloway and Thacker's argument.
Life in twenty-first-century media networks reveals something that has
perhaps always been the case, but that has never been so insistently manifest: agency is *resolutely not* the prerogative of privileged individual actors.
Whether taken individually or as nodes in a network, agency must be re-
conceptualized in a fundamental way. Specifically, we must rethink agency
as the effect of global patterns of activity across scales in networks, where
absolutely no privilege is given to any particular individual or node, to any
level or degree of complexity.

To address this imperative, Galloway and Thacker suggest that we define
networks in terms of "edges." They also insist on the "unhuman" aspects
of networks and suggest that "our understanding of networks is *all-too-
human*." As they see it, the dominant coupling of an individualist perspective on action and the privilege of the human as hermeneutic agent causes
us to overlook the actual functioning of networks and to neglect the radical
dispersal and distribution of agency that occur in networks.

I accept the spirit of this position without embracing it to the letter.
Against Galloway and Thacker's blanket dismissal of the "human" as such
(as if there were such a thing), I want to stress the need for a fundamental rethinking of the human and of human experience as a non-optional complement to the new figure of the network. Such a rethinking will require us to
abandon the all-too-facile opposition of the human and the unhuman, and
to theorize the human—and all forms of agency that can be predicated of
the human—in relation to the elemental, indeed, *as part of the elemental*.
To grasp the place of the human within today's media networks, and to
appreciate how these networks actualize a properly *elemental* conception
of the human, we must adopt a *radically environmental perspective* encompassing human activity as one element among others: such a perspective
views human agency just as it does any other type of agency, namely, as
internally differentiated, dispersed across various scales and operational divisions, and implicated in and immanent to a total, multi-scalar cosmological situation. Far from being an autonomous source of power somehow cut
off from the rest of the environment—from the elemental—human agency
operates *as a configuration of the elemental*. Like other forms of agency, it

emerges within larger configurations of the elemental, which are not distinct in kind from other, formally homologous configuration(s).

One crucial corollary of such a radical environmental perspective is a fundamental generalization and reconceptualization of subjectivity. Indeed, reconceptualizing the human as part of the elemental has radical consequences for how we theorize both media and subjectivity. To be precise, such reconceptualizing implicates subjectivity—though perhaps not "subject-centered" subjectivity—in the very functioning of twenty-first-century or "atmospheric" media. Exemplified by networks, atmospheric media operate through the radical technical distribution and multi-scalar dispersal of agency. Yet to grasp how networks technically distribute and disperse agency, we must retain some role for subjective experience, and, thus, as I shall argue, some role for phenomenology (albeit in a reformed, post-Husserlian instantiation).

This imperative will require a more specific supplementation of Galloway and Thacker's position. For if Galloway and Thacker take the important step of rejecting the object as the privileged focus of media theorization—and this goes far toward explaining the contemporary appeal of their work—they fail to recognize the corollary imperative to reconceptualize subjectivity: what is required—and what I shall attempt to develop here—is an account of subjectivity that does more than simply mirror the dispersed and multi-scalar operation of networks. Simply put: subjectivity must be conceptualized *as intrinsic to the sensory affordances that inhere in today's networks and media environments.* In our interactions with twenty-first-century atmospheric media, we can no longer conceive of ourselves as separate and quasi-autonomous subjects, facing off against distinct media objects; rather, we are ourselves composed as subjects through the operation of a host of multi-scalar processes, some of which seem more "embodied" (like neural processing), and others more "enworlded" (like rhythmic synchronization with material events). In today's media environments, that is, subjectivity is neither set off against a (media) object world, nor different in kind from the microprocesses that inform it. It is, rather, a certain organization—what philosopher Alfred North Whitehead calls a "society"—of other, more elemental processes, *all of which are subjective in their own right.*

Twenty-First Century Media

My aim in using the rubric "twenty-first-century media" is to specify what makes the new forms of media prevalent in our world today different in substantive ways from their predecessors. Encompassing everything from social media and data-mining to passive sensing and environmental microsensors, twenty-first-century media designate media following their shift from a past-directed recording platform to a data-driven anticipation of the future.

Readers familiar with my previous work will know that I have for some time been interested in exploring how the advent of the digital computer as the general platform for media interrupts the circuits linking media and experience: specifically, given that computational processes occur at time frames well below the thresholds constitutive of human perceptual experience, they seem to introduce levels of operationality that impact our experience without yielding any perceptual correlate.

While this situation remained relatively benign so long as it directed our focus to machine-generated photographs or the material specificity of hypertext fictions, it has become markedly less benign over the past decade as Google has consolidated its monopoly over Internet searching and data aggregation, in the process perfecting a system for extracting data-value from our every web search; as Facebook has consolidated its monopoly over sociality on the Internet, in the process perfecting a system for extracting consumer profiles ripe for delivery to advertisers; and in general, as today's media industries have honed methods for mining data about our behavior that feature as their key element the complete bypassing of consciousness, the direct targeting of what I shall call the "operational present" of sensibility.

To address the challenges posed by these developments, we must face them head-on. This task will require us to utilize the affordances of the very technologies that are responsible for marginalizing our sensory experience. And to do this, we will need to find ways of deploying the very operations of data-gathering and computational sensing most responsible for marginalizing consciousness in the service of a fundamental reengineering of sensory existence. Such a reengineering is explicitly "pharmacological" in the sense lent the term by Jacques Derrida and Bernard Stiegler.[2] Like writing—the originary media technology—twenty-first-century media involve the simultaneous amputation of a hitherto internal faculty (interior memory) and its supplementation by an external technology (artifactual memory). And yet, in contrast to writing and all other media technologies up to the present, twenty-first-century media—and specifically the reengineering of sensibility they facilitate—mark the culmination of a certain human mastery over media. In one sense, this constitutes the specificity of twenty-first-century media. For if twenty-first-century media open up an expanded domain of sensibility that can enhance human experience, they also impose a new form of *resolutely non-prosthetic* technical mediation: simply put, to access this domain of sensibility, humans must rely on technologies to perform operations to which they have absolutely no direct access whatsoever and that correlate to no already existent human faculty or capacity. That is why pharmacology, as it obtains in relation to twenty-first-century media, calls for a radical reengineering of human experience that welcomes the assistance of computational data-gathering and analysis, and embraces the qualified yet undeniable demotion of certain aspects of human experience—sense perception and consciousness—that it brings with it. This loss of agential human powers can only be recompensed by the expanded sensory contact with "worldly sensibility" that twenty-first-century media make possible. Exploring contemporary opportunities for such pharmacological recompense—for expanded sensory contact with the world—constitutes the main investment of my study.

Environmental Subjectivity, or the Reformed Subjective Principle

In order to develop the theoretical resources necessary for describing this pharmacological reengineering of human experience, I will turn repeatedly to the process philosophy of the early twentieth-century philosopher Alfred North Whitehead. For my purposes, Whitehead's most important contribution is his articulation of an ontology of becoming that is neutral in relation to the human-nonhuman divide, even as it aims ultimately to explain human experience. For this very reason, Whitehead's philosophy furnishes a foundation upon which we can theorize the reengineering of human experience as a positive development: specifically, Whitehead's perspective helps us see how the shift catalyzed by twenty-first-century media—the shift from agent-centered perception to environmental sensibility—yields an enhanced human contact with worldly sensibility.

At the core of my interest in Whitehead is a very important claim about human experience in relation to a larger domain of experience—what I am calling, with emphatically purposeful reference to the phenomenological tradition, "worldly sensibility." Because this is a claim that will reappear many times in this study, let me give it a name—the claim about access to data of sensibility (CADS)—and let me try to explain it more fully. Put in the form of a thesis, CADS can be stated as follows: Human experience is currently undergoing a fundamental transformation caused by the complex entanglement of humans within networks of media technologies that operate predominantly, if not almost entirely, outside the scope of human modes of awareness (consciousness, attention, sense perception, etc.). I have already described and shall continue to describe this transformation as a shift in the economy between human-addressed media and twenty-first-century media. (By human-addressed media, I mean media that correlate *directly* to human modes of sensory experience and cognitive processing; by twenty-first-century media, though of course this remains to be demonstrated, I mean media that are only *indirectly* correlated to human modes of experience, or, to put it in the more precise conceptual framing I shall develop more fully below, media that involve technical operations to which humans lack any direct access.) The idea, then, is that human experience is undergoing change caused by our entanglement within contemporary media environments, and that the directionality of this transformation inverts the long-standing privilege held by humans as the well-nigh unique addressee of media.

I do not, by any means, want to say that twenty-first-century media dispense with human experience, as so many recent and contemporary media theorists have said; rather, I want to suggest that today's media indispensably involve human experience, but that the avenue of their impact on human experience and of their implication of humans within their operationality has shifted from a direct to an indirect modality. Put otherwise, I want to claim that media impact the general sensibility of the world prior to and as a condition for impacting human experience. This situation is both revealed to us *and* intensified by the computational technologies constituting twenty-first-century media, and this peculiar combination of revelation and intensification allows us to be quite specific about the agency of twenty-first-century media: *at one and the same time*, twenty-first-century media *broker human access to* a domain of sensibility that has remained largely invisible (though certainly not inoperative) until now, *and*, it *adds to* this domain of sensibility since every individual act of access is itself a new datum of sensation that will expand the world incrementally but in a way that intensifies worldly sensibility.

I shall in what follows refer to this particular feature of twenty-first-century media as their inherent or constitutive *doubleness*: their simultaneous, double operation as both a mode of access onto a domain of worldly sensibility and a contribution to that domain of sensibility. Although there are certainly anticipations of this particular feature (including some that I will discuss below, for example, Étienne-Jules Marey's chronophotographic practice, Hermann Helmholtz's braintime experiments, and photography following Vilém Flusser's account of how the photographic apparatus integrates its user into its technicity), what is relatively singular about the constitutive doubleness of twenty-first-century media—and what justifies my designation of twenty-first-century media as marking a certain, though certainly non-absolute, break with past media systems—is their sheer ubiquity: we now live in a world where the very media that give us access to events outside the scope of our conscious attention and perception—what I shall call "the operational present of sensibility"—are now typically events that simultaneously contribute to the growth of this very domain of sensibility. I shall consequently specify the constitutive doubleness of twenty-first-century media as their capacity for the "data-propagation of sensibility," the fact that data *about* sensibility is simultaneously data *of* sensibility.

With this formulation, the relation between twenty-first-century media and the philosophical project of phenomenology—a relation that will feature centrally in this study—comes to the fore in a particularly acute manner. For the doubleness of twenty-first-century media marks a certain advance in relation to debates concerning intentionality that has profound consequences for the latter's historical correlation with consciousness. To the extent that they centrally involve data processing, twenty-first-century media bring together an intentional relationship to sensibility (the fact that data is *about* sensibility) with a nonintentional relationship to sensibility (the fact that data *is* sensibility). Without getting bogged down in debates that feature precisely this relationship between the intentional and the non-intentional, whether these be within the originary discussions of Husserl's *Logical Investigations*, or between Bergson and Husserl, Raymond Ruyer and Husserl, or Deleuze and Husserl,[3] let us specify that what is important here is the way that the doubleness of twenty-first-century media, insofar as they involve an "aboutness" *and* a "just being," combine in one technical operation what cannot be so combined in the operation of consciousness.

This difference encapsulates the advantages of a technical, as opposed to a conscious, presentification of the data of sensibility as I shall develop it in this study. Specifically, a technical presentification of such data is *about* that data (it presentifies it for being capable of receiving such a presentification—proximately a computer, mediately, the contemporary human consciousnesses to which it is, as I shall put it, fed-forward), but it is also, in turn, data in its own right, data that will support a further act of presentification. What, in the philosophical tradition, is a radical opposition between two modes of consciousness's Being (intentional or "absolute," to use Ruyer's term) becomes, in and through the operationality of twenty-first-century media, a functional, and as we will see, a processual, relationship. With this functionalization, moreover, the relationship between aboutness and being, between data as access to sensibility and data as sensibility, undergoes a certain reconceptualization through its anchoring in temporalization: aboutness is linked to being in an incessant oscillation, where each act of access onto sensibility creates a new unit of sensibility that itself calls forth a new act of access that creates a new unit of sensibility, and so on, as Whitehead would put it, until the "crack of doom."[4]

Without belaboring this account of the specificity of twenty-first-century media, an account that will concern us throughout this study, let me simply mention here how this essential doubleness, this technical functionalization of the philosophical opposition of aboutness and being, holds the key to the value of the philosophical account that will concern me most centrally, namely, Whitehead's process philosophy; how it anticipates the shift from what Whitehead calls "symbolic reference" (the referral of sense perception or presentification to its causal source in the "withness of the body") to what I call "machinic reference" (the capacity of data to presentify the very relation between access to and production of sensibility, between aboutness and being); and finally, how it thus furnishes to consciousness, in the form of feed-forward circuits, some indirect presentification of the operationality of sensibility, of the worldly process that, despite being the source for consciousness's being, remains fundamentally opaque to its intentional grasping.

Beyond simply describing the essential doubleness and the ensuing data propagation of sensibility, however, my aim here is to take stock of the historical impact of the media revolution that it fuels. As I see it, twenty-first-century media catalyze a shift in the economy of experience itself, a shift from a media system that addresses humans first and foremost to a system that registers the environmentality of the world itself, prior to, and without any necessary relation with, human affairs. On this score, what I am calling the "data propagation of sensibility"—the fact that the act of accessing sensibility itself produces new data of sensibility—is the source for nothing less than a fundamental media-driven transformation in human experience itself. The self-propagating, self-escalating increase in non-perceptual sensible data generated by twenty-first-century media profoundly affects the economy of experience, such that our (human) experience becomes increasingly conditioned and impacted by processes that we have no direct experience of, no direct mode of access to, and no potential awareness of. This is why access is perhaps *the* key operation performed by twenty-first-century media, and thus why the claim about access to data of sensibility (CADS) is so central to the essential doubleness (i.e., the specificity) of twenty-first-century media and to the story of their advent that I shall unfold here.

Before I follow the trajectory developed here as it converges with Whitehead's neutral account of experience, let me, as a note of caution of sorts, underscore what it is I am saying and also what I am emphatically not saying. I am saying that twenty-first-century media, which differ in crucial ways from earlier media (and from much contemporaneous media as well), are fundamentally transforming human experience and the conceptualization of human experience. I am not, however, saying or in any way implying that human experience simply and abruptly ceases to be what it has been up to now, that humans have somehow changed in a way that leaves behind what they have changed from. Rather, I shall argue emphatically that we still live the world through attentional consciousness and sense perception, and that we still experience media that address us through these modes. What has changed is that we can now acquire a far richer understanding of the broader environmental confound that is in play independently of the modes of access furnished by the higher-order processes and that provides the "ground" from which they arise. In concert with Whitehead, who describes his philosophical goal not as a critique of consciousness but as a re-embedding of consciousness in a far richer context of the causally efficacious lineages that have produced it, what I am interested in describing here are the ways that twenty-first-century media—precisely by their capacity to access the data of our shared sensibility with the world—provide both a broader and a richer account of the "achievement" (to use Whitehead's felicitous term) that is the human, and an account, specifically, that begins, not by separating the human from the world, but rather by seeking to discover how the human is in the deepest sense *of the world*. On such a view, human experience cannot be considered to be an achievement solely due to the human, but, on the contrary, must be seen to encompass a plethora of agencies, both "human" and "nonhuman," and to exist first and foremost as a dimension of a larger production of a complex environmental process, where such distinctions (e.g., human-nonhuman) can only hold provisional status, in the sense that they correlate with concrete, higher-order developments of more generic processes.

With this explanation, we come to the first reason for my appeal to Whitehead: the imperative for an account of experience that is neutral concerning any possible divisions between human and nonhuman, as well as animate and inanimate, and that is capacious enough to account for the ways in which these supposedly foundational and categorical divisions in fact involve complex overlappings of different levels of experience, none of which is intrinsically more worthy than others. Whitehead's "reformed subjective principle" gives a name to the shift from an agent-centered perceptual modality to an environmental sensibility that lies at the heart of twenty-first-century media. The fruit of his re-interrogation of Descartes's great break with the Western philosophical tradition, Whitehead's reform of subjectivity aims to balance the solipsism of modern, post-Cartesian subjectivism with "an 'objectivist' principle as to the datum for experience"; to do this, Whitehead stresses the necessity of recognizing that every datum of experience is composed of external things *that are nonetheless immanent in subjective occasions of experience.*[5] In effect, Whitehead's reformed subjective principle aims to restore a balance to experience that, despite being introduced by Descartes, was initially lost with his own development of his break, and whose loss thus flavors modern philosophy from its very

onset. As Whitehead sees it, "Descartes's discovery on the side of subjectivism requires balancing by an 'objectivist' principle as to the datum for
experience."[6] Put in more straightforward terms, Descartes's indubitable
cogito must be reconnected to its "objective" source: the worldly material,
the "objective datum," catalyzing its emergence.

A large part of Whitehead's reform of modern subjectivism centers on
his rejection of the Cartesian substance-quality model of the subject in favor of a "processual subjectivism" that not only ranges across all scales of
matter but that, in an important sense to be developed, emerges from the
bottom up. For Whitehead, that is, subjectivity is not an experience limited
to certain kinds of beings (humans, higher animals, etc.); nor is it typically
characterized by consciousness. Rather, subjectivity is an element in *all* dimensions of actuality, and indeed can be said to characterize higher levels of
being or "societies" (where it qualifies the internal unification of actual entities) *only because it qualifies the actual entities themselves.* For Whitehead,
in short, if there is subjectivity at the highest levels of being, there must be
subjectivity all the way down. Clearly, the very meaning of subjectivity is up
for grabs here.

Whitehead's scheme introduces a certain relationality, or even perhaps
a relativity, into the issue of subjectivity: there are no purely subjective or
purely objective occasions of experience; all occasions necessarily have both
objective and subjective elements. The radical relationality of being on
Whitehead's account can ultimately be traced to his radically environmental perspective on agency: as he sees it—and this is, to my mind, one of his
most inspiring and beautiful thoughts—every actual occasion implicates
the entirety of the universe, whether through actual engagement (via "positive prehension") or through active exclusion (via "negative prehension,"
which, crucially, is a form of exclusion *that is still a relation*). By rendering
the subjective-objective divide fundamentally relational, such a radically
holist perspective decouples it absolutely from any privilege accorded the
human, human individuals, and human subjectivity.

Elemental Subjectivity

By thinking media and subjectivity through Whitehead, we will be able to
grasp their fundamental co-implication or mutual immanence at a far more
"elemental" level than the level where we encounter the higher-order subjectivity characteristic of human experience. And, importantly, we will be
able to grasp precisely how contemporary media and dispersed, multi-scalar
subjectivity are bound together not via some external relation, but as two
components of a new sensory reality. In this respect, Whitehead's general

approach to subjectivity—his general attribution of it to every occasion in the universe—forms a crucial complement to Galloway and Thacker's generalization of networks as the "objective" (though not object-focused) structure of the "elemental." The permeation of impersonal, sub-macroscopic subjectivity across scales directly parallels the dispersal of agency across networks that marks the elemental character of contemporary media. Taking off from this complementarity, I would suggest that Whitehead's speculative philosophy—precisely because of its insistence on the universality of subjectivity—furnishes the basis for a re-anchoring of human experience within media networks that have become substantially decoupled from direct human perception.

As we will discover, the ultimate ground for the continued significance of subjectivity in an ever-increasingly data-fied (or, in Whitehead's terms, "objectified") world is the irreducibility of temporality, or, more precisely, the irreducibility of a minimal temporal gap between occasions of experience. In the final instance, it is this minimal temporal gap that will help us counter the position of those media theorists, from Kittler to Galloway and Thacker, who, in distinct yet ultimately similar ways, correlate contemporary digital media with some fantasized end of the human. Put more precisely—and more affirmatively—this temporal gap of subjectivity, insofar as it inheres in the data-fication operated by contemporary technics and insofar as it forms the materiality of sensibility, holds the promise for a reinscription of human experience within the very objecification that allegedly renders it superfluous.

On this score, I would not disagree with Galloway and Thacker's diagnosis of our contemporary situation when they write that the "twentieth century will be remembered as the last time there existed nonmedia." Nor would I reject their prognosis for the future: "In the future there will be a coincidence between happening and storage. After universal standards of identification are agreed on, real-time tracking technologies will increase exponentially, such that almost any space will be iteratively archived over time. . . . Space will become rewindable, fully simulated at all available time codes."[7] To this account, I would, however, want to add the notion that this new reality—the total manipulability of mediated or recorded space—itself calls forth the irreducible temporal gap just mentioned; within the total mediation Galloway and Thacker envision, the minimal temporal gap between occasions of experience is precisely what will remain "proper" to subjectivity as such, including human subjectivity. Far more important than defining a division of "the lived environment . . . into identifiable zones and nonidentifiable zones," this new condition of total recording and trackability will foreground irreducible subjective temporality—though not necessarily the temporality of a time-consciousness—as the source for novelty within an increasingly data-fied and archived world.

For this reason, I am not, as are Galloway and Thacker, "nostalgic . . . for a time *when organisms didn't need to produce quantitative data about themselves*, for a time when one didn't need to report back."[8] I am not nostalgic for such a time precisely because the subjectivity and agency of the human, as well as the subjectivity and agency of the nonhuman—far from standing against the quantitative—now more than ever *requires quantification*. More precisely, any specific operation or performance of subjectivity—human or otherwise—correlates with and emerges on the basis of the generalized subjectivity that inheres *even within*—and, in light of the massive proliferation of computing in our world today, *perhaps especially within*—quantitative data. Whitehead's work helps us to appreciate the irreducible sensory dimension of even the most inert, objectified or "data-fied" occasions of experience: literally swathed in a multi-scalar and dispersed sensory surround, our (higher-order) subjectivity acquires its power not because it incorporates and processes what is outside, but rather through its direct co-participation or sharing in the polyvalent agency of myriad subjectivities. Our distinctly human subjectivity is the result of a complex assemblage of overlapping, scale-variant microsubjectivities functioning distinctly and autonomously. Within such assemblages, these microsubjectivities can be said to exist in "operational overlap" with one another (where operational overlap, as we shall see, precisely does *not* mean "emergence").

A Neutral Theory of Experience

If Whitehead's reform of subjectivity and critique of consciousness can help us resituate human subjectivity within a more encompassing environmental sensory confound where we can begin to address its complex heterogeneous basis, his more immediate value for reconceptualizing experience in light of twenty-first-century media lies in the more "objective" aspects of his speculative empiricism. Rather than the account of nonsensuous perception or symbolic reference, it is the cosmological dimension of Whitehead's project that most directly helps us to overcome the anthropocentrism of our theorizing. For Whitehead's aim is not simply to reground consciousness or human experience on a more inclusive foundation, but rather—first and foremost—to develop a speculative metaphysical account of the way things must be (or alternatively, the way the world must be) in order for experience to be what it is. This goal leads him to develop a complicated and still contentious account of the speculative domain of "actual entities" or "actual occasions." Such entities or occasions are the truly real things that lie at the basis of all experience but that—and this is what makes them speculative—cannot themselves be experienced directly.

Actual entities or occasions are created through a process called "concrescence" in which they "prehend" everything that has been created up to that moment in the development of the universe. (More or less synonymous with "grasping," prehension can either be positive, when an actual entity in concrescence, or an "actuality-in-attainment," takes in as part of its content some element of the settled world or world of "attained actualities"; or it can be negative, in which case it rejects an element of the settled world, but in rejecting it *still creates a relationship with it*.) Concrescence is guided by a "subjective aim" that unifies the disparate elements prehended by the incipient actual entity; when the process of prehending is completed, the concrescence reaches satisfaction, at which point, the phase of "transition" occurs; in transition, the actual entity reenters the universe or, more precisely, is added to the multiplicity of the universe, making the latter a many + 1. This process of concrescence occurs incessantly, although not within time, and whenever it occurs, a novelty is added to the settled world, making it richer as a world and as a source for the genesis of new actual entities. The canonical interpretation of Whitehead, which is largely justified by his own writings, holds that only concrescence is creative because it is only in concrescence that actualities wield their subjective power; once they "perish," undergo transition, and enter the settled world, actualities become merely objective (or superjectal), meaning that they become passive and inert and can only become creative again if they are taken up by future concrescences of new actual entities.

Much of my own understanding of Whitehead's value for theorizing experience today depends on rejecting elements of this canonical picture. Indeed, at the very heart of my enterprise is a claim for inversion (CFI). The claim for inversion urges us to view Whitehead's account of concrescence *not* as the be-all and end-all of his account of process, *but rather as one component within a larger model of process* in which the "worldliness" of the world, what I shall call "worldly sensibility," plays a crucial and irreducible role. More precisely, the claim for inversion contends that we should invert the orthodox understanding of creativity provided by Whitehead and ratified by virtually all of his commentators: rather than looking to concrescences as the sole source of creativity, we must view them as vehicles for the ongoing production and expansion of worldly sensibility, as instruments for the expression of a creative power that necessarily involves the entirety of the superjective force of the world. Far from operating as the exclusive agents of the creative process, as they do for almost all of Whitehead's commentators, concrescences on my understanding are nothing more nor less than a speculative means to explain the production of superjects or, even more precisely (keeping with Whitehead's stress on process), of superjectal relationalities (webs of objectified, i.e., "data-fied" prehensions) that constitute worldly sensibility.

I shall come back to this claim about inversion in great detail below; for the moment, however, the canonical picture presented above will serve perfectly to illustrate the complexity of Whitehead's speculative enterprise: his description of the oscillation between concrescence and transition of actual entities produces a model of the metaphysical structure of existence that is both *pre-experiential* and foundational for *experience per se*, which is to say, for the experience of all experiential entities or "societies" (Whitehead's term for assemblages of actual entities and/or other societies), ranging from the most "micro"-level phenomena, for example, quantum decoherence, to the most "macro"-level phenomena, for example, geological and cosmological processes. In other words, whatever account of experience one builds up on the basis of Whitehead's metaphysical scheme will have to be a theory of experience that not only does not begin by privileging human experience but that is, at a very deep level, *neutral* concerning the specific qualities of its "subject." It is, to reiterate the point I am trying to make here, precisely this neutrality that makes Whitehead valuable for the task of theorizing the experience of twenty-first-century media: with the emphasis he places on causal efficacy, Whitehead provides an account of experience that not only is multi-scalar and heterogeneous but is capable of addressing media *non-anthropocentrically*, *non-phenomenologically*, and *non-prosthetically*. As will become clear in what follows, this account of experience will allow me to characterize sensibility—or, more precisely, worldly sensibility—as a domain of experience that is more fundamental than the divisions that ultimately lead to the enthroning of the human as "experiencer par excellence."

A Different Whitehead?

With its aim of emphasizing how Whitehead's neutral account of experience meets certain experiential challenges posed by twenty-first-century media, the radically environmental account of experience I seek to develop here engages Whitehead in a manner that differs fundamentally from most recent deployments of his work by cultural and media theorists.

Two elements in particular inform this difference:

First, in contrast to those contemporary engagements with Whitehead that are marked by a strong antihuman flavor, and that draw on elements of his philosophy most suited to such a position, I attempt to deploy his neutral theory of experience in order to decenter—*but not to dispense with*—the perspective of the human. On Whitehead's neutral theory of experience, the human no longer stands against everything else; rather, exactly like everything else, each human being is a particular organization or composition of actual entities. In this sense, the human not only enjoys no de jure privilege, but it is able to provide a (partial) perspective on experience only on account of its particular organization. That is why the aim of Whitehead's philosophy is precisely to bring consciousness into line with the heterogeneous and multi-scalar Being-of-the-world, or, as he puts it, to perform "the self-correction by consciousness of its own initial excess of subjectivity."[9] Indeed, I consider Whitehead's "reformed" commitment to consciousness—and to a fuller picture of the human capable of explaining why it is the highest achievement of the universe—to be among the most important elements of his work. Again, the payoff of Whitehead's philosophical reform of consciousness is to resituate consciousness—and the human with it—within the world; following such a procedure, we can simply no longer speak in terms of distinctions like human-nonhuman.

That is why, in marked contrast to many of Whitehead's contemporary rejuvenators, I am interested in how his radically environmental and ontologically neutral account of experience can *enhance* human experience *precisely by throwing into question many of our received notions about the human*—including the privilege of (agential) perception over (environmental) sensibility. As I see it, what is ultimately most valuable about Whitehead's thought is how it compels us to rethink the human as an inseparable part of a larger environmental sensory confound. The conjunction with twenty-first-century media, which addresses the environmental sensibility to which we belong prior to and independently of any address to properly human perception, furnishes a compelling reason to bring out this core element of Whitehead's philosophy.

On this score, and for the sake of theoretical clarity, let me directly and explicitly repudiate any allegiance of my argument with contemporary accounts, in research areas like the "new materialism" and "speculative realism" (or object-oriented ontology), that promote an account of the world, whether in the guise of nonhuman actors (Jane Bennett), objects (Graham Harman), or the ancestral (Quentin Meillassoux), that seeks to eschew contact with humans. To put it bluntly, I don't believe such an aim is tenable, and I further believe that Whitehead's work shows us why, insofar as it undertakes a radical deterritorialization of experience from the framework of human affairs that ultimately—and as it were, inexorably—yields a far more complex account of the human, and indeed of the universe itself *as an entity (the supreme society) that necessarily includes (or as I prefer to say, implicates) humans within it and within each and every element comprising it.*

Upon hearing me state this view, one of my students began to speak of "human dust" that permeates everything in the universe (the reference was to Carl Sagan's notion of "star stuff"), and I have come to like this metaphor quite a lot. It helps us see precisely where the proponents of today's theoretical antihumanisms go wrong in the assumptions they make about humanness. Bluntly put, they assume that humans are, and have to be, substances, or consciousnesses, or minds, or subjects, or whatever else they are keen to denounce, rather than elements, what Whitehead would call "actual entities," that are prehended by other processes, be they atoms or land formations, cells or weather patterns, legal judgments or effects of global warming. They fail to entertain a possibility that is crucial for Whitehead, namely that the dust of the universe implicates the human in its every speck and particle, without requiring the actual presence of any traditionally embodied humans or human consciousnesses.[10] And these same proponents of antihumanism further assume that humans have to be treated as somehow separate from the rest of the universe, as ultimately detached from non-human processes (including those with which they maintain relations), and as in need of "correlation" (to use the Kantian concept denounced by Meillassoux and his followers) to overcome their isolation.

I want to suggest—and I believe that Whitehead's neutral ontology of organism is the proof for this—that once we give up these faulty assumptions concerning the human, once we embrace an environmental view of the human informed much more by the human's participation (or implication) in other becomings than by any myopic focus on its own becoming, the pathos surrounding the construction of those distinctions dear to today's antihumanists (e.g., human-nonhuman, human-object, human-slime mold, etc.) will simply fall away. For if the human is implicated in every element of the universe (although certainly not as a consciousness taking it as its object or a representation taking it as its correlate), then what is at issue when an event is thought, or rather when it is tracked, from the perspective of an electrical power grid, or of edible matter, or of metal is only a shift of emphasis—and not a theoretical revolution. What is more, the type of deterritorialized thinking that results is not a thinking without the human, but a thinking in which the human figures as a component in some alterior or "alien" process operating according to its own logic, and emphatically *not* as the focus or the ground on which such a process can be materialized or made to appear.[11] Don't get me wrong: I am for the moves that Bennett and Harman and even Meillassoux make; it is just that I see them as exemplifying (or at least calling for) a mode of thinking that has already solved the "human-nonhuman problem," as it were, rather than one that seems stuck in place in the face of its perceived need to erect itself against some phantom figure of humanness.

If twenty-first-century media provide an opportunity to reform our understanding of the human, as I shall argue they do, that is precisely because of their role as catalysts for the latter's complexification: faced with the necessity to deploy technologies of data-gathering and analysis in order *simply to make contact with the present of sensibility*, we humans must come to embrace a new condition of technical distribution as our norm. And faced with the reality that we are implicated in processes that we neither control, directly enjoy, or even have access to, we humans cannot but come to appreciate our participation in a cosmology of process, which is to say, to embrace our superjective implication in a plethora of processes of all sorts and at all scales. To the extent that this participation is indelibly implicated in the allegedly nonhuman processes Bennett inventories, in the withdrawal of objects Harman theorizes, or in the deployment of mathematics Meillassoux undertakes, the promiscuous implication of humans in a vast range of worldly processes would itself appear necessary to give substance to these contemporary accounts of nonhuman agency. With Whitehead, the aim should be to complexify the human by multiplying its connections, not to wall it off as a helplessly imperializing intentionality that cannot but turn the alterior into its own proper content.

Returning now to the thread of my presentation, the second element that differentiates my account of Whitehead from the Whitehead renaissance is my willingness to submit Whitehead's philosophy to *philosophical* critique. Notwithstanding my general fidelity to Whitehead's perspective, I believe that a number of his philosophical commitments are not (or are no longer) tenable. For this reason, I engage in a philosophically transformative criticism that differs markedly, at least to my mind, from what most of Whitehead's contemporary re-inventors have proposed. Recent years have witnessed a plethora of explorations engaging Whitehead in a host of contemporary theoretical debates; these range from explorations of the value of Whitehead's philosophy for social theory (Michael Halewood) to applications of his theory of perception to neuroscientific research (Steven Meyer) and much in between, including studies of Whitehead's theory of extension in relation to contemporary sound culture (Steve Goodman) and of his contribution to contemporary architectural theory and practice (Luciana Parisi) and to dance and movement studies (Stamatia Portanova). In all of these cases, and in others equally central to my interests (Brian Massumi, Erin Manning, and Steven Shaviro), what critics discover in Whitehead is an ally for their diverse efforts to intensify the operation of perception and the scope of the aesthetic.

No matter how productive such work is, however, none of it quite manages to engage *philosophically* with Whitehead; and indeed, with some notable exceptions, these explorations overwhelmingly tend to treat Whitehead's thinking as fully formed, as effectively black-boxed. The result is that none of these critical appropriations actually deploys the resources afforded by Whitehead's philosophy to their full extent or in their full radicality. In large part, the reason for this restricted scope is the tactical or instrumental nature of these invocations of Whitehead: each of these critics positions Whitehead's philosophy, often in concert with elements of Deleuze's thought, in the role of ontological ground for some account of experience as becoming. They thus borrow piecemeal from Whitehead—stressing discrete elements of his philosophy such as prehension, nonsensuous perception, concrescence, and so forth—without an adequate consideration for the larger consequences of Whitehead's radical reform of philosophy, including its crucial implications for our understanding of consciousness and the human. The result, as I see it, is a kind of myopia about Whitehead's purposes, an overly intense focus on particular aspects of his work at the expense of a consideration of the larger project of philosophical reform.

What follows from this double limitation of the contemporary Whitehead renaissance is a peculiar situation: a mode of criticism that is at once too philosophically conservative in its method and too "theoretically" radical in its commitment to antihumanism. Despite appearances, these two limitations actually go hand in hand, for it is precisely because of their myopic investment in some particular element of Whitehead's work, without adequate consideration of transformations that must be performed on it, that critics are able to enlist Whitehead in the service of philosophical antihumanism. In contrast, what I propose is a Whiteheadian engagement with twenty-first-century media that puts the very meaning of the human into question. Indeed, such questioning of the human constitutes the ultimate rationale behind my conjunction of Whitehead with twenty-first-century media: for it is the subterranean sensory operation of the latter that calls for the radical potential of Whitehead's philosophy. In this respect, my project differs from many others today for, *far from treating the human as a static, black-boxed, and moribund concept,* I seek precisely to transform the human by subjecting it to the force of the environmental outside that has been made both salient and accessible by twenty-first-century media: insofar as the latter call into play elements of worldly sensibility that are *within the human* even if they do not (and cannot) belong to the human, they bring out hitherto unacknowledged elements of human experience, and in this sense make possible a veritable reinvigoration of the human. As the first study to situate Whitehead's contribution within the field of media, *Feed-Forward* excavates the deep affinity between new affordances of twenty-first-century media and certain untapped potentials of human becoming that are made salient by certain elements of Whitehead's philosophy. My argument is simply and literally that these new media affordances provide a new perspective on Whitehead's philosophy of organism and his philosophical reform of human subjectivity. Where Whitehead shows that consciousness can and must be reformed, I hope to show, in parallel fashion, that the human can and must be reformed.

Two Paths out of Sense Perception

To illustrate how my engagement with Whitehead differs from that of the current Whitehead renaissance, let me focus for a moment on Whitehead's reform and expansion of the Western philosophical doctrine of perception. For me, the key issue concerns what we make of Whitehead's reform, or, more specifically, how we can radicalize his reform in ways that cut against his own purposes and address the challenges of our contemporary mediasphere. Here we anticipate what will become one of the major themes of my study: the imperative to radicalize Whitehead's own expansion of perception, to move not simply from "sense perception" to "nonsensuous perception," as Whitehead does, but from "nonsensuous perception" all the way to what I shall call "non-perceptual sensibility." As we shall see, Whitehead's focus on perception—notwithstanding his important reform of it—remains centered on human modes of perception; indeed, the very distinction of sensuous from nonsensuous sensation can only be made if consciousness is taken as a frame of reference. Divesting Whitehead of this residual bias—one of the key claims of my study—liberates a preperceptual worldly sensibility that cannot be preferentially correlated with any particular form of perception.

It would involve no exaggeration to say that Whitehead's reformed doctrine of perception constitutes one of the most—if not indeed *the* most—cathected sites for recent critics. Developed mainly in his lectures in *Symbolism* and in *Process and Reality*, Whitehead's expansion of perception centers around his conjoined effort to criticize the limitations of sense perception (what he calls "perception in the mode of presentational immediacy") and to reground it in a broader mode of perception, "perception in the mode of causal efficacy" (which he later, in *Adventures of Ideas* and, in my opinion reductively, rechristens "nonsensuous perception"). Unprecedented in the history of philosophy before Whitehead and reminiscent of explorations of bodily perception by Maurice Merleau-Ponty and other more recent philosophers, perception in the mode of causal efficacy designates a vague, inchoate form of perception of the causal background of experience itself and is fleetingly glimpsable in moments when we recognize that we "see with our eyes" or "touch with our hands." Whitehead's development of the distinction between sense perception and perception in the mode of causal efficacy aims to fill out the picture of perception, to position sense perception in its narrow and properly philosophical sense against a far broader material background, the host of material processes—the causal efficacy—that informs *and produces* its eventual emergence.

On the basis even of such a simplified explication (and I return to the topic of perception below in chapter 2), we get a sense of what's at stake in Whitehead's reform of perception and why it has found such a deep resonance with today's cultural and media critics: by opening up perception, beyond sense perception proper, to the material processes that do not manifest in sense perception but that nevertheless are necessary for its occurrence, Whitehead significantly broadens the scope of what figures into the sphere of perception.

For cultural theorists and media critics like Brian Massumi, Erin Manning, Luciana Parisi, and Steve Goodman, Whitehead's broadening of perception facilitates an exploration of the "just-before" of perception, a way of thickening the present of perception by folding into it its *immediately past* causal efficacy. The payoff of this line of thinking is succinctly illustrated by Parisi's exploration of bionic technologies, by which she means technologies that extend the sensory capacities of embodied human beings. What such technologies afford is a capacity to "feel thought" before it becomes available to sense perception: bionic technologies are, Parisi argues, "crucial for extracting sensing potentials below and above frequencies of habitual sensory perception. . . . [They] directly connect with the causal field of sensation, accounting not simply for sensory-motor perception, but, more importantly, for the causal intricacies of the physical and the nonphysical, whereby thought itself is felt."[12] Notwithstanding the fact that Parisi does develop a specification of Whitehead's notion of "nonsensuous perception" that takes seriously and attends concretely to the way in which contemporary sensory technologies mediate the thickening of the present, the expansion of affectivity that occurs when thought itself is felt—when thought feels itself *before* its own happening—remains narrowly focused on the immediate just-past of the present moment, the half second preceding sense perception. As I shall argue at length below, this understanding simply repeats, and in effect ratifies, Whitehead's own reductive rechristening of perception qua causal efficacy as "nonsensuous perception"; by so doing, Parisi—in concert with Whitehead himself—simply jettisons the crucial "vector character" of perception, the way that lineages of causal efficacy stretch far into the background of perception, and not just to its most immediate just-past. By expanding Whitehead's own reductive conceptualization of causal efficacy as nonsensuous perception, Parisi's account compromises what is, to my mind, potentially one of the most fundamental contributions of Whitehead's philosophy for thinking the experiential challenges posed by twenty-first-century media: its capacity to embrace media's impact on the domain of sensibility beyond the limited scope of a "nonsensuously thickened" perceptual moment.

That is why Parisi's treatment of perception perfectly illustrates the thoroughly "affirmative character" that characterizes contemporary critical deployments of Whiteheadian terms and concepts. Parisi's work—and on this score it can stand in for a host of contemporary efforts to make Whitehead speak to our media situation—evinces little if any recognition that certain of Whitehead's positions must be critically interrogated, that the situation created by twenty-first-century media calls for more than a simple application of already solidified concepts.

Toward a Human-Implicating Materialism

Nowhere is this affirmative character more clearly manifest than in what is certainly the most substantial account to date of Whitehead's relevance for contemporary cultural theory, Steven Shaviro's book-length study of Whitehead's contribution to post-Kantian aesthetic thought. Shaviro's *Without Criteria* develops as the unfolding of an interesting thought experiment: What would the situation of cultural theory be today if Whitehead, rather than Heidegger, had provided the cornerstone for post-structuralism and the developments that have ensued in its aftermath? Noting that two more different kinds of thinker would be hard to find, Shaviro proleptically characterizes the payoff of his counterfactual experiment as a wholesale shift in critical terrain:

> If Whitehead were to replace Heidegger as the inspiration of postmodern thought, our intellectual landscape would look quite different. Certain problems that we have been overly obsessed with would recede in importance, to be replaced by other questions, and other perspectives. What Isabelle Stengers calls a "constructivist" approach to philosophy would take precedence over the tasks of incessant deconstruction. Whitehead's thought has a kind of cosmic irony to it, which offers a welcome contrast both to the nar-

cissistic theorizing to which the heirs of Heidegger are prone, and
to the fatuous complacency of mainstream American pragmatism.
Whitehead's metaphysics is a ramshackle construction, continually
open to revision, and not an assertion of absolute truths. It stands
outside the dualities—the subject or not, meaning or not, human-
ism or not—with which recent theoretical thought has so often bur-
dened us. Whitehead both exemplifies, and encourages, the virtues
of speculation, fabulation, and invention.[13]

Shaviro's study should be understood as a contribution toward making this
proleptic projection a reality. The "critical aestheticism" he constructs by
reading Kant and Deleuze through Whitehead is meant to open possibilities
that have been closed off by the Heideggerian paradigm, and that speak to
practices in digital film and video, neuroscience and biogenetic technology,
and post-Fordist capitalism. By approaching these and like practices with an
eye to how they implicate affect and singularity, we will—so Shaviro assures
us—open broader and more robust contexts for assessing their impact on
our living and understanding.

Notwithstanding its seductive counterfactual lure, Shaviro's project remains largely historicist in focus and centered on assessing contemporary
cultural developments with the newly liberated tools bequeathed us by Whitehead. Thus, despite (or perhaps because of) the personal transformation
informing his study (he reports shifting perspective from reading Whitehead
through Deleuze to reading Deleuze through Whitehead), Shaviro's contribution centers around the task of making Whitehead useful for reassessing
the untapped legacy of aestheticism from Kant to Deleuze and, proleptically
here and in a promised volume to come, for assessing the operation of culture *as it already exists today and can be projected to develop tomorrow*.
Throughout this work, the relation of Whitehead's philosophy to the culture it will help mediate thus remains fundamentally external and markedly
conservative: its role is simply to provide a better basis than that of our post-
Heideggerian postmodernity for evaluating cultural objects and processes.
In this respect, Shaviro's account severely limits the scope of Whitehead's
contribution to contemporary culture: specifically, Whitehead's contribution is deprived of any role *in the determination of* how those objects and
processes are composed and how they function.

By correlating Whitehead's philosophy with twenty-first-century media,
and by approaching this conjunction as a challenge—the very experiential
challenge posed to us by our contemporary media developments—I am proposing what amounts to a different kind of experiment, one inspired not so
much by a "philosophical fantasy" as by a reckoning with materiality in its

most concrete, historically and technically specific contemporary manifestations. Put another way, it is media in their concreteness—and not some fantasized and retroactively installed revision of our critical tradition—that call for a contemporary reinvention of Whitehead: the challenge is posed by the address and materiality of contemporary media, and the invocation of Whitehead responds directly to this challenge. That is why, in a world linked together by multi-scalar computational networks and increasingly populated with intelligent sensing technologies ranging from environmental sensors to the smart phones and other portable devices we now carry with us as a matter of course, experience simply is not what it used to be: far more of what goes on in our daily lives is carried out by machines functioning at their own timescales, meaning outside of our direct perceptual grasp but in ways that do significantly affect our activity. I want to propose that Whitehead's constructivism can lend a specificity to such a techno-historicist claim about contemporary experience, but, even more fundamentally, I want to propose that constructing or composing experience through Whitehead's theory opens crucial opportunities for expanding experience in novel and creative ways. Far from leading inexorably to some anti- or post-human scenario, such opportunities open up human-directed, human-philic, or, as I shall prefer to say (for reasons to be explicated below), *human-implicating* folds of the increasing technical incursions that are now reshaping our lives.

Here we return again to the neglect among many of Whitehead's contemporary critics of his qualified though unequivocal embrace of human consciousness and to the corollary necessity to rethink the human on the basis of a neutral ontology of experience, which is to say, on the basis of its belonging to a larger sensory confound, its implication within complex lineages of causal efficacy. The single-minded fervor with which Whitehead's contemporary critics embrace discrete elements of his critique of received philosophical accounts of perception—most notably, his concept of "nonsensuous perception"—causes them to overlook, if not actively dismiss, the ongoing importance of higher-order modes of human operation within Whitehead's work. For Whitehead, that is, the philosophical reform of perception does not aim to *replace* human experience with asubjective affectivity or any other "nonhuman" experiential modality, but rather to fill out the picture of human experience by embedding higher-order operationality and, most fundamentally, consciousness, within the broader context of its causal efficacy, within the worldly sensibility from which it comes.

Let us return to this issue of nonsensuous perception in order to open up a second path of its development that, in contrast to the microscopic focus on the pre-feeling or pre-anticipation of perception, follows the vectors of causal efficacy beyond a point where perception, even in its "nonsensuously thickened" operation, can be said to be in play. What such a path reveals is, I want to suggest, the operation of a sensibility that is prior to the division of the subject from the world, meaning prior to the cut that creates perceptual transcendence, and that envelops the human within its broader operation. Initially opened by some of Whitehead's developments in *Process and Reality*, such a path gets definitively closed off when Whitehead rechristens perception in the mode of causal efficacy "nonsensuous perception." For with his rechristening, Whitehead effectively identifies causally efficacious perception with—and, I would argue, limits it to—the immediate past of sensory perception: "that portion of our past lying between a tenth of a second and half a second ago."[14] By ratifying this redefinition of causal efficacy as nonsensuous perception, today's critics follow Whitehead in foreclosing the far more radical and more interesting implications of his nuancing of perception: they effectively abandon the potential of Whitehead's analysis for opening direct contact with the domain of causal efficacy *beyond perception*. Though it informs perception in both its modes, this domain *does not and cannot appear through (human) perception*; indeed, it can only be accessed *indirectly* by humans, through the technical supplement afforded by biometric and environmental computational sensing.

Underscoring the contrast with perception in all its forms, I propose to rename this domain of causal efficacy proper (i.e., causal efficacy independent of its filtering through perception, even in that mode of perception Whitehead calls "causal efficacy") "worldly sensibility." Insofar as contemporary microcomputational sensing and data-gathering technologies are able to capture a wealth of data from worldly sensibility—including data about our own implication in it—and feed this data forward into a future or just-to-come moment of conscious perception, they operate to reground the human on the basis of a *non-anthropocentric* account of the world and of the environmental dimension that is at issue in any and every event, including events involving humans. In this way, the more radical development of causal efficacy I advocate supports a model for the technical distribution of sensibility whereby humans, with their limited sensuous *and their limited nonsensuous* perceptual capacities, are given "digital insight" into their own robust sensory contact with the world. The potential for this insight to be useful—because it enhances the intensity of experience and because it can guide behavior in the future—is what gives me hope that there is indeed a pharmacological recompense to twenty-first-century media.

Consciousness must accordingly be placed within the larger context of causal efficacy informing its operation, and it must be subjected to critique in the Kantian sense of taking on board the limits of its functioning; but the key point is that these moves help to remake consciousness so that it can continue to be a crucial resource for human experience in the twenty-first century. The notion of "feed-forward" that I have just mentioned and that I shall introduce more fully below captures this situation perfectly: because perceptual consciousness is simply left out of the loop when data-gathering and passive sensing capacities grasp the "operational present" of sensibility at time frames from which conscious activity is excluded, this operational present can only be made available to consciousness in a future anterior time frame, by being presented *after the fact* to a consciousness that, with respect to the present's operationality, cannot but arrive too late on the scene. To put it more simply, consciousness has to be repurposed to function in the networked regimes characteristic of twenty-first-century media: no longer at the center of the present *of sensibility*, consciousness can only impact the actual happening of sensory presencing *indirectly* and in a *proleptic* or *anticipatory* mode, by planning for new prescencings of sensibility in the future. Consciousness's input is henceforth restricted to shaping or modulating the future happening of sensory presencing so as to occasion or elicit desired (future) experiences of its own. More precisely still, it is only by strategically deploying technical intervention to modulate the inaccessible operational present of sensibility that consciousness can induce certain kinds of experience. No longer coincident with the operational present of sensibility, consciousness can only pre-engineer, as it were, its own emergent or just-to-come experiences.

Repurposed in this way, consciousness takes on what, contrasted with its near-absolute privilege in the history of Western philosophy, cannot but appear to be a more humble role as modulator of a sensory presencing that takes place outside its experiential purview. For this reason, "understanding twenty-first-century media" must certainly mean something altogether different from what Marshall McLuhan meant when he chose to call his famous study of media as the extensions of man *Understanding Media*.[15] For media in their twenty-first-century vocation simply do not impact experience in a way that could be an *object* for understanding, not even for bodily understanding; instead, they impact the domain of worldly sensibility on the basis of which understanding, and all higher-order events of hermeneutic meaning, arise as such. Yet neither can media in their twenty-first-century vocation be limited to the role of providing infrastructure—the "non-hermeneutic materiality"—for acts of meaning, as media theorist Friedrich Kittler would have it. Viewed from our contemporary perspective, even this critical-material position would appear to give too much to the hermeneutic paradigm: blinded by its obsession with the non-hermeneutic body, Kittler's media science remains incapable of pursuing its most radical insight—that higher-order, complexly embodied human operations have been fundamentally displaced in a world of microtemporal computational media.

To appreciate the transformation now under way, we require a more far-reaching break with the hermeneutic tradition—one that entertains the possibility for a dethroning of embodied consciousness as privileged locus where non-hermeneutic materialities (the so-called materialities of communication)[16] can exercise their corrosive force. The repurposing of consciousness for the twenty-first century—and, specifically, for its future-modulating supervisory role—sounds the final death knell for phenomenology's animating dream: the dream of a consciousness capable of experiencing its own presencing *in the very moment of that presencing—consciousness's dream of living the "now" of its happening.* This dream is everywhere manifest in Husserl's work, up to and including his final struggles (in the C-*Manuscripts* from 1929–34) with the impasse of an "absolute time-constituting consciousness" (the "living present"); indeed, this phenomenological dream of consciousness's coincidence with itself comprises the theoretical kernel of the project for a phenomenology of constitution, a project that remains alive—long after Husserl's demise—in forms as diverse as Derrida's deconstruction (which problematizes, but does not displace, the *philosopheme* of the self-coincidence of consciousness) and Michel Henry's phenomenology of absolute immanence (which shifts the very terrain of constitution to materiality, but only by rendering the operation of self-affection absolutely paramount).

Departing from these and other paths taken by the philosophical inheritors of Husserlian phenomenology, I want to embrace the opportunity twenty-first-century media present for reinventing phenomenology. I want, that is, to show how twenty-first-century media concretize the theoretical program developed on the margins of phenomenology by alternate, more radical, and, in some sense, properly *post*-phenomenological extensions of Husserl's legacy. These extensions of Husserl all share the fundamental conclusion—which simultaneously announces the end of the phenomenological project proper—that worldly temporalization happens beneath, if not in some sense *prior to*, the (temporal) experience of individual time-consciousnesses. More specifically, twenty-first-century media make this conclusion—a conclusion central to the otherwise diverse work of Eugen Fink, Jan Patočka, and Merleau-Ponty—into an everyday reality: for with the full permeation of media into the infra-empirical infrastructure underlying and informing our daily activity, we encounter a situation where technically modulated agencies will always already have activated microtemporal sensory affordances of the environments encompassing—and facilitating—

our doings, well in advance of showing up, at a far higher level of organization, as "contents" of our consciousnesses. Among the central challenges posed to us by this new reality is the question concerning what becomes of consciousness: How can consciousness continue to matter in a world where events no longer need it to occur, and, indeed, where they occur long before they manifest as contents of consciousness?

This question exposes the substantial affinity that exists between Whitehead's philosophy of organism and what I would propose to call "the post-phenomenological afterlife of phenomenology." Indeed, Whitehead's recognition that the narrow bandwidth of consciousness is the crucial problem motivating his reform of philosophy is nothing less than the catalyst for the reconstruction of consciousness's role within an expanded, radically environmental perspective on becoming. The question of how to bring out this dimension of Whitehead's philosophy lies at the very heart of my efforts to develop its affinity with twenty-first-century media; in effect, this affinity poses a crucial empirical challenge to Whitehead's philosophy: specifically, it calls for further clarification of the relations between macroscale consciousness following its Whiteheadian critique and the agency of microscopic experience that (though certainly a key element of Whitehead's systematic philosophy) becomes massively expanded and concretized following the widespread dissemination of contemporary sensor technologies into our everyday lifeworlds.

Whitehead, Media Critic?

As I have sought to stress, the conjunction of Whitehead with twenty-first-century media involves far more than a simple application of Whitehead's philosophy for rethinking the recent history of cultural theory and particular cultural objects and processes. In schematic terms, my transformative reading of Whitehead involves a rehabilitation and expansion of the domain of potentiality as the most expansive source for process in the universe. The project I undertake here thus involves a set of nontrivial, though I hope to convince you, ultimately compatible, transformations of certain key aspects of Whitehead's thinking. Composing contemporary experience with and through Whitehead calls on us to reconceptualize some elements of his theory of perception and of his account of "real potentiality" in light of some other aspects of his thought, for example, the relativization and pluralization of scales entailed by his monist ontology of actual entities. The result of this reconceptualization will be a series of key (and for readers schooled in the orthodoxy of Whiteheadian criticism, perhaps counterintuitive) arguments, all of which lend support to the claim for inversion (CFI) that lies at the heart of my engagement with Whitehead. (Again, the CFI views concrescences not as the pinnacle of Whitehead's account of creativity, but as elements within and as instruments for the production of worldly superjects, which are the true source of experiential creativity.)

For the moment, let me simply enumerate some of the most important of these arguments:

1. Potentiality is ontologically more fundamental than actuality.
2. Potentiality operates within actuality and contrasts with all conceptions of virtuality.
3. Potentiality is rooted in the superjectal power of the settled world.
4. Potentiality operates through intensity which comprises the product of contrasts of settled actualities.
5. Concrescence is subordinated to potentiality insofar as it is catalyzed by a "dative phase" generated by contrasts of settled actualities.
6. The extensive (or vibratory) continuum provides a general sensibility that qualifies the operation of superjects (in contrast to eternal objects that qualify concrescences).
7. Eternal objects lose their status as eternal and their role as the source of "pure potentiality" and acquire a new, more restricted status as products of the flux of experience.
8. Non-perceptual sensibility emerges as central insofar as it designates how humans are implicated within a worldly sensibility that is not relative to any particular perceiver and that exceeds the scope of perception in both its Whiteheadian modes.

I furnish this enumeration of transformations not to overwhelm you and even less with the expectation that these claims will make sense to you now. Rather I furnish it simply to give body to my general claim that any contemporary engagement with Whitehead must be a transformational engagement. Each one of these claims accordingly represents a transformation that correlates to some potential in Whitehead's cosmological ontology and that is made both possible and necessary by the experiential challenges posed by twenty-first-century media.

Consequential as it is, this conclusion only serves to highlight the anomaly of my venture here, the fact that my deployment of Whitehead to address challenges of twenty-first-century media implicates him in an area of study—media—about which he had scant little to say. More than that

even, my venture makes Whitehead's work speak to a media-driven historical transformation of experience that would seem to be about as far away
from his more properly metaphysical concerns as anything could be. If there
is, as I hope to convince you, a thorough consistency to this conjuncture of
Whiteheadian process philosophy and contemporary media culture, that is
because more is at issue in it than a mere "positivistic" application of certain
theoretical concepts to an empirical domain: what *is* at issue is a deep affinity
between a revolutionary experiential paradigm and a radical philosophical
reform of experience. My inspiration here is the bidirectional relationality
between a philosophical corpus that remains open to further development
and a contemporary empirico-cultural-technical situation: thus I remain
convinced that we can learn as much from thinking Whitehead's philosophy
through twenty-first-century media as we can from thinking the new vocation of contemporary media through Whitehead's speculative empiricism.

In accord with this understanding, my study will begin by focusing on
Whitehead's contribution to a neutral, non-anthropomorphic theory of experience. Only once this has been put in place will I attempt to reinsert
the human within the larger theory of experience, an endeavor that, as we
shall see, will involve a certain productive conjunction of Whitehead with
what I have called the "post-phenomenological afterlife" of phenomenology. In each of the four chapters to follow, I devote myself to unpacking
four distinct, yet intimately interrelated aspects of Whitehead's speculative
empiricism that are essential for developing a neutral theory of experience
capable of explaining the impact of twenty-first-century media on worldly
sensibility and the reconceptualization of the human this facilitates. These
four aspects are prehensity, intensity, potentiality, and sensibility.

Chapter 1, "Prehensity," sets out the terms for the affinity between
Whitehead's speculative empiricism and the experiential challenges posed
by twenty-first-century media. Its purpose is to explicate Whitehead's won-
derful notion that every actuality prehends the entirety of the universe (or,
alternatively, that the entirety of the universe informs each new actuality),
and to flesh out how it facilitates the development of a radically environmental perspective of worldly sensibility that, in turn, provides some pharmacological recompense for the loss of the centrality of human perceptual
consciousness.

Chapter 2, "Intensity," focuses on Whitehead's philosophy of organism
as a "neutral" or radically environmental account of experience. Its central
aim is to liberate the figure of the "superject" from the constraints placed
on it by Whitehead and by the majority of his commentators; the result is
a picture that accords superjective power to the settled world: as the source
of "real potentiality," the settled world catalyzes—*from the environmental*

outside—the genesis of new actualities and informs—*again from the environmental outside*—the durational existence of societies at all scales.

Chapter 3, "Potentiality," explores the expansion of causal efficacy that is generated by data-intensive media. Its central aim is to thematize the potential for contemporary microcomputational sensors to directly mediate the domain of sensibility and thereby to facilitate a form of indirect human access to this domain, via the operation of "feed-forward." Feed-forward names the operation through which the technically accessed data of sensibility enters into futural moments of consciousness as radical intrusions from the outside: it is, I shall suggest, the principal mode in which contemporary consciousness can experience—in the phenomenological sense of *live through*—its own operationality.

Chapter 4, "Sensibility," takes stock of the larger consequences of this expanded, and specifically technical, agency of the superjective environment by exploring Whitehead's conception of the world as vibratory continuum. Its central aim is to reconceptualize "real potentiality" (the potentiality of the settled or superjectal world) as a mode of actuality that is more fundamental than the production of new actual entities and whose effects can be found in the "predictive analytics" informing the operation of today's culture industries.

Finally, in a short conclusion, I return to the singular situation in which twenty-first-century consciousnesses increasingly find themselves, namely, as supervisors and modulators of material and temporal processes to which they lack direct access, but upon which their experience is built and out of which they themselves arise. By exploring media critic and artist Jordan Crandall's performance event *Gatherings* (2011), I sketch a phenomenology of implication—centered on the notion that humans are implicated within larger sensory environments—as an alternative to more orthodox phenomenological accounts that insist on the necessity of a transcendent subject to be the recipient of the world's manifestation. The payoff of this phenomenology of implication—and more broadly of the entire study it culminates—is an account of the world as capable of sensing itself and of human sensing as a mode of such self-sensing.

If I have chosen to forgo a more detailed excavation of the affinities of Whitehead's philosophy with the post-phenomenological afterlife of phenomenology, it is precisely so I can focus my energies here on explaining why Whitehead is the philosopher par excellence of twenty-first-century media and of their impact on human experience. I am convinced—and hope here to convince you—that Whitehead's philosophy is made more interesting and more incisive by the transformations catalyzed by its conjuncture with twenty-first-century media, and also that twenty-first-century media be-

come more accessible and more pertinent by way of their intellectual mediation through a transformed Whiteheadian process philosophy. More than a
simple application of Whitehead's philosophy to twenty-first-century media
or a simple description of twenty-first-century media as exemplifying certain Whiteheadian commitments, what I hope to have accomplished here is
a bidirectional transformational coupling between a theoretical corpus and
a contemporary material and informational revolution where each is made
more complex and more intense by its distorted reflection in the other.

1

Prehensity

The analysis of an actual entity into "prehensions" is that mode of analysis which exhibits the most concrete elements in the nature of actual entities. This mode of analysis will be termed the "division" of the actual entity in question. Each actual entity is "divisible" in an indefinite number of ways, and each way of "division" yields its definite quota of prehensions. A prehension reproduces in itself the general characteristics of an actual entity: it is referent to an external world, and in this sense will be said to have a "vector character"; it involves emotion, and purpose, and valuation, and causation. In fact, any characteristic of an actual entity is reproduced in a prehension.

Actual entities involve each other by reason of their prehensions of each other. There are thus real individual facts of the togetherness of actual entities, which are real, individual, and particular, in the same sense in which actual entities and the prehensions are real, individual, and particular.

I have adopted the term "prehension" to express the activity whereby an actual entity effects its own concretion of other things.

Alfred North Whitehead, *Process and Reality*

From Object to Objectile

Efforts to theorize the operation of media in our world today are enframed by contrasting conceptions of the "technological object" that can stand as figures for two quite distinct philosophical traditions and that provide two divergent sets of resources for accessing and assessing media's experiential impact.

At one extreme lies contemporary French philosopher Bernard Stiegler's understanding of the technical temporal object—exemplarily, cinema in the age of global, real-time audiovisual fluxes:

> The program industries, and more precisely the media industry of radio-televised information, mass-produced temporal objects that are heard or viewed simultaneously by millions and sometimes by tens, hundreds, indeed millions of millions of "consciousnesses": this massive temporal coincidence dictates the new structure of the event, to which correspond new forms of consciousness and of collective unconscious.[1]

At the other extreme lies Gilles Deleuze's conceptualization of the technological object as "objectile":

> This new object we call *objectile*. As [architect] Bernard Cache has demonstrated, this is a very modern conception of the technological object: it refers neither to the beginnings of the industrial era nor to the idea of the standard that still upheld a semblance of essence and imposed a law of constancy ("the object produced by and for the masses"), but to our current state of things, where fluctuation of the norm replaces the permanence of a law; where the object assumes a place in a continuum by variation; where industrial automation or serial machineries replace stamped forms. The new status of the object no longer refers its condition to a spatial mold—in other words, to a relation of form-matter—but to a temporal modulation that implies as much the beginnings of a continuous variation of matter as a continuous development of form.[2]

Contracting a tradition running from Husserl (if not, indeed, from Hume) to Derrida, Stiegler's project confronts the great Husserlian figure of time-consciousness with its necessary technical supplementation. In his exuberant rejuvenation of Husserl's project, which simultaneously marks the limits of the latter's analytical scope and methodological rigor, Stiegler lays bare time-consciousness's dependence on technical objects that can neither be safely reduced to contents of consciousness (following the famous method of phenomenological *epochē*) nor seamlessly assimilated into Husserl's bipartite schema for conceptualizing memory as (primary) retention and (secondary) recollection. As Stiegler sees it, technical (temporal) objects introduce a third, *tertiary*, layer of memory that, far from being a mere degradation of secondary recollection, in fact makes possible the very interplay between primary and secondary modes of memory. It is only once we have the possibility of experiencing the *exact same temporal object more than once*, Stiegler argues, that we can properly fathom the bidirectional traffic between retention and recollection. Thus, a new experience of hearing a song or seeing a film a second (or *n*th) time cannot but be impacted by our previous memory of hearing or seeing that same song or film; that is why, insists Stiegler, our new experience differs from our first or earlier experience. In sum, our earlier experience of hearing or seeing selectively impacts our new experience in a way that can be generalized to memory as such. Conversely, our (secondary) memory of the experience is also selectively impacted by each new experience of hearing or seeing the same technical temporal object, in a way that modifies its future impact on new experiences following a pattern that ultimately turns out to display a tightly knit recursivity.

Culminating a quite different tradition stretching from Leibniz to Whitehead and ultimately to himself, Deleuze's conception refuses the instrumentalization of the technical object that constitutes the first step in Stiegler's account. Far from enlisting the technological object as a surrogate capable of objectifying the immanent flow of time in consciousness *for the purpose of consciousness's reflective self-evaluation*, Deleuze begins by according the object a material agency of its own. Following this reconceptualization, the object enters into a much more intimate contact with the flux of matter that it "objectifies": rather than capturing matter in a static form, as a "spatial mold" that temporarily transcends or suspends the temporal flux, the object becomes a process that continuously indexes the material flux and, in so doing, offers a perspective on variation. The changed status of the object thus implies a "profound change" in the status of the subject:

> A subject will be what comes to the point of view, or rather what remains in the point of view. That is why the transformation of the object refers to a correlative transformation of the subject: the subject is not a sub-ject but, as Whitehead says, a "superject." Just as the object becomes objectile, the subject becomes a superject. A needed relation exists between variation and point of view: not simply because of the variety of points of view . . . , but in the first place because every point of view is a point of view on variation. The point of view is not what varies with the subject, at least in the first instance; it is, to the contrary, the condition in which an eventual subject apprehends a variation.[3]

It is important that we appreciate what is at issue here: far more than a simple contrast between subject- and object-centered conceptions of the technological object, Deleuze's characterization effectively conjoins subjectivity to the broader worldly processes within which it arises. For this purpose, Deleuze's reference to Whitehead is neither spurious nor tenuous: indeed, beyond the concrete figure of the superject, which will play a crucial role in my argument here, Whitehead's general ontology promotes a radically environmental perspective on process. Such a perspective stands at the farthest imaginable extreme from orthodox Cartesian (and orthodox phenomenological) subjectivism. According to it, the entirety of the universe informs any and every becoming. Thus, what may look like autonomous operations of subjects are in actual fact aggregates of multiple and heterogeneous, overlapping agencies complexly imbricated with the total situation or environment at the given moment of their occurrence.

When he positions the superject as the subjective correlate of the becoming-objectile of the object, Deleuze does more than simply invoke this cross-scalar conception of subjectivity. Indeed, he correlates the operation of superjection with the process of technical modulation. In this way, he manages to attribute agency directly to the temporal modulation of the technological object. This temporal modulation operates directly on the subjectivity that inheres in the power of superjects to impact future becomings, both at the level of concrescences and at the level of events. That is why Deleuze's attribution of agency to temporal modulation contrasts markedly with Stiegler's embrace of the technical object's transcendence of consciousness. It involves more than mere surrogacy (the object performing the work of consciousness); indeed, it involves nothing less than a becoming-subjective of the object. On Deleuze's account, it is matter itself, or, more precisely, the modulation of matter introduced by the technological objectile, that calls the subject—qua point of view on a material variation—into being and, importantly, into being *as an "effect" of its own materiality*.

What hangs in the balance between Stiegler's and Deleuze's positions then is nothing less than the possibility for the technical object to exercise material agency of its own. That is why the two positions, and the two passages with which I began, define what amount to two extremities on a continuum of media. With its focus on the correlation between media objects and higher-order cognitive processes, Stiegler's work addresses one end of the spectrum of contemporary media experience: what it means that media mediate the temporal flux of conscious experience and of life itself. With its invocation of a direct modulation of matter, Deleuze's work begins at the other end: it seeks to explore how media might impact experience without being channeled through delimited, higher-order processes. The point of the contrast between these two positions is not, however, to proffer two options for thinking technics. Rather, they relate to one another as Newtonian to Einsteinian physics: what Stiegler demonstrates about consciousness is nothing other than a limit case of the far broader material operation of technics following Deleuze's account. The point is not to decide between these two perspectives, as if one were simply right and the other wrong, but rather to deploy them together, though asymmetrically, with the goal of generating a more inclusive continuum that positions media's impact on experience as the correlate of a disparate and heterogeneous, multi-scalar and expanded—indeed, properly "post-phenomenological"—phenomenology.

Twenty-First-Century Media

Precisely such a continuum is at stake in the operation and experience of what I propose to call "twenty-first-century media." By twenty-first-century media, I mean to designate less a set of objects or processes than a tendency: the tendency for media to operate at microtemporal scales without any necessary—let alone any direct—connection to human sense perception and conscious awareness. This tendency is in large part the result of the revolution in media instigated by digital computation: today's microsensors and smart devices allow for an unprecedented degree of direct intervention into the sensible confound. For the first time in history, media now typically affect the sensible confound independently of and prior to any more delimited impact they many come to have on human cognitive and perceptual experience.

In this sense, twenty-first-century media pose a challenge that is new. They challenge us to construct a relationship with them. On this point, they differ markedly from earlier media. Unlike the various forms of recording media typical of the nineteenth and twentieth centuries, where the coupling or synchronization of media system and human sense perception formed something of a telos, if not indeed a constitutive presupposition, twenty-first-century media not only resist any form of direct synchronization but question the viability of a model of media premised on a simple and direct coupling of human and media system. Faced with the environmental effects of today's media—effects that, by definition, occur outside our awareness—we must work to expose the complex networks through which environmental media impact experience and to construct relationships that afford some grasp of, if not indeed some distinct agency over, their operation.

While this environmental dimension has led some contemporary media theorists to characterize contemporary networked media as "inhuman" (Galloway and Thacker), I would strongly oppose any move to link the promise of new media to some fantasized transcendence of the human as a form of life and would argue instead that it introduces a massive complexification in the networks that now link not just machines with machines and humans with networked machines, but also *humans with other humans.* Within the hybrid domain opened by this complexification, the very possibility to rethink experience as such—and to intensify *our* specifically *human* experience—depends on our capacity to forge connections with the microtemporal processes that, despite evading the grasp of our conscious reflection and sense perception, nonetheless impact our sensory lives in significant ways.

There are, to be sure, many facets to this shift in the address of media, and we shall have occasion to explore a number of them in what follows. Let me focus for the moment on the changed and still-changing situation of human experience in the wake of the microcomputational revolution. Because they primarily and directly address the vibratory continuum that composes the world, twenty-first-century media must be said to impact experience through embodied and environmental sensory processes that are peripheral to consciousness and sense perception. More simply still, twenty-first-century media impact the environment, including our bodily environment, before impacting—and, in part, as a way to impact—our higher-order sensory and perceptual faculties. This situation is precisely what informs—and makes imperative—the claim about access to data of sensibility (CADS) introduced above: specifically, it is because the impact of media makes itself felt, as it were, prior to the constitution of "human-addressable" agents, that recourse must be made to technical operations capable of accessing and intensifying the domain of sensibility itself.

What this means, to say it yet another way, is that we can no longer take for granted the correlation of media and human experience that has informed media history up until today. Whereas the technical media characteristic of the nineteenth and twentieth centuries, for example, photography and cinema, primarily address human sense perception and experiential memory (and I say "primarily" to indicate both that there is no technical necessity involved here and that there are significant exceptions), twenty-first-century media directly shape the sensory continuum out of which perception and memory arise. If they are not, as Kittler would have it, essentially or fundamentally indifferent to the human, twenty-first-century media are certainly hybrid in their address, in the sense that they operate both micro- and macrotemporally, directly on microsensory experience and, by way of various *aesthetic* mediations, indirectly on higher-order sense perception and consciousness.

This hybridity or double-valenced operationality of twenty-first-century media was recognized early on by the pioneers of digital media studies. In his groundbreaking study *The Language of New Media*, Lev Manovich makes the crucial distinction between digital simulations (or emulations) and digital syntheses, where the salient point concerns whether new media objects or processes exploit the affordances of the computational environment. In schematic terms, simulations merely reproduce the appearance of a non-digital object whereas syntheses create new objects that are concretely and often complexly anchored in their digital infrastructure. For present purposes, my interest in this distinction centers less on the materiality of new media objects than on the experiential dimensions of digital media in their contemporary techno-social configuration. What new kinds of experience do the microtemporal and microsensorial operations of digital syntheses solicit, and what resources do we require not simply to theorize them, but indeed to *live* them?

Today, new media do not simply nor even primarily center on "the computer," as they arguably did when Manovich wrote his pioneering study. The period between 1999 and 2014 has witnessed the explosive growth of mobile media and the distribution of the computer into the lived environment. This is a story with which we are all intimately—and experientially—familiar. We still use computers, to be sure, but we also rely increasingly on the mobile computational devices and smart phones that we now typically carry around with us. The transition to the paradigm of mobility—and from computing as the deliberative use of a portable computer to computing on the fly in so-called ubiquitous computational networks—involves more than a shift of technical platform and the swapping of some bigger machines for other smaller ones.

More important than these material technical changes considered in isolation are the social and cultural developments with which they are inextricably connected. It is notable, for example, that we now use our computational devices not only, and perhaps not even primarily, to perform specialized activities like creating spreadsheets or word processing documents or even searching the Internet, but also to gather information on the fly and to share it with others. Our mobile technologies are currently in the process of transforming the function of recording: no longer solely or primarily a technical process for memorializing human experience, as it largely was in the cinematic age, recording now typically operates in the service of connection—to provide information that is practically oriented and useful only for a short time—and it occurs at levels of technical operation that are by definition beyond the scope of human awareness. Needless to say, this shift in our use of media is accompanied—and indeed is made possible—by a massive expansion in the interaction of machines with other machines. Thus, well before we even begin to use our smart phones in active and passive ways, the physical devices we carry with us interface in complex ways with cell towers and satellite networks; and preparatory to our using our digital devices or our laptops to communicate or to acquire information, the latter engage in complex connections with wireless routers and network hosts. In providing the infrastructural support for our use of media, this on-the-fly, or "real-time," machine-to-machine interfacing constitutes something qualitatively new about twenty-first-century media.

To understand the experiential shift at issue here, let us focus on how the operation of recording is modified in twenty-first-century media networks. In nineteenth- and twentieth-century media, recording operates, again *primarily* though by no means exclusively, at the level of experiential unities and in the service of individual and cultural memory;[4] typical forms of recorded media include individual photographic frames, still photographs, cinematic moving images, and continuous scanning of a video raster. In today's media networks, by contrast, recording operates primarily at the level of sub-experiential and microtemporal unities and in the service of future-directed, often non-deliberative (or better: not traditionally deliberative) action in the present; typical forms include bits of computational data and fine-grained inscriptions of analog fluxes. Moreover, recording now operates predominately in the service of communication between machines necessary for the operation of our smart phones and other microcomputational devices.

Bluntly put, the model of recording as the durable inscription of traces of personal experience simply no longer applies (or applies only derivatively) in most of its contemporary instances. Put in terms that are at once and indelibly sociocultural *and* technical: recording now occurs through and in the service of extremely short circuits of experience and, as such, no longer serves to support the kinds of reflective experience and memory that could still be adequately mediated by recording technologies like cinema and even video. What hangs in the balance here is the very "essence" of recording: no longer oriented by the aim and the technical problematic of capturing durational traces of human experience, recording now operates in the service of myriad small-scale technical processes necessary to construct the connections that underlie contemporary media networks. If the interface with the human element remains in play—and I want to argue in the most forceful terms that it does—it has lost its directness. Rather than being the "content" of media, as it once was, human experience must be composed of molecular behavioral traces that record incremental dispositions rather than integral experience. In sum: what gets stored by today's media are no longer human experiences themselves but bits of data that register molecular increments of behavior and that do not in themselves amount to a full picture of integrated human "lived experience."

Critics have of course already directed some significant attention to this difference. One important example is film theorist David Rodowick, who, in his recent elegy for film, has eloquently argued that digital recording technologies lack a direct connection to the kinds of qualitative experience—most centrally, durational experience—that characterize a certain vision of human existence.[5] For my purposes here, what is important is the implication, vaguely present in Rodowick's study, that digital recording as such (and not simply digital *cinematic* recording) fundamentally modifies the scope and operation of recording.[6] Largely despite its intentions, Rodowick's study beautifully demonstrates how digital recording ruptures the long-standing correlation of technical recording capacities with human experience: we now live in media environments in which synchronization with experiential time—or, more precisely, with the long circuits of lived experience—no longer constitutes the dominant function of technical media. In this media environment, recording has, as it were, come into its own: indeed, now that it typically operates at the microtemporal scales of the computational processes that support it, recording tends to undermine the very higher-order experiential syntheses it once mediated.

German media critic Wolfgang Ernst links this shift in the operation of recording to the figure of the archive. Citing Gerd Meissner, who twenty years ago presciently observed that "computer technology is made for information processing, not for long-term storage," Ernst correlates computization with the end of the archive or, alternatively, with the figure of the "anarchive": "The 21st century," he writes, "will increasingly be an epoch that exceeds the archive. With data-streaming and network-based communication, the perspective shifts: the privileged status accorded in Western civilization to 'permanent' cultural values and traditions—the cultural ROM [Read-Only-Memory], as it were—is increasingly giving way to a dynamic exchange, a permanent transfer in the most literal sense."[7] A certain technical displacement lies behind this shift in perspective: the advent of the anarchive marks the displacement of a technical system supporting static, long-term information storage directly accessible to and manipulable by humans in favor of a technical system oriented by dynamic processes of permanent regeneration that "operate at the speed of electricity itself."[8] Following this shift, the function of storage is fundamentally redirected from the problems of the archive proper—of access to already-created information—to the more immediate tasks concerned with the actual generation of information in real time. Ernst finds a concrete illustration of this shift in the figure of the Internet: "The use of the term 'archive' in the Internet . . . indicat[es] a shift of emphasis to real-time or immediate storage processing, to fast feedback. Thus, the so-called Internet 'archive' becomes radically temporalized [and temporalized, we might add, at radically microtemporal scales]. It is rather hypertemporal than hyperspatial, based on the aesthetic of immediate feedback, recycling and refreshing, rather than on the ideal of locked-away storage for eternity."[9] What the Internet archives, if the concept of the "archive" can even still be deployed here, are the extremely short circuits, the host of microscale technical operations, that make up the global network of computers supporting its World Wide Web.

To address the changed role of experience in such an altered storage environment, Ernst invokes Foucauldian "counter-spaces": "isolated islands of archival storage" that will "retroactively remain"; "monumental and material resistance against dynamic and permanent reorganization of binary data, counter-practices in this age of general digitization driven by economical force."[10] For Ernst, these heterotopic spaces are already a thing of the past, as the very meaning of the archive has been decoupled from its long-standing, historical correlation with human experience. Today's archive describes the technical conditions for the operation of computer networks and thus provides tech support for the technical regimes out of which human experience will be composed:

> In the digital domain, the archive in the strict cybernetic (i.e., "governmental") sense returns, even more rigorously than ever, particularly in the form of the laws governing technological and electromathematical communication. Source codes and protocols reign on the level of programming languages in computers; so do the registers (an original archivological term) on the level of the central processing unit (CPU) within computer hardware. Physically and logically (that is: technologically) the archive rules in media culture. . . . With mathematized machines (the "computer"), the archival regime returns more mightily than ever, but this time *it does not depend upon being processed by human archivists and users*, but rather is coupled with electronic materialities.[11]

With its capacity to "perform according to its own laws," the computational archive would appear to mark a moment in the history of technical media in which human experience is simply left behind.[12]

It is at this conjuncture that Rodowick's work can be made to intervene in a useful way. Insofar as it isolates a desire for media to mediate *human* experience, Rodowick's pathos-laden elegy of analog film can motivate us to discover new ways to forge long circuits of lived experience precisely on the basis of the dynamic, real-time operation of anarchival recording. Indeed, what Rodowick's Jekyll and Hyde account of digital recording makes particularly salient is the necessity for *a supplementary layer of mediation* between technical recording and human experience: where mediation once named the technical inscription of human experience, today mediation must be redirected to the task of composing relations *between* technical circuits *and* human experience. Elsewhere, I have sought to explicate this singular situation of digital technics in terms of a claim about mediation itself: rather than mediating the content of experience (or experience as content) and rather than mediating the content of a former medium, contemporary media mediate the technical conditions of mediation itself. Thus, if it is the case that technical media now operate through microtemporal loops that are below the threshold of conscious attention, as Rodowick convincingly claims, a supplementary stage of mediation is required to bring their operation into our purview.

One of the examples I have elucidated in this context is an art website called Flickeur.com that simply grabs images "randomly" (i.e., following a randomization program) from Flickr.com and combines them, again using "randomly" selected cinematic transitions, into a potentially infinite film.[13] Through the gradually emergent differences between this digital media object and a traditional cinematic object—aesthetic differences that *can* be experienced by consciousness—Flickeur.com affords viewers a perceptual interface onto the microscalar processes of computational selection and composition—a mediation of mediation itself. This mediation, however, and the perceptual access it affords, comes at an experiential cost: it requires a temporal disjunction of perception from operationality. Thus, by the time they become available to our perception, the microscalar processes that form the infrastructural basis for whatever properly human experience might occur will always already have happened. Simply put, their operationality belongs to a different level of temporalization than any ensuing and retrospectively constructed perceptual interface.

In the current context, I am less interested in the technical specificity of digital technics—and the particular demands it institutes for media reflexivity—than I am in the broader experiential impact of twenty-first-century media. More than just a technical form among others, twenty-first-century media broker a shift in experience itself, a shift as much social and sensory as technical. Put another way, the operation of mediating contemporary technical media *for the purposes of making it salient for our traditional modes of experience* (i.e., for consciousness) can now be understood to be but one small part of the practical and theoretical work required to reconfigure the correlation of contemporary media with experience. What such work requires, as I have been suggesting here, is nothing less than a fundamental reconfiguration of experience itself. In the face of twenty-first-century media networks, we need a *neutral* theory of experience that applies to humans and nonhumans alike, and that broaches the divide separating the animate from the inanimate. Experience can no longer be restricted to—or reserved for—a special class of being, but must be generalized so as to capture a vast domain of events, including everything that happens when machines interact with other machines in today's complex media networks, everything that happens when humans interface with these networks, and also, of course, everything that happens when humans self-reflect on these interactions. Put another way, the scope of experience must be broadened to encompass not simply what it has always encompassed—higher-order modes of experience and lower-order, bodily modes to the extent these bubble up into higher-order ones—but a veritable plurality of multi-scalar instances of experience that extend, along the continuum of what White-head calls "causal efficacy," from consciousness all the way down to the most rudimentary aspects of our living operationality and all the way out to the most diffuse environmental dimensions of a given sensory situation. Twenty-first-century media, in short, call on us to trade in our univocal model of experience—a model that, no matter how open to the "precognitive," cannot but channel everything through *our* experience, which is to say through higher-order modes of experiencing—for a massively plural and differentiated model where experience must be reconceived as the composition of multiple overlapping levels of sensation and where each of these multiple levels retains some degree of sensory autonomy.

Let me be perfectly clear: my point is not that we no longer experience media at the level of our consciousness. My point, rather, is that such experience, when it happens, can no longer be presumed to be some kind of default synchronic correlate of media, the privileged recipient or object of mediation as such. Faced with twenty-first-century media, we can ask a simple yet absolutely crucial question that is long overdue: Why should media operate in a way that is exclusively targeted to consciousness? Because they address experience at sub-perceptual, subconscious levels, twenty-first-century media provide the impetus for us to suspend the long-standing correlation of experience with (higher-order) human experience and to focus instead on the heterogeneity and multi-scalar scope of experience as it operates all along the continuum of causal efficacy from the most elementary events (e.g., quantum decoherence) all the way up to the most cosmic. Throughout this expansion, the very meaning of experience will necessarily be in play, for it can no longer simply be assumed that we—that is, we formerly privileged human beings—determine the bounds of its scope.

From Consciousness to "Human-Implicating" Experience

This suspension of consciousness's privilege, however, does not betoken its irrelevance so much as its redescription. If consciousness no longer exercises an unquestionable privilege as the stable, substantial hub of experience, it nonetheless continues to operate, as it has always done—as one level of subjective operationality among a host of others. Indeed, as I shall argue at length below, conscious experience of twenty-first-century media increasingly occurs as the result of a complex compositional process involving digital techniques of data-gathering and granular synthesis that facilitate the "feeding-forward" of multiple experiential sources into a potential future synthesis within consciousness.

This reconfiguration of higher-order experience, of the experience of consciousness as phenomenology from Husserl onward has defined it, will have significant theoretical consequences. Indeed, it will require us to rethink in the most radical way imaginable the historical correlation between living experience and the temporal modality of the present: not only will we need to reconceptualize the present *of consciousness* as an accomplishment that is in some crucial sense *always-to-come*, but we will also, and perhaps more fundamentally still, need to embrace the coexistence of multiple experiential presents—multiple, partially overlapping presents from different time frames and scales—as what composes the seemingly more encompassing, higher-order syntheses of consciousness.

Where the question concerns its impact on human—or, as I shall prefer to say, at the risk of a certain expressive barbarity, "human-implicating"—experience, one crucial challenge posed by twenty-first-century media is how to understand the co-functioning that constitutes this hybridity. How can we model the operational overlap that occurs when higher-order cognitive and perceptual faculties function alongside microsensibilities that, though peripheral to their modes of "awareness," are nonetheless central to the total situation in which they are implicated? Answering this question will require us to discover new resources that will permit us to address media's impact on human experience beyond the boundaries of the object-centered and body-centered models we have relied on to date. For, as I have already suggested, today's ubiquitous computational environments and bionic bodily supplementations operate more by fundamentally reconfiguring the very sensory field within which our experience occurs than by offering new contents for our consciousness to process or new sensory affordances for us to enframe through our embodiment.[14]

If these media systems help us—embodied, minded, and enworlded macroscale beings that we are—to access and to act on the microtemporal-

ity of experience, they do so *precisely and only because they bypass con-*
sciousness and embodiment, which is really to say because they bypass *the*
limitations of consciousness and embodiment. That is why, in stark contrast
to the technical object theorized by Stiegler and also, to an extent, the technological objectile at the heart of Deleuze's baroque conception of matter,
the "object" of twenty-first-century media, if it can even be said to have one,
is the very domain of sensibility itself. Whatever else it betokens, twenty-
first-century media centrally involve a massive expansion in, as well as a
fundamental differentiation—a "heterogenesis"—of, the interface between
human being and sensory environment.

One absolutely crucial element of this expanded scope of media in its
contemporary form is the certain demotion to which it submits the concept
of perception. Because the impact of twenty-first-century media occurs in
large part peripherally to or entirely outside of perception, we can no longer continue to accord perception the privilege it has held in the history of
Western philosophy, which, incidentally, is the same privilege that anchors
most contemporary (as well as most historical) thematizations of media.
Twenty-first-century media are largely environmental in their scope, which
means that they affect the materiality of experience at a level more elemental
than that of perception; more precisely, they impact experience by shaping
the ongoing worldly production of sensibility that constitutes the sensory
confound out of which perception proper can in turn arise.

One of the crucial claims I shall advance in this book concerns the displacement of perception in favor of sensation—or rather of what I shall
call "worldly sensibility"—that results as a necessary experiential correlate
of twenty-first-century media. *Wikipedia* defines perception as "the process
of attaining awareness or understanding of the environment by organizing
and interpreting sensory information."[15] This definition perfectly captures
the difference between perception and sensation as I understand it and as it
is important here: perception characterizes the operation of a system that is
distinct from an environment, and it involves an awareness based on some
activity performed by that system on the sensory information it gathers
from the environment. In this respect, we can say that perception operates
at a higher level of organization than sensation, and that sensation is more
"atomic" than perception insofar as it involves specific sensory relations
between a sensor and an environment prior to and to some extent independently of their integration into the more unified operation of perception.

To the extent that it motivates a resurgence of sensation—or rather
of sensibility—and a concomitant demotion of perception, twenty-first-
century media create an experiential situation that hearkens back to the
nineteenth-century efforts to isolate the sensory materiality of experience

using objective techniques of measurement.[16] Together with the entire legacy of nineteenth-century psychophysics, these efforts were derailed by phenomenology in its classical formation. With its stress on the inseparability of sensation from a perceptual or intentional context, the phenomenology of Husserl, Heidegger, and Merleau-Ponty made it impossible to speak about sensation without anchoring it in a higher-order system to which its function was necessarily subordinate. Thus, Husserl focused on the integration of the *hyle* into intentionality; Heidegger spoke of "contexts-of-involvement" and emphasized the hermeneutic circle underlying any sensory experience; and Merleau-Ponty fundamentally reoriented the entire phenomenological project in terms of the "primacy of perception," albeit a bodily one.[17]

A crucial subterranean materialism nonetheless traverses the history of phenomenology and makes possible a different, far more complicated account of the fate of sensation following its psychophysical heyday. The fruit of this materialism, which emerges out of the tortured meditation on time that Husserl carried out until his death, is a conception of worldly temporalizing—dubbed "de-presencing" (*Entgegenwärtigung*) by Husserl's final assistant and putative heir, Eugen Fink; as I shall understand it here, de-presencing designates a primordial worldly sensibility constituting the source for all higher-order sensory and perceptual experience. In this respect, it shares much in common with Merleau-Ponty's final conception of the reversibility of the flesh and furnishes a concrete account of how this reversibility (as we shall see below in chapter 4) depends on a temporal difference that cannot be the property of a transcendent subject. One of the fundamental claims of my study is that this "minor" legacy of phenomenology—a legacy that marks the limits of the classical phenomenological project and inaugurates its afterlife as a post-phenomenology of sensibility—correlates with the material impact of twenty-first-century media.[18] The very worldly sensibility that constitutes the fleeting object of Husserl's final ruminations on time, and that finds a positive formulation in Fink's de-presencing and in Merleau-Ponty's reversibility, is precisely what is currently being expanded, intensified, and made accessible by the media on which we are becoming ever increasingly dependent.

In light of this development, I shall be led to claim that what twenty-first-century media mediates is sensibility itself, and that this operation of mediation—in stark contrast to the mediation of our sense organs (McLuhan) or of our past experience (Stiegler)—occurs, as I've said, largely outside the purview of perception. What this means is that twenty-first-century media, rather than mediating our qualitative experience itself, mediate *the sensory basis for such experience*. This situation imposes a crucial critical limit on the operation of media that we must treat with respect: twenty-first-century media only impact higher-order forms of experience, such as sense perception or consciousness, *indirectly* or at a remove. Their more fundamental, immediate impact is on worldly sensibility itself. In order to access and account for twenty-first-century media's mediation of the sensory basis for experience, we will thus need to develop a neutral model of experience that, in contrast to classical phenomenology (but informed by its post-phenomenological afterlife), not only does not rely exclusively or even primarily on perception, but that can, as it were, go "beneath" perception in order to address the causal infrastructure of experience directly.

With his (already-mentioned) distinction between two "pure" modes of perception—perception in the mode of causal efficacy and perception in the mode of presentational immediacy—Whitehead furnishes the starting point for developing such a model. As its proximate purpose—to refute Humean skepticism—attests, Whitehead's expansion of perception takes the important step of anchoring perceptions *within the material universe where causality reigns*. For Whitehead, that is, perceptions (whether in the mode of presentational immediacy or causal efficacy) are never simply subjective creations ("ideas" or "impressions") that transform the fleeting appearances of material reality into certain subjective contents; rather, perceptions are themselves caused *by the very same kind of shift that causes all events in the universe's becoming*.[19]

With this observation, Whitehead introduces precisely what is required to move from a perception-centered account of experience to a broader understanding of sensibility as the concrete texture of experience across the board. One of the key efforts of this study will be to develop such an understanding—which, as mentioned, I call "worldly sensibility"—by radicalizing some of Whitehead's claims. In particular, it will be necessary to contest Whitehead's restriction of the material impact of causal efficacy to the status of "contents of perception": simply by conceptualizing this material impact as a form of *perception*—perception in the mode of causal efficacy—Whitehead in effect restricts it to a form that fits into the orthodox phenomenological conception of perception. No matter how much it expands our understanding of experience, Whitehead's broadening of perception to encompass causal efficacy beyond sense perception remains biased toward the form of perception characteristic of higher-order experiential operations and of the beings capable of performing them. More simply put: the payoff of Whitehead's expansion of perception is a broadening of the scope *of perception*, not an extension of it to address its non-perceptual source in worldly sensibility.

Despite Whitehead's own tendency to treat causal efficacy—often in explicit contradiction to what he claims about it—as *a mode of perception* rather than a material force of the universe, we can, however, take from his theory the absolutely crucial idea that the causal lineages informing events, including events of perception, open different paths toward accessing the properly sub-perceptual impact of twenty-first-century media. To the extent that they either inform us about the sensory agency of matter or extend our capacities for sensation beyond the scope of perception, today's smart phones and microsensors introduce an unprecedented opportunity for us to probe the hitherto "black-boxed" processes of causal efficacy that White-head champions as the motor of process at all scales. With today's digital and bio-informational technologies and processes, we encounter a sphere of objectivity that is itself highly subjective—that is capable not simply of startling dynamic becoming of its own, but also of providing feedback about this dynamic becoming both in itself and insofar as it interpenetrates the becoming of other subjective processes.

We can get a sense for what is at stake here—and also why Whitehead may have sold himself short—by recalling the philosophical origins of his expansion of perception. For this purpose, it is crucial to acknowledge that Whitehead develops his conception of causal efficacy, and his more specific claim that it constitutes a distinct mode *of perception*, in order to dissolve Humean skepticism. Whereas Hume restricted the operation of causal-ity to the status of an idea (the idea of an impression), Whitehead insists on the irreducible materiality of causal lineages that, he demonstrates convincingly, is felt through the "withness of the body." It is by means of vague, and vaguely self-referential, perceptions, such as the perception that I see with my eyes or that I touch with my hand, that the causal efficacy of worldly sensibility can enter directly into the sphere of human awareness. If perception in the mode of causal efficacy resolves Humean skepticism, it does so because it attests perceptually to the *material causal lineages* that exist and have force outside of the realm of impressions, ideas, and ideas of impressions—outside the domain of sense perception proper. Beyond supporting an alternative mode of perception, and indeed as the very rea-son why they can do so, these material lineages of causal efficacy designate ontologically efficacious events that have direct impact on our experience independently of, and at levels more primitive than, the higher-order percep-tions (including perceptions "in the mode of causal efficacy") that emerge from them.

This material efficacy of causal lineages becomes particularly crucial in the context of twenty-first-century media, which, as I have suggested, oper-ate predominately at microtemporal scales and thus largely evade the grasp of perception, whether this is understood as sense perception proper *or as perception in the mode of causal efficacy*. Bluntly put: there simply is no direct conscious *or* bodily correlate of the sensory effects of twenty-first-century media. This situation poses a direct challenge to phenomenological models of media, for as a result of the microtemporal address of today's media, we can no longer gain access to their impact either by analyzing a technical temporal object that furnishes a surrogate for the flux of time through consciousness (Stiegler) or by excavating how they affect the withness of the body (Whitehead). In this respect, it may well be that our currently fashionable models for analyzing the impact of media have reached a point of critical exhaustion: neither consciousness-centered nor bodily-centered approaches seem capable of grasping the level of materiality and the sensuous heterogeneity at issue in twenty-first-century media. To appreciate why will require us to delve more deeply into the technicity of twenty-first-century media and, in particular, to grapple with the specificity of their "pharmacological" dimension.

The End of Pharmacology?

More than any other figure, French philosopher Bernard Stiegler deserves credit for laying bare the pharmacological basis of technics. Following in the wake of Jacques Derrida's reading of technics in "Plato's Pharmacy," Stiegler has made the *pharmakon*—the Greek term that names both a poison and its remedy—the central figure for theorizing the correlation of technical media with human being. In his reading of this figure, Stiegler convincingly demonstrates how technical media, beginning with the invention of writing as conveyed in the Myth of Theuth in Plato's *Phaedrus*, operate through an essential duplicity whereby they give back to the human a remedy for what they take away. The case of writing stands as the paradigm for this pharmacologic: in the very act of harming the operation of (internal) memory (because it removes the need for memory practice), writing extends the scope of memory (by supplementing it technically or, more precisely, by exteriorizing it into a technical support).

A similar pharmacological structure appears to lie at the heart of twenty-first-century media: at the same time as it demotes perceptual consciousness from its privileged position as arbiter of experience, twenty-first-century media furnish a means for humans to access the very experience that would appear to have been lost in the wake of that demotion. And yet this pharmacological structure differs in an important respect from writing and other previous technical media. For, whereas writing, standing in for technical media as such, *directly* gives back what it takes away, exchanging a "natural" source of memory for an "artificial" one, twenty-first-century media involve an exchange of experiential modalities that is also an exchange of temporal scales of experience: what we lose in the way of *perceptual* grasp of our environment, we regain through an expanded and microtemporal *sensory* contact with the world that, in itself, *does not have a perceptual dimension and that does not need to develop one in order to yield experience.* The newly accessible sensory contact with the sensible world constitutes an *indirect* recompense for the waning of the powers and centrality of perception, where the term "indirect" is meant to signal that this recompense does not so much restore a lost capability as develop a different one in its place.

In contrast to writing and other previous technical media that are themselves the pharmacological recompense for the changes they bring about, twenty-first-century media thus require a technical supplement *in order to make good on their pharmacological promise.* Because their pharmacological recompense—expanded and microtemporal *sensory* contact with the world—cannot be experienced directly through any mode of human self-reference, a technical interface is necessary, as it were, to *translate* the sensory expansion into a form that can be experienced through human self-reference. And even more fundamentally, what is involved in this unprecedented pharmacological situation is a *technical distribution of experience* that couples human operations with machinic operations in a functional system where the "meaning" of the experience—the payoff of the pharmacological recompense—is "proper" neither to the human nor to the machinic component, and therefore cannot be understood exclusively from one or the other perspective. Rather than exteriorizing and forming a technical surrogate for some already up-and-running human faculty, twenty-first-century media directly impact worldly sensibility *and at the same time* operate as a technical presentification of *the actual causal efficacy* of that sensibility. As such, they furnish a means of access to the efficacy of sensibility that, crucially, *is not a perceptual means of access.* Twenty-first-century media in effect bypass the older mediation via embodiment—the gradual bodily assimilation of the preperceptual—in favor of a more direct, in some sense radically disembodied, surrogacy.

On this new paradigm of human co-functioning with technics, machines are necessary to register and interpret the sensory data constituting experience, and such data encompass events that are "environmental" in relation to an experiential center (data about the environment in which sensation occurs) as well as events that directly involve the embodiment of such a center (e.g., biometric data that cannot be accessed directly by means of perception and consciousness). With twenty-first-century media, in short, we witness the advent of a media system that no longer directly mediates the human senses or any other *faculty* specific to human experience (e.g., memory). In a fundamental break with the lineage of media prosthetics that runs from

Plato via McLuhan to Derrida and Stiegler, twenty-first-century media directly mediate the causal infrastructure of worldly sensibility. Whatever impact they have on human experience specifically is a part of this larger mediation: by mediating worldly sensibility, twenty-first-century media simultaneously modulate human sensibility, as it were, beneath the senses.

As mentioned above, to mediate human experience in accordance with the "traditional" vocation of media, twenty-first-century media require a supplementary layer of mediation that can connect their "primary mediation" (their mediation of the causal efficacy of sensibility) with whatever necessarily delayed impact they may go on to have on higher-order human modes of experience (memory, perception, etc.). Because it is literally what facilitates our interface to the sensory continuum, this supplementary layer of mediation is the source for whatever compensation accompanies the disenfranchisement of perception. Thus, in addition to—and, in an important sense, to the side of—their direct impact on the sensory continuum, twenty-first-century media also expand our access to this sensory continuum: because of their specific technicity, they are able to gather data about microtemporal dimensions of sensory experience that simply could never appear *as such* to consciousness, or, more precisely, that belong to what I shall call the "operational present" of sensibility, a present to which consciousness has no "natural" access.

What transpires is a *doubling or splitting of media's operationality*: on one hand, twenty-first-century media mediate the sensory continuum in which all experience, human included, occurs; on the other, twenty-first-century media function as media for humans—as media in its traditional sense—when and insofar as they *presentify* the data of sensibility in ways that humans can perceive. I cannot emphasize enough the centrality of the temporal dimension of this second, supplementary mediation and of the elements of experience it mediates. Indeed, one way to capture the singularity of the pharmacological dimension of twenty-first-century media would be to foreground the way in which it bypasses the slow time resolution of consciousness in order to maximize our material contact with and operational agency over the sensory continuum.

On such an understanding, it is precisely because twenty-first-century media exceed the temporal bounds of sense perception that they can expand experience: for while perceptual consciousness can only experience microsensory sensibility once the latter bubbles up into its operational window, the technical sensors now ubiquitous in our lived environments are able to capture experiential events directly at the microtemporal level of their operationality and—*independently of consciousness's mediation*—"feed them forward" into (future or "just-to-come") consciousness in ways that can influence consciousness's own future agency in the world. Otherwise put, while embodied consciousness can only wait for microsensory experience to become embodied and to generate emergent effects of self-reference, the microtemporal data gathered from worldly sensibility makes it possible to deliver this sensibility to consciousness artifactually and with a shorter delay than the resolution time required for it to arise through the "organic" channels that forge consciousness. In sum, the direct gathering of data from behavior allows for action on that data, or action informed by that data, at an earlier moment than any emergent effect possibly could: the direct gathering of data facilitates action in time frames far more condensed that those characteristic of the lived time of perceptual (and preperceptual) consciousness.

Recalling the comparison with writing will help us appreciate the significance of the radical *exteriority* of the technical supplement that is central to twenty-first-century media's pharmacological recompense:[20] if writing made up for the loss of interior memory by introducing an exterior or artificial memory surrogate, twenty-first-century media compensate for the loss of conscious mastery over sensibility by introducing machinic access to the data of sensibility that operates less as a surrogate than as a wholly new, properly machinic faculty. Or again, if writing allows access to experiences that have never been lived by consciousness, to invoke the theme of Husserl's *Essay on the Origin of Geometry* (as well as Derrida's and Stiegler's extensions of it), today's technical sensors facilitate the feeding-forward of data capturing sensory micro-experiences that not only have never been factually lived by consciousness, but that—because of their microtemporality—fall outside the domain of that which can be lived by consciousness. For this reason, contemporary data of sensibility can be defined as data that *cannot be directly lived* by consciousness.

I cannot stress this last point enough: the data made available to consciousness by today's microsensors capture experiences that not only were not, *but can never be*, lived by consciousness. This singularity of twenty-first-century media serves to differentiate it from writing and other previous technical media. Indeed, this singularity represents the generalization of a minor tradition in media theory, dating back at least to the nineteenth century, that conceptualizes the technical distribution of experience as a cofunctioning of autonomous machinic and human elements each possessing its own domain of sensation. Standing at the head of this minor tradition is none other than Étienne-Jules Marey, the French psychophysical researcher who pioneered the "graphic method" for gathering data about human and animal behavior and who went on to develop chronophotography as a technical alternative to human observation.

The crucial point about Marey's practice—and a point of stark differentiation from the superficially similar work of the English Eadweard Muybridge—concerns the autonomy it grants to the machinic element. As photography historian Joel Snyder has very astutely grasped, Marey's aim is not to develop technical prostheses that extend the range or efficacy of human perception and observation; his aim, rather, is to develop machinic sensors *that possess sensory domains of their own*:

> Marey did not conceive of his precision instruments as impartial mediators substituting for and improving upon an observer's eye or an illustrator's hand. His mechanically originated graphs and photographically generated pictures are visualizations of displacements charted against precisely determined units of time. These movements fall outside the scope of human detection and accordingly, their inscriptions cannot be characterized as especially accurate visualizations of what might otherwise have been registered by an illustrator or scientist. To put this in slightly different form: in . . . Marey's experimental work there is no place (literally or figuratively) for human intervention, nothing for a mediator to mediate, no conceptual room into which a scientist might enter and intervene, not because instruments substitute accurate, mechanically produced data for the unreliable, humanly generated variety, but because the displacements registered by mechanical monitors and traced by clockwork-driven inscribers *fall outside the scope of human sensibility*. Consequently, they do not permit even the possibility of human intervention.[21]

What is at issue in Marey's media practice is resolutely not a prosthetic operation of surrogacy, but the veritable inauguration of new, *properly technical* domains of sensation. In this sense, Marey's machines are the precursors of the complex machinic networks that supplement human operations today by participating—as autonomous agencies—in the distribution of sensibility beyond perception. Indeed, Marey's conceptualization of machines already grasps everything necessary to understand how today's smart phones, wireless devices, computational microsensors, and Internet networks interface human experience with new domains to which it lacks direct, perceptual access: for Marey, Snyder continues, "machines can be constitutive of their own field of investigation—one in which substitution is not at issue. These tools can provide access to an unknown world—to a new province of study *generated by the instruments themselves*."[22]

With his appreciation for the radical sensing potential of machines, Marey's example helps us to conceptualize—and also lends an important historical dimension to—the model of technical distribution of experience that, I want to suggest, is required if we are to grasp the sensory affordances of twenty-first-century media *as affordances*, that is, as opportunities for us to expand and intensify *our* experience. For what Marey's example makes salient is the way in which graphic and chronophotographic technologies open new dimensions of experience that operate *alongside* perceptual consciousness and that impact it at the level of sensibility, but that can only be accessed by perceptual consciousness in the form of external or environmental data about its own past behavior. In this respect, Marey's work constitutes a significant precedent for what, I suggest, now forms a general condition of experience in twenty-first-century media environments.

Unequal Deliberation Time

Some significant differences do, however, distinguish this generalization from its nineteenth-century precedent. Of particular interest for my purposes here is the role of time. For Marey, time was central for the expanded scope of machinic sensibility, and his chronophotographic machines operated as mediations of the operational time of sensibility whose purpose was to make this latter, properly machinic, phenomenon accessible to human (visual) perception. In this sense, Marey's work conforms to the pattern of what historian of science Henning Schmidgen has called the "braintime experiment": the deceleration of a microtemporal phenomenon (whether it be microtemporal visual sensing or microtemporal neural processing) so that it can be presentified, after the fact and artifactually, to a consciousness that remains, constitutively, too slow to grasp it directly.

In the contemporary context, the insulation from worldly pressures that characterizes these scientific experiments has been lost, along with the possibility to decelerate a microtemporal operationality that appears to have left the time of consciousness in the dust. Indeed, in the face of contemporary data capitalism, time itself becomes an agent of surplus value extraction that operates within a system structurally dedicated to exploiting the imbalance between microtemporal, machinic sensibility and human consciousness. Where it had earlier been a variable allowing for interchanges between distinct domains of sensibility, time today has become a source of pressure that lends overwhelming advantage to today's sophisticated culture industries in their efforts to sway consumer decisions, or, more exactly, to produce such decisions without any dependence on conscious desires and deliberation.

In preparation for exploring this "post-experiential" paradigm of sensibility (the focus of chapter 3), let me try to characterize the generalized condition in which time exerts pressure on experience today. I am thinking of situations, increasingly numerous in our contemporary world, in which the opportunity, or indeed the necessity, to act comes before any human capacity to act deliberatively; in such situations, responses are literally required *before* perceptual consciousness will have had time to arrive at a deliberative result that emerges "naturally" on the basis of its embodied processing of microtemporal sensory data. I am thinking, specifically, of situations where our contribution to technically distributed perceptual systems in which we are implicated must happen in the "real time" of a technical process, in a technically artifactual time that is literally too fast for consciousness, that operates "beneath" the time of conscious awareness.

The supreme example of such a situation may well be contemporary military (Defense Advanced Research Projects Agency or DARPA) research on "operational neuroscience," where human consciousness and attention are bypassed entirely in favor of a complete instrumentalization of the human brain. The project focuses on improving the task of pattern recognition as it informs the reading of satellite images by trained experts. Human experts in recognizing targets of interest in satellite images, such as military bases or bomb-making facilities, are hooked up to EEG machines that take readings of their neural activity as they rapidly view micro-sections of images. Rather than waiting for these human experts to report on their observations, as was traditionally the case, information is extracted directly from the neural firing patterns captured by these readings; this technique—which leaves the human, or at least the human as an experiencing entity, entirely outside the informational circuit—yields a massive acceleration in the identification of targets of interest. Moreover, in a further elaboration of the dehumanization at work in this operationalization, the human element is no longer even confronted with a whole image or a recognizable territory: today these experts only see cut-up sections of such images flashed before the eyes at a rate of ten images per second.

Even if the ultimate purpose of this operationalization of the human brain is the protection of human beings, its very possibility opens up the terrifying specter of a total sidelining of conscious deliberation in the development of future human-machine convergences. Despite its broadly "humanistic" intent, an intent it shares with other empirical applications (e.g., systems designed to alert soldiers in the field to imminent dangers by directly tapping into their neural activity in real time), what this example brings home is the reality that, in many instances of action in the world today, it is the slow resolution time of human attention that creates informational bottlenecks.

A more mundane allegory of the same phenomenon would be action-based video gaming, and speed gaming in particular, from the machini-matically recorded speed runs on *Quake* to contemporary competitions involving highly skilled and highly trained players operating at extremely fine-grained temporal micro-intervals. In this situation, players are called upon to execute moves that cannot be premeditated and that emerge without cognitive awareness playing any operational role whatsoever; and while the training necessary to perform in these conditions involves repetition—repetition that leads to embodiment—what exerts the pressure to perform in the microtemporal moment is not simply the player's desire to improve (as is the case, for example, in sports training generally), but the machinic microtemporal operationality of the game engine, the fact that the game keeps moving on, and that it does so beneath the threshold of ordinary human perception.

This example perfectly conveys how our technoculture puts increasing demands on us to act in the absence of any prior awareness and without sufficient time for conscious deliberation. If we generalize this principle, we can begin to see how the combination of specified time frames and massive capacities for data collection together underwrite a system in which we cannot but experience a certain degree of cognitive opacity. Because it typically involves capitalist industries compelling consumer responses, I shall describe the impact of this combination of temporal pressure and unequal resources via the "principle of non-equal deliberation time"; this principle states that the capacity for—indeed, the luxury of—deliberation has come ever increasingly to lie on the side of capitalist institutions, to the point perhaps of becoming its exclusive prerogative. More precisely, this principle of non-equal deliberation time designates the situation, typical of our contemporary world, in which the decisions of individual cultural consumers can be manipulated—and in some sense effectively "preprogrammed"—as a result of the "digital insight" into behavioral motivation that microcomputational sensing affords corporate interests. With their capacity to gather massive amounts of data about our likes and dislikes—data to which we individual consumers of today's digital commerce have little or no access—today's culture industries benefit from a massive informational imbalance: they offer us stimulation, an instrumentalized perversion of what Whitehead calls "lure for feeling," that directly solicits "our" microtemporal, subconscious motivation, and that completes its solicitation long before any output appears in and to consciousness.

The temporal pressure that characterizes this situation of unequal deliberation lends a contemporary urgency to the autonomy of the machinic supplement that characterizes the technical distribution of experience within twenty-first-century media environments. For it is precisely because today's data and culture industries can bypass consciousness and go directly to behavioral, biometric, and environmental data that they are increasingly able to capture our "attention" without any awareness on our part: precisely because it places conscious deliberation and response out of play, microtemporal behavioral data that evades the oversight of consciousness allows today's data and culture industries to accomplish their goal of tightening the circuit between solicitation and response. And it is for the very same reason—namely, that conscious deliberation is increasingly sidelined from the scene of cultural solicitation—that the impact of twenty-first-century media is and can only be felt *indirectly* and *after the fact* by higher-order modes of human experience, and only then in large part because of feed-forward loops that literally mediate the data of causal efficacy (as measured, calculated, and analyzed by twenty-first-century media) for future consciousness *to factor into its activity-to-come.*

If we have any hope of intervening into this media-assisted, capitalist operationalization of our desire, we will have to introduce new methods for developing "footing" within such instrumentalized circuits. The older methods central to various programs in cultural studies—decoding and demystification, culture jamming and resignification, and so forth—are, despite their undeniable contributions, powerless in the face of the brutal functionalism of today's media-savvy marketing firms and data companies. They are powerless, that is, as material interventions into cultural production, for whatever deliberative reappropriation of cultural processes and products such practices carry out necessarily happens after the fact and to the side of the main impact of the cultural product and of the overwhelming resources that today's capitalist data and culture industries bring to the task of "pre-anticipating" our responses. This disjunction of reappropriation from impact is brought home by the marginalization of conscious deliberation as an element of decision-making: to the extent that cultural reappropriation occurs *as a deliberative decision to do something with a given cultural product*, it always occurs too late and, in a sense, simply misses the mark. For with their sophisticated methods for targeting the infrastructural elements that inform our responses, today's data and culture industries are increasingly able simply to cut our conscious deliberation out of the loop.

I cannot emphasize the temporal basis of this predicament strongly enough: whatever agency is produced through acts of cultural reappropriation is necessarily subsequent to the operational impact of the cultural products it would resignify or divert. The real action, in other words, is elsewhere, or rather "elsewhen": it occurs, that is, in the microtemporal, and massively researched, details of our sensory-material solicitation by contemporary cultural institutions. Cultural industrial products and processes now typically encompass a massive "environment" of data collection and processing—a "data milieu"—as an integral factor informing their causal efficacy. And while it may be possible for individual cultural agents to engage with such data milieus to various degrees (though, to be sure, never with anything like the resources wielded by the data and culture industries themselves), such engagement can only occur through a temporal disjunction from the operationality of the cultural product or process: it is necessarily "after the fact." The resulting scenario involves a distinct displacement of our agency: acting through our conscious grasp of situations, we simply cannot have direct *operational or "real-time"* access to the data milieus of cultural products. In light of this increasing data-fication of cultural products and processes, coupled with the general acceleration of culture as such, we thus find ourselves faced with the imperative to respond—to take deliberate action and to make conscious decisions—*in situations where deliberation is no longer the relevant mode of response and where consciousness is no longer the relevant level of experience.* Faced with such situations, we cannot but experience a certain cognitive opacity as our consciousnesses perpetually—and vainly—struggle to "catch up" to what is happening.

There is, however, an important flip side to this loss of mastery. For the very same technologies that inform the acceleration of culture and the capitalist conquest of deliberative time can be used to "technically distribute" our own cognitive operationality in ways that can expand our agency without requiring such expansion to be registered—operationally or in real time—by consciousness. The importance of this properly pharmacological dimension of contemporary technoculture cannot be overemphasized: in their conquest of deliberative time, today's data-driven culture industries develop research tools and techniques that can also be deployed in the development of delayed cognitive-perceptual systems rooted in the power of data and the capacity for feeding it forward. If such technically distributed systems afford us the means to regain some agency over the operational moment of cultural impact, what I shall term the "operational present of sensibility," this agency comes at a certain cost: the pride of place formerly occupied by consciousness.

Human-technical couplings that bypass consciousness are already in operation in our world. Consider the supplementation of the human perceptual system with devices designed to indicate when levels of insulin get dangerously low or when seizures are likely to come on. These kinds of devices bypass consciousness in their gathering of data: by mediating various elements of bodily activity, such devices can be said to operate directly at the level of causal efficacy. These devices meet the challenge posed by the combination of massive and multi-scalar informational complexity and fine-grained temporal acuity: because of their capacity for gathering data from bodily processes *in their operational presencing, as they are actually occurring*, these devices are able to overcome the opacity of consciousness, and thus to supplement consciousness with insight—"digital insight"—in which it can never directly participate but in virtue of which it can, subsequently, act.

To move from such highly specialized medical devices to the everyday smart devices we now carry around with us, we need only expand the scope of our imagining. How, we must ask, can the paradigm instanced by these medical devices be generalized to tasks involved in our everyday perceptual and cognitive interchange with the world? As a first step toward such a generalization, let us take note that medical devices like those just mentioned are simply black-boxed mechanisms that bring the force of digital insight into the closest possible proximity to the technical recording of data. They are not different in kind from technologies like the "sociometer" designed by Sandy Pentland and his colleagues at the Human Dynamics Lab at MIT. The sociometer, to which I return in detail below, is a portable device capable of registering a plethora of biometric and environmental data about business negotiations. What Pentland's research has revealed is just how much "information" gets exchanged beneath the purview of conscious attention; comparing after-the-fact, introspective reports with the data gathered by the sociometer, Pentland and his colleagues have found that decisions about salary negotiations and promotions are often made in the very first moments of interaction, long before conscious evaluation would have had a chance to come to any kind of deliberative resolution. For Pentland, the payoff of this finding lies in the possibility to inform negotiators *before the fact* about the nonverbal level of decision-making; his aim is to give participants conscious awareness that there is more involved in decisions than the perceptually accessible verbal content of their interactions, and to give them the opportunity to adjust their future behavior accordingly.

Generalizing from this research, we could imagine a version of Pentland's sociometer that, rather than feeding data forward in anticipation of a conscious reckoning to come, instead executed actions designed to steer the direction of negotiations *in their operational present*. Here, the black-boxed mechanism driving this immediate feed-forward loop would constitute the fruit of such "future" conscious deliberation, which rather than remaining to come in some not-yet-happening deliberative moment, would be retrojected into an operational present that eludes the grasp of consciousness. As with the medical devices just mentioned, the result would be a supplementation of consciousness with "digital insight" such that its longer-circuit response gets foreshortened and effectively anticipated, in a certain sense, *before it happens*.

Environmental Sensibility, or the "Digital Nervous System"

Let us now return to that other important facet of the changed experiential situation generated by twenty-first-century media: the imperative for us to reboot our perspective on human experience. In order to break with the subject-centered accounts of modern philosophy, which access the world through some form of subjective givenness, we must adopt a radically environmental perspective on experience that is capable of grasping the total power—what, with Whitehead, we might call the "prehensiveness"—of the universe at any and every given moment. On such an account, higher-order faculties of human operationality can no longer be treated as privileged modes of experience, but are themselves implicated in—and are emergent along with, or, better, out of—more encompassing situations that bring elemental dimensions of human embodiment as well as properly environmental factors to bear on the happening of (human) experience.

As we shall see, it is Whitehead who helps us appreciate both the need and possibility for such a radically environmental perspective: with his conception that the entirety of the universe is implicated in any new becoming, Whitehead furnishes what is required for us to think the total environmental situation as the complex causal ground ("the real potentiality") for new experience. This conception that the entirety of the universe is implicated in any new becoming constitutes *the most important speculative element* in Whitehead's ontology: without being directly accessible to experience—no perspectival entity can grasp the total situation from which it precedes—this speculative conception explains how activity, and thus experience, arises on the basis of the "real potentiality" of the universe at every moment of its development. My effort to adapt Whitehead's speculative empiricism for theorizing twenty-first-century media can thus be understood to be an expansion of his own program for reforming philosophy: "Philosophy," he writes at the beginning of *Process and Reality*,

> is the self-correction by consciousness of its own initial excess of
> subjectivity. Each actual occasion contributes to the circumstances
> of its origin additional formative elements deepening its own pecu-
> liar individuality. Consciousness is only the last and greatest of such
> elements by which the selective character of the individual obscures
> the external totality from which it originates and which it embodies.
> An actual individual, of such higher grade, has truck with the total-

ity of things by reason of its sheer actuality; but it has attained its
individual depth of being by a selective emphasis limited to its own
purposes. The task of philosophy is to recover the totality obscured
by the selection.[23]

We might think of the media theorist's task as cognate with this more properly philosophical task. Thus, where Whitehead focuses on laying bare the
metaphysical structure for the clarification of radically environmental experience, twenty-first-century media challenge us to move outside our "excess
of subjectivity" in a far more practical, directly experiential register.

How, we must ask, can we appropriate Whitehead's fundamental metaphysical insight into the total relatedness of any situation for the purposes
of theorizing twenty-first-century media's experiential impact? Just as any
new actuality speculatively "prehends" the totality of the universe as it exists at the moment of its becoming, so too must any new experiential event
advance the becoming of a given "society" (by society, again, Whitehead
means any experiential assemblage, from an atom to a geological process)
by processing the "real potential" that belongs to the settled world at the
moment of its composition (or more precisely, if more technically, to the entirety of the attained actualities comprising that settled world). The system
of twenty-first-century media as I have sought to explicate it here—as radically environmental in its mediation of sensibility—perfectly embodies this
correlation of the ongoing advance of experiential societies with a reserve
of potentiality belonging to the actuality of the total situation at every stage
in that advance. Because it broadly impacts the total situation of worldly
sensibility—the "real potentiality"—informing the creative advance of a
given society (e.g., a human bodymind), this system of twenty-first-century
media necessarily brings to bear on that creative advance what, from the
perspective of any given society, can only be a potentiality; yet, as implicated
within the larger situation from which it emerges, this potentiality not only
is fully actual (it is the potentiality of the attained actualities constituting
the settled world) but has the power to act *in itself*, without being channeled
through the delimited subjectivity of the particular society that is the human
bodymind. Capturing the impact of that activity, without falling back into
our familiar modes of subjectivity, is the task in front of us.

The affinity between this philosophically rooted environmental perspective and the concrete effects of today's media networks lies at the heart of
my intervention. The implication of human bodyminds into larger causal
networks of actuality, which act on them as a force of potentiality, would
seem to parallel the process through which human experience is becom-

ing increasingly enmeshed into what Pentland has called a "digital nervous system":

> It seems that the human race suddenly has the beginnings of a working nervous system. Like some world-spanning living organism, public health systems, automobile traffic, and emergency and security networks are all becoming intelligent, reactive systems with sociometer-style sensors serving as their eyes and ears. The evolution of this nervous system will continue at a quickening speed because of Moore's law and basic economics. The networks will become faster, the devices will have more sensors, and the techniques for modeling human behavior will become more accurate and detailed. The combination of this evolving nervous system with models of social physics will soon lead to the ability to engineer our societies and entire culture.[24]

With the advent of such a digital nervous system, humans become implicated within larger causal and technical networks in relation to which they can no longer claim any kind of transcendence. What is crucial about such implication is the way it expands agency beyond the subject-centered perspective of any delimited entity or society, thus rendering it a function of the total environment involved in any given social event. Insofar as any such total environment is structured through the potentiality it possesses but that is only made accessible by digital technologies, we can say that potentiality itself mediates the expanded contact we humans enjoy with a vibratory continuum that appears—precisely because of technical mediation—to possess agency of its own. In this sense, the digital nervous system is simply the ultimate consequence of the innumerable feed-forward loops that are generated through the technical surrogacy of embodied causal efficacy.

Despite its superficial affinity with McLuhan's notion of a global electronic nervous system, Pentland's concept speaks to a world in which media can no longer be restricted to a prosthetic function. Indeed, the digital nervous system Pentland envisions is one in which media technologies directly mediate the causal efficacy of worldly sensibility itself. Accordingly, whatever impact this digital nervous system will have on our experience will occur not through any direct link between its sensory affordances and our higher-order faculties, but rather through supplementary layers of mediation that constitute what I shall understand as "calculative affordances of its data gathering capacities." Twenty-first-century media impact us sensorily just as they do every other entity in the world—through the subjectively heterogeneous, microtemporal processes of causal efficacy that constitute all forms of worldly becoming. But we—that is, we higher-order human bodyminds—only come to understand this impact at a remove from its operationality and with a constitutive delay, by way of feed-forward loops that send its meaning—a meaning co-substantial with its causal efficacy—forward and into our awareness, as it were, from the "objective" outside.

Worldly Temporalization

The experiential situation just outlined—of human experience operating within and constituting part of larger networks of experience—is in some important sense historically unprecedented. While human life has been characterized by exteriorization and technicity from its origin, as Bernard Stiegler (following French paleontologist André Leroi-Gourhan) has argued convincingly, it is only in the wake of the computational revolution that sensibility acquires agency of its own—and becomes addressable—independently of higher-order perceptual processes. Twenty-first-century media thus institute a form of technical distribution of human experience that is directly informed by this autonomy of sensibility, and that differs from earlier forms of technical distribution precisely on this account. Whereas pre-computational forms of technical distribution, what Andy Clark aptly calls environmental "scaffolding," were directly intended to off-load tasks that would otherwise need to be performed on the inside of a cognitive system, the distribution at issue today typically involves coupling with technical processes that remain cognitively inscrutable to humans: twenty-first-century media technically distribute experience by correlating humans with sensors and other microtechnologies that are capable of gathering data from experience, including *our own* experience, that "we ourselves" cannot capture. Such data can be either bodily or environmental; the important point is that they operate on scales and at sensory thresholds that remain beyond our grasp. The data gathered by our microsensors thus literally put us into recursive loops—what I shall call "feed-forward loops"—with aspects of our own experience to which *we would otherwise have no access whatsoever*.

With respect to human experience, the challenge this situation poses is singular. For with the shift in the scale and scope of the technical distribution of our experience comes a certain displacement of "self-reference" as what anchors experience. Because technical distribution now involves an expansion of experience that literally exceeds the resources of human perception, it is no longer possible to reference experience exclusively on the higher-order faculties that have long been associated with the human. This means that we must renounce the position of mastery we have long accorded ourselves and instead take our place within the larger environmental networks of sensibility that generate experience. At the same time, however, we must not rush to abandon the qualitative integration that has long characterized—and resolutely still does characterize—our distinctly human experience. The task, as Whitehead so clearly sees, is to encompass the larger scope of causal efficacy that underlies and informs consciousness, not to abandon consciousness altogether in favor of its causal infrastructure. For although consciousness has an extremely "narrow-bandwidth" grasp of worldly sensibility, it constitutes the very pinnacle of nature's development: as Whitehead stresses repeatedly, consciousness is characterized by a maximum of both intensity and discernment. Thus, despite its qualified displacement in our twenty-first-century media ecology, consciousness remains a crucial—perhaps *the* crucial—factor for understanding the singularity of human experience as it is being transformed by contemporary media networks. It is through consciousness alone that we achieve a qualitative appreciation for media's impact on sensibility. And it is through consciousness that we attain agency to shape future opportunities for experience.

The challenge posed by twenty-first-century media therefore calls on us to recalibrate our phenomenology of human experience in order to account for its imbrication within such environmental networks. As I have already suggested, this will require us to develop a model of human experience as fundamentally hybrid, as a composition of higher-order perceptual self-reference and lower-order bodily and environmental sensibility mutually functioning in operational overlap. While Whitehead's ontology will prove crucial for developing the radically environmental dimension of this hybrid agency, it is the corpus of phenomenology—and in particular, Edmund Husserl's lifelong meditation on the constitution of time-consciousness—that will help us grasp the particular impact such an environmental dimension has on human self-reference. With its focus on the correlation of temporalization and subjectivity, phenomenology furnishes a model that, once adapted for the situation of experiential hybridity, will help us pinpoint the new configuration of subjectivity in relation to twenty-first-century media. Indeed, the end point of Husserl's meditation on time-consciousness is precisely a recognition of the limitations of the constituting power of consciousness and of the need for supplementation by an environmental agency. At issue in Husserl's final thinking on time is nothing less than the toppling of the very trajectory motivating it—the quest for an absolute constituting time-consciousness—in favor of a more primordial worldly temporalizing, what his student and final assistant Eugen Fink calls *Entgegenwärtigung* or "de-presencing." With this culminating development, phenomenology acquires the resources, as well as the necessity, to reenter the "natural world" from which it originally withdrew, and to do so through the route of radical immanence whereby the temporal gap or "objectification" qualifying subjective temporal experience (which is expanded beyond the bounds of consciousness, into the domain of the microtemporal) can be directly correlated with—or better, situated inside of—the primordial temporalizing of worldly sensibility.

With its focus on the qualitative dimension of human experience, even as it shifts from the macroscale of time-*consciousness* to the microtemporal scale of non-perceptual sensibility, phenomenology furnishes crucial resources for excavating precisely how the complex temporality of operational overlap generates human experience. In particular, phenomenology will help us assess the significance of what I shall call the "surplus of sensibility" that is generated through the technical production of sensibility. This surplus of sensibility designates that part of microsensory intensification generated by twenty-first-century media that exceeds the short-term, instrumental circuits instituted by contemporary cultural capital. In this way, it exposes the underside of the instrumental operation of today's culture industries: the ineliminable experiential dimension of the probabilistic data-gathering that informs the continuity of the contemporary lifeworld. The surplus of sensibility shows that, in addition—and prior—to being instrumentally delimited and quantified elements of a data computing system, recorded behavioral traces are traces of elements of sensory life. The surplus of sensibility thus shows that there is always more sensory potential to data than what gets captured by the techniques central to today's culture industries or what, with Nigel Thrift, we can call the "microbiopolitics" of contemporary capitalism.[25]

If one source of this surplus is the holism of life, the very dimension that Whitehead's speculative conception of the total situation introduces, another—and this emphatically underscores the deep compatibility of sensibility and quantification—is the productivity of data-mining itself, the fact that computational data analysis actually generates new sensibilities and new relationships between sensibilities. As one information scientist puts it, data-mining differs "from ordinary information retrieval in that the information which is sought does not exist explicitly within the database, but must be 'discovered'"—or, indeed, *produced* by analytic operations.[26] The key point here is that such discovery or production creates a surplus of sensibility *to the precise extent that it exceeds the narrow instrumentality of capitalist cultural industries.* That is why this surplus furnishes the potential for counterdeployments of data that have the production of intensity as their aim. And it is also why phenomenology—retooled as a post-phenomenology of sensibility—forms such a key resource for such production: insofar as it opens access to sensibility beyond any direct presentation in perception, phenomenology is able to put humans into contact with the surplus of sensibility from which the potential for experiential intensification stems.

Once it is expanded to encompass the microtemporal scale of non-perceptual sensibility, phenomenology will be capable of addressing the "subjective" side of the relation between data and sensibility without needing to channel it through a subject proper, through a *consciousness* of time. The phenomenology of time-*consciousness* will thus give way to an asubjective— or, more precisely, to a non-subject-centered—phenomenology of time that focuses on the correlation between worldly temporalizing ("de-presencing") and the temporal ecstasis of human experience (the impression-retention-protention complex). Insofar as human temporalizing, on this account, becomes a correlate of the very relationality that constitutes worldly sensibility, phenomenology itself will acquire a fundamentally different status from that accorded it by the Husserlian *epochē*: far from constituting the reduction of the objective sphere to a domain—consciousness—that brackets fluctuating sensations in favor of apodictically secure lived experiences, phenomenology will be more fully and directly anchored within worldly sensibility itself. More precisely, phenomenology will address temporalizing as a single yet internally differentiated phenomenon: refusing the division constitutive of its orthodox articulation—the division that accords human beings the power to constitute time—this rejuvenated, post-phenomenological phenomenology will implicate human consciousness, along with the rest of human sensory life, *within a larger sensory confound* that is always in operation *along with* it.

This reformed picture of phenomenology converges to a great extent with the project of Czech phenomenologist Jan Patočka, who, in a reprise of Husserl's original motivation in the *Logical Investigations*, sought to develop an asubjective phenomenology of manifestation capable of overcoming its orthodox subjective basis. On this account, worldly manifestation, not subjective certainty, comprises the core of phenomenology: when the world manifests itself in "appearances" or "adumbrations," it is manifesting itself *as it is*. In this way, Patočka's account manages to restore the autonomy of appearance. In contrast to the canonical Husserlian position, which views adumbrations as partial appearances of objects that require fulfillment, Patočka's account collapses the ontological distance between object and appearance: the partial manifestation simply *is* the object as it appears to a being capable of receiving its appearance. On this understanding, in other words, appearance *is* being, and there is no possibility to decouple the partial manifestation of the world from its concrete mode of being. Accordingly, far from involving a conversion of an objectivity into a subjectivity, of worldly materiality into a subjective (and intrinsically unreliable) appearance, manifestation is in itself a thoroughly "objective" process. The fact that the world happens to manifest itself to human subjects does not change this in the least: the partial manifestation of the world in forms assimilable to human subjects is itself part of the "objective" structure of worldly manifestation, not some compromise or supplement introduced by the specific capacities (and limitations) of (human) subjects.

With its defining identification of appearance with being, Patočka's phenomenology of manifestation repudiates the entire structure of the model of phenomenology—the canonical Husserlian model—developed on the basis of the *epochē*. For Patočka, what is at stake in phenomenology is not the securing of an apodictically certain domain of interiority (consciousness or time-consciousness) but the objective, material manifestation of the world. On his reformed view, phenomenology does not address "lived experiences" or "contents of consciousness." On the contrary, it concerns a sensible confound that manifests itself independently of any such forms of experience (lived experiences or contents of consciousness), even if these may in fact emerge, as supplementary developments, at later, no longer properly phenomenological stages.

With this "objective" or material account of phenomenology, Patočka's philosophy furnishes the basis for a treatment of temporalizing as a unitary, if highly differentiated and complexified, phenomenon. Far from being the function of a rarified subjective consciousness producing its own apodictically secure contents, temporalization always happens first and foremost in the world and, indeed, *as worldly temporalization*; as such, temporalization includes the production of internal contents of consciousness as one of its crucial, if derivative, dimensions. For Patočka, then, as for Fink (and possibly also for the final Husserl of the *C-Manuscripts*), the world itself must temporalize *in order for consciousness to temporalize*. Worldly depresencing is the condition for—and indeed is the very materiality of—all temporalization.

If Patočka's development of Husserl's project foregrounds the operation of worldly temporalizing, it also helps us to redescribe the role of the human or of what, adapting Heidegger's term, he calls *Dasein*, within the larger processual domain of manifestation. Indeed, with its focus on humans as *recipients* or *receivers* of manifestation, Patočka's asubjective phenomenology manages to articulate the primordial *implication* of human agency, and thus of human experience more broadly, within larger networks of worldly sensibility.[27] I shall explore the specificity of such agential implication, as contrasted with any transcendental form of subjectivity, in relation to both

Patočka and Merleau-Ponty in my conclusion below; for the moment, however, let me emphasize how Patočka's privileging of the process of worldly manifestation undoes the central tenet of Husserl's phenomenology of constitution. What this privileging establishes is that human activity—far from comprising the *source* for temporalization and thus for experience—is rather the *result* of, indeed *part* of, a more fundamental process of worldly temporalizing: lacking the autonomy it has on Husserl's (orthodox) account in terms of constitution, human temporalization occurs as a *participation* in larger worldly temporalizations. Indeed, Patočka's phenomenology allows us to specify two distinct levels of what we might call "the causal efficacy of worldly temporalizing": on one hand, an "objective" level at which humans, insofar as they are sensory beings, are *part of worldly sensibility*; and on the other, a higher-order, subjective level at which humans generate experience, and indeed experiential forms, of their own (perceptions, lived experiences, illusions, etc.) through self-reference, which is to say, through self-differentiation from worldly sensibility.

Insofar as these layers coincide with the hybridity of human experience introduced above, Patočka's phenomenology gives an account—and thus furnishes an example—of how we humans can be "collectives" composed of higher-order agencies functioning in operational overlap with more primordial processes of worldly sensibility impacting us both bodily and environmentally, but in some crucial sense prior to the very division of subject and world that informs the higher-order processes and that typically qualifies our status as human subjects. From this perspective, we are emphatically not distinct, substantial subjects that exist independently from the sensory confound with which we are at every moment in contact, but are rather heterogeneous compositions in ongoing and highly complex individuation with and within this confound, following the powerful conceptualization of French philosopher Gilbert Simondon.[28] Specifically, we are compositions of forces from different ontological levels, compositions of forces that impact us at fundamentally divergent stages of organization.

The Contemporary Perversion of Pharmacology

Having now clarified how twenty-first-century media open a new, properly post-phenomenological and non-prosthetic phase of technical distribution in which human experiencers become implicated in the larger, environmental processes to which they belong but to which they have no direct access via consciousness, let me now specify how this development correlates with the pharmacological history of technics. As I see it, the inauguration of a post-phenomenological, non-prosthetic phase of technical distribution brings with it the potential for a fundamental expansion of human agency over the sensory conditions of human experience. With the smart devices and microsensors now populating our lifeworlds, we have an unprecedented capacity to access aspects of our experience—aspects ranging from properly environmental elements to dimensions of bodily experience—that would otherwise remain beyond the grasp of our modes of perceptual awareness. This potential has, however, remained largely untapped or, rather, has been left to capitalist culture industries to exploit; with their generalized imperative to gather and analyze data in order to create highly specific, closed-loop circuits between the past behavior of consumers and their probable future activity, today's culture industries have largely co-opted the open potential of twenty-first-century media.

This in itself makes twenty-first-century media a site of political contestation. Against the sway of the contemporary culture industries, we must struggle to preserve the open potentiality of twenty-first-century media and to deploy them toward ends that are not narrowly instrumental but that are "humanistic"—in some very broad and general sense—because they are generative of a heightened intensity of human experience or some other enhancement of human life. We must, in other words, struggle for the liberation of the "surplus of sensibility"—or, more precisely, for access to the inherently liberated and excessive surplus of sensibility—that, as we have seen, attaches to the production of new relationalities through data-gathering and analysis. The target of such struggle is the reduction that lies at the heart of this contemporary capitalist imperative: the reduction of general potentiality—the potentiality stemming from the sum of attained actualities constituting the settled universe (what Whitehead calls "real potentiality")—to a fully instrumentalized deployment of potentiality in a narrow coupling with specific functional ends.

This political struggle is made all the more difficult—and, at the same time, all the more imperative—by the contemporary perversion to which twenty-first-century media, fueled by the hyper-acceleration of data-gathering and analysis, subject the pharmacological trajectory of media. In the wake of today's tightly controlled media circuits, it is no longer necessarily the case that media change yields an unambiguous recompense; indeed, with the capacity to extract exploitable data from even the most minimal human activity, whatever recompense today's media systems afford would seem to be "contaminated" from the start.

A function of the success of the just-named reduction of general potentiality, this perversion of media pharmacology typifies twenty-first-century media as such, insofar as it is generically or tendentially characterized by a split between micro- and macroscale operationality. In the wake of this operational split, twenty-first-century media have ushered in new possibilities to address—and to manipulate—experience beneath the level of human (conscious or perceptual) awareness. Informed by increasingly rigorous neuroeconomic study, contemporary advertising aims to capture our attention without our awareness, to manipulate us subliminally and outside of our control;[29] and today's digital networks possess the capacity to gather and to exploit all kinds of data without us having any knowledge, and, to a great extent, any possibility for knowledge, of such activity. As a consequence of this operational split and the resulting possibilities for data-gathering and manipulation, the long-standing pharmacological "pact" that has characterized the history of media from writing to cinema would seem to have been broken or, at the very least, rendered obsolete: simply put, what we get back has no possibility to compensate for what we give up.

Consider again the difference between writing and today's "social media." In the case of writing, as I have already observed, there is a direct correlation between the "poison" and the "remedy": what writing takes away (the exercise that preserves "internal" memory's capacity) is directly compensated for by the gain it brings (memory's expansion via a technical supplement operating as "external" or "artificial" memory surrogate). The key point is that the correlation of dispossession and recompense at issue here is, as it were, *built in to the sociotechnical development that is writing.* The loss and gain are simply two sides of a single coin: one follows directly from the other, and they both concern the same integral (human) faculty.

This simple correlation no longer obtains in the case of a social-media network like Facebook. Facebook, as many readers will certainly be aware, is currently (circa 2014) the most popular social-networking website in the world (or, at least, in the Western world); in addition to making available information pertaining to each user's identity, Facebook offers its users the possibility to conduct many communicative activities that were formerly performed separately from one another: users can send e-mail; receive automated reminders; participate in group discussions; play games; post photographs, videos, and other sources of information about themselves and their friends; and so forth. Like other social-media platforms, Facebook seeks to operate as a single gateway to the entire digital universe and has its impressive market share to show for its success.

If we conceptualize Facebook in terms of the pharmacological basis of media, we discover a far more complicated situation than what we find in the case of writing or, for that matter, cinema. With Facebook, it is far more difficult to say exactly what is gained and what is lost, and indeed, the answer differs depending on the operational "level" to which the question is addressed. In the case of computational platforms like Facebook, we must differentiate between a "service" and a "data" level, and must distinguish the operation of two pharmacologies: a pseudo-pharmacology that gives users functionality (efficiency of information gathering and dissemination) in exchange for data extraction, and a "perverted" pharmacology that gives corporate interests a treasure trove of data prime for capitalization.

For the majority of Facebook's ever-expanding user base (1.28 billion users at the end of April 2014), what is gained is the capacity to publicize one's activities efficiently, to centralize communications, and to acquire information about a vast network of other people, both in the present and from the past. What is lost is control over one's (digital) memory since, as some dramatic recent stories have made altogether clear, digital traces are just as permanent as the networks hosting them. The capacity to preserve and disseminate information, once it is posted, is a function of the network, not of the user.

That is why, for Facebook's executives, what appears to be a pharmacological structure at the level of the user is simply the surface, what Kittler once called the "eyewash," of a deeper pharmacological figure centered on data collection and analysis.[30] What Facebook's executives gain from the effectively closed-circuit integration of communication functions is a massively expanded capacity to gather data about its users, a capacity that includes access to traces of *all of their (online) activity*. While this disjunction between the "service" and the "data" elements of Facebook was thrust into the spotlight by the recent uproar surrounding the changes in the company's privacy provisions, the question of who owns the information it gathers is, in a sense, subordinate to the more general issue of the sheer capacity it and similar information platforms have to collect personal information on such a massive scale and without the awareness of their users.

With respect to the question of Facebook's pharmacological status, two crucial points need to be made. First, both elements of this disjunction are made possible by the same technical infrastructure: it is *one and the same* data network that allows users to share and access information *and* that facilitates the gathering of massive amounts of information concerning user behavior. Second, the fact that behavior necessarily generates data traces supports a pharmacology that is, in some significant sense, out of balance: because the experiential affordances of social networking have no direct correlation with their technical basis, there is no longer anything to guarantee the pharmacological economy of loss and gain that has characterized media from writing to cinema. Indeed, we must speak of gains and losses in relation to two distinct registers, the experiential and the operational. And with respect specifically to the disjunction between these registers, we must recognize the imbalance involved: in the case of Facebook and similar social-media platforms, if not of the Internet as such, a loss at the level of user experience (users' control over their "memory") is the price to be paid for a recompense that obtains *not* at the level of user activity but rather at the infrastructural or systemic operational level (the company's capacity to gather and exploit data traces of user activity).

The perversion in the pharmacological basis of twenty-first-century media stems directly from this disjunction between experiential and operational registers. Indeed, with respect to a social-media network like Facebook, it is difficult even to say whether what we gain compensates in any way at all for what we lose, since what we gain *doesn't appear to have any common ground*—outside of a shared technical basis—with what we lose. How can we even begin to compare the social affordances of Facebook, affordances that structure our communication with the world, with the far less immediately—and self-referentially—tangible dangers of widespread data-gathering? What we *can* say is that the experiential affordances of Facebook cannot possibly counterbalance the loss of control over data generated by user activity *for the simple reason that there is no direct experiential connection between them*. From the macroscale standpoint of Facebook's 1.28 billion users, the production of data traces is purely incidental to the connectivity it affords (or, more precisely, it is a factor whose only relevant impact is its role in optimizing connectivity); and from the microscale perspective of the data-mining itself, what users actually do is purely incidental to the sheer production of digital data traces.

The ensuing situation of pharmacological imbalance, which I have sought to describe here, perfectly captures the political stakes of the digital revolution. Indeed, twenty-first-century media platforms like Facebook—and, indeed, the Internet as such—would seem to lend a crucial concreteness, as well as a necessary corrective, to Kittler's purposefully polemical and highly contentious claims that digital technologies already can and increasingly will operate autonomously from human beings and that our contemporary entertainment systems are simply the optional surface effects of a ruthlessly inhuman technical development. Eschewing the Manichean polarization of humans and machines that lends pathos to Kittler's admittedly seductive vision,[31] what a platform like Facebook (or, for that matter, the Internet as such) renders manifest is the purely instrumental correlation of *entertainment* (or "service") and *operationality* (or "data"): Facebook's experiential affordances are precisely what facilitates the collection of data; yet, no matter how distant the ensuing data-mining might be from the experiential dimension of user activity, it remains in necessary correlation with human interests. The political dimension thereby underscored concerns access to and control of data—the very data generated as an unavoidable consequence of activity within digital networks. Far from it being an instance of a digital network operating in some fantasied autonomy from human interests, then, what is at issue here is the calculated extraction of data that, though generated by user activity, operates to serve the interests of the network itself or, more exactly, the "special interests" controlling the network.

In light of this situation, which typifies the development of Internet enterprises circa 2014, let me orient my project around a fundamental political principle. What I shall call the "principle of data neutrality" states that, despite the seemingly closed-circuit nature of the majority of today's digital networks, the potential offered by twenty-first-century media for data collection, analysis, and prediction—and especially for the feeding-forward of data into ongoing experience—is a potential that is, and must be made to remain, fundamentally *common to all, publicly accessible, and open to multiple uses*. Whatever politics will ultimately emerge from the theorization of twenty-first-century media will have to grapple with the thorny issue of how to preserve (or restore) this commonality, accessibility, and openness of media in a world dominated by special interests whose livelihoods are strictly coupled to their success in appropriating data for their own private gain. This task is further complicated by the "intrinsic" tendency of digital technology to accelerate the oscillation cycles of, and thus to shorten, the circuits linking users' behavior and data networks: as we have already seen, this technical pressure toward acceleration introduces a fundamental disparity of resources, and specifically of time for deliberation, which places users at a massive disadvantage: as users are compelled to make decisions in ever-narrowing time windows, their opportunities for deliberative reckoning are diminishing. Put another way, deliberation shifts from being an activity that happens at the moment of reception or, in its incalculable aftermath (to invoke Derrida's take on so-called real-time media networks),[32] to an activity that happens—that can *only* happen—in a fundamentally anticipatory mode, *before* any encounter with a cultural object or media network. And while we can perhaps refrain here from accusing contemporary data capitalism per se of instituting a technically driven, structural antidemocratic authoritarianism, we can acknowledge the fundamental dromological disparity between technical progress and democratic deliberation that informs such a position: with its dromological imperative, technology appears to "favor" the elimination of post-encounter or receptive deliberation.[33]

In the wake of this double pressure on the commonality, accessibility, and openness of data, we must refine the aim and scope of political resistance. While recognizing—contra Kittler—that our contemporary digital networks are *our* networks, that is, inventions fundamentally correlated with our ongoing evolution, we must also recognize that our behavior is ever more subject to surveillance, analysis, and indeed informatic exploitation by the information systems in which we increasingly choose (or are compelled to "choose") to participate. Rather than endorsing Kittler's purposefully polemical dystopian view—of a frighteningly antihuman machinic future—we would perhaps do better to invoke the more wide-ranging, and in this respect perhaps more nuanced, position of Czech media historian and philosopher Vilém Flusser. For Flusser, specifically, the "apparatus" designates a shift in the hierarchy between humans and technologies whereby the human, operating in a feedback loop with the machine, acquires (or, rather, is forced to take on) the role of information provider in the service of improved performance of the apparatus itself:

> Certainly for the time being, most apparatuses are not so completely automatic that they can get along without human intervention. They need functionaries. In this way, the original terms *human* and *apparatus* are reversed, and human beings operate as a function of the apparatus. A man gives an apparatus instructions that the apparatus has instructed him to give. In this way, a powerful flood of programs is unleashed, a flood of software with which people no longer pursue any particular intention but rather use to issue instructions as a function of an earlier program. As these programs become more complex and clever, they demand faster, smaller, and cheaper apparatuses, more congenial hardware. And so one generation of apparatuses after another appears. With each new generation, human intention recedes further into the background—the intention, that is, that produced the first generation of apparatuses.[34]

While this reversal has not (yet) completely left the human behind, neither at the time of Flusser's writing (1983) nor today, this situation calls for a certain kind of cultural criticism—a criticism that faces up to the changed relationship of human and apparatus. The point is not to reject the reversal chronicled in this passage and, over a greater historical trajectory, in Flusser's theorization of images, but rather to accept it, and indeed, to make it the very basis for critical intervention.

With its anchoring in an analysis of the photographic apparatus, Flusser's media theory has the undeniable advantage of providing a long history of and rich context for the contemporary moment of user integration into digital data networks. Thus the shift Flusser chronicles—the qualified subordination of the user into the technical system—begins already in the nineteenth century and in relation to technologies that can hardly be called "digital."[35] Yet despite the time of his writing (1983), Flusser sees quite clearly how the photographic apparatus effectively anticipates the developments we have been chronicling here: "the camera," he states, "will prove to be the ancestor of all those apparatuses that are in the process of roboticizing all aspects of our lives, from one's most public acts to one's most innermost thoughts, feelings and desires."[36] The longer historical trajectory Flusser proleptically provides for our contemporary moment allows us to be extremely specific concerning the singularity of digital technology: far from directly causing a wholesale reversal in human-machine interrelations, digital technology can only claim to have accelerated such an already-in-process reversal, albeit in an exponential manner.

It is, however, this acceleration that makes all the difference, as Ian Ayres repeatedly emphasizes in his popular study *Supercrunchers*: it is not so much the mathematical techniques for data analysis that are new, but the capacity to crunch data on the massive scales afforded by digital computation. In example after example, ranging from predictive analysis of wine vintages based on weather data to the Oakland A's experimentations with data analysis in evaluating player performance and potential, Ayres paints a compelling picture of the computer's revolutionary contribution to a new paradigm of knowledge.[37] In his account of the "new calculative sense" or "qualculation" that emerges from the contemporary acceleration of calculation, critical geographer Nigel Thrift concurs: "But what seems certain is that the sheer amount of calculation going on in the world has undergone a major shift of late as a result of the widespread application of computing power through the medium of software to the extent that many quite mundane human activities are now shadowed by numerous, often quite complex, calculations. Calculation, in other words, is becoming a ubiquitous element of human life."[38] From my perspective here, it is precisely this digitally facilitated exponential acceleration of calculation that introduces the disjunction of a heterogeneous microtemporal scene of experience from the macroscale figures of experience—perception, consciousness, deliberation, attention, awareness, and so forth—that have dominated media theory up to now. Thus, while the microtemporal domain of sensibility has always fringed the macrotemporal domain of human activity, it is only now—following our development of computational capacities for accessing it—that this domain can catalyze a veritable shift in the "economy" of experience, a deprivileging of perception in favor of sensibility.

To appreciate why this shift offers a potential pharmacological recompense for the data-fication of experience, we must focus on the role microtemporal experience plays in the political project I have proposed here. Insofar as it facilitates access to microtemporal agencies of sensibility or "microconsciousnesses,"[39] the data-fication of sensibility performed by twenty-first-century media potentially yields a massive expansion in the scope of experience itself that entails, among other effects, an expanded agency on the part of human beings. Having already encountered this expansion in the figure of the "surplus of sensibility" introduced by digital networks, we can now appreciate its complex pharmacological basis: far from being a strict correlate of a technically instigated loss, this expansion occurs as the accidental side effect or leftover of a technical change. Moreover, if this surplus can provide human beings with a "power" of experience, that is only because and to the extent that it can make use—can facilitate alternate use—*of the very same technical systems of data collection and analysis* that produce it in the first place, and that produce it, importantly, as an incidental by-product of an effort to lock human behavior into ever-shorter circuits with data networks. To make good on this opportunity, on this alternate deployment of the technically constituted surplus of sensibility, we must rely on the very networks that seek to exploit our sensibility for their own gain. With this situation clarified, we can now properly appreciate the pharmacological imperative to redress the pharmacological imbalance that informs twenty-first-century media: this imperative enjoins us to use the technologies of data capture, analysis, and prediction to create a feed-forward structure capable of marshaling the full productive potentiality of data—its commonality, accessibility, and openness—in order to improve, indeed to improve by *intensifying*, our experience.

Sensibility and Quantification

Responding to this singular pharmacological imperative requires that we accept our imbrication within data networks, our qualified subordination to the functional optimization of the apparatus, and the more general data-fication of sensibility and experience that paradoxically seems to form both their cause and their consequence. If Flusser again helps us to conceptualize what such a position might entail, that is because he appreciates how the apparatus implicates our activity in its own functioning and continuous evolution: "All apparatuses," he claims, "have a program by which they program society to act as part of a feedback mechanism. . . . The photographic industry learns automatically from the actions of those taking snaps (and from the professional press that constantly supplies it with test results). This is the essence of post-industrial progress. Apparatuses improve by means of social feedback."[40] Apparatuses improve by means of social feedback—isn't this the very principle behind today's social media? On this score, how can we fail to recognize Flusser's prescience here, given how much more advanced the feedback structure is in today's digital networks, where the capacity to gather information structures their very operation?

Indeed, if the integration of social feedback into the apparatus reaches a critical threshold with twenty-first-century media, it calls for us neither to indulge in dystopian paranoia, no matter how purposefully polemical it might be (Kittler), nor to adopt a defensive tactics of nonexistence (Galloway and Thacker). Rather, following Flusser's lead, we must rethink the scope of human agency itself in order to take stock of its tight correlation with technics.[41] What this task requires is an appreciation—and an acceptance—of the contemporary phase in our historically evolving "subordination" to the apparatus. Only in this way will we be able to recognize, understand, and make use of the deepened infiltration of technics into life that occurs with the shift to twenty-first-century media.

To assess what such a deepened infiltration entails, let me conclude this discussion by turning to a fuller consideration of the media philosophy of Bernard Stiegler. As I have been developing my argument here, twenty-first-century media pose a direct challenge to Stiegler's project *because they address experience at a level that eludes consciousness and the role of surrogacy that Stiegler accords the technical media object.* (Remember that the central investment of Stiegler's rejuvenation of the Husserlian technical object is its temporal homology with the time of consciousness: in the flux of today's media objects, we are literally presented with a objectification of the temporal correlation of our own consciousness and perceptual experience.) To the extent that it impacts worldly sensibility directly, without being channeled through higher-order human perceptual experience, twenty-first-century media simply do not register on an account like Stiegler's. It is nonetheless important to reconstruct Stiegler's model in a bit more detail, for the model of media experience I am seeking to develop here emerges in a way as an effort to make good on this gap in Stiegler's consideration of technics.

No critic has more thoroughly and convincingly laid bare the deep correlation of human life and technical culture: from the first volume of his *Technics and Time* to his recent study of attention and technics (*Taking Care*), Stiegler has explored the coevolution of technics and life and has successfully articulated a powerful neo-phenomenological model of media centered around the adaptation of the Husserlian figure of time-consciousness for thinking contemporary "technical temporal objects" and their role in mediating our subjectivity. Stiegler's work is important in the present context precisely because of his commitment to the continued relevance of phenomenology, and through it, to the continued operation of higher-order human agency following the technical distribution of precognition that is now ubiquitous in our world today. In this respect, Stiegler's is an important voice of dissent that stands against the tide of much of contemporary media criticism which, in my opinion, all too readily welcomes the wholesale dissolution of consciousness, sense perception, attention, and other higher-order human faculties in favor of a free-floating circulation of somehow not-yet and never-to-be human affect. With his contention that technics impacts human life first and foremost by contaminating the innermost intimacy of human time-consciousness, Stiegler retains a crucial commitment to the integrity of human agency. Accordingly, even at moments when he does seem to recognize the specificity of twenty-first-century media—its operation at levels and in time frames beneath those of consciousness—Stiegler focuses his attention almost exclusively on how interaction with microtemporal technics impacts higher-order human experience.

This focus forms both the strength and the weakness of Stiegler's work. With his appreciation for the specificity of contemporary digital technics, Stiegler is in principle ready and able to recognize the necessity for rethinking human agency along the lines suggested above: namely, as a hybrid composition of overlapping processes—of which consciousness is simply one among others—operating at different timescales and levels of complexity. And yet he is prevented from doing so because of his overly narrow conception of time-consciousness, which is equally to say, because of his fidelity to a certain Husserl: the orthodox Husserl of the phenomenological *epochē*. There is, in other words, a fundamental tension at the core of Stiegler's position: while his analysis of technics pinpoints its operation beyond the *grasp of consciousness*, his argument for technical contamination *retains consciousness as the exclusive site for thinking technics*.[42]

The source of this tension will, ultimately, turn out to be the restrictive scope of the phenomenological model that Stiegler appropriates from Husserl. Indeed, the difficulties Stiegler encounters when seeking to theorize twenty-first-century media parallel the difficulties Husserl faced in his lifelong efforts to theorize the "absolute time-constituting" level of time-consciousness: just as Husserl repeatedly bumped up against the aporia of a consciousness unable to ground the primordial impressionality (the non-egoic hyletic moment) from which it somehow spontaneously arises, so too does Stiegler repeatedly encounter the incapacity of time-consciousness, figured as the correlate of a discrete technical temporal object, to thematize the preperceptual, precognitive elements of twenty-first-century media's experiential impact.

I insist on this parallel here precisely to underscore how the reconstruction of what I earlier called the "minor" legacy of phenomenology will put

us in a position to redirect Stiegler's key insight into the technical founda-
tions of phenomenology toward a broader account of the experiential impact of contemporary media. For just as the exhaustion of the constituting
power of time-consciousness points to the necessary operation of worldly
"de-presencing," and with it to the operation of a sensibility prior to human subjectivity proper, so too does this exhaustion of time-consciousness
require us to jettison the narrow figure of the "temporal object," even in
its contemporary technical instantiation, in favor of a more expansive conception capable of grasping the experiential impact of technics in all of its
disparateness and heterogeneity. Indeed, my reconstruction of a properly
post-phenomenological theorization of time—a reconstruction rooted in
Husserl's final work in the *C-Manuscripts* of the early 1930s and in Fink's
and Patočka's respective developments of it—is aimed specifically to address the experiential predicament of human subjectivity in the face of a
technical mediation of experience that now targets the sub-perceptual and
precognitive basis of time-consciousness, rather than the contents of time-
consciousness proper.[43]

The resulting reconfiguration of how human temporalization is produced on the basis of—and indeed *as part of*—a broader worldly de-
presencing has some important parallels with Whitehead's understanding of
how perception, both "sensuous" and "nonsensuous," emerges on the basis
of—and again *as part of*, as a certain *channeling of*—a broader production of sensibility that occurs equally through the continual genesis of new
concrescences and through the ongoing power of the settled world of superjects. The crucial point in both cases is not simply that human subjectivity
is a resolutely hybrid phenomenon, a complex operational overlap of time-
consciousness with microtemporal events that are both endogenous and environmental; rather, the most crucial point is that human subjectivity qua
operational overlap is composed on the basis of—indeed through and as
part of—a far broader worldly sensibility, itself also in continual production. In this sense, debates over how macroscale time-consciousness relates
to its microtemporal components or (equivalently) how presentational immediacy arises out of a nonsensuous background—which is to say, those
debates that have tended to occupy Whitehead's recent commentators—
properly belong to a later stage of analysis, and address a higher order of
being, than the far more primordial production of sensibility. Before we
can even raise these kinds of higher-order questions, the ongoing process
of worldly de-presencing (of superjective reproduction) will always already
have taken place. In this sense, questions pertaining to human modes of
perceiving arise only on the basis—as concrete organizations—of the primordial sensibility of the world.

In conclusion, let me restate my broad claim about media: contemporary media, or that part of it I am calling twenty-first-century media, impact this primordial level of sensibility—impact the worldly production of sensibility—without any direct correlation with their distinct and equally significant impact on higher-order perceptual experience. One crucial—and, in some meaningful sense, truly new—set of questions twenty-first-century media pose to us thus concerns *our very access to this primordial impact*: How can we assess, let alone find the language to talk about, something in which we, higher-order human agents, are only tangentially or peripherally, and even then only subsequently, belatedly, implicated? Can we truly think and experience the environmental processes composing worldly sensibility without channeling them through our own delimited modes of experience? And what specific new opportunities for self-understanding arise following the reinsertion of our activity within the total sensory confound?

2 Intensity

The doctrine of the philosophy of organism is that, however far the sphere of efficient causation be pushed in the determination of components of a concrescence—its data, its emotions, its appreciations, its purposes, its phases of subjective aim—beyond the determination of these components there always remains the final reaction of the self-creative unity of the universe. This final reaction completes the self-creative act by putting the decisive stamp of creative emphasis upon the determinations of efficient cause. Each occasion exhibits its measure of creative emphasis in proportion to its measure of subjective intensity.   **Alfred North Whitehead, *Process and Reality***

A Radically Environmental Agency?

What motivates my invocation of Whitehead in this study is the imperative, posed to us by the challenges introduced by twenty-first-century media and made salient in our above discussion of Galloway and Thacker, to develop a theory of experience capable of accounting for preperceptual, worldly sensibility and the implication of humans within it. Indeed, it is precisely to address the broad phenomenological issues that emerge from the conjunction between twenty-first-century media and philosophical models of experience that Whitehead's philosophy of organism will prove invaluable. More precisely, Whitehead will help us supplement phenomenological accounts of experience with an ontological conception of total environmental agency. At stake in this supplementation is nothing less than the capacity for phenomenology to overcome its historical, and in some sense constituting, correlation with human perception; once this limiting correlation is overcome, phenomenology, as we shall see, will become free to address worldly sensibility more generally, including the sensibility of inanimate entities.

Whitehead's curious ontology of atomic entities will furnish a "neutral" ground for the expanded scope of phenomenology; specifically it will allow us to think the happening of situations from a perspective that includes, but that is not exclusively (or even primarily) channeled through, human modes of agency. In this sense, the theorization of a neutral (or radically environmental) ground forms a real condition for conceptualizing the experiential impact of twenty-first-century media in all of their heterogeneity and, at least potentially, in their entirety—in what I would prefer to think of as their "total environmentality." For if twenty-first-century media do indeed catalyze a tendential shift in the primary locus of experience from higher-order operations like consciousness and perception to more elementary sensory operations, and if they do so in part at least (and somewhat paradoxically) because they make such sensory operations newly accessible to our higher-order understanding, then a radically environmental conception of agency becomes necessary not just to address what lies beyond the perspective of this higher-order understanding but also, crucially, to grasp what informs its concrete operationality.

In this chapter, I shall turn my attention to philosophical interrogations of the basic structure of Whitehead's metaphysics of experience in order to unpack the promise of his account for a "neutral" or radically environmental theory of experience. To that end, I shall closely follow the reading of intensity proposed by philosopher Judith Jones and shall seek to position this reading as the basis for a fundamental reevaluation of Whitehead's work that focuses on adapting it to the new challenges posed by our contemporary world and specifically by twenty-first-century media.[1] According to Jones (who, to be clear, does not herself relate Whitehead to media), "intensity" (one of the nine "categoreal obligations" introduced in *Process and Reality*) should be elevated—in the place of "creativity" itself—to the status of the "ultimate" in Whitehead's speculative philosophy. Among the more fundamental stakes of this bold and counterintuitive reading is a contestation over what constitutes the source for novelty in Whitehead's philosophy: Jones's reading calls for the displacement of the canonical account that correlates novelty exclusively with the speculative operation of "concrescence" in favor of an account that discovers crucial sources for novelty within the *experience* of "societies," and specifically, in the production of contrasts that generate and maintain societies. (Again, for Whitehead, societies are assemblages of actual entities—or more precisely, of attained or "superjected" actual entities—that share a common causal lineage; in principle, societies would encompass all forms of experiential assemblage, from quantum actualizations to the cosmic expansion of the universe.)

Central to Jones's radicalization of Whitehead is her liberation of the superject from its subordinate status within Whitehead's metaphysics, as this has been developed—or, perhaps more accurately, simply ratified (largely on the basis of *Process and Reality*)—by the majority of his critics. On the canonical picture, the superject designates the operation of an actual entity, following the completion of its concrescence (or more simply, following *its* completion), as an element of the settled world to which it is added; in becoming a superject, the actual entity undergoes what Whitehead calls "objectification"—a transformation from the status of subjective entity ("actuality-in-attainment") to an objective element of the world ("attained actuality"); with this transformation, the actual entity loses its active, subjective power and becomes an inert, passive, and now past entity (Whitehead refers to it as objective "data") available for revivification in new concrescences of new actual entities.

For Jones (who, with Jorge Nobo, Isabelle Stengers, and Didier Debaise, is among Whitehead's most astute *philosophical* commentators), this canonical picture is inadequate and potentially even misleading. As Jones sees it, the superject holds a potential that remains unrealized in Whitehead and in his critical reception: specifically, the superject possesses a lingering agency—indeed, a lingering *subjective* agency—*in and for itself*, which is to say, in its role as objectification of a former concrescence or actuality-in-attainment. The subjective power (meaning a capacity for action and a certain presentness)[2] associated with the actual entity during its genesis (concrescence) *bleeds* or *seeps* into the contribution the actual entity makes to the settled world: "superject" is simply the technical name Whitehead gives to this seepage.

Jones's radical reading of Whitehead facilitates the conceptualization of a radically environmental agency that exists alongside any delimited subjective becoming. The key to such an environmental agency is the operation of the superject as a worldly element of power or subjectivity that exerts its influence or impact on situations *independently of any subject or subjective unification, narrowly considered*. Ultimately, this environmental capacity of the superject will allow for a fundamental rejuvenation of the phenomenological project of time-consciousness in a way that capitalizes on the displacement of consciousness in favor of worldliness (the fruit of Fink's conception of *Entgegenwärtigung*—"de-presencing"); specifically, the superject will "retain" the power of the now past subjective element (actual entity-in-attainment) from which it results, and it will wield that power, not as an

element of a "time-consciousness" or any other interior, intimate, subjective agency, but *as an element of worldliness itself*. Before we follow this line
of deterritorialization to its end point, however, let me focus on a more elementary point concerning the superject's qualified autonomy: what does it
mean to argue, as I shall do here (following Jones), that the superject wields
agency independently of the narrowly subjective entity that was responsible
for bringing it into the world?

My main task in this chapter will be to answer this question by con-
sidering various complications it raises for Whitehead's metaphysics, not
least of which is the status of the speculative itself; what we shall find is
that we, like all other commentators on Whitehead, will need to make a
decision concerning how to understand what I shall call the "speculative
ban" in Whitehead: the prohibition against invoking or appealing directly
to actual entities to explain experiential events and societal processes. For
my part, I will argue that the ban must be maintained, though in a restricted
sense that allows us to exploit to its fullest the distinction Whitehead draws,
but doesn't develop sufficiently, between actualities-in-attainment and attained actualities. (Briefly, actualities-in-attainment designate the phase of
concrescence by which new actual entities are produced; attained actualities
designate the stage when new actual entities are added to the world, thus
expanding the data of the settled world.) Specifically, I shall argue that the
speculative ban applies to actualities-in-attainment, but not to attained actualities: it forbids any direct reference to the former as experiential entities,
that is, beings capable of perception.

This heterodox reading of the economy between the speculative and the
experiential facilitates an understanding of Whitehead's speculative empiricism as a "speculative phenomenology." Specifically, it lets us see that actualities are, in effect, two-sided: they are at once and inseparably both speculative (when they are viewed from the perspective of their concrescence) and
empirical (when they are viewed from the perspective of their participation
in the potentiality of the settled world). And, indeed, in line with Whitehead's focus on explaining experience (which positions his speculative philosophy as an explanation of what the structure of the cosmos must be for
experience to be what it is), I will argue that the speculative side of actualities provides—and is intended to provide—an account of the structure of
reality that is necessary to explain why and how attained actualities operate
experientially in the ways that they do.

If this means, ultimately, that I will choose to accord a certain privilege to attained actualities, that is partly—but only partly—because my
interest here is resolutely experiential: my aim is to adapt Whitehead's phi-

losophy for thinking the experiential realities introduced by twenty-first-century media. With Judith Jones, I feel comfortable maintaining that Whitehead—his apparent disinterest in the post-Kantian continental tradition notwithstanding—would have welcomed the neutral or asubjective phenomenologizing attempted here as a complement to—and as one, if not *the*, key payoff of—his speculative project.[3] And, indeed, one of my central aims in this chapter will be to demonstrate how the privileging of attained actualities goes hand in hand with Jones's liberation of the superject from the subordination to which Whitehead, despite his own pronouncements, effectively submits it. If, that is, attained actuality is the site from which we must begin in the effort to adapt Whitehead for thinking twenty-first-century media, it is not simply because this is the structure of experience that correlates with Whitehead's speculative account of the genesis of actualities. It is also—and, indeed, more importantly—because it constitutes the site where Whitehead's work achieves its most radical consequences for a fundamental rethinking of experience as neutral or asubjective: as the key elements through which attained actualities generate worldly sensibility (or "real potentiality"), superjects generate a dispersed, environmental, non-subject-centered subjectivity. For this reason, as well as for their crucial contribution to the composition of experiential societies—societies that are, as we shall see, constitutively coupled to, indeed imbricated within, an environmental surround from which they are only transiently or tactically separable—superjects (and the attained actualities whose "subjectivity" they express) constitute the truly revolutionary offering of Whitehead's philosophy, at least where it is a question of understanding twenty-first-century media.

The idea that superjects hold a potentiality far beyond the constraints Whitehead imposes on them is absolutely crucial for the claim for inversion (CFI) that structures my engagement with Whitehead's speculative philosophy. For if, following CFI, the speculative account of concrescence proffered in *Process and Reality* is ultimately no more than a vehicle to explain how it is that actualities are added to the world—both as new elements in themselves *and* as sources for further creation (both speculative and experiential, i.e., societal)—then what becomes most fundamental are the concrete elements of creative process, namely, liberated or objectified prehensions, aka superjects. I would even venture to say that the philosophical position I share with Jones and Jorge Nobo—that attained or superjectal actualities are the true heroes of Whitehead's speculative thinking—*requires an embrace of the claim for inversion in some form*: one simply cannot do justice to the double force of the superject (to influence subsequent actualities and to inform societal becomings at all levels) while continuing to uphold the exclusive privilege Whitehead (and most of his commentators) seem to reserve for concrescence as the sole source of creativity and agent of process.

The Speculative Ban

To set the context for my unpacking of the radical potential of the superject, let me return for a moment to the recent surge of interest in Whitehead by literary and cultural critics, and specifically to the interest of some of these critics in Whitehead's value for theorizing contemporary media. As already suggested, these critical explorations have opened new and important avenues for exploring the specificity of contemporary media. Thus, cultural theorists Brian Massumi and Erin Manning ask how Whitehead's conception of "nonsensuous perception" can help us understand the way the present is "pre-anticipated" by the immediate past; Steven Shaviro explores the affinity between Whitehead's emphasis on repetition and the role of sampling and recycling in contemporary media culture; literary critic Steven Meyer tracks parallels between Whitehead's expanded conception of perception and the perspectives opened by contemporary neuroscience; and media theorist Luciana Parisi and sound theorist Steve Goodman ask whether Whitehead's notion of the extensive continuum can support a radical conception of the computational and vibratory basis of culture. All of this activity, which touches only on certain highlights of the recent attention accorded Whitehead,[4] contributes to a veritable renaissance of Whitehead scholarship that has literally expanded his thinking beyond its narrow philosophical legacy and opened it up for a host of cultural theoretical deployments.

As a way of further specifying my claim that Whitehead's ontology furnishes a neutral basis for conceptualizing twenty-first-century media's impact on worldly sensibility, let me try to clarify its key contrast with what may appear to be similar claims concerning Whitehead's value for thinking media today. My claim hinges on a careful differentiation—one I make in concert (at least to a point) with philosophical readers of Whitehead from Ivor Leclerc and Nobo to Stengers and Debaise—between two distinct domains of philosophical exploration: the speculative and the experiential. In my opinion, Didier Debaise gives the clearest account of this crucial distinction, which he places at the very heart of his argument for Whitehead as a "speculative" (rather than a radical) empiricist. In making this argument, Debaise (here following Ivor Leclerc) insists on the necessity of preserving the categorical difference between the "microscopic" domain of *ontological* constitution and the "macroscopic" domain of empirical events (note that "macroscopic" and "microscopic" do not here characterize different levels of phenomena, as they typically do; rather they name distinct domains of being: the experiential and the speculative, the phenomenal and the metaphysical, respectively). For Debaise, as for Isabelle Stengers preceding him,[5] this difference accounts for the singular force of Whitehead's philosophy: its paradoxical aim is to give an account of experience not by "going to the things themselves" (following the path of phenomenology), but by developing concepts to describe that to which we can have no perceptual or sensory access whatsoever, but that is speculatively necessary for things to be as they are.

In his effort to defend the centrality of this enabling division in Whitehead's philosophy, Debaise indicts the entire French reception of Whitehead, from Jean Wahl to Deleuze, for its failure to make and maintain a firm differentiation of speculative from experiential. As Debaise sees it (again following Stengers), every French philosopher to have embraced Whitehead has done so in the name of a misguided identification of actual entity with event;[6]

> *Actual entities are not events.* This question of events must be situated elsewhere, in what Whitehead calls 'societies.'. . . J. Wahl, and Deleuze in his wake, have confused actual entities and societies: two very different things, of which the qualities, in *Process and Reality*, are practically [*quasiment*] opposed. The first are in effect 'abstract' and do not correspond to anything in our experience: they belong to a level qualified as "microscopic." The second are "concrete events," events that we experience in our perception, in our sensations, in our desires, etc.; they form a "macroscopic" level. With the thought of individuation, we are exclusively at the "microscopic" level, a level that is in no case the object of our experience, whether in the form of an empirical object or an intentional object. No doubt the examples of Wahl and Deleuze retain their force, but far from explaining or giving an account of prehension, they can only at best be taken as incitations of what Whitehead calls a "leap of the imagination," a leap into a pure abstraction. It is technically false to say that a "rock" or a "life" are "prehensions," but they evoke what must be thought at the level of actual entities.[7]

There is in Whitehead's mature philosophy no question more vexing than that of how to understand the relation of the speculative to the experiential. Yet this relation is absolutely crucial for a proper understanding of the qualified autonomy of the superject, and thus equally crucial for my effort to find in Whitehead's philosophy the basis for a radically environmental approach to the event.

Because of my commitment to expanding the role played by the superject in Whitehead's philosophy, my decision on the speculative ban must diverge—though I hope only partially—from Debaise's more categorical separation. For me, rather than forbidding any appeal from experience whatsoever, the speculative ban should be restricted to the side of actual entities—actualities-in-attainment—that concerns their speculative genesis or concrescence. Thus, while a description of an event in terms of concrescence would fall under this ban, an appeal to the superjective agency of attained actualities would not. Indeed, with this division in place, we can begin to appreciate how the speculative ban on appealing to the concrescence of actualities *actually serves to facilitate* the experiential power they possess qua attained actualities or superjects. Or to put it another way, we can see how the speculative ban forms a key component of the claim for inversion, for it operates in conjunction with the worldly force of the superject. The speculative ban on concrescence and the experiential power of superjects are simply two sides of a single process that, not surprisingly, generates a two-sided actual entity (one that is indelibly *both* actuality-in-attainment *and* attained actuality). In this sense, the restriction I place on the scope of the speculative ban has the express purpose of facilitating experiential appeal to the attained actualities or superjects that are produced through speculative concrescence. The world they construct is the domain of phenomenology, though of a non-subject-centered, worldly, and in some sense speculative sort.

Were I to synopsize my position in relation to the plethora of recent work on Whitehead, I might say that I take from Debaise a respect for the sway of the speculative ban, while concurring with the cultural and media critics who draw on Whitehead concerning the importance of making his philosophy speak to the experiential realities of the twenty-first century. Debaise's criticism of the French tradition of Whitehead scholarship underscores the necessary caution that must be taken not to confuse or conflate the speculative and the experiential. There is clearly some meaningful and irreducible sense in which this distinction is absolutely crucial to Whitehead's philosophy and to all efforts that make use of it to think contemporary culture and media. Yet, as I have just outlined, everything depends on how this necessity is understood. Let's put Debaise and Stengers at one end of a continuum: for them, there simply can be no experiential appeal to the speculative whatsoever. At the opposite end of the same continuum, let us put Shaviro, Massumi, Manning, Parisi, and others: in their zeal to make

Whitehead relevant for analyzing contemporary experience (and in several cases, because of a certain fidelity to Deleuze), these critics run headlong into the very error denounced by Debaise—the historically French error of identifying actual entity with event.

The Debaise-Stengers position insists on drawing a stark division between the metaphysical and the phenomenological. For it, actual entities are through and through speculative, meaning they are withdrawn absolutely from any possible or real experience: they are what is necessary for there to be experience, but what cannot in themselves be experienced. On this account, the speculative ban would logically have to apply to actual entities tout court, meaning to attained actualities as much as to actualities-in-attainment. But, importantly for what is to follow, this apparently wholesale endorsement of the speculative ban does not mean that these philosophers are indifferent to experience: over against actual entities qua purely metaphysical entities stand "societies" (assemblages of actual entities), and, for Debaise and Stengers, it is to societies that we must turn when and if we want to focus on experience proper.

The position of Shaviro and his comrades either rejects or overlooks the categorical division between the metaphysical and the experiential in its bid to deploy Whitehead's metaphysical account of the genesis of actual entities as a resource for explaining experiential processes. This position recurs to the legacy of the French tradition of Whitehead scholarship, adding what amounts to a new chapter in the mistaken identification of actual entity and event.

To get a sense for the guiding concern of this position, one need only consider Shaviro's willingness—indeed, his eagerness—to address experiential events as prehensions, that is, as achievements of actual entities in concrescence:

> To avoid the anthropomorphic—or at least cognitive and rationalistic—connotations of words like "mentality" and "perception," Whitehead uses the term *prehension* for the act by which one actual occasion takes up and responds to another. Clear and distinct human sense perception, as it is conceived in the classical philosophical tradition from Descartes to the positivists of the twentieth century, is one sort of prehension. But it is far from the only one. Our lives are filled with experiences of "non-sensuous perception": from our awareness of the immediate past, to the feelings we have of "the '*withness*' of the body" (*Process and Reality*, 312). "We see the contemporary chair, but we see it *with* our eyes; and we touch the contemporary chair, but we touch it *with* our hands" (62). Or again, "we see *by our eyes*, and taste *by our palates*" (122). In the same

way, "a jellyfish advances and withdraws, and in so doing exhibits some perception of the causal relationship with the world beyond itself; a plant grows downwards to the damp earth, and upwards to the light" (176). These are all prehensions. For that matter, the earth prehends the sun that gives it energy; the stone prehends the earth to which it falls. Cleopatra's Needle prehends its material surroundings; and I prehend, among other things, the Needle. A new entity comes into being by prehending other entities; every event *is* the prehension of other events.[8]

A strong Deleuzian influence permeates Shaviro's position here: beyond the direct reference to Deleuze's own account of prehension in *The Fold*, Shaviro's account makes a "decision" to forgo any detailed engagement with the complexities involved in crossing the speculative ban in order to secure a non-anthropomorphic perspective. In a move that recurs, mutatis mutandis, in all of the other cultural and media critics mentioned here, prehension and concrescence are embraced for their potential to escape from human-centered modes of perception and, crucially, are treated *as if* they could have direct experiential functions.

Despite the vast differences in their respective understanding of Whitehead, neither position—that of Debaise-Stengers or that of Shaviro and comrades—strikes an adequate balance between the speculative and the experiential. Indeed, both positions—though for precisely opposite reasons—fail to grapple with the double or two-tiered status and function that Whitehead accords actual entities as "actualities-in-attainment" on one hand, and as "attained actualities" on the other. At the one extreme, Debaise and Stengers place both sides of actual entities in the domain of the speculative. And at the other extreme, Shaviro and comrades simply efface the speculative ban and proceed as if actualities were empirical through and through.

To be fair to these critics and to recall the incompleteness and spirit of openness of Whitehead's philosophy, I should point out Whitehead's own failure to clarify how the double status of actualities relates to the speculative dimension of his metaphysics. Notwithstanding what I take to be its central importance for the very task Whitehead takes on (the task of clarifying the necessary structure of reality for experience to be what it is), the double status of actualities appears only tangentially in relation to the definition of the actual entity that Whitehead offers at the end of the section of *Process and Reality* on "Process." There Whitehead writes: "To sum up: There are two species of process, macroscopic process, and microscopic process. The macroscopic process is the transition from attained actuality to actuality-in-attainment; while the microscopic process is the conversion of conditions which are merely real into determinate actuality. The former process effects the transition from the 'actual' to the 'merely real'; and the latter process effects the growth from the real to the actual."⁹ Despite its clear subordination here to the distinction between microscopic and macroscopic process, and despite Whitehead's clear privileging of actuality-in-attainment, the correlation of attained actuality and actuality-in-attainment is absolutely crucial for understanding the full scope of the actuality of actual entities. For actual entities are not actual only when they are in concrescence, but are equally actual—though in a different mode (the mode of potentiality)—when exerting their "dative" force on what will go on to yield new concrescence.

If it is the case that actual entities are two-sided—that they are at once speculative and empirical—then neither Debaise's perhaps overly rigorous commitment to the speculative status of actualities, nor Shaviro's unintentionally heedless embrace of a nonhuman, molecular account of experience qua prehension can do justice to the potentiality of Whitehead's conceptualization. By refusing the speculative altogether, Shaviro deprives himself of the very resources provided by Whitehead's speculative scheme: all that remains on his account is a souped-up empiricism. Homologously, by foreclosing all possibility for a crossing from the speculative to the experiential, Debaise loses sight of an important source of experience—the experiential creativity of attained actualities. What ultimately compromises both appeals is their inability to appreciate the particular combination of two-sidedness and oneness that characterizes Whitehead's view of actuality: as we shall see, actualities acquire their empirical power from their concrescence, but they exercise this power entirely in the domain of experience—*as* attained actualities. Put another way: if the purpose of Whitehead's speculative scheme is to account for how the world must be in order for experience to be what it is, then the speculative account of actualities—the account of their concrescence—is precisely what is necessary to explain how they can generate experience the way they do, that is, as attained elements of actuality. Far from exercising any power directly, concrescences are the explanation for how actualities have power to exercise in the first place—the concrescences of actualities-in-attainment explain how attained actualities can, as elements in societies and as environmental factors, compose the ongoing course of experience.

With their respective conceptualizations of intensity and the primacy of the dative phase, Jones and Nobo help to redress Whitehead's own failure to develop the potentiality of his account of actual entities. In this respect, their interventions allow us to flesh out a position that carves out a space somewhere in between the rigorous defense of actualities as speculative and the heedless embrace of them as empirical. As my above discussion has made clear, the crucial component of any intermediary position must be a revised understanding of the power of actualities to impact experience, that is, the operation of attained actualities once they have been reentered into the world. Having already contrasted Jones's radicalization of Whitehead's understanding of the superject with the canonical view that privileges concrescence, we can now see clearly why the distinction central to the canonical view—between actual entities that are in some sense present and invested with subjective power and actual entities that have become past, inert, and objectified data—simply has, and can have, no other purpose than that of driving a wedge between actual entities in some allegedly proper sense and objectifications of actual entities that render them *mere reflections* of their former selves. What hangs in the balance for the canonical interpretation is the very legitimacy of a view that actual entities-in-attainment are the *only true* actual entities.

Any such view becomes incoherent, and thus illegitimate, as soon as we restore the superjective dimension of the settled, objective world to its rightful status. Here I follow in the footsteps of Jones, for whom the orthodox picture of actual entities as subjective becomings (as concrescences) requires counterbalancing by a restoration of the ontological power of the settled world of former actual entities, now superjects, as they act on future concrescences both as elements of experiential societies of all sorts and as environmental elements (the two descriptions being simply two "views" of the same situation). Following such a restoration, any effort to demarcate true (because ontologically productive) actualities from merely inert and passive ones must fail: superjects wield the subjective power of the attained actualities whose very existence and operation it is the job of speculative metaphysics to explain. In a sense, the elucidation of the structure of concrescence has no purpose other than this: concrescence is necessary to explain the creation of the attained actualities that compose the world. (This, again, is the basis for the *claim for inversion* that is guiding my reading of Whitehead.) Viewed in this way, superjects constitute the mode in which the future inhabits the present following the category of subjective intensity; or, put more concisely, superjects are speculative in origin and experiential in effect. They constitute an *irreducibly experiential* element that is paradoxically located *within* Whitehead's speculative scheme: as the lingering (or proleptic) subjective power of attained actualities, actualities that have (or will have) undergone objectification and are (or will be) separated from their subjective geneses, superjects constitute the very elements with which experiential societies are composed. Superjects are thus the source of power for all composition of experiential societies, of environmental influences, and thus of events as such.

The restoration of superjective attained actualities to their role as source of experiential power catalyzes a certain phenomenologizing of Whitehead's philosophy of organism. The fundamental principle at issue here is the empirical origin of the power to impact experience, which applies just as much to the operation of concrescence as it does to the formation of societal compositions. For even when we narrow our focus to concrescence, certainly the most speculative element in Whitehead's scheme, we are confronted with the operation of a minimal affectivity—reactivity to a datum in the "dative phase" preceding concrescence proper—that can only be understood phenomenologically. Accordingly, although the process of concrescence remains properly speculative, the occurrence of concrescence concerns the broadly phenomenological domain of sensibility: every concrescence is catalyzed by a physical "gift" of data from the settled world or experience, what Nobo calls the "dative phase," which has the paradoxical—but *crucial*— consequence of making "objectification" the *source for*, rather than (as on the canonical account) the result of, concrescence. As Nobo explains:

> This formulation of the nature of a physical prehension begins to make evident, the majority of Whitehead's interpreters notwithstanding, that the subjective activity of an actual occasion is subsequent to the activity whereby the past actualities are objectified, or repeated, in the novel occasion and are in that fashion data for the novel occasion's subjective activity. The objectifications, in other words, are data derived, by means of a reproductive activity, from the novel occasion's correlative universe of completed, or settled, actualities. But the subjective activity of the novel occasion is in no way involved in the derivation or production of the objectifications. The subject does not create the objectifications; it merely reacts to them.[10]

Like Jones, Nobo places his emphasis squarely on the operation of attained actualities, and what he adds to our discussion thus far is a clarity concerning the role of the objective datum. Everything begins with the dative phase, when the physical repetition of a datum of the settled world—an assemblage of attained actualities or superjects—manages to bootstrap itself into an incipient concrescence. For Nobo, such an emphasis stems directly from Whitehead's own account of objectification: "This is one reason why the completed actualities are always said by Whitehead to be objectified *for*, rather than *by*, the novel subject."[11] What follows is the startling conclusion that speculative concrescences themselves have *experiential origins*: they are sparked into becoming by the repetition of objectified elements of the settled world.[12]

Judith Jones comes to a similar conclusion on the basis of the crucial role intensities play as the "reasons for the sustenance of the orders that occur in nature":

> The conditions of order, whereby fully determinate subjects of adequate intensity emerge where they are needed and constitute the world of which we are aware when we look out the window at the breezy colors of an autumn afternoon, or when we accelerate particles in a physics laboratory, impose themselves on the observer as well as on the entities so ordered. Given the questions in empirical science from which Whitehead began his metaphysics, this is not far-fetched. One might object that this reduces metaphysics to a sort of sophisticated phenomenology that attempts to describe how reality must be, given how we experience it. . . . It is unlikely that Whitehead would be troubled by this notion: he never denied the ultimately experiential origins and endpoints for metaphysical explanation.[13]

The account of phenomenology that results from the primacy of experience in Whitehead's metaphysical scheme—what I shall call "speculative phenomenology"—is both asubjective and microtemporal. In this respect, it differs markedly from phenomenology in its orthodox understanding. By shedding its hitherto constitutive correlation with "time-consciousness" and with an "inner domain of apodictic truth," phenomenology becomes available to characterize the operation of the world in all its heterogeneity as it continually creates its own ongoing flow.

Yet the operation of the speculative persists through this phenomenologization, even if it takes on a more narrow or specific role. Restricted to the concrescence of actual entities, the speculative ban ensures that experiential events are attributed to experiential causes: attained actualities provide the elements of societies as well as data for new concrescences. Such an understanding respects the speculative ban that is crucial to Whitehead's philosophy and that serves to differentiate it from a radical empiricism of the Jamesian sort: in this way, it preserves the disjunction between the speculative explanation of how actuality must be in order for experience to happen and the account of experience actually happening. My proposal for a third position on the continuum defined above thus opposes the mere dismissal of the speculative-experiential distinction by Shaviro and others. Yet, it does so less as an end in itself—as it often seems to be in Debaise-Stengers—than as a correlate of a robust speculative phenomenology that it in some sense makes possible. By enjoining us against appealing to actual entities-

in-attainment in our efforts to describe experience, this third position maintains the speculative ban, but—and this is the crucial point—it does so in a way that does not restrict our capacity to make use of attained actualities to analyze experience. That is precisely why the speculative ban goes together with a massive expansion in the scope of phenomenology, an embrace of the asubjective phenomenology of the world itself. The radicalization of the superject as proposed by Jones—its capacity to wield subjective power independently of any subject narrowly considered—simply is the result of this newly prominent operation of attained actuality, the fruit of its resolutely *experiential* creativity.

Prehending the Experiential

Despite my criticism of Debaise, my specification of the scope of the speculative ban could be said to resonate, at least in a general way, with the overall picture of Whitehead that he sketches, even if he does not himself develop the fundamental significance of the distinction between the actual entity's two sides. Indeed, what Debaise criticizes in the French tradition is not the mere invocation of actual entities to describe experience, but rather the *illegitimate* appeal to the *genesis* of actual entities for this purpose. In this sense, the emphasis Debaise places on the speculative centers on the operation of actualities-in-attainment and confirms the differentiation between speculative and experiential as I have been developing it here. In fact, as we shall see, Debaise himself develops the productivity of attained actualities (without explicitly marking their distinction from actualities-in-attainment) in terms of the "disjunctive world," and he devotes the third and final chapter of his book to an explication of Whitehead's account of experience in terms of the composition of societies.

The same cannot be said for the other position, thus far identified with Shaviro's work, which *does* make explicit—and, I contend, illegitimate—appeal to concrescence and genesis in order to characterize experience. A particularly clear example comes by way of cultural theorist Luciana Parisi's recent effort to align Whitehead's theory of perception with contemporary sensory enhancements. In a provocative and compelling theorization of what she calls "technoecologies of sensation," Parisi correlates bionic technologies that extend human sensibility in "non-presentational" ways, such as neuromorphic chips, cochlear implants, and synthetic retinas, with Whitehead's theory of perception. Bionic technologies, Parisi writes,

> seem crucial for extracting sensing potentials below and above frequencies of habitual sensory perception. Indeed, bionic tech-

nologies seem to directly ingress sensuous and nonsensuous perception, or, as Whitehead remarks, perception of immediate presentation (sensory perception of the here and now) and perception
of causal efficacy (thought perception of the there and then). Bionic
technologies seem to directly connect with the causal field of sensation, accounting not simply for sensory-motor perception, but,
more importantly, for the causal intricacies of the physical and the
nonphysical, whereby thought itself is felt. Bionic technologies thus
count neither as mechanical extension nor as digital dematerial-
ization of the physical sensorium. Rather, the bionic sensorium is
above all implicated in the machinic extension of the non-physical
and physical capacities for feeling, entailing the rearrangement of
sensation at the shortest span of time. Thus, bionic technologies
are not simply the sensory enhancement of cybernetic systems
media, humans, animals—but more importantly are in the process
of constituting a veritable technoecology of sensation—a machinic
intricacy of organic and inorganic milieu of information sensing
preceding sensory perception, resulting in an inarticulate sensation,
that is, an unframed feeling.[14]

Understood as a general claim about technology, Parisi's analysis here would
seem to converge with the tendential shift in the address of twenty-first-
century media discussed above. In particular, her emphasis on "perception
in the mode of causal efficacy" mobilizes the very element of Whitehead's
speculative empiricism that, as I suggested above, would seem entirely apt
to characterize the imbrication of media with a subrepresentational and
nonconscious realm of sensibility: before and entirely independently of any
higher-order sensory perceptions they might ultimately help facilitate, bionic technologies, like digital technologies more generally, operate directly
on the causal field of sensibility. They quite literally create new technoecologies of sensation.

When, however, Parisi goes on to invoke Whitehead's concept of "prehension" to characterize the mode of sensation that occurs in such technoecologies, she takes what appears to be an unnoticed—and what, in my
view, is clearly and indisputably an *illegitimate*—leap across the speculative
divide. "Symbiosensation," she writes, "is the machinogenesis of a novel
relatedness between organic and inorganic milieus of information sensing:
a concrescence, to borrow from Whitehead, the growing of 'novel togetherness' of actual occasions, the felt nexus of distinct societies or worlds across
scales and milieus, adding new dimensions of nonphysical feeling to the
body. Symbiosensation is not direct perception, but prehension."[15] Notwith-

standing her entirely laudable intention to correlate symbiosensation with a mode of sensibility that would be more environmental than any imaginable mode of perception, Parisi's argument violates the speculative ban: for by explicitly characterizing the sensory affordances of contemporary technoecologies using the terminology Whitehead reserves for the speculative genesis of actual entities, she makes direct appeal to the speculative in order to describe experience.

Fallout from this categorical error manifests in Parisi's tendency to mix elements that belong to categorically distinct levels of analysis. Such mixing occurs, for example, when Parisi characterizes symbiosensation as a "concrescence" *in the very gesture of describing* it as "the felt nexus of distinct societies or worlds." Here, that is, she describes symbiosensation *at one and the same time* as an actuality-in-attainment (a concrescence) and as an assemblage of attained actualities (a society). If we are to preserve any sense for Whitehead's carefully articulated distinctions, we simply cannot endorse any claim that positions symbiosensation *simultaneously* as a speculative process occurring in concrescence and as an empirical process through which societies are composed, and that does so *without any recognition whatsoever of the category mistake it involves.*

What we have learned from our above exploration of Debaise's indictment of the French tradition, and our specification of the extension of the speculative ban, should warn us to proceed with caution here. It is, we now know, simply illegitimate to analyze experiential entities like "nexuses" or "societies" as if they were speculative concrescences (processes that occur by means of a speculative genesis); and it is furthermore unclear what such an analysis could even accomplish, given that the speculative account of actualities operates through an entirely different logic than their experiential description. If nothing else, what Parisi's confusion ultimately brings home—by way, as it were, of a demonstration by failure—is the importance of distinguishing experiential entities (nexuses, societies, attained actualities) from speculative concrescences. And what we learn from her account is just how important it is for us to focus on the former if we are to develop a robustly experiential, "symbiosensory" dimension of Whitehead's philosophy.

That is why, notwithstanding her own fundamental confusion concerning the status of the entities she so freely mixes, we can endorse the broad intent of Parisi's analysis and the imperative that it expresses for developing an experiential side to the operation of prehension. For if Parisi errs in equating symbiosensation with prehension, she is entirely correct—and indeed prescient—in suggesting that Whitehead can help us to theorize a domain of sensibility that is radically environmental and that is in some sense more primitive than perception (including perception in the White-headian "mode of causal efficacy"). Thus, in a move that will help us adapt Whitehead's work for thinking the singularity of twenty-first-century media, Parisi effectively suggests that worldly sensibility—what she calls "symbiosensation"—makes itself felt *at the level of prehension*. Yet to cash in on this suggestion, we will need to supplement Parisi's analysis by doing for prehension something akin to what Jones and Nobo do for the actual entity: we will need to develop an internally complexified or doubled account of prehension capable of preserving its particular speculative "purity" while also making good on its undeniable experiential significance.

Such a development, to be sure, flies in the face of Whitehead's understanding of prehension, even if it ultimately strengthens the account of sensibility his philosophy facilitates. For Whitehead, the term "prehension" has a technical specificity and precision: prehensions are relationships involving "actual entities" and "eternal objects" that are formed during the concrescence (subjective becoming) of any and every new actual entity.[16] They name the form of relation through which a given actual entity—more precisely, an actuality-in-attainment—grasps, both positively and negatively, the entirety of the settled universe (the disjunctive plurality of attained actualities) at the moment of its genesis.[17] For Whitehead, that is, prehension clearly designates a form of relationality that properly belongs to the speculative explanation of the concrescence of actual entities and that can only metaphorically be carried over to the domain of experience, to characterize (for example) a particular sensation or feeling.[18]

Far from being some sort of direct precursor to, let alone a synonym for, sensation or perception, prehension thus designates what is a very specific and predominately physical form of relationality—a form of relationality that occurs as a reaction to causal efficacy, or, more precisely, to the "dative phase" of physical prehension so compellingly theorized by Nobo. This reaction, which sparks a new actuality into becoming, yields a series of phases of prehension that occur prior to the emergence of any perception of its occurrence and in a speculative reserve from the temporal world; these phases culminate in the unification of prehensions around the "subjective aim" driving concrescence. We can thus conclude that, in its proper usage, prehension constitutes an element of Whitehead's speculative ontology, a key part of the conceptual arsenal that accounts for the existence of actual entities, or, more precisely, for the becoming of being at the "microscopic" (pre-experiential) scale. When Parisi speaks of "symbiosensation" as if it were some direct feeling of such "microscopic" prehensions involved in the speculative concrescence of actual entities, she commits an unmistakable category mistake that mirrors her above-discussed mistake. Indeed, as I've already noted with respect to concrescence, Parisi commits precisely the category mistake Debaise denounces in the French reception of Whitehead: she treats the *speculative* unification of prehensions by actual entities in concrescence as if it were simply equivalent to the *experience* of sensing.

Once again, however, what is undeniably a shortcoming of Parisi's analysis actually harbors a lucid insight. For just as soon as we jettison her references to concrescence, Parisi's position begins to outline the possibility of according prehensions an experiential purchase, the power to operate superjectally and in the domain of experience. Though it does not alter the necessity to distinguish prehensions from perceptions, this possibility accords perfectly with my conviction that prehensions must be liberated from their restricted role in Whitehead's speculative scheme. That is why, insofar as they spark new actualities into becoming, prehensions not only cannot be withdrawn from the experiential world but must be positioned as the very source for contrasts that generate intensity. Like the actual entities to which they initially belong, prehensions are objectified and reentered into the world as elements possessing superjectal subjectivity: just as actual entities obtain new activation as superjects (attained actualities), so too do the prehensions "originally" bound to a specific concrescence come to enjoy new life as liberated worldly relationalities.

In analogy with the distinction between actualities-in-attainment and attained actualities, we will thus need to distinguish a speculative account from an experiential operation of prehension: in speculative entities, prehensions designate relationalities constituting the content and the unity of an actual entity in concrescence, while in experiential ones, they operate as empirical relationalities that in fact constitute attained actualities following their objectification and reentry into the settled world. What we have said about attained actualities thus holds equally for objectified prehensions; indeed, once they lose their internal unifying aim, which only obtains during concrescence, attained actualities become largely indistinguishable from assemblages of attained prehensions. Indeed, attained prehensions are the elements of attained actualities, and, as such, they constitute the relational texture of the settled world not just for future concrescences of new actualities-in-attainment (where concrescence is understood as unification of prehensions), but also for all *experiential* compositions of higher-order societies, from the most elementary (atoms, electrons, protons, etc.) to the most complex (human bodyminds, the cosmos, etc.). Like the attained actualities they in effect compose, attained prehensions exist in the world in the form of superjectal remainders, and indeed, they are—or rather, they *become*—micro-agents of experiential events.

Having now introduced this experiential side of prehension, let me turn once again to the topic of twenty-first-century media in order to explore how they expand the causally efficacious operation of what we might call "worldly prehensiveness." To the extent that they address experience at levels beneath perception and consciousness, twenty-first-century media operate through preperceptual attained prehensions; in this way, they both reveal the experiential import of prehension and potentially give us new, *non-perceptual* modes of access to it. Such a mode of non-perceptual sensibility is, I would suggest, precisely what is at issue in Parisi's call for new, unframed modes of sensation: what "symbiosensation" requires is a potential to access worldly sensibility independently of its subsequent impact on our higher-order modes of experience, independently, that is, of its effect on perception.

To the extent that they afford such access, twenty-first-century media expose the fundamental phenomenological dimension of Whitehead's philosophy: more precisely, twenty-first-century media furnish access to the primordial encounter that occurs in the dative phase. They thus lay bare the existence of worldly sensibility prior to—and at the very heart of—any and all higher-order emergences. In this respect, the phenomenology of sensibility differs categorically from all subject- or ego-centered phenomenologies: here the operation of sensibility occurs prior to any experiential unification in a subject.

If this phenomenological dimension accounts for the broad affinity linking Whitehead's thought to phenomenology in its post-phenomenological phase, his emphasis on the fundamental continuity of experience across all scales serves to specify the contribution of his distinctly speculative phenomenology: Whitehead's phenomenology is a resolutely neutral phenomenology capable of addressing contemporary experience and the specific forms of environmental mediation that inform it. For Whitehead, this experience ranges from the superjective power of the simplest attained actualities, together with the prehensions composing them, all the way up to the highest forms of contrast found in processes of perception, consciousness, and symbolic reference. This continuity is a complex, or internally differentiated, and locally discontinuous one. More precisely, it is a *continuity of indirection* whereby each successive level reorganizes lower-level processes as part of its own operation but, importantly, without subsuming those processes or compromising their specific autonomy. For this reason, Whiteheadian phenomenology constitutes a radically environmental and hybrid phenomenology, one that accords the capacity of experience to all levels of becoming, to all societies, from atoms to geological processes. This phenomenology finds its fundamental principle in the deprivileging of perception in favor of sensibility, which "belongs" first and foremost to the world. And it acquires its principle of expression from what I shall call "operational overlap," the coexistence alongside one another of disparate and quasi-autonomous "levels" of process that do not get sublated in any upward-directed telos of emergence. On this understanding, we can grasp the human being in a new way, as a set of overlapping levels that remain, in some nontrivial sense, autonomous from, and in temporal heterogeneity with, one another: in human agency, higher-order, self-referential modes like perception overlap with bodily and environmental modes of sensibility that paradoxically retain their autonomy and exert their own proper impact on the total experiential situation even as they also form the components of such higher-order modes.

Intensity

Philosopher Judith Jones's careful rehabilitation of the concept of "intensity" in Whitehead offers the philosophical basis for a neo-phenomenological account of environmental experience that expands its import to all forms of becoming. In Jones's view, intensity designates the ultimate causally efficacious ground for all experience: as the product of material contrasts generated by superjects (by the settled world of objectified actualities), intensity directly expresses the force of superjective agency (worldly de-presencing) and reveals it to be—from the standpoint of experience—*more fundamental than the subjective concrescences of new actual entities.*[19] In this sense, intensity lies at the basis of the continuity-through-indirection that characterizes Whiteheadian phenomenology; more specifically, because intensity differentially expresses the qualitative dimension of sensibility across all levels of experience, it can help us develop a phenomenological account rooted *in the experience of sensibility itself*, not—as is the case for orthodox phenomenology from Husserl to the Merleau-Ponty of *Phenomenology of Perception*—in the *perception of* that experience. In this sense, it is through intensity that the sensibility of the world is first felt: intensity is the first qualification of worldly sensibility or, more precisely, of the "shocks" or "primal impressions" that inaugurate it. To the extent that intensity—and not perception—constitutes the proper qualitative correlate of prehension, intensity is precisely what is at stake experientially in twenty-first-century media's direct mediation of worldly sensibility.

Jones's study of intensity is, in essence, an extended consideration of the centrality of Whitehead's eighth categoreal obligation, "the category of subjective intensity," in his mature philosophy. This category specifies the being of the "subjective aim" of the concrescence of an actual entity and applies it both to the subject but also to the future-directed superject:

The Category of Subjective Intensity. The subjective aim, whereby there is origination of conceptual feeling, is at intensity of feeling (a) in the immediate subject, and (b) in the *relevant* future. This double aim—at the *immediate* present and the *relevant* future—is less divided than appears on the surface. For the determination of the *relevant* future, and the *anticipatory* feeling respecting provision for its grade of intensity, are elements affecting the immediate complex of feeling. . . . The relevant future consists of those elements in the anticipated future which are felt with effective intensity by the present subject by reason of the real potentiality for them to be derived from itself.[20]

As this definition makes clear, intensity designates the experience by the "present subject" (which simply means the actual occasion for the experience) of two correlated feelings: the present qualification of the contrasts informing the actual occasion and the real potential for them to qualify future occasions that are no longer narrowly subjective but are worldly, which is to say, superjective. It is with this duality in mind that we can appreciate Jones's correlation of intensity with the concept of "ecstatic individuality"; as Jones explains, ecstatic individuality "asserts that an entity exists with the ontological status of *its* subjectivity *to* some degree in every subject in which it comes to have influence (and, to an extent, in every subject from which it originally derived)."[21] On this point, her reading resonates strongly with Deleuze's mobilization of the superject to characterize the agency, and specifically the future agency, of the technological objectile and the ongoing process of modulation shaping its evolution; what is key for Deleuze, as for Jones, is the capacity for a subjective variation to reach out beyond itself and impact the becoming of other entities. On this account, the superject, the former actual entity following its objectification and (re)entry into the settled world of experience, *continues to wield the "subjective" power* that, for Whitehead and the majority of his commentators, exclusively characterizes the pre-experiential operation of concrescence.

As I have already suggested, this understanding of intensity—as a power that exceeds the individual actual entity in concrescence—requires a crucial corrective to Whitehead's conception of actual entities, a corrective that draws from Debaise's (and Stengers's) embrace of the speculative, though it is developed most fully by Jones. Specifically, it requires us to reject Whitehead's claim—a claim that has become canonical in the secondary literature—that an actual entity in concrescence, once it achieves its "satisfaction" (i.e., once all its prehensions are carried out), simply "perishes." Inherited from John Locke, this account of the perishing of individual actualities following their objectification functions to explain the "objective immortality" of attained actualities, their belonging to the settled world as inert data awaiting future revivification. From my perspective, and also for Jones, this account effectively strips actualities of their properly superjective dimension, by which I mean their capacity to operate as environmental subjectivities within the domain of experience. We must reject Locke's account of perishing, together with Whitehead's adoption of it, precisely in order to preserve this environmental operation of subjective power that, as I am arguing here, constitutes one of the crucial achievements of Whitehead's philosophy. It is precisely, as Jones points out, Locke's account of perishing that lies behind Whitehead's denial of temporal intensity to individuals, which amounts to a denial of causality from actual entities to other actual entities and also, crucially, from actual entities to higher-order societies of actual entities (and societies of societies). "Whitehead," insists Jones, "was mistaken to think that intensive, evaluative individuality had to be confined to a radically perishing conception of presentness. The way Whitehead (and consequently his interpreters) ontologizes the past, present, and future operates at a separate, more abstract analytical level than the actual process of temporalization."[22] Eschewing the consequences of Whitehead's inheritance from Locke, Jones's emphasis on intensity thus allows for a reconceptualization of the subject-superject and licenses—and, I would say, even requires—a certain post-phenomenological phenomenalizing of Whitehead's radically environmental ontology.

The core of this post-phenomenological phenomenalizing is the claim for inversion. The CFI calls on us to reverse the priority Whitehead accords concrescence in favor of the "yield" it produces, that is, the addition of new superjective elements to the settled world, elements that possess subjective power of their own and that provide new sources for experiential process. In the present context, we learn that this inversion is both informed by and encompasses a transformation of Whitehead's own understanding of the temporal intensity of actualities: far from perishing upon completion, actualities in fact only begin to become efficacious, to impact worldly sensibility and to wield the force of the sensible, once they have been phenomenalized. Understood as such, phenomenalization emerges as a synonym of sorts for Whitehead's "objectification," only with its core valuation reversed: that is, whereas objectification marks the moment when the subjective force of an actuality ceases, and when that actuality becomes part of the world's inert data, phenomenalization lays stress on the subjective power of attained actualities, and indeed suggests that their proper subjective power is in fact a superjective one, that is, a power deriving from the dispersion and potentiality of process.

This view of phenomenalization, and of its potential to subsume White-headian "objectification" into an account that inverts Whitehead's core commitment to concrescence, is supported by Jones's account of process. For my purposes here, the key claim of Jones's study concerns the way in which past actual entities can impact the genesis of new actual entities: she insists that they have active not passive, living and not just inert, subjective agency, even (or indeed, especially) in their existence as superjects. In this respect, Jones's account furnishes the very mechanism by which the superjects constituting the settled (or "de-presencing") world come to impact both future concrescences *and* experiential compositions at all scales.

On this point, Jones's account stands in stark contrast to Whitehead's stated position. For Whitehead, each actual entity is related to the entirety of the universe because it either "positively" or "negatively" prehends data from all past actual entities and determinateness from "eternal objects." (Again: positive prehensions are feelings received into and unified within the developing subjective occasion; negative prehensions exclude data from this occasion and thus cannot be feelings although they make a contribution to the actual entity or, as we shall see, convey intensity to it; eternal objects are "pure potential" for the specific determination of fact, and include things like color and other sensory qualities as well as other unchanging abstract qualities of the universe.) On Whitehead's account, actual entities become connected to one another *externally*: through a process of "transition," completed actual entities "perish" as actual and become "objectified" as inert and passive data available for subsequent concrescing actual entities. Following their own proper concrescence, actual entities can, that is, only continue to exercise agency passively, by being taken up (prehended) as content in the concrescence of future actual entities.

As Jones views it, this characterization significantly impoverishes the role played by past actual entities in future concrescences: it restricts the superjected element of subjectivity to the status of simple replication of inert past content. To remedy this, Jones proposes a reading of Whitehead that accords agency—specifically, the power of intensity—to the superject; more than the mere inclusion of past actual entities (and eternal objects) as contents of a new concrescencing actual entity, the superject is permeated by the lingering agency—the intensity—of the past actual entities it includes, and its crucial contribution is to exercise this agency in the future-to-come. "It is my thesis," Jones announces at the outset of her study,

> that the functioning of an existent in another existent must be as-cribed to the internal account *of the first existent*, as much as it is to be ascribed to the present self-constitution of an entity in concres-

cence. The fully determinate feeling characterizing the "satisfaction" of any occasion includes elements whose sources lie in *other* entities that to some significant extent retain their character as determinate unities of feeling *in themselves* even as they are objectified in a present concrescence. The objective functioning of one thing in another, in other words, never completely loses the subjective, agentive quality of feeling that first brought it into being. The "accidents" or "tricks" of an actuality's insinuation in another remains a real and passional element in the satisfaction of that other entity.[23]

What is ultimately at stake in Jones's argument is a general claim about actuality that applies as much to experiential entities as it does to speculative ones. Simply put, her thesis postulates the existence of a permeability between the subject and the superject—a seepage of the former's proper power into the latter and a reentry of this power into new subjective geneses and societal compositions—that has a bearing on the composition of experiential entities as much as it does on the concrescence of new speculative entities. Such a reading allows us to redress what we can only call (with a touch of irony, to be sure) the subjective bias of Whitehead's orthodox account: by restoring the subjective power to the superjective dimension of process, this account strikes a balance between concrescence and objectification that is necessary to explain the creativity of worldly process. Nothing less is at stake in what I am calling the claim for inversion: the marshaling of Whitehead's account of concrescence as an element in a larger account of process.

One important consequence of the permeability between subject and superject concerns the scope of causation. On account of the extrasubjective function of subjective power central to Jones's revaluation of Whitehead's account of intensity, the power of causation can no longer be neatly divided into a form of causality (final causality) that characterizes actual entities in concrescence and another form (efficient causality) that characterizes experiential nexuses and societies. Rather, as Jones points out, "the analysis of causal interaction is primarily concerned with intensity and only secondarily with other formal considerations as to the entity as subject-superject." From this, she immediately goes on to conclude that many of the problems involved in correlating the speculative and the experiential would have been avoided "had Whitehead developed a vocabulary whereby the work of final and efficient causality could have been described in terms related to 'order' as intensive actualization."[24] Ultimately, what Jones means to underscore here is that actual entities in their speculative genesis (i.e., actualities-in-attainment) are themselves necessarily implicated in causal orderings of nature. If, as I put it above, concrescence is the speculative account necessary to explain how attained actualities compose experience, then actualities-in-attainment are nothing other than the necessary flip side of the attained actualities that compose experiential entities at all scales.

That is why Jones can conclude by privileging the causal basis of actuality: "When we speak of entities we are rarely if ever referring to free-floating self-determiners outside of some temporal organization denoted by the term 'nexus.' That is, actual entities are found in paths of causal transmission of characteristics such that discernable orders are present in nature."[25] With this conclusion, Jones's analysis converges with that of Debaise, in the sense that both clearly discern the primacy of nexuses and societies within the experiential domain: although both include provision for according causal power to attained actualities and liberated prehensions (even if neither quite grasps the radical implication of this provision), they recognize that causal power is typically expressed through the participation of actualities in higher-order compositions, which is to say, in durational entities of higher complexity.

This conclusion concerning the primacy of nexuses and societies follows directly from Whitehead's own enumeration of four "grounds of order" which serve, among other things, to correlate intensity with the causal exfoliation of actual entities in temporal nexuses. These grounds of order are:

(i)   That "order" in the actual world is differentiated from mere "givenness" by introduction of *adaptation for the attainment of an end*.

(ii) That this end is concerned with the gradations of intensity in the satisfactions of actual entities (members of the nexus) in whose formal constitutions the nexus (i.e., antecedent members of the nexus) in question is objectified.

(iii) That the heightening of intensity arises from order such that the multiplicity of components in the nexus *can enter explicit feeling* as *contrasts*, and are not dismissed into negative prehensions as *incompatibilities*.

(iv) That "intensity" in the *formal constitution* of a subject-superject involves "appetition" in its *objective* functioning of a superject.[26]

Nowhere in Whitehead's speculative work is the centrality of experience more thoroughly clarified than in this highly complex, yet in some sense deceptively simple, enumeration. In commenting on this passage, what I would hope to convey is a sense for how Whitehead's understanding of the speculative—far from forming some alternate dimension (e.g., a virtual plane)—constitutes *nothing more nor less than a component in his account of experience*. We get a first statement to this effect when Whitehead contrasts "adaptation for the attainment of an end" against "givenness." From this, we learn that Whitehead's speculative account aims to provide something more "active" than phenomenological accounts of thrownness or facticity: every new event of experience, regardless of its scale, constitutes an accomplishment of novelty that is not fully explicable in terms of its gathering of experiential elements, but that involves a genuine ontological creativity. Events do not arise as gifts of Being, as they do on a Heideggerian account, but are themselves created as elements of Being in the very process of their experiential becoming. What this means is that the speculative domain cannot "preexist" the experiential and that it is, in fact, ultimately nothing more than a dimension of the experiential: what has to be—or better, what has to be created—in order for experience to be what it is.

Whitehead further specifies the "differentiated oneness" of the speculative and the experiential in points (ii) and (iii) where he effectively fleshes out the relationships that allow him to claim, as he does in (iv), that the intensity generated in the "formal constitution" of an actuality (i.e., in its concrescence) correlates with the "appetition" of the superject. What we find in the concrete specificities of these relationships is a complex crisscrossing between the speculative and the experiential. Thus, from (ii), we learn that the "end" (final cause) of the formal constitution of the actual entity, far from being a finality purely immanent to that entity's concrescence, is "concerned with" (by which I understand Whitehead to mean, partially composed of) the intensity of the attained actualities constituting the members of the nexus in question. What this means, in effect, is that the finality governing the formal constitution—the finality allegedly reserved for the speculative process of concrescence exclusively—is at least partially (if not predominately) informed by the experiential power of the nexus in question. More simply put, the telos of every concrescence is shaped by the experiential intensity of the particular nexus that concretizes its conditions of adaptation: its subjective aim is literally motivated by this intensive shaping. Indeed, Whitehead effectively tells us in (iii) that the generation of intensity among the components of the experiential nexus is the factor that determines whether given elements of the universe "enter explicit feeling as *contrasts*" or "are dismissed into negative prehensions as *incompatibilities*."

Here we encounter a situation that can only create a paradox for both the Debaise and the Shaviro camps: according to this situation, the determination of whether an element is prehended positively or negatively (and recall that for Whitehead prehension occurs in concrescence) is made not by a factor internal to the process of concrescence *but rather by the intensity among the elements of the settled world that adapt the process for the attainment of an end.* What makes this situation paradoxical is that concrescence cannot account for its own process: far from being exclusively motivated by an internal aim, concrescence is always beholden to an *external* situation, which is to say, to an experiential reality whose attainment it supports.

In her analysis of the four grounds of order, Jones emphasizes the transmission of feelings that forms the source of power motivating concrescence. Indeed, in a direct parallel to Nobo's correlation of the onset of concrescence with the worldly repetition of physical prehensions (the "dative phase"), Jones singles out the "phase of 'conformal feeling'" that constitutes an emergent entity's reaction to worldly causality in its zero degree: "A concrescence involves first a phase of 'conformal feeling,' which denotes primarily the reproduction in the novel entity *of feelings belonging to other entities in the concrescent subject's world.* Whitehead calls this the stage of 'physical feelings,' wherein there is genuine 'transmission' of feelings from actuality to actuality. The sense of reproduction meant here is the new subject's feeling for itself, a feeling that markedly belongs to the being of another entity. This is the *essence of causal influence in its barest form.*"[27] Jones notes that these feelings, which "bear in themselves reference to the actualities whose objectifications they are," furnish the source for new entities in the world, and thus for the new concrescences that compose these new events. As what amounts, within the terminology of phenomenology, to de-subjectified radicalizations of phenomenological heteroaffections, these feelings "are incorporated into the new entity in the guise of *their intensities.*"[28] The causal transmission, which is also to say the "otherness," at the very root of concrescence, turns out to be nothing less than a *transmission and othering*—a transmission through othering—by intensity.

If we take on the full force of Jones's development here, then the power of causation as intensity forms a continuity, as it were, across the speculative-experiential divide; as such, it serves to link the concrescence of actual entities to their experiential power in a way that resonates with, and seems to corroborate, our above specification of the scope of the speculative ban. Despite their reserve in relation to the domain of experience, actualities-in-attainment are themselves catalyzed by the very same forces—the forces of contrasts generative of intensity—that also catalyze the composition of experiential entities at all levels of complexity. This means that the power of causation ultimately concerns intensity understood as a force of relationality linking actual entities into "nexuses," or "paths of causal transmission of characteristics such that discernable orders are present in nature." Insofar as it is expressed through intensity, through the fundamental experience informing all orderings of nature, causality operates in one and the same way regardless of whether it applies to the dative phase of an incipient concrescence or to the complex composition of a human consciousness.

In the process of rereading Whitehead to make his thought consequent with this fundamental valuation of intensity, Jones deconstructs several of the key differences that have dictated commentary on his philosophy; these include the divisions between concrescence and transition, between public and private, and, as mentioned, between efficient and final causation. For my purposes, none of these deconstructions is more significant than that between temporal ecstasis (the past/future) and the present, for it is precisely here that we get the clearest sense for why Whitehead's speculative empiricism is compatible with a post-intentional, asubjective phenomenology of sensibility. Although Jones does not herself develop the implications of her argument concerning intensity for a potential reconciliation of Whitehead with the post-Husserlian phenomenological tradition, her comments on temporalization and the clear and acknowledged Heideggerian roots of "ecstatic individuality" help us to grasp what is at stake here. On Whitehead's stated account, which restricts agency to concrescing actual entities, time is effectively deprived of power: more precisely, it is rendered a subordinate effect of the extensive relations that are established between actual entities following the oscillation between concrescence and transition, satisfaction and objectification. As Jones sees it, such an account can do no more than yield an inert atomism, one in which the power of actualization is restricted to the developing subjective occasions and in which all further individualities, including past experience and all higher-order societies, are mere derivatives from this primary ontological power.

By contrast, to develop an "atomism of connected individuals," what is required is an extension of agency to the superject, which is to say, a conceptualization of agency as an imperishable intensity that actively connects individuals in temporalized relations. In short, if intensity is the true "ultimate" of Whitehead's empiricism, as Jones wants to claim, then time cannot be the derivative product of external relations between actual entities, but is and must be itself a co-ingredient of the active causal operations that generate intensity. The inversion of Whitehead's philosophy spearheaded by Jones's reading calls on us to differentiate two orders of time—intensive and extensive time. While the latter designates the worldly time that is created by the incessant oscillation of concrescence and transition—which is to say, by process itself—the former names the force that fuels the oscillation itself. Put another way, Jones's account situates time squarely within the domain of intensity. We can easily anticipate what such a reading of Whitehead will bring to the project of developing a post-Husserlian, post-phenomenology of sensibility: by making time and sensation elements of intensity rather than correlates of consciousness, it not only thoroughly de-anthropomorphizes the process of temporalization, but perhaps more monumentally, also vastly expands its scope, scale, and degree of heterogeneity.

"Non-perceptual Sensibility"

Let us now return to the topic of Whitehead's value for theorizing twenty-first-century media. Bearing in mind Jones's exciting reconceptualization of superjective agency as the power of intensity, we can now pinpoint even more precisely the source of the conceptual confusions in Luciana Parisi's argument concerning symbiosensation. Following Deleuze and the French tradition he culminates, Parisi effectively dissolves the distinction between microscopic and macroscopic processes in the sense Whitehead gives these terms (where the microscopic, again, refers not to entities at small scales but to the speculative operation of actualities, i.e., to concrescence, while the macroscopic encompasses experiential entities at all scales, i.e., nexuses and societies). That is why Parisi can so easily move from perception to prehension and, indeed, why she feels justified in simply identifying "symbiosensation" with prehensive feeling. What we have learned from Jones, however, complicates this picture of simple identification: insofar as it mediates both forward in time (or causal lineage) and upward in complexity, intensity explains how properly speculative microscopic processes always already possess a macroscopic side—or, perhaps better, a macroscopic potentiality—independently from the experiential entities (nexuses and societies) in which they participate. In this respect, Jones's account affirms the reality of experience within both domains of process. And it does so, importantly, not by positing a monolithic figure of sensation that remains qualitatively the same across levels, but rather by embracing the concrete differences—indeed the actual contrasts—constitutive of distinct orders of complexity.

Put another way, the operation of intensity recognizes a degree of indirection in the forward and upward movements it facilitates: thus, "perception in the mode of causal efficacy"—Whitehead's term for the vague perception that informs and characterizes animal life—emerges on the basis of causal lineages of attained actual entities effectuated through objectification, but crucially *as a higher-order, macroscopic—and indeed, properly societal— experience of these lineages* that is distinct from the individual attained actualities constituting them.[29] That is why it is crucial to emphasize, as I have sought to do in my account of Whitehead's expansion of perception, that *perception* in the mode of causal efficacy *is not coequal to causal efficacy as such, in the entirety of its operationality*, and also that worldly sensibility *simply is causal efficacy minus the dimension of perception*. And the individual attained actualities constituting causal lineages, as we have seen, are themselves objectifications, in the domain of macroscopic causal efficacy, of microscopic actualities-in-attainment; indeed, as objectifications of the microscopic concrescences, they introduce actual entities into the domain of causal efficacy that underlies the genesis of all experience at all levels.[30]

Similarly, and further up the line as it were, "perception in the mode of presentational immediacy"—Whitehead's term for sense perception in the strict sense—emerges on the basis of causal efficacy, but again as a higher-order experience of these macroscopic lineages that is distinct from the vague causal processes constituting them. With each "ascent" to a higher level of organization, possibilities for intensity increase and come increasingly under the control of narrowly subjective or subjectively unified processes. The pinnacle of this causal ascendance is a third, synthetic mode of perception, "symbolic reference," that correlates presentational immediacy with its causal sources in a way that not only brings clarity to and agency over the vague and emotion-laden domain of causal efficacy but that in so doing maximizes intensity. Symbolic reference, writes Whitehead, "lifts the meanings" of the causally efficacious elements of our world "into an intensity of definite effectiveness."[31] It thus comprises what Jones calls "an extreme case of the eliciting of intensities that occurs at all levels of process."[32]

We can now see why the continuity of indirection characteristic of Whitehead's radically environmental ontology constitutes the experiential mechanism for diverse qualitative sensation, and thus for subjective intensity, across the board. The margin of indirection between distinct agents of experience correlates with a certain autonomy of process and ensures that lower-level societies are not simply engulfed by or assimilated into higher-order ones, but continue to exert their own proper power of intensity, as it were, *alongside* such emergences. Indeed, without this margin of indirection characteristic of the transversal operation of intensity as it crosses thresholds of complexity, all possibilities for expanding sensation would simply collapse. For without indirection, the agency of the superject at any given level of complexity could not act "upward," as it were, *without being wholly absorbed* into a higher order of subjective process. Indirection thus allows intensity qua superjective agency to contribute to objectifications at higher levels without losing its causal anchoring in its "originary" milieu of becoming. Still more simply: indirection allows superjective processes to impact higher-order processes *as microscopic subjective agents*, as the properly experiential power of speculative actualities. That is why indirection introduces the very principle of subjective heterogeneity—the simultaneous operation of subjectivity, indeed of distinct subjective processes, at heterogeneous scales of experience.

The error Parisi commits when she identifies symbiosensation with prehensive feeling thus ends up repeating the error of modern philosophy tirelessly denounced by Whitehead: the error of subjectivism, or the overvaluing of "sense perception" ("presentational immediacy") as the exclusive means of access to process. Paradoxical as it may appear given her explicit intention to expand the bounds of perception, Parisi's identification of symbiosensation with prehension cannot but culminate in the elevation of the subject of perception as *the exclusive arbiter of* the impact of causal efficacy (and by extension, of the microscopic causal lineages informing it). With this elevation, the subjective heterogeneity of sensibility collapses, leaving only the cognitive end point to show for its operation. This is precisely why Parisi's entire argument for symbiosensation is ultimately aimed—and cannot but be aimed—at unpacking the causal processes that *directly and immediately contribute to the generation of sense perceptions.* Like Erin Manning, who also draws on Whitehead to access what she calls the "preacceleration" of perception, and like Brian Massumi, who speaks of a "thinking-feeling" as an intensification of the present of perception,[33] Parisi's aim is less to expand the domain of sensation that lies outside the bounds of—and occurs prior to and independently of—perception, than it is to fold the sensory preconditions for perception *into perception itself.*

This becomes clear, for example, when Parisi recapitulates the ecological scope of symbiosensation: "Far from defining a prosthetic extension of sensory-motor perception, a machinic, ecological conception of the sensation of movement, or proprioception, rather points to a nonsensuous perception of movement whereby an ecologically expanded body (an already bionic body) is ready to feel motion before the sensory perception of actual movement."[34] Despite the explicit break with the sensorimotor model of perception, Parisi's liberation of a "proto-sensory" background operating behind sense perception constrains the agency of the proto-sensory—of intensity—to what informs an eventual sense perception. Intensity is thereby reduced to what is produced in and by the resulting sense perception, which is to say, it is stripped of the subjective heterogeneity accruing to it through the multileveled causal lineages that run all the way down, as it were, to the microscopic.

Parisi's inability to embrace intensity in the role Jones accords it—as a forward- and upward-directed agency of the superjective—goes together with her characterization of this proto-sensory "preinteraction" as "*nonsensuous* perception." In making this characterization, Parisi, in concert with other prominent cultural critics who have recently turned to Whitehead, chooses to telescope the force of causal efficacy in terms of the immediate past of sense perception. With this move, Parisi is, in effect, simply following in the footsteps of Whitehead himself, who, as we have seen, introduces "nonsensuous perception" as a gloss on *Process and Reality*'s "perception in the mode of causal efficacy." As the following passage from *Adventures of Ideas* makes clear, Whitehead's proximate aim in doing so is to stress the poverty of sense perception; in accord with this aim, nonsensuous perception is proffered as a way of expanding the scope of perception beyond what is offered to the senses:

> This wider definition of perception [wider than the narrow definition based upon sense perception, sensa, and the bodily sense organs] can be of no importance unless we can detect occasions of experience exhibiting modes of functioning which fall within its wider scope. If we discover such instances of non-sensuous perception, then the tacit identification of perception with sense-perception must be a fatal error barring the advance of systematic metaphysics. . . . The evidence on which . . . interpretations [of barren sensa like a patch of red] are based is entirely drawn from the vast background and foreground of non-sensuous perception with which sense-perception is fused, and without which it can never be. We can discern no clear-cut sense-perception wholly concerned with present fact. In human experience, the most compelling example of non-sensuous perception is our knowledge of our own immediate past. I am not referring to our memories of a day past, or of an hour past, or of a minute past. Such memories are blurred and confused by the intervening occasions of our personal existence. But our immediate past is constituted by that occasion, or by that group of fused occasions, which enters into experience devoid of any perceptible medium intervening between it and the present immediate fact. Roughly speaking, it is that portion of our past lying between a tenth of a second and half a second ago.[35]

It should be clear from Whitehead's focus on the very immediate past that his frame of reference here remains that of *consciousness. Despite his aim to expand perception beyond the scope of its "present,"* Whitehead cannot seem to embrace the complex layerings informing the "vector character" of experience—the many levels of experience sedimented beneath and causally informing sense perception—in any other way than through the perspective of consciousness. If "nonsensuous perceptions" are memories, they are memories that are "immediate" in the same sense that Husserlian "retention" is immediate: nonsensuous perceptions remain part of the complex of sense perception that generates consciousness qua time-consciousness.

As I see it, this perspective—and, specifically, the narrowing of the vector character of causal efficacy to nonsensuous perception—compromises precisely what is most exciting about Whitehead's expansion of perception in *Process and Reality*, namely, the way it opens the possibility to follow the causal lineages that culminate in sense perceptions all the way back to their origins in sensibility. What such a possibility affords—especially now that it can be made operational with the assistance of twenty-first-century media—is an opportunity to shift our perspective on experience in a fundamental way. For with the access to the domain of sensibility afforded by today's media, we no longer need to position consciousness as the sole arbitrator of experience; rather, with today's technologies for data-gathering and analysis, "machinic reference" displaces "symbolic reference" as the operation whereby the data of causal efficacy gets presentified. Machines literally stand in for consciousness within the circuits through which we gain access to worldly sensibility.

If this displacement expands the scope of presentification well beyond the domains of sense perception, it also exposes the paradox that informs Whitehead's restriction of the scope of causal efficacy to nonsensuous perception: to wit, nonsensuous perception is only nonsensuous *from the standpoint of the perceiving subject's presentational immediacy.* In order to characterize it as "nonsensuous," Whitehead must adopt, and effectively ratify, the very perspective he is seeking to criticize and expand: the perspective of sense perception (perceptual consciousness) as the sole perspective through which the data of causal efficacy can be accessed. That is why, as I suggested above, the access given to the domain of causal efficacy *by* perception (i.e., perception in the mode of causal efficacy), despite its undeniable advance over sense perception, constitutes what amounts to a massive restriction on the power and scope of causal efficacy itself (i.e., causal efficacy independent of perception): when we perceive that we see with our eyes or touch with our hands, what we experience is a fleeting perceptual glimpse of the causal efficacy of sensibility as it enters into the scope of consciousness. As we will see in chapter 4, this is the precise impasse to which Merleau-Ponty came in his own efforts to move beyond a duality of subject and object, and the entire Cartesian legacy of modern philosophy; a fully consequential thinking of the reversibility of the flesh requires an abandonment of any "transcendental" role of a subject: to liberate causal efficacy and to position it as the operation of worldly sensibility itself requires us to accord the power of sensibility to the world itself, independently of its perceptibility to consciousness, whether as immediacy or as causal background (withness of the body).

In the place of nonsensuous perception, which only obtains meaning in relation to the perspective of sensuous perception (it is nonsensuous pre-

cisely and only because it is no longer sensuously present to consciousness),
I propose that we characterize the sensibility at issue here—causal efficacy
in its multiple, heterogeneous, and multileveled causal lineage—as *non-
perceptual* sensation." Non-perceptual sensation (or more precisely, non-
perceptual sensibility) designates sensation that, to paraphrase Whitehead,
is directed at, and subsequently from, the superject, and that acts outside
and beyond the scope of the original subjective becoming from which it
proximately resulted and also outside or peripherally to any new narrowly
subjective process (new concrescence) to which it may contribute, as it were,
from the side of the environment. Put another way, non-perceptual sensibility embraces the entire "vector character" of perception going along causal
lineages that run all the way back to its origin: in direct contrast to the
Whitehead of *Adventures* and to his recent inheritors, the concept of non-
perceptual sensibility *marks the refusal to reduce this vector character to
what immediately precedes sense perception* (i.e., nonsensuous perception).
As a radicalization of Whitehead's expansion of perception in *Process and
Reality*, non-perceptual sensibility follows the causal lineages informing
perception in the mode of causal efficacy to the point of their culmination,
and the dissolution of perception itself, in worldly sensibility. We can thus
conclude that non-perceptual sensibility is superjective subjectivity, and
vice versa, or, alternately but equivalently, that worldly sensibility *simply is
causal efficacy without perception.* By rejecting the constraining and disin-
genuous move to retain "sense perception" as the sole basis for arbitrating
what counts as sensuous, together with the collapse of perception in the
mode of causal efficacy into nonsensuous perception, non-perceptual sensibility thus expands the scope of sensibility itself that is its basis: specifically,
it places perception into relation with its non-perceptual source, its basis in
worldly sensibility and superjective subjectivity.

The contribution non-perceptual sensibility makes to the task of theorizing the experiential impact of twenty-first-century media will recur as a
central investment of my exploration of Whitehead and of phenomenology in the chapters to follow. Because it expands the scope of causal efficacy precisely by opening access to worldly sensibility independently of
consciousness, twenty-first-century media place non-perceptual sensation
on center stage; indeed, the conceptualization of sensation beyond sense
perception—of sensation *as intensity*—becomes imperative if we are to
grasp the experiential impact of twenty-first-century media. For if today's
sensor technologies let us access sensory events in which our experience is
implicated independently of and prior to any distinct perception that might
emerge from such events, they effectively call into being a "new" (or, more
exactly, a dormant and as yet untapped) potential for directly experiencing

worldly sensibility. This is precisely the potential of non-perceptual sensation. One key task for us in what follows will be to articulate how this
potential, which is largely synonymous with intensity as we have analyzed it
above, can form the cornerstone of an asubjective and, in some meaningful
sense, *post-phenomenological*, phenomenology of experience. How, we will
need to ask, can we conceptualize intensity as the qualitative correlate, or,
perhaps more precisely, the material element, of non-perceptual sensation?

Such an exploration dovetails perfectly with the shift in the address of
twenty-first-century media as we have analyzed it thus far. For if today's
ubiquitous computational environments and bionic bodily supplementations reconfigure the very sensory domains in which we live and experience, they do far more than simply intensify sense perception by infolding
into it the proto-sensory. Rather, today's media technologies directly impact worldly sensibility *by shaping the very production of intensity at the
infraperceptual level.* They thereby modulate possibilities, and open new
possibilities, for experiencing the heterogeneous superjective subjectivity of
sensory intensity, and also, for gaining access to and accounting for such
experience *in ways that do not recur to perception as ultimate arbiter.* What
is at stake in twenty-first-century media is in no sense a mere prosthetic
enhancement that operates at a single level of sensory integration and that
leaves our sensory circuits intact. Rather, today's media effectuate nothing
less than a pluralization and a radical scale-heterogenesis of sensibility: a
multileveled introjection of superjective agency that renders intensity—not
sense perception—the ultimate qualitative correlate of experience.

The Societal Basis of Phenomenology

Recalling our point of departure in the recent Whitehead renaissance, we
can now clearly grasp two facts: first, that what lies behind the upsurge
of interest in deploying Whitehead for addressing contemporary media is
some conviction about the value of his philosophy for analyzing experience
beyond the narrow bandwidth of perception; and second, that the respective
efforts to develop Whitehead's expansion of perception are hampered by a
conceptual confusion, namely, the tendency to draw on Whitehead's speculative account of the genesis of actual entities in order to explain experience.

It is perhaps only now that we can fully appreciate how this tendency
goes together with a marked neglect of the specific resources—the concepts
of nexus and society—that Whitehead expressly develops for the purpose
of analyzing experience. Indeed, we can now understand that Whitehead's
entire speculative apparatus—meaning both the speculative account of the

concrescence of actual entities and the speculative ban on any direct appeal to *their genesis* to explain experience—is really nothing more than a mechanism for grasping his account of experience *in terms of nexuses and societies*. This fundamental shift of perspective calls for a reassessment of the Whitehead renaissance. It is not simply, as I suggested above, that the protagonists of today's Whitehead renaissance *should have* focused on nexuses and societies as the proper place to address experience in Whitehead's philosophy. It is rather that Whitehead's entire philosophy, including its speculative components, is constructed *precisely in order to account for the genesis of a robust phenomenological domain* composed of societies and nexuses at all scales of being. The speculative ban, and the restricted speculative domain it serves to "protect," furnish what is necessary to construct a superjective or "worldly" phenomenology of experience centered in the operation of nexuses and societies at all scales of temporal and organizational complexity. The speculative ban allows us—indeed, *requires* us—to position the domain of attained actualities (superjects and liberated prehensions) as the most fundamental elements of Whitehead's philosophy. This domain, the settled world or "disjunctive plurality" (Debaise), constitutes the basis for all societal compositions, and is, as such, the ultimate payoff of Whitehead's metaphysical enterprise: it informs the "real potentiality" of an actual world of experience that is always unique and uniquely creative.

Given that media operate through and within experience, there is ample reason to concentrate our effort to think media through Whitehead (and Whitehead through media) on the correlation between his theory of societies and the dispersal of sensibility central to twenty-first-century media. As we shall see, societies support an account of time binding that is rooted not in some privileged internal domain of experience but rather in the resonating intensity of their component entities. In this way, societies explain temporal unification or synthesis as an effect of environmental forces: for if an experiential society is defined—and is able to perdure in time—by and through the determinate intensity shared by its members, this intensity itself is generated by the environment provided to its component actualities by the society. As we will see, this environmental dimension correlates perfectly with the dispersal of sensibility central to twenty-first-century media.

Let us begin our exploration of Whitehead's conceptualization of societies by noting that when Whitehead speaks of "societies," he uses the term in an odd and narrowly technical sense: a society is a set of actual entities (more exactly, of attained actualities) and/or of other societies of actual entities (societies of attained actualities) *that are united through the sharing of a common form and causal history*. Societies are experiential entities that arise at scales from the nano to the cosmological: they are literally the *how* of experience, and in this sense, they compose the phenomenality of all experience, whether or not it is centered on human beings.

Yet societies, it is important to emphasize, are more than mere aggregations of actual occasions; they are sets of attained actualities that are brought together and that perdure as unities *in virtue of a shared intensity and ongoing causal efficacy*. Although composed ultimately of attained actualities, the formation and endurance of societies—the process of becoming-society—contributes something crucial that makes them *more than mere sets* of such actualities. At the same time, societies require the speculative withdrawal of actual entities, for it is this withdrawal of their genesis that makes actualities qua attained actualities available for multiple societal compositions: precisely because they are not themselves generated within or through the experience of any society, attained actualities can participate in multiple processes of intensity at multiple scales at the same time, or, as I shall prefer to put it, can operate in "operational overlap" with one another.

This particular "promiscuity" of attained actualities, made possible by the speculative withdrawal of their genesis, forms the source for the experiential heterogenesis central to societal composition. And it is this heterogeneity—the capacity for attained actualities to participate, as "real potentiality," in multiple and diverse societal compositions—that furnishes the basis for the robust phenomenology of sensibility I have sought to develop here. This capacity furnishes a mechanism for actual entities to enjoy ongoing coupling within larger compositions, and this coupling is the basis both for the creation of experiential societies at all scales of being and for the participation of the same actual entities in multiple societies at variant scales.

It is precisely this correlation between the speculative withdrawal of actualities and the robust phenomenology it generates that licenses Debaise to characterize Whitehead's philosophy as a "speculative empiricism." At stake in this characterization is the potential to ground experience on a non-anthropocentric speculative or metaphysical structure:

> "Actual entities" are at the heart of speculative thought. They permit us to say not what existence is insofar as it is undergone, experienced, or lived, but what existence is *as such*, in its proper reality, "in itself.". . . No example, no evocation which originates in our experience, can give an account of what an actual entity is, because this concept cannot be inscribed within anything that appears evident or familiar to us. Everything transpires as if, for Whitehead—though he remains very allusive on this question and we can only engage in a hypothesis—existence, defined in terms of the actual

entity, were precisely *that of which we do not have and cannot have experience*. The confusion between the ultimate elements of existence and experience is "the error that has derailed European metaphysics from the epoch of the Greeks" [citing *Adventures of Ideas*, 267]. This error . . . has consisted principally in transposing to the level of ultimate principles of existence what has been given in our experience, to favor relations of resemblance and analogy. The result is that, in the end though implicitly, the first principles of metaphysics have, for the most part, only been more or less unconscious generalizations of experience, and more particularly of visual experience. It is against this projection, against this transposition of *our* modes of experience into the heart of an existence that is not constituted on the model of what matters to us, that Whitehead seeks to return the distinction to its originary ground [*ramener la distinction au premier plan*].[36]

With his keen understanding of Whitehead's aim to correct the subjective projection that has "derailed European metaphysics from the epoch of the Greeks," Debaise immediately seizes on precisely what is most exciting about Whitehead's project *both for the reform of metaphysics itself* and *for the expanded and dispersed account of experience it facilitates*: it calls for reconceptualizing experience as "neutral" in relation to any narrowly human phenomenology.

I am particularly interested in how these two aspects of Whitehead's reform of philosophy coincide: the expanded and de-anthropomorphized theory of experience is ultimately nothing if not the flip side, the necessary correlate, of the purification of metaphysics, the purging of its all-too-human basis.[37] It is the articulation of a metaphysics of existence "not constituted on the model of what matters to us" that makes possible—and in some sense necessary—the "neutral" theory of experience I have been attempting to develop here. Indeed, the projection that has derailed metaphysics finds an experiential parallel in the error that has derailed the phenomenology of experience: what Whitehead's criticism of consciousness demonstrates is just how much *our* modes of experience have been imposed on the broader field of experience that is not constituted on the model of what matters to us.

Contextualized in relation to twenty-first-century media, Whitehead's neutral ontology of experience helps to expose the "phenomenological error" that, in my opinion, informs much theoretical work in media studies today. Like the category error denounced by Whitehead, this error involves the transposition of *our* modes of experience into the heart of *other* modes of experience—specifically, *technical* modes of experience—that are not constituted on the model of what matters to us. This error occurs, for instance, when we narrow the experiential impact of computational media to their effects on the composition of an image, which leaves out the experiential dimensions of various microtemporal computational processes. And, more broadly, it occurs whenever we impose our perceptual regimes as the basis for media forms, as we do, for example, when we restrict the impact of color (say, the redness of Jean-Luc Godard's *Weekend*) to its inflection of specific events in a film, which leaves out its more direct and more diffuse impact on the spectator's general "mood."

Far from being a dry metaphysical edifice removed from the concrete texture of experience, Whitehead's conception of the speculative serves expressly to theorize what is needed to explain experience but that cannot be accessed via experience itself. We can grasp the specificity of this commitment to the speculative most clearly at moments when Whitehead characterizes his aim as "the elucidation of immediate experience." This elucidation, he specifies, "is the unique justification for thought; and the starting point of thought is the analytical examination of the components of this experience."[38] What we learn from this specification is just how central a role Whitehead's reform of experience plays in his philosophy generally: it is precisely what motivates his recourse to metaphysical clarification, which is to say, his embrace of the speculative as such. On this score, it is noteworthy that critics, like Debaise and Jones, who hold quite distinct views concerning the role of speculation, nonetheless concur in their assessment of Whitehead's aim: for both, Whitehead's overriding aim simply is to explain experience.[39]

The key role Whitehead accords the reform of experience helps to explain the contribution societies play within his neutral ontology of experience. Societies constitute the ultimate end of Whitehead's entire speculative scheme: as the creations of the "promiscuity" of attained actualities, societies are literally what create experience. As if in recognition of precisely this point, Debaise grants societies pride of place in his assessment of Whitehead's speculative empiricism. As he astutely discerns, societies compose a myriad of worlds, *all of which are made of the same stuff—actual entities.* In this sense, they directly express the experiential heterogenesis facilitated by the speculative withdrawal of actual entities:

> In the framework of speculative thought, one could say that the worlds [of experience] all require the notion of the actual entity, that they are all composed, despite their heterogeneity, of the same stuff. . . . No world of experience can claim a direct resemblance to actual entities. They are so many specific modes, particular organi-

zations. Whitehead introduces a technical term to express the elements of these worlds of experience that do not correspond directly to actual entities. He calls them "societies." We must understand the term "society" in a very broad sense, without implicit reference to the meaning it has in ordinary language. We will designate as "societies" realities as different as an atom, a cell, an impression, an object, an individual, and even a civilization. Everything that *makes* experience and everything *of which* there is experience can be called a society. . . . The concept is at the center of a very particular form of empiricism at issue in *Process and Reality* since it essentially aims to construct a concept of experience that would emanate from speculative thought.[40]

As this account makes clear, the "motor" for the experiential heterogenesis facilitated by the composition of societies is precisely the availability of actual entities (attained actualities) to participate simultaneously in multiple, and indeed in countless, nexuses and societies. And what facilitates this availability, as I have already indicated, is the speculative withdrawal of the *genesis* of actual entities, the nonavailability of their concrescences to experience: it is precisely because actual entities come to be *outside of extensive time* that they do not get used up through their participation in experiential entities. Paradoxically, actual entities remain available—as potentiality—for innumerable experiential compositions precisely because of their originary nonavailability or non-belonging to experience.

   This means that the "disjunctive plurality," what Debaise glosses as the "pure disjunction of already existent actual entities,"[41] is composed of actual entities qua attained actualities. With this specification—that attained actualities are the stuff of the disjunctive plurality—we are in a position to appreciate why societies are more than mere sets or aggregations of attained actualities. They are the result of resonances—both systemic and environmental—that bind certain actualities together in enduring processes of various extents and that add something to their status as elements of the disjunctive plurality. And with this new specification, we are furthermore in a position to appreciate how this situation—itself the necessary implication of Debaise's account—requires a fine-tuning of his understanding of the disjunctive plurality. For Debaise, a society is an "aspect" or "trait" of the mode of existence of actual entities; "a society," he writes, "is an aggregation [*un amas*], a collection, or, more exactly, a being-together of actual entities," and what gives rise to societies is a process of emergence fueled by actual entities: "Everything happens as if a certain manner of being of actual entities produces at another scale [meaning the macroscopic scale of experience, in its specific opposition to the microscopic scale of speculative actual entities] emergent qualities that are distinct from them. 'Societies' are in fact effects of actual entities."[42]

What Debaise doesn't specify here, but what could helpfully be specified, is that this conceptualization of societies as effects of actual entities makes sense only if we understand actual entities to be attained actualities, which is to say, only if we introduce the key distinction between actualities-in-attainment and attained actualities into Debaise's account of the disjunctive plurality. Understood with the requisite degree of precision, the disjunctive plurality simply is a plurality of attained actualities existing as real potentiality for new concrescences *and* for societal compositions. So long as Debaise's account fails to introduce this crucial distinction between the two sides of actualities, it risks falling into the very trap that Debaise works so hard to denounce: the historically French error of lending experiential agency to speculative entities. Once the distinction is introduced, however, we can see that Debaise locates the source for experiential events in the proper place—namely, in the superjective subjectivity of actualities, or, still more precisely, in the potentiality they attain via their objectification as attained actualities. And with his clarification of how this potentiality generates the intensities that compose societies, Debaise contributes something crucial to my effort to phenomenologize Whitehead: specifically, he conceptualizes the disjunctive plurality as a metastable source teeming with potentiality and attributes the power of societies to the superjective resonances animating them.

If societies are "effects" of actual entities, it is precisely because they are compositions of attained actualities that bind temporally, or processually, through superjective resonances rather than through some internal, unifying principle of organization. The differentiation of the two sides of actual entities thus explains how societies arise on the basis of a transposition of scale by actual entities. Indeed, we might even want to say that attained actualities (and the "liberated" prehensions comprising their relationality) act as mediators between the speculative and the experiential: they are simultaneously the *result of* speculative genesis and the *components of* experiential societies. Not only does such an understanding correlate perfectly with Debaise's own characterization of the disjunctive plurality,[43] but it is absolutely critical if we are to avoid trivializing the role of experience in the composition of societies: all of the power exercised by experiential entities comes from their cumulative superjective subjectivity, from the lingering and world-directed force that lies beyond—or better, *in front of*—their speculative geneses.

Although Judith Jones, like Debaise, does not explicitly mark the distinction between actualities-in-attainment and attained actualities, her account of societies in terms of intensity explicitly posits an experiential source for the formation of societies: societies are compositions of super-jected actualities and the experiential prehensions liberated by their addition to the settled world. For this reason, Jones is able to grasp, perhaps more clearly than Debaise, the concrete source for the genesis and perdurance of societies; specifically, she understands why the "defining characteristic" common to members of a society is not *and cannot be* generated as an internal principle of unity, on the basis of some formal "being-together" of (speculative) actual entities. Rather, societies are composed, and thus given definition, through the operation of actual contrasts—contrasts that are themselves *generated experientially out of the disjunctive plurality* and that serve to make this plurality the source of "real potentiality" for future con-crescences *as well as* for compositions of experiential societies of all sorts. In this sense, Jones's clarification can help us appreciate what is at stake in Debaise's characterization of the disjunctive plurality as a domain of poten-tiality: the power of the settled universe (i.e., attained actualities) to generate experiential entities of all sorts.

To make her case, Jones stresses the second requirement of a society on Whitehead's definition, namely his stipulation that in addition to a shared "defining characteristic," which we now understand to be generated experi-entially, a set of entities is a society "in virtue of the presence of the defining characteristic *being due to the environment provided by the society itself.*"[44] For Jones, this requirement is crucial: it allows us to grasp what the experi-ential process of societal composition brings to the account of experience, what it *positively adds* to experience; and for this reason, it answers with a helpful degree of specificity the question of why a society is more than a mere aggregate of actualities. Indeed, far from being mere emergences from some other domain of existence (the speculative or microscopic domain), societies come into being by bootstrapping themselves out of *more primitive or unorganized experiential* entities (the liberated or superjected prehen-sions and attained actualities constituting the disjunctive plurality) which henceforth operate environmentally in relation to one another. If societies are more than mere aggregates of actual entities, that is because, as properly experiential entities, they introduce elements that simply cannot be reduced to the status of mere emergent effects of a speculative logic. More precisely still, it is because they benefit from a mutuality of shared intensity and en-vironmental relationality that can be equated neither with a mere aggrega-tion of actual entities nor with a formal "being-together" in virtue of some internal binding principle.

Jones's clarification of why societies are not mere aggregates in either of these senses makes the worldly status of their constituting prehensions altogether patent. What binds the elements of a society together is not a narrowly subjective, internal element, but the way in which worldly elements—attained actualities and prehensions—mutually provide an environment for one another:

> The individual entities of a society would not have the intensities they do without the massiveness of emphasis provided by the collective of entities in a genetic relationship. In other words, the society provides the environment that is procurative of the desired intensity. The inheritance of feeling has a cumulative result that defies [the] characterization of the society as a mere aggregate. The society's contribution is cumulative in two senses, each of which has to do with the achievement of intensity of feeling. The first sense is that the possibility of prehension of the components of the actual world that form the society in question is by reason of their *compatibility for contrast*; an identical intensity will not obstruct and thereby attenuate itself. *Thus there is real inclusion of multiple elements (actualities) that proffer the same intensity.* The integral intensity achieved is massive. . . . The second sense in which the society's contribution is cumulative is that . . . a shared characteristic will be attributed to a nexus as a real entity. . . . This will also produce a massiveness of feeling that is more than an acknowledgement of a multiplicity.[45]

To understand why a society is more than a mere aggregate, Jones reiterates, we need only consider the way that social order is maintained and, specifically, the way that societal organization is built upon the "total prehensiveness" that informs the genesis of actualities in every concrete instance: "Each actual entity really includes, via repetition and structuring according to the conditions of intensity, its entire past world, in this instance under forms of dominant intensities repeatedly transmitted. . . . Thus actualities in their feeling of their actual worlds, *particularly in social orders*, are engaged in a process that is 'the cumulation of the universe and not a stage play about it' [PR 237]."[46]

Societies, the Experiential Basis of Speculative Phenomenology

While I shall return to Jones's account of cumulation via intensity below in chapter 3, where it will play the crucial role of expanding the scope of worldly de-presencing to encompass the totality of the universe at each moment of its operation, for the moment I want to return to the point from which I began—namely, the imperative to focus on societies, the crucial concept informing Whitehead's account of experience, as we seek to develop the affinities between his theory and twenty-first-century media. For it is Whitehead's account of experience through societal composition, and ultimately through the creativity of superjected prehensions, that positions the experiential production of intensity as a heterogeneous and multi-scalar expansion of worldly sensibility.

Given the operative reduction that lies at the heart of much recent work on Whitehead—the collapse of the speculative onto the empirical—it is not surprising that the centrality of societies gets overlooked by his contemporary commentators. To give an example of this neglect, and specifically to illustrate how it is directly correlated with the reduction of the speculative, let me focus on Steven Shaviro's deployment of Whitehead in *Without Criteria*, his book-length study of Whitehead and modern aesthetics from Kant to Deleuze. What I specifically want to bring out is how Shaviro finds himself compelled to undervalue—and, despite what he himself says, to undervalue in a nontrivial, indeed, massive way—the distinct and crucial contribution of societies *as experiential entities*. Bluntly put, Shaviro's decision to promote actual entities as exclusively experiential—as events—renders him utterly unable to grasp the singular role societies play *as complex experiential entities*, as, literally, *compositions of intensity*. Like Parisi, Shaviro postulates a direct correlation between experience and the speculative operation of Whitehead's account of concrescence; that is why he characterizes events as prehensions and promotes nonsensuous perception as a movement from perception proper to prehension.[47] Yet more clearly than is the case with other contemporary critics, Parisi concluded, Shaviro's failure to recognize any non-collapsible distinction between the speculative and the experiential—between entities and events—leaves him unable to appreciate the categorical difference between occasions and societies, and thus without any of the resources necessary to capitalize on the key role societies play in Whitehead's philosophy.

This conclusion is all the more striking in that it follows directly from an effort on Shaviro's part to inject a degree of precision into his account:

> However, I am being a little sloppy here. In *Process and Reality*, Whitehead strictly distinguishes between *occasions* and *events*, and between *entities* and *societies*. He "use[s] the term 'event' in the more general sense of a nexus of actual occasions, inter-related in some determinate fashion in one extensive quantum. An actual occasion is the limiting type of an event with only one member" (73). At the limit, an event may be just one particular occasion, a single

incident of becoming. But more generally, it is a group of such incidents, a multiplicity of becomings: what Whitehead calls a *nexus*. A nexus is "a particular fact of togetherness among actual entities" (20); that is to say, it is a mathematical set of occasions, contiguous in space and time, or otherwise adhering to one another. When the elements of a nexus are united, not just by contiguity, but also by a "defining characteristic" that is common to all of them, and that they have all "inherited" from one another, or acquired by a common process, then Whitehead calls it a society (34). A society is "self-sustaining; in other words . . . it is its own reason. . . . The real actual things that endure," and that we encounter in everyday experience, "are all societies." Whitehead sometimes also calls them *enduring objects* . . . . To summarize, an "occasion" is the process by which anything becomes, and an "event"—applying to a nexus or a society—is an extensive set, or a temporal series, of such occasions. This contrast between individual becomings, and the progressive summation of such becomings, is crucial to Whitehead's metaphysics.[48]

Far from introducing a *distinction* between the process of speculative becoming and that of experiential composition, this account promotes what can only be described as a *continuum* between them—a continuum that, not surprisingly, operates exclusively at the experiential level or that, more precisely, models the speculative, as Debaise puts it, on "resemblance and analogy." No more legitimate than it was in the case of Parisi, Shaviro's reduction of the speculative to the experiential is a direct result of his adherence to Deleuze's (and the French tradition's) understanding of Whitehead as a thinker of the event.

Yet Shaviro's more detailed reconstruction of Whitehead on the basis of this reduction gives us crucial insight into how the reduction of the speculative effectively *compromises the phenomenological promise* of Whitehead's account of experience in terms of societies. Recalling Debaise's criticism of the French tradition, we can see precisely how Shaviro's adherence to Deleuze causes him to overlook the crucial distinction between actual entities as the "ultimate reasons" for experience and societies as the agents of experience.[49] This is precisely why we find Shaviro characterizing Whitehead as a straightforward empiricist, even if of a radical, or, as he puts it, a "very special," sort: Whitehead, states Shaviro, "is a secular and naturalistic thinker, but one of a very special sort. He rejects supernatural explanations, holding to what he calls the *ontological principle*: the claim that 'actual entities are the only *reasons*,' that 'the search for a reason is always the search for an actual fact which is the vehicle of that reason.' For 'there is nothing which floats into the world from nowhere. Everything in the actual world is referable to some actual entity.' This means that empiricism is ultimately correct: *all our knowledge comes from experience, and there is nothing outside experience, or beyond it.*"[50] Shaviro's abrupt shift from an account of the ontological principle to the conclusion that all knowledge comes from experience (the first principle of orthodox empiricism) makes clear just how much his understanding depends on a massive, if unacknowledged, slippage from actual entities as the "only reason" for experience to actual entities as the concrete contents of experience. Shaviro, it appears, fails to understand the distinction at the very heart of Whitehead's speculative scheme: that the ultimate "reasons," that is, the metaphysical bases, for experience *are not and cannot be given in and through experience*, but must be constructed speculatively as the way things must be in order for experience to be what it is. There is a crucial distinction between the actuality of actual entities ("actual facts") and the actuality of the empirical world ("actual world"), which means that what Whitehead says, when he emphasizes that "everything in the actual world is referable to some actual entity," is the precise opposite of what Shaviro understands: for Whitehead, the referral at issue here is a speculative operation by which what is or can be experienced correlates to some reason, some actual entity, that cannot itself be directly experienced.[51]

What ultimately explains Shaviro's conflation of the speculative and the empirical—his complete neglect of the speculative ban—is his failure to recognize any salient distinction between actualities in their two modes of operations, between actualities-in-attainment and attained actualities. Without such a distinction, Shaviro simply lacks the means to do what he wants to do—namely, to move from "actual facts" to the "actual world." And he also lacks the resources to grasp what is truly at stake in Whitehead's speculative empiricism: namely, the operation of a real potentiality *within* the actual that precedes and catalyzes the genesis of actual entities, and in this way, ensures their participation in experience *despite their inaccessibility to experience*. Put another way, it is only by way of a distinction between actualities-in-attainment and attained actualities that one can escape the trap Whitehead (no doubt, inadvertently) poses when he suggests that "an actual entity is the limiting type of an event with only one member." For this claim to be true, let alone coherent, the actual entity to which it refers *must* be an attained actuality expressing its superjective subjectivity, as an isolated unit, independently from any societal correlation with other attained actualities. This society of one is composed like all other societies—out of attained actualities (in this case, one attained actuality), not out of actualities-in-attainment. Contra Shaviro, then, we must conclude that a society with one member *can never be equivalent* to a single actuality-in-attainment: only an attained actuality, operating superjectively in the temporal world of experience, can compose such a numerically minimal society.

We can now perhaps see more clearly how the distinction between the two sides of actual entities that I have been developing here, a distinction introduced but never fully developed by Whitehead, constitutes an absolutely central piece in his philosophical enterprise. More specifically, we can see how this distinction allows Whitehead to develop a speculative empiricism, and how the development of this latter allows us to articulate a rigorously speculative phenomenology. For, with their properly experiential status, attained actualities constitute a mediating layer capable of—and indeed necessary for—correlating, while simultaneously keeping distinct, the properly speculative operation of concrescence and the robustly experiential operation of societies. On this understanding, societies are not directly connected to the operation of concrescence that generates new actual entities and do not constitute unifications of prehensions. Rather, societies only ever engage with attained actualities, which is to say, with actual entities that have been objectified and added to the settled world. From the experiential perspective—the perspective of the nexuses and societies that constitute the events of experience in every instance—actual entities are always already objectified, always already part of the disjunctive plurality.

We can now grasp precisely how Shaviro's promotion of actual entities as exclusively experiential—as simply equivalent to events—leads him to overlook the crucial function of societies in Whitehead. For if all actual entities were in fact events and if they were only distinguishable from societies through the operation of aggregation, then societies would be nothing more than mere sets of actual entities. In this sense, it is as if Shaviro simply *has no need for societies*: he can approach the domain of experience directly in terms of actual entities as events. As mere aggregations of such entities, societies make—and can make—no significant contribution of their own.

With this conclusion in place, we can now appreciate why Debaise and Jones are able to recognize the crucial role played by societies in Whitehead's empiricism: because both critics do mark a difference between (speculative) actualities-in-attainment and (experiential) attained actualities (even if neither names this distinction explicitly), and because they both differentiate between the disjunctive plurality of attained actualities and the organized plurality of societies, they are able to offer accounts that, to varying degrees, manage to pinpoint the concrete contribution of societies. As we have seen, this appears most clearly in Jones, who positions societies as the achievements of intensity-generating contrasts among attained actualities and who characterizes their temporal (experiential) consistency not just in terms of a "defining characteristic" but also, and more importantly, in terms of their delimitation of an "environment"—a specific portion of the disjunctive plurality of attained actualities in which intensity can be generated. For Jones, the key issue is how the intensity generated through contrasts among attained actualities (superjects) actualizes real potentiality in ways that create and sustain societies of actual entities. As the experiential source for intensity, real potentiality constitutes a domain of worldly sensibility that logically, if not indeed temporally, precedes the formation of societies, and as such, constitutes a "condition of real potentiality" for their ongoing ontogenesis. Much of the force of this approach, as I will argue at length in the next chapter, comes from its capacity to preserve the power of prehensions as a dimension of the real potentiality of the settled world, which is to say, as a power independent from their restricted participation in the subjective unification of concrescence.

Far from offering a flat ontology of experience, as many commentators would have it,[52] Whitehead's philosophy introduces nuanced distinctions between different levels of being that are crucial for the coherence of his neutral account of experience. With this observation, we come back to the specificity of societies, and to the key question concerning what they add to the actual entities they assemble. Following Jones's understanding of intensity as the glue that binds societies into durational entities, we can now appreciate what it means to say that societies bootstrap themselves into being; more than mere sets of actual entities externally unified by their participation in a "route of inheritance" or internally unified by their convergence around a subjective aim, societies comprise the ongoing and continuously renewed accomplishment of entities catalyzed into being by their reactive processing of external, worldly contrasts into shared intensity. Far from being mere aggregations of individual atomic units of experience, "nothing more than sets of actual occasions," as Shaviro puts it, societies are enduring compositions of objectified actual occasions which, through their endurance, compose causal lineages *that themselves come to wield agency*, or, more precisely, that allow the superjective force of superjected prehensions to express itself directly, from the position of the environmental outside.[53] Societies, in short, are compositions of intensity.

Just Noticeable Difference

Given our long-standing bias in favor of higher-order faculties like sense perception, it should be self-evident that a fundamental and protracted retraining of our sensorium will be required for us to "learn" to experience intensity via self-reference, which is to say, in a way that correlates it with some integrated subjective experience. One key point I hope to make here is that microcomputational sensor technologies can help us in this task by supplementing our quite limited means of "presentifying" the causal efficacy of media across scales: technologies for measuring and recording biometric data (including heart rate, galvanic skin response, brain wave, and other internal data), together with technologies for measuring locational and environmental conditions more broadly, can make available to our deliberation information that we literally cannot perceive. Because they effectively take the place of consciousness as the channel for accessing bodily and environmental operations, biometric and environmental sensing technologies open a certain recursivity between "us" and our microscale (or sub-perceptual) embodiment, the robust couplings between our embodiment and the environment, and elements of the environment taken in and for themselves. In sum, today's future-oriented "presentational" media hold forth the promise of a fundamental, and potentially empowering, shift in the ecology of perception: by accessing data that is inaccessible to perceptual consciousness and by presentifying it artifactually for consciousness, they not only displace the perceptual subject from its long-standing role as the ultimate experience-intensifier, but in the process, massively expand the source for experience-intensification.

While much of the impact of this technical supplementation of perception will remain cognitive in the sense that it concerns our knowledge of the actual causal basis of our own experience, twenty-first-century media, as I have been suggesting here, also exert a fundamental sensory impact in the sense that they expand our contact with the environmental outside (worldly sensibility). Part of the sensory pedagogy at issue here must accordingly involve learning to experience qualitative (sensory) intensity without it being fully integrated into and subordinated to unified, higher-order perceptual experiences. As I see it, this dimension of twenty-first-century media will only truly become a reality when (and if) we begin to live in "atmospheric" media environments where the microtemporal qualities of experience—precisely those qualities now targeted by neuroeconomics and today's technically sophisticated marketing strategies—become independently addressable and fully manipulable. A crucial political and technical challenge that will necessarily come to the fore as we begin to develop such environments centers on whether and how we can gain agency over the power of these microtemporal qualities of experience, and on whether and how we can safeguard our expanded openness to worldly sensibility from corporate takeover: will the atmospheric media systems of the future provide opportunities for open-ended intensification of our experience, or will they remain exclusively focused on instrumentally targeting specific effects aimed at making our "desire" legible for exploitation by others?

Despite the "still-to-come" status of such atmospheric environments (and of answers to questions concerning their development), certain contemporary media artworks can help us get a sense of their potential for generating intensity through technical manipulation of microtemporal sensory qualities. One such work is Chris Salter's recent *Just Noticeable Difference*, an installation-environment that seeks to catalyze liminal experiences of sensibility at the point of indifference between individual embodiment and environmental sensory affordance. To accomplish this aim, *JND* invites visitors to enter a large box where they encounter a fusion of near darkness with sound, tactile vibration, and color-changing light operating at different perceptual thresholds. Visitors experience the environment individually by lying on their backs on a custom floor lined with twelve full-frequency "tactile sound" actuators normally used in commercial or home-cinema seats to deliver low frequency vibrations. These actuators produce both audible vibrations and what Salter dubs "almost sub audio vibrations" that vary from extremely subtle to extremely intense. The environment attains its aesthetic aim by placing the user's ongoing experience of these vibrations into resonance with itself, in a way that creates contrasts ranging across perceptual scales and, as a result, a differential experience of intensity. This sensory resonance results from the setting into play of a technical circuit that generates positive or open-ended feed-forward of qualitative data: the visitor's bodily movements, which range from fidgeting to large body motion, are measured in real time by a wireless network of resistive paper-based sensors; this data then subtly affects the behavior and intensity of a partially scripted composition of vibration, sound and light directly under and around the body; and the experience of this composition recursively impacts the production of new contrasts and new embodied intensity.

The environment of *JND* places the visitor into real-time sensory resonance with her own just-past experience not as a cognitive content but as a quantum of intensity, which is to say, as it is logged and objectified as technical data of sensibility. By placing the visitor into direct, responsive resonance with the superjects generated by just-past, now objectified actual occasions, the work gives her what I would venture to call "superjective agency" within her ongoing sensory experience through the medium of intensity. These superjects continue to express their subjective force in ways that impact the visitor's ongoing subjective becoming, but importantly, *without becoming a part of that subjective becoming*, or, alternatively, *while remaining part of the world's sensibility*. They thus mark a transfer of subjective power—

from subject-centered subjective processes in the narrow sense to the larger sensory worldliness within which such processes arise—at the very same time as they facilitate a real-time sensory experiencing *of this very transfer*. Put another way, *JND* increases access to intensity by putting the visitor into direct contact with a rich and heterogeneous source for experiential intensification. Not only is this contact neither brokered nor constrained by consciousness or perceptual subjectivity, it occurs through the medium of intensity, which is to say, through the agency of now completed, superjected subjective becomings as these effectively "haunt" or "contaminate" higher-order experience from the environmental outside, furnishing them crucial inherited sources for the experience of contrast from which intensity arises.

By effectuating contrasts that do not happen at the behest of consciousness, *JND* "interpellates" a sensory agency that cannot in any simple sense be qualified as belonging to the visitor, and indeed as being "personal" in any way, but that she will likely experience as coming from the outside, as a more or less unsettling intrusion into her sensory awareness of her own sensibility. What the work effectuates, I want to suggest, is a dissociation of sensa—sound, color, light—experienced as *content* from the same sensa experienced *as*, for want of a better term, the *"how" of experiencing*. In this respect, Salter's environment makes common cause with much of the work done in the microsound audio art community, work that centers on the subliminal sensory impact of granular sound particles that cannot be directly experienced at the level of perception.[54] Specifically, Salter's work resonates with microsonic practices that engage microsounds to flavor the "how" of hearing and thereby create sensory contrasts that cannot be experienced as contents but only as intensity. In this way, it shifts the terrain for our adaptation to the technical conditions of life by displacing recording (and the problematic of tertiary memory) in favor of technically mediated sensory resonance. Thus, where cinema or analog recording, following Bernard Stiegler, constitutes a laboratory for exploring the temporal selectivity constitutive of consciousness, *Just Noticeable Difference*, and the process of digital granular synthesis it deploys, proffer a laboratory for exploring the experience of intensity as it is "caused"—*not* by consciousness reflecting on itself—but by *the objectile, or superjective, elements of past causally inherited and embodied experiences being reanimated, acting again or continuing to act, in new sensory experiences*, and in the service of the revelation of the impersonal basis of sensory intensity.

While works like *Just Noticeable Difference* might seem to occupy the outermost fringes of our contemporary media culture, the experiential affordances they introduce are absolutely central to the future of our human technogenesis and the political struggles over the development of technical media. For, as I see it, whatever hope we might have to develop a proper pharmacological recompense for the contemporary cultural-industrial data-fication of our lives lies in the possibility to reform our phenomenology in the most radical ways, to develop experiential modalities that exploit the very affordances offered by the technical colonization of the microtemporal for our own ends. In sum: if there is a properly "humanistic" opportunity concealed in contemporary data-fication, our capacity to make good on it will depend upon our success at learning to experience through intensity and at creating atmospheric media environments that facilitate such experi-ence as the basis not just of certain fringe aesthetic experiences but of every-day life in all of its sensory richness and heterogeneity. This recompense, in short, will hinge on our capacity to exploit, for our own ends of experien-tial intensification, the "surplus of sensibility" generated by contemporary technologies for data-gathering and passive sensing; if we must cede our direct agency over the "operational present" of sensibility, as I shall argue in chapter 4, we can gain something back by learning how to intervene in and to shape this operational present in ways that will modulate how sensibility will impact us once it reentered—or, as I would have it, *fed-forward*—into the far slower phenomenological time frames of our conscious, sense per-ceptual experience.

3 Potentiality

> Thus each actual entity, although complete as far as concerns its microscopic process, is yet incomplete by reason of its objective inclusion of the macroscopic process. It really experiences a future which must be actual, although the completed actualities of that future are undetermined. In this sense, each actual occasion experiences its own objective immortality.
>
> This extensive continuum expresses the solidarity of all possible standpoints throughout the whole process of the world. It is not a fact prior to the world; it is the first determination of order—that is, of real potentiality—arising out of the general character of the world. . . . This extensive continuum is "real," because it expresses a fact derived from the actual world and concerning the contemporary actual world. All actual entities are related according to the determinations of this continuum; and all possible actual entities in the future must exemplify these determinations in their relations with the already actual world. The reality of the future is bound up with the reality of this continuum. It is the reality of what is potential, in its character of a real component of what is actual. **Alfred North Whitehead, *Process and Reality***

Datasense

Only at your "debriefing" do you become aware of the plethora of data generated by your own just-past interaction with a potential future employer. As far as you had been concerned—that is, until the impact of this debriefing took root—things had gone pretty smoothly. You noticed the generally benign countenance of your interlocutor and the relative ease with which conversation seemed to flow. You noticed that things seemed to bog down a bit when the discussion turned to collateral benefits but took heart that this lull passed quickly and that the conversation appeared to end on an up note. In general, you felt up-beat about the whole thing and confident that something good would come out of it.

Given the opportunity to peruse the wealth of data generated by your interaction—and registered by a small portable device you were wearing around your neck—you cannot but see things a bit differently. Examining the biometric, behavioral, and environmental data registered by this device—data which captures information about your body movement, your nonlinguistic social signals, your location in space, even your physical proximity to your interlocutor—you now have a far more fine-grained and multi-modal access into your own just-past experience. You can now see how the periodic micro-movements of your limbs conveyed a message of discomfort and how your global body positioning indicated distraction or aloofness. You can now see how the paratactic rhythm of your speech suggested anxiety or ambivalence and how your efforts to effect a benign countenance instead conveyed a lack of concern and engagement. Whether or not you are able ultimately to correlate this wealth of data with the simple outcome of the interview, you have been put on alert that there is much more to any interaction—and to any experience—than what can be grasped by consciousness and retrieved by introspection.

Before examining the research project from which the example is abstracted—MIT researcher Sandy Pentland's explorations of business negotiations using a digital device called a "sociometer"—let me foreground the specificity of the experience just presented. What happened in this imagined experience is an encounter between two humans and data registering the "blooming buzzing confusion" (to borrow William James's rich metaphor) of the total sensory situation in which their encounter took place; mediating between one of these humans (the "you" of the example) and this data is a digital device, a "sociometer," that in reality has the responsibility for converting elements of the total sensory situation into data that can be experienced by the human (by "you")—which is to say at the level of the higher-order, perceptual consciousness characteristic of human experience, what you would typically think of as "your" experience.

Yet despite its address to "you," this digitally mediated and digitally enhanced experience differs fundamentally from the kinds of experience that have been proffered, by me and by others, to illustrate the impact of digital technology on our conceptualization of media. Specifically, it names an experience that cannot be "had" by a "you" *at the moment of its occurrence*, but that can only be reappropriated by the "you" (by human perceptual consciousness) after the fact. It thus contrasts markedly—as an experience *and* as an exemplar of media's impact on experience—with the haptic perception of Robert Lazzarini's *Skulls* that can only be felt bodily, or with the expansion of perceptual presence effectuated by Bill Viola's *Quintet of the Astonished*.[1] If both of these examples constitute instances of a heightening of sensation that, ultimately, *could be felt or otherwise directly lived by consciousness*, the situation now in front of us offers something altogether different: the possibility of experiencing something not immediately available to consciousness. Exemplary of what I am calling twenty-first-century media, the experience facilitated by Pentland's sociometer is a fundamentally *hybrid experience*—an experience that combines human sensing with machine sensing and introduces a delay between the operationality of this sensing and the future moment in which it will be fed-back—or rather *fed-forward*—into consciousness.[2]

Twenty-first-century media impact our experience *indirectly, sensorily, and at multiple scales*. In so doing, they constitute a "force" which should compel us to rethink how experience operates and what it is: for where sense perception and consciousness once reigned essentially uncontested as arbiters of all of the sensory world, of what counts from that world, we are now able to access, if not directly to encounter, sensibility in its generality and heterogeneity. Largely because of its technically facilitated capacities to impact the actual temporal and spatial frameworks in which sensibility is produced and to gather data about this impact, twenty-first-century media furnish an occasion for us to broaden our understanding of what experience is and perhaps has always been.

My aim in deploying the second person address in the above example is precisely *to underscore the failure of personal consciousness* (the general addressee designated by the "you") as a means for grasping the experiential impact of twenty-first-century media. Now that our technologies can capture the sensory dispersal at the root of all experience, we can no longer privilege a single, higher-order access to this sensibility: in today's highly mediated world, there really is no simple and direct conscious correlate of experience.[3] And if experience is the composition of multiple layers of sensibility, functioning in "operational overlap" with one another, then experience can no longer be held to occur in a simple present, whether understood as purely perceptual (Husserl) or radically impressional (Michel Henry), as shot through with non-presence (Derrida) or thickened into a "specious present" (James). Indeed, it is as if experience today were *always already deconstructed*, and deconstructed in a way that doesn't simply introduce non-presence into a single present, but that *multiply de-presentifies presence*, that spreads sensory experience across a host of overlapping timescales. Our technical access into microtemporal sensibility reveals experience to be *dispersed temporally* across a plethora of presents, each of which correlates to a particular level of experience (in principle from the quantum to the geological) that, though it can only be "artifactually" separated from the global composition to which it contributes, nonetheless possesses some degree of experiential autonomy.[4] Accordingly, if there is no content to the you-awareness of the situation described above, at least at the time it is actually occurring, it is because the causal efficacy informing this situation is spread across a set of presents, a set of quasi-autonomous sensory events, that can only be gathered and assembled together for presentational experience once they are fed-forward into a future synthesis-to-come of sense perception or consciousness. In itself, the present you-awareness at issue in this example is manifestly insufficient to access the heterogeneous causal efficacy of the interaction it describes.

This dispersal of experience—and of the experiential present—calls into operation what I propose to call the "feed-forward" structure of experience. This feed-forward structure dictates that disparate elements of higher-order (human) experience—each one of which is an experience in its own right—become unified for presentation to consciousness only through their convergence around a just-to-come future moment. On the model of experience that correlates with twenty-first-century media—a model rooted in the sensory heterogenesis and plurality at the heart of experience—sensory life sheds its dependence on presentation in sense perception and consciousness and becomes directly addressable and presentifiable by artifactual, technical means. Accordingly, the "feed-forward" structure of contemporary experience comprises two distinct elements: (1) the causal and material autonomy of sensation, and indeed of distinct levels of sensibility, in relation to any higher-order presentation; and (2) the redescription of sense perception and consciousness as constitutively after the fact, and hence futural or just-to-come, *effects* of more primordial events of sensation or worldly sensibility.

Feed-forward in the sense I am developing it here must be distinguished operationally from the cybernetic concept of feedback, and also from the concept of feed-forward that is used in neuroscience (as a counterpart to feedback) to describe the pathway of sensations downward from the brain to the sensory nerve endings. What is at stake in both these latter conceptualizations (notwithstanding their differences) is an operation that occurs *internally to a system* and *for the purpose of maintaining system function.* By contrast, what is at stake in the specifically technical feed-forward structure at issue here is a radical introjection of data of sensibility gathered and analyzed by a technical system (twenty-first-century media) into a vastly different techno-biotic system (supervisory consciousness) not for the purposes of the maintaining of this latter system's functioning, but for the purposes of expanding its own access to and (potentially) its agency over the material elements of its own situation. Homeostasis thus gives way to intensification, as compounding feed-forward loops begin to spiral outward in what can only be described as an expanding resonance—but importantly, an expanding *external* resonance[5]—between consciousness and its total situation.

The feed-forward structure at issue here is directly correlated with—and indeed is concretely instituted by—the operation of contemporary microcomputational sensors. Because of their capacity to *stand in for* consciousness, to *take the place of* sense perception in the operations of registering sensory data, coupled with their sheer ubiquity, today's technical circuits facilitate a largely unprecedented perspective on experience: they allow "direct" engagement with the sensory experience underlying perception (where direct means: not channeled through higher-order processes). As a result of such direct engagement, our contact with the materiality of the world undergoes a massive expansion that encompasses two separate though intimately correlated developments. On one hand, *our perceptual access to the world* undergoes expansion: today's microsensors, functioning as surrogates for our on-board modes of perception, facilitate the registration and eventual presentification of a far greater share of worldly sensibility than can be accessed and presentified through sense perception. On the other hand, and precisely because of this increased access, *worldly sensibility itself* is expanded: following what amounts to a potentializing of the actual (what Whitehead calls "real potentiality"), more of our multi-scalar and radically heterogeneous contact with sensibility becomes available as material that can be acted on, which is to say, as part of what constitutes actuality.

With this excavation of the feed-forward structure of contemporary consciousness, we return again to the claim for access to the data of sensibility (CADS) that, as I have already more than once suggested, constitutes the hinge linking Whiteheadian process philosophy and contemporary technical media. Here, in the sections to follow, we will take a more concrete look at how data propagates sensibility, and how this data propagation of sensibility shifts the economy between human-addressed media and twenty-first-century media. Again, however, let me caution that the point is not to choose between these two, as if embracing the challenges posed to us by twenty-first-century media necessarily entailed abandoning media in their more traditional operations. My point, rather, is that we increasingly experience media on a two-tiered platform—exemplified by my earlier excavation of the structure of Facebook—in which perceptually accessed media are doubled, expanded, and displaced by media operating in the deep background, beyond the grasp of sense perception, conscious attention, and even affective attunement or dissonance. If our moment marks a certain stage in the gradual and ongoing shift from human-addressed to environmental media, it is one that focalizes the productivity of data as a source for sensibility, and in so doing, lays bare the positive side of the data-fication currently sweeping through the cultural domain.

Drawing on its analogy with Whitehead's account of process, we can describe data propagation of sensibility as a kind of second-order oscillating process that, expanding Jones's deconstruction of the empirical-speculative divide, brings the operation of speculation, concretized in the form of media, into the domain of experience. Like Whitehead's account of the incessant oscillation between concrescence and transition, every act of accessing the data of sensibility is itself a process that creates new sensibilities— sensibilities that are, in turn, added into the extant data of sensibility. This process of data propagation of sensibility perfectly captures the way that potentiality (Whitehead's "real potentiality") correlates with the superjective dimension of process: far from being an inert source for computation, as it is often understood to be, data is quite literally teeming with potentiality, and specifically, with potentiality that—though part of the settled world—has a speculative relation to experience understood as the experience of consciousness. That is why, as we shall see shortly, data-mining and data analytics do not simply calculate a preexistent space of possibilities, but literally *create* new relations and thus new information (new data) as a result of their operation. And that is also why, when push comes to shove, we must supplement the orthodox account of the speculative explicated above (in my discussion of Debaise in particular) with a slightly different account: the speculative as a dimension of experience that evades grasp via extant modes of experience and that literally introduces—that, as it were, *forces the creation of*—new experiential modes.

Two factors merit particular attention here. Let us first consider the link between this analogy between Whiteheadian process and computation and the claim for inversion (CFI) that has structured my approach to Whitehead. Following this analogy, computation can certainly be likened to concrescence, but data cannot so easily be equated with transition: far from being inert and passive, as it would be following Whitehead's adoption of Locke's account of "perpetual perishing," data wields the lingering subjective force of attained actualities—the real potentiality of the settled world (the disjunctive continuity) that "hosts" the always excessive, hence potential, force of superjects (the subjective power of attained actualities). By way of concretizing the operation of process in a datified world, the analogy thus manages to enact the inversion of Whitehead's account of process: it thereby renders computation/concrescence a mere instrument for realizing the potentiality of already-actual data/settled world, a realization yielding new data that can claim a double superjective agency (as data added to extant data/settled world, on one hand, and as data informing the creativity of concrete events or societies, on the other).

Following directly from this double superjective agency is a second noteworthy feature of this analogy between process and computation: its expression of a certain empirical subsumption of the speculative. The crucial point to emphasize here is that the relation between computation and data constitutes a process that *is* speculative, but not in the way that Whitehead claims for concrescence—as (following Debaise's explication, discussed above) an operation that is withdrawn from the domain of experience as such, that which can never be accessed empirically. Rather, the speculative element here—computation (or technical processes for accessing and operating on the data of sensibility)—is fully part of the domain of experience writ large, even as it remains speculative in relation to specifically human (and perhaps more broadly, to living) modes of experience. In this respect, we can perhaps think of the data propagation of sensibility as exemplifying a third arena of process, one that operates at a "higher level" than the microscopic domain where actualities come into being but at the same time at a "lower level" than the macroscopic processes of perception. What such a folding of the speculative back upon itself ultimately points to is a relativizing of the speculative that goes hand in hand with Jones's critique of Whitehead's devaluation of the temporal reality of process: if, as Jones suggests (and as we explored above), Whitehead would likely be amenable to a phenomenologizing of his speculative scheme, what precisely hangs in the balance is the economy between the speculative and the empirical.[6] Giving up the priority of the former, and the concomitant privilege accorded concrescence, permits a different emphasis, one that links the speculative to the potentiality of worldly sensibility, to the fact of its excess *in relation to any delimited process of actualization*. On this account, the speculative effectively undergoes revaluation *from the perspective of experience*: without losing its reserve in relation to any given experience, the speculative comes to coincide with the worldly sensibility that, I am arguing, constitutes the imperceptible background, the font of causal efficacy, for perceptual activity. If, in the end, this empirical subsumption of the speculative does not violate the speculative ban as we earlier developed it (restricting it to actualities-in-attainment or concrescence), that is not only because of its status as analogy, but also because it chips away at the privilege, and also the autonomy, of concrescence itself: on the account I am developing here (and following the claim for inversion), concrescence is a vehicle for explaining how worldly sensibility propagates by way of processes at all levels; it is emphatically *not* the single and all-important metaphysical *source* for actuality Whitehead takes it to be.

To tease out the significance of this dissolution of the divide between the speculative and the empirical, I shall now turn to a concrete affinity between Whitehead's account of process and the data propagation of sensibility. My focus in this chapter will accordingly concern the concrete connectives linking the revolution in "passive" sensing that characterizes twenty-first-century media with Whitehead's critique of modern subjectivism and the ensuing liberation of "causal efficacy" from its debilitating ties to various modern avatars of the subject (including Whitehead's own "nonsensuous perception"). What unites these quite disparate phenomena is a shared commitment to developing modes of access—in the former case technical, in the latter speculative—to the teeming, multi-scalar and heterogeneous domain of sensibility that lies at the heart of experience, but that evades presentification in sense perception and consciousness. While the payoff of this commitment will include a reformulation of the operation of these latter, higher-order faculties—a reformulation that places them *back in the sensory flux in which they belong*—what shall concern me in this and the next chapter is the way in which, in both cases, it opens a material domain, worldly sensibility or "non-perceptual sensation," that has been relegated, in the history of modern philosophy as well as in media theory, to the noumenal status of that which can only be presumed to exist, but not encountered phenomenologically, or otherwise experienced.

As I have already had occasion to suggest, the description of this material domain in terms of "causal efficacy" is the ultimate payoff of Whitehead's differentiation of two "pure" modes of perception (causal efficacy and presentational immediacy) and the critique of modern subjectivism within which it functions. Far more than just a revisionary account of perception that includes the vague experience of the "withness of the body," the true accomplishment of Whitehead's move here is to expose the operation of a worldliness that does not depend on its presentification to human modes of experience for its existence. Likewise, this material domain—worldly sensibility—centrally informs the operation of twenty-first-century media, which as I have been claiming here, impact experience in a plethora of ways and at a host of scales, most of which lie beneath the threshold at which higher-order cognitive operations take place. That is why my concern here is precisely with how contemporary media themselves directly contribute to—or more exactly, how they expand—worldly sensibility, both by opening it up to human access and by increasing the sheer quantity of sensation in the world.

As I have already suggested and shall argue in more detail below, this situation—twenty-first-century media opening access and directly contributing to the domain of causal efficacy—facilitates a complete reversal in perspective on the issue of how consciousness/sense perception correlates with its causal infrastructure. In the wake of this reversal, we no longer need to treat worldly sensibility solely as a *preperceptual* causal basis *for perception* and can rethink perception in a most fundamental way—as itself an *effect* of worldly sensibility. If such a fundamental reconceptualization of the economy linking perception and sensibility becomes possible, it is precisely because our technical capacity to register data of causal efficacy allows us to stop subordinating sensibility to a culminating moment of perception: in contrast to thinkers (Whitehead included) who have felt compelled to treat sensibility as what is preparatory to perception—utilizing creative terms like "preacceleration," "thinking-feeling," and "symbiosensation" (all of which are glosses on Whitehead's term "nonsensuous perception")—we are now able to address worldly sensibility *in itself* and in relation *to its own force*, independently of any ensuing perception. In short, perception is no longer needed to enframe the causal efficacy of sensibility, and it is no longer needed to provide access (by way of what, with James, we might call "fringe" experience)[7] to this efficacy; indeed, insofar as it is decoupled from the force of sensibility, perception becomes available for what I am here trying to theorize as the operation of "feed-forward": projecting causal efficacy forward into future activity, and specifically, into the future of perceptual consciousness deliberating on its own future activity.

Let us now consider the payoff of the direct access to worldly sensibility afforded by contemporary microcomputational sensors. This payoff is, as I have already had occasion to suggest, a massive expansion in the material efficacy of sensibility, both as it implicates humans and as it operates in excess of the scope of human activity. Today's ubiquitous media and passive sensors can register massive amounts of data concerning the sensibility of human embodiment (heart rate, galvanic skin response, brain wave activity, etc.) as well as the sensibility of environmental factors (ambient temperature, amount of light, humidity, etc.) that may or may not bear on situations involving human activity. The cumulative result of such data-gathering is a shift in focus where sensibility is concerned, from an agent-centered perspective to a broad, environmental one, which I shall try to theorize, in line with Whitehead's beautiful thought that each actuality prehends the entire universe, as the "total situation" underlying and informing any event.

To address this broad, environmental perspective, this total situation, we will need to position the concept of "non-perceptual sensibility" both as an inversion of Whitehead's "nonsensuous perception" (together with all of its contemporary avatars) and as a synonym for "worldly sensibility." Non-perceptual sensibility, we now learn, is what is at stake in the various societies and subsocieties that constitute elements of integrated human embodiment but do not embody higher-order characteristics (for example, the immune system, the neural network of the brain, the cellular system, etc.), and it is also what is at stake in microsensory computations that register data and the vast networks of predictive calculation that today's creative industries have built up on the basis of this data. And with respect to Whitehead's philosophy more generally, non-perceptual sensibility is what is at issue in—what is needed to conceptualize—Whitehead's extension of experience and of subjectivity to all scales of eventality, from the atomic to the geological. In this sense, and despite its apparent opposition to the privilege Whitehead lends perception in the analysis of causal efficacy, non-perceptual sensibility is central to cashing in on the promise of Whitehead's own account of the "total situation"—the notion that every actual entity prehends the entirety of the universe—for the analysis of experience in all its manifold richness.

I shall return to this topic below, following a deeper exposition of the correlation linking the environmental dimension of twenty-first-century media with Whitehead's critique of modern subjectivism. For the moment, and to give a sense for what is to come, let me emphasize simply that non-perceptual sensibility names a mode of diffuse sensation—enjoyed, differentially, to be sure, by every experiential entity—that occurs beyond the grasp of sense organs understood as embodied (or, more broadly, as artifactualized) processors of data from the world. In this sense, my argument resonates strongly with James Gibson's ecological psychology,[8] even if it substitutes sensibility for perception as the means for the "direct" channel—or mode of de-differentiation—between humans (and other experiential entities) and the environmental outside.

For this reason, I find Jerry Kang and Dana Cuff's claim that microcomputational sensation introduces what amounts to a new sense organ both suggestive and ultimately overly restrictive of the correlation at issue here. In their 2005 assessment of pervasive computing, Kang and Cuff go so far as to stress pervasive computing's capacity to sense information previously unavailable, only to correlate this capacity with sensation as it has traditionally been understood, that is, as sense perception:

> By being bathed in such data, we augment our experience of reality with layers of contextually relevant information. It is as if human beings were granted an additional "sense" in addition to sight, hearing, taste, smell, and touch—a sort of sixth sense, a datasense. Preliminary implementations of such augmented reality already exist. For instance, contractors can walk through construction sites with

a visor that paints a digital overlay of the approved architectural drawings on the building in progress. . . . The above examples involve collecting information by authenticating an individual's identity and referencing it to extant databases. But PerC's [Pervasive Computing's] animation—its sensing powers in particular—could allow for datasense to collect types of information previously unavailable. For instance, sensors could collect infrared data, which can speak volumes. A childcare center may strictly prevent drop-offs of children with fever. An employer may guess that a job applicant is pregnant. A border official may profile visitors for SARS.[9]

Notwithstanding the rather ominous nature of their examples, all of which attest to the pervasive correlation of pervasive computing with control, Kang and Cuff's account of datasense opens a perspective that will prove crucial to my effort to expose the deep affinities linking twenty-first-century media and Whitehead's critique of philosophical subjectivism. For their very willingness to conceptualize the affordances of pervasive computing in terms of sensation—and of sensation, at least initially, beyond perception—opens a perspective that permits, or, more precisely, that requires, the *direct* correlation of data and sensation, outside of or beyond the mediating operation of human consciousness. It is this perspective that will be at issue in what follows. Thus, even if we will need to trade in Kang and Cuff's agent-centered approach for the environmental perspective of "data milieus," their notion of datasense provides a crucial springboard for my endeavor to grasp the sensibility of pervasive computing as radical potentiality.

Data Milieu

Let me accordingly begin my account of Whitehead's reformed subjective principle by asking what "datasense" might mean within his thinking. To answer this question, I propose that we take Whitehead at his word when he describes "attained actualities," actual entities following their "objectification" and entry into the settled world, as "data." "Data" for Whitehead functions similarly to impressions in the empiricist (and, we might add, phenomenological) tradition(s): they provide the basic elements out of which experience is constituted. As Whitehead puts it, "In the organic philosophy the 'data of objectifications' are the nearest analogue to Hume's 'simple impressions.'"[10] In taking the place of impressions, however, data of objectifications (or attained actualities) lay stress on the material or causal force of the actual world: "The 'objectifications' of the actual entities in the actual world, relative to a definite actual entity, constitute the efficient causes out of which *that* actual entity arises."[11] I want to hold on to this correlation of data and causal efficacy—which forms the basis for Whitehead's "solution" to Humean skepticism—as we reconstruct Whitehead's critique of modern subjectivism and seek to clarify the role that his theory of perception plays within it. For it is this correlation of data and causal efficacy that ultimately informs the environmental agency at issue in Whitehead's thinking: independently of their former or subsequent belonging to a delimited subjective (or agential) becoming, data themselves possess objective material force. Or, put more concisely and more elegantly: data are superjective and superjects are made of data. That is why the correlation of twenty-first-century media and causal efficacy does indeed constitute a new *datasense*, to anticipate the conclusion to come, but only so long as this latter is understood in contrast to sense organs as internal processors of sensory information and indeed to any agent-centered (perceptual) perspective. Under these constraints, *datasense* becomes effectively synonymous with *data milieu*.

Returning to my opening question concerning the place of datasense in Whitehead's reformation of modern subjectivism, I can now be more direct: datasense constitutes a surrogate form of what Whitehead calls "symbolic reference." Developed in a chapter of *Process and Reality* as well as his 1926 lectures on *Symbolism*, symbolic reference, as I have already had occasion to mention, designates the activity of correlating the two "pure" modes of perception—perception in the mode of presentational immediacy and perception in the mode of causal efficacy—that typifies normal everyday lived experience. Symbolic reference, Whitehead explains,

> is the interpretative element in human experience. Language almost exclusively refers to presentational immediacy as interpreted by symbolic reference. For example, we say that "we see the *stone*" where *stone* is an interpretation of *stone-image*: also we say that "we see the *stone-image* with our eyes"; this is an interpretation arising from the complex integration of (i) the causal efficacy of the antecedent eye in the vision, (ii) the presentational immediacy of the stone-image, (iii) the presentational immediacy of the eye-strain. When we say that "we see the stone with our eyes," the interpretations of these two examples are combined.[12]

Symbolic reference involves the attribution of sense perception (presentational immediacy) to some less "clear and distinct" perception of the material basis informing it (causal efficacy). As a surrogate for symbolic reference, datasense displaces the *direct, human* correlation of the two modes of perception, a correlation that occurs by way of a "common form,"[13] in favor of an *indirect, machinic* correlation—what we might call "machinic reference"—that involves the capacity of sensors to register a plethora of data of causal efficacy unavailable to any narrowly perceptual mode of causal efficacy and to present such data, after the fact, to perceptual consciousness.

This expansion and externalization of the (distinctly human) operation of symbolic reference is, however, only one element of the broader technical expansion of the operation of causal efficacy. Beyond offering a surrogate for symbolic reference, datasense impacts the materiality of the world, as I have been arguing here, in ways that do not directly concern higher-order human activity: specifically, datasense involves the *production of sensibility by data-gathering operations*. In this respect, datasense operates directly on causal efficacy quite independently of any activity of perception, whether in the mode of presentational immediacy *or* in the mode of causal efficacy. And this is why it impacts experience in ways that remain inscrutable to human perception.

Here again we come upon the need to broaden the account of experience afforded by Whitehead's organic philosophy beyond the confines of the operation of perception. For despite its significant contribution to our conceptualization of human activity, perception on Whitehead's account, as applied (for example by Steven Meyer)[14] to the conceptualization of the neural operationality of the brain, presents only a very partial picture of how computation impacts materiality. To grasp why this is so, I shall resituate Whitehead's inspired revision of perception (i.e., his introduction of perception in the mode of causal efficacy) within the larger context of his critique of modern subjectivism. Once it is so resituated, Whitehead's expansion of perception, and whatever correlation it may have with datasense, will appear as an element, and in some sense as an instrument, of a greater expansion of sensibility—Whitehead's causal efficacy (here as distinct from the perception of it, from perception in the mode of causal efficacy)—that coincides with his reform of modern subjectivism. The payoff of this move, with respect to datasense, is to liberate data-gathering from any dependence on perception, and thereby, to position data-gathering as an independent producer of sensibility (causal efficacy) in its own right.

Causal Efficacy

Among the identifying characteristics of perception on Whitehead's account, none is more crucial than its disparateness: for Whitehead, as we have seen—and here he stands opposed to the vast majority of his predecessors—perception bears no special affinity with human conscious experience or even human experience per se, but occurs across the vast range of the universe's multifarious processes and indeed crosses over the living-nonliving divide. In the case of human perception, this disparateness entails a deprivileging of consciousness as the final product and orienting point of philosophical analysis of perception. Rather than beginning from consciousness and asking how it is possible, Whitehead positions consciousness as the most restricted, though also most complex, practical accomplishment of a causal lineage that spans across countless scales of existence and that forms a continuum linking the most elementary physical processes with the highest-order mental process yet achieved. On such a view, far from being the simple and unique accomplishment of one level of human activity (e.g., consciousness), any and every experience of a human being is actually the accomplishment of a very complex series of partially overlapping processes occurring at different scales and in different time frames.

Though Whitehead does not directly address this level of complexity in his account of perception, it is—or so I shall argue—one of the most fundamental implications of his philosophy of organism when it is a question of theorizing the composition of human experience. Whitehead's already-introduced differentiation of two "pure modes" of perception opens the terrain on which such complexity can be theorized. As we have seen, these two modes are not so much different ontologically (i.e., different in kind) as different in function (two dimensions of a single activity). The first, "perception in the mode of presentational immediacy" (hereafter PMPI), is perception in its traditional sense, namely "sense perception." This form of perception characterizes higher-order experience and has generally been understood to be the result of the processing of information taken in by our sense organs. To this commonplace concept of perception, Whitehead adds "perception in the mode of causal efficacy" (PMCE). Whitehead describes this mode of perception as "vague" and "ill-defined," and cites as examples experiences of recognizing that we "see *with* our eyes," "taste *with* our palates," and "touch *with* our hands." Perception in the mode of causal efficacy occurs, in short, when we manage to perceive the causal processes that underlie sense perception.

These two so-called pure modes of perception do not designate separate perceptual faculties, but rather two aspects of a single process that culminates in the mixed or hybrid mode of perception, namely symbolic reference. Insofar as it involves the co-referral of the two pure modes of perception to one another, symbolic reference can only take place *because of the continuum between the two pure modes.* As Whitehead explains, "Presentational immediacy is the enhancement of the importance of relationships which were already in the datum, vaguely and with slight relevance. This fact, that 'presentational immediacy' deals with *the same datum* as does 'causal efficacy,' gives the ultimate reason why there is a common 'ground' for 'symbolic reference.' The two modes express the same datum under different proportions of relevance."[15] For my purpose here, what is most crucial about Whitehead's bi-(or tri-)partite account of perception, is the distinct primacy he lends to PMCE over the higher-order form of perception that we ordinarily identify with perception per se. As I shall understand it here, this primacy reflects the materiality of causal efficacy: the power or force that causal efficacy possesses in itself, *independently of any perceptual operation.* In this respect, PMCE is unlike PMPI which "requires the more sophistical activity of the later stages of process, so as to belong only to organisms of a relatively high grade"; indeed, PMCE reaches all the way down to the simplest levels of experience: "The perceptive mode of causal efficacy is to be traced to the constitution of the datum by reason of which there is a concrete percipient entity. Thus we must assign the mode of causal efficacy to the fundamental constitution of an occasion so that in germ this mode belongs even to organisms of the lowest grade."[16] As a "direct" reaction to the causal efficacy of the world, PMCE is literally responsible for the fact that there is perceptual experience in the first place. In this "material" role, perception extends well beyond the bounds normally associated with it: it occurs whenever there is an experience of the causal processes informing experience, or, in more technical terms, whenever there is a feeling *of* the "subjective" vehicle of the prehensions constituting the causal infrastructure of a given entity's experience.

But certainly the most important consequence for my purposes here is the continuum Whitehead's account introduces *within the perceptual—or as I shall prefer to say, the sensory—experience* of any given entity. For if sensation arises in relation to the entirety of the causal basis of experience, and if the vast majority of this sensory experience is beyond the range of sense perception (and perceptual consciousness), the resources bequeathed us by the philosophical tradition for conceptualizing sensation are manifestly inadequate. Sensation, or rather sensibility, to put it simply, largely evades the grasp of perception; or alternatively, perception captures only that part of sensibility which can be rendered as sensations. A solid grasp of the limited scope of perception and of the ubiquity of sensibility is, as we shall see shortly, precisely what is at stake in Whitehead's criticism of Hume (and his rejection of Kant's solution to Humean skepticism). What follows from Whitehead's account is a general restriction on the operation and value of sense perception: sense perception can no longer be—and indeed, *should never have been*—positioned as the privileged mode of access to our worldly sensibility. It is this concrete criticism of modern subjectivism that leads me to postulate the operation of non-perceptual sensibility at the heart of human experience: non-perceptual sensibility, we can now appreciate, constitutes a consequential development of the logic behind Whitehead's own expansion of sensation into the domain of causal efficacy. And while it will be important to understand why Whitehead did not himself develop this logic to its end point, far more central for the current task is to appreciate how the technical expansion of sensibility makes Whitehead's neutral theory of experience more powerful, both in itself and in the context of our ubiquitously mediatized world.

As I indicated above, this specific task calls on us to extend the correlation of data-gathering and sensation beyond the operation of symbolic reference as Whitehead conceptualizes it. In this extended context, we will see that the purpose of Whitehead's expansion of perception is not simply to refine the operation of perception but also, and I would argue, more fundamentally, to make worldly sensibility accessible to human modes of experiencing—or, still more precisely, to make it accessible independently of its impact on human perception, or, again, in a way that doesn't channel it through higher-order human faculties. That is why non-perceptual sensibility, far from deviating from Whitehead's concern, effectively culminates the expansion of experience central to *Process and Reality*: non-perceptual sensation makes it possible to address experience at the level of its sensory disparateness, *before it is synthesized into perceptual unities*, including unities, like the inchoate feeling that I see *with* my eyes, that contribute to higher-order organization even if they lie somewhere beneath overt conscious awareness. Described in Whitehead's terms, non-perceptual sensibility lets us address the "responsive phase" of an experience, in which "subjective sensations associated with barely relevant geometrical relations" are experienced directly.[17]

Whitehead is unequivocal in defining the scope of causal efficacy. It extends to all determinations involved in the concrescence of actual entities but not to the creativity that concrescence introduces *into the world*:

> The doctrine of the philosophy of organism is that, however far the sphere of efficient causation be pushed in the determination of components of a concrescence—its data, its emotions, its appreciations, its purposes, its phases of subjective aim—beyond the determination of these components there always remains the final reaction of the self-creative unity of the universe. This final reaction completes the self-creative act by putting the decisive stamp of creative emphasis upon the determinations of efficient cause. Each

occasion exhibits its measure of creative emphasis in proportion to
its measure of subjective intensity.[18]

This specification of the scope of causal efficacy constitutes yet another
instance in which Whitehead restricts creativity to the process of attainment and denies it to attained actuality. In direct contrast, Jones's reading
of intensity *as creativity* allows us to break down the division introduced by
Whitehead here, since it understands intensity less as a *symptom* of something else than an *operation*—indeed, the fundamental operation—of efficient causation.[19] From Jones's perspective, as we have seen, the intensity
introduced into the world by concrescence manifests causal force independently of the operation of concrescence. One consequence of this conclusion is that causal efficacy operates *in the experiential domain*; and, on this
point, Whitehead and Jones indeed stand united: for both, causal efficacy
spans the continuum from the objectification of the simplest actual entities
to the highest forms of presentational experience.

What this means is that the materiality of causal efficacy vastly exceeds
the (and our) perception of it. Not only must causal efficacy as material process be distinguished from its perception by humans (or, for that matter, by
any other perceiving entities), but the issue of how to access its materiality
must be rethought fundamentally, such that it can no longer be channeled
through and can no longer be made to depend on human perception. Causal
efficacy characterizes the complex networks of materiality that *in every case*
ultimately lead back to attained actualities and the liberated prehensions
they release into the settled world. Some (a tiny minority) of these networks
become accessible to perception in the mode of causal efficacy, and an even
smaller number, to perception in the mode of presentational immediacy.
But the vast majority of them remain *beyond the grasp of perception*; they
generate dispersed data of sensibility that falls through the cracks of sense
organs, and in this respect approximate what Deleuze once called "transcendental sensibility," though with the important difference that they are
not in fact transcendental since they do not fall outside what is accessible
to experience or, alternatively, outside the actual. Understanding worldly
sensibility as a specifically non-perceptual mode of experience thus becomes
imperative.

On this score, it is significant that Whitehead turns to pre-Kantian
philosophers from Descartes to Hume, whereas Deleuze invokes Leibniz and the post-Kantian legacy of his thought (notably in the figure of
Solomon Maimon). The driving principle of Whitehead's reconstruction
of seventeenth-century philosophy is the restoration of "objective actuality" as the counterpart to—and indeed as a necessary component of—

subjectivism. This restoration refocuses the locus of philosophical analysis from the subjective mode of givenness of an experience to the subjective enjoyment of an objective actuality.

In the Beginning Was the Datum

In his articulation of the "reformed subjective principle," Whitehead attributes this objective dimension directly to the *datum* of experience: "Descartes' discovery on the side of subjectivism requires balancing by an 'objectivist' principle as to the datum of experience." The error of modern subjectivism, an error initially made by Descartes himself and later ratified by both Locke and Hume, is to have subsumed the objectivity of the datum *within a subjective mode of givenness*. In this way, Descartes's initial discovery of objective actuality is effectively compromised from the very start:

> Descartes modified traditional philosophy in two opposite ways. He increased the metaphysical emphasis on the substance-quality forms of thought. The actual things "required nothing but themselves in order to exist," and were to be thought of in terms of their qualities, some of them essential attributes, and others accidental modes. He also laid down the principle, that those substances which are the subjects enjoying conscious experiences provide the primary data for philosophy, namely, themselves as in the enjoyment of such experience. This is the famous subjectivist bias which entered into modern philosophy through Descartes. In this doctrine Descartes undoubtedly made the greatest philosophical discovery since the age of Plato and Aristotle. For his doctrine directly traversed the notion that the proposition, "This stone is grey," expresses a primary form of known fact from which metaphysics can start its generalizations. . . . But like Columbus who never visited America, Descartes missed the full sweep of his own discovery, and he and his successors, Locke and Hume, continued to construe the functionings of the subjective enjoyment of experience according to the substance-quality categories. Yet if the enjoyment of experience be the constitutive subjective fact, these categories have lost all claim to any fundamental character in metaphysics.[20]

In Whitehead's reconstruction, Descartes is thus in conflict with himself: his radically new understanding of the constitutive subjective fact simply cannot be reconciled with his adherence to the Aristotelian doctrine of substance. The dead end of this legacy plays itself out in the skeptical empiri-

cism of Hume, which in this respect can be understood as an attempt to
suture the fault line between two incompatible philosophical doctrines:

> Hume—to proceed at once to the consistent exponent of the
> method—looked for a universal quality to function as qualifying
> the mind, by way of explanation of its perceptive enjoyment. Now if
> we scan "my perception of this stone as grey" in order to find a uni-
> versal, the only available candidate is "greyness." Accordingly for
> Hume, "greyness," functioning as a sensation qualifying the mind,
> is a fundamental type of fact for metaphysical generalization. The
> result is Hume's simple impressions of sensation, which form the
> starting-point of his philosophy. But this is an entire muddle, for
> the perceiving mind is not grey, so grey is now made to perform
> a new role. From the original fact "my perception of this stone as
> grey," Hume extracts "Awareness of sensation of greyness"; and
> puts it forward as the ultimate datum in this element of experience.
> *He has discarded the objective actuality of the stone-image in his
> search for a universal quality*: this "objective actuality" is Descartes'
> "*realitas objectiva*."... What [Hume] has done is to assert arbi-
> trarily the "subjectivist" and "sensationalist" principles as applying
> to the datum for experience.[21]

As defined at the beginning of *Process and Reality*'s chapter "The Subjectivist Principle," from which these two passages have been drawn, both of
these principles describe reductions of the datum for experience. The subjectivist principle states that the datum in the act of experience "can be adequately analyzed purely in terms of universals" and the sensationalist principle (which "acquires dominating importance, if the subjective principle be
accepted") states that "the primary activity in the act of experience is the
bare subjective entertainment of the datum, devoid of any subjective form of
reception." This, Whitehead clarifies, is "the doctrine of *mere* sensation."[22]

What Hume accomplishes, in a move that only compounds Descartes's
initial reduction, is to correlate the substance doctrine with sensationalism,
such that the datum for experience is given for subjective enjoyment in the
form of a universal perceived by a substance. With this move, as the above
passage makes clear, Hume effectively discards objective actuality, and with
it the capacity for the datum of experience to furnish an objective reality
that, rather than being given subjectively, is what is enjoyed by the subject
and what, in being so enjoyed, comes to make up a constitutive subjective fact.

We should accordingly understand Whitehead's reformed subjective principle as an attempt to restore *the autonomy of the datum for experience.* Whitehead makes as much clear in his own characterization of the specificity of his philosophy of organism: "The philosophies of substance," he writes, "presuppose a subject which then encounters a datum, and then reacts to the datum. The philosophy of organism presupposes a datum which is met with feelings, and progressively attains the unity of a subject. But with this doctrine, 'superject' would be a better term than 'subject.'"[23] What I want to emphasize in this characterization (which, we should not fail to note, would seem to ratify Jones's reading of subjectivity as intensity and her concomitant privileging of the superject) is its focus on a primordial domain of subjective experience—"worldly or superjectal sensibility"—that precedes and makes possible the experience of any unified subject whatsoever.

It is precisely in the name of such a dispersion of sensibility that Whitehead aspires to construct a "critique of pure feeling" that would supersede the Kantian critiques. Whereas Kant, following Hume, "assumes the radical disconnection of impressions *qua data*" and "therefore conceives his transcendental aesthetic to be the mere description of a subjective process appropriating the data by orderliness of feeling," in Whitehead's organic philosophy Kant's "Transcendental Aesthetic" is revealed to be nothing more than "a distorted fragment of what should have been his main topic." What the aesthetic should have analyzed is *feeling as the primordial reception of the objective datum*: "The datum," Whitehead continues, "includes its own interconnections, and the first stage of the process of feeling is the reception into the responsive conformity of feeling whereby the datum, which is mere potentiality, becomes the individualized basis for a complex unity of realization."[24] Here, the work of sensibility prior to the emergence of unified sense perceptions—the very domain of Deleuze's transcendental sensibility—is itself made empirically accessible and empirically consequential, though certainly not through higher-order modes of perception.

For my purposes, it is absolutely crucial that Whitehead describes this primitive level of feeling, which modern physics first makes it possible to access, as being concerned *not with sense perception* but with *sense reception.* For if sense perception characterizes a higher-order, unified subjective experience of the datum for experience, sense reception designates *the sensibility of the datum itself*, sensibility as objective actuality. "In sense-reception," Whitehead explains, "the sensa are the definiteness of emotion: they are emotional forms transmitted from occasion to occasion."[25] Or again, "emotions conspicuously brush aside sensations and fasten upon the 'particular' objects to which—in Locke's phrase—certain 'ideas' are '*determined.*'" This situation calls for an inversion in our received understanding of sensory objectification: "The confinement of our prehension of other actual entities to the mediation of private sensations is pure myth. The converse doctrine is nearer the truth: the more primitive mode of objectification is via emotional tone, and only in exceptional organisms does objectification, via sensation, supervene with any effectiveness."[26] Part of what informs this inversion—and here we get a concrete sense of Whitehead's radicality—is the correlation of emotional tone with "gut reactions"; "if we consider the matter physiologically," Whitehead notes, we see that "the emotional tone depends mainly on the condition of the viscera which are peculiarly ineffective in generating sensations."[27] At stake in sense reception, and in what I am calling non-perceptual sensibility, is a visceral mode of engagement that is not only common and impersonal but also more primordial and more fundamental than any agent-referenced, private sensations.

With this in mind, it is certainly not without significance that Whitehead identifies the reformed subjective principle as "merely an alternate statement" of the "principle of relativity." This latter principle, he notes, "states that it belongs to the nature of a 'being' that it is a potential for every 'becoming.'"[28] The subject is always a subject-superject, or really, as Jones helps us to grasp, is fundamentally and primordially a superject. In making this identification, Whitehead seeks to combine the subjectivist position that "the whole universe consists of elements disclosed in the analysis of the experiences of subjects" with the restored objective actuality of the datum for experience. We can now appreciate precisely how objective actuality impacts experience: rather than being a content of subjective activity, as it is on (orthodox) phenomenological as well as empiricist models, it constitutes *the objective (or efficient) cause of* subjective activity and *retains its status as objective data* throughout and beyond the experience. At the same time, however, we must also accept that "apart from the experiences of subjects," there would be, as Whitehead memorably puts it, "nothing, nothing, nothing, bare nothingness."[29]

By emphasizing the relativity of the agency in play here, the potential of the subject-superject to participate in the becoming of other entities, Whitehead manages to retain the Cartesian discovery—the discovery of the constitutive subjective fact—while at the same time maintaining the objective reality or power of the datum. As he puts it in a passage already cited, the datum is met with feelings, and only progressively attains the unity of a subject: it elicits visceral reactions *before it becomes a subject*. Or, in other words, there is sensory subjectivity—non-perceptual sensibility—*before* there is prehensive unification and sense perception.

This same objective reality or power of the datum helps Whitehead resolve the impasse of Humean skepticism. Hume is right, Whitehead clarifies, to adopt the subjectivist bias of modern philosophy; he is right that nothing can be brought into philosophy that is not "discoverable as an element in subjective experience" and he is right that causation must be "describable as an element in experience." Where Hume goes wrong is when he denies the objective power of the datum, the visceral dimension of its operation as "lure for feeling": "The point of the criticisms of Hume's procedure is that *we have direct intuition of inheritance and memory*: thus the only problem is, so to describe the general character of experience that these intuitions may be included. It is here that Hume fails."[30]

By maintaining the autonomy of the datum, and by treating its objective power at the primitive level of feeling (non-perceptual sensibility), Whitehead's philosophy can thus succeed where Hume's fails:

> In contrast to Hume, the philosophy of organism keeps "this stone as grey" in the datum for the experience in question. [Hume, you will recall, treats it in terms of the universal "greyness," which is predicated of the substance, stone.] It is, in fact, the "objective datum" of a certain physical feeling, belonging to a derivative type in a late phase of a concrescence. But this doctrine fully accepts Descartes's discovery that subjective experiencing is the primary metaphysical situation which is presented to metaphysics for analysis. This doctrine is the "reformed subjective principle.". . . Accordingly, the notion "this stone as grey" is a derivative abstraction, necessary indeed as an element in the description of the fundamental experiential feeling, but delusive as a metaphysical starting-point. This derivative abstraction is called an "objectification."[31]

Here we encounter yet another instance calling on us to distinguish metaphysical analysis from experiential analysis: for although it may be an "abstraction" from the subject's enjoyment of the datum for experience which, for Whitehead, constitutes the basis for metaphysics, objectification is, in another sense, the very causal basis for that constitutive subjective fact. This very point is precisely what Whitehead's correlation of sense reception with the superject establishes: the datum is met with feeling long before it gives rise to subjective enjoyment.

Returning to the question of what "datasense" means in the context of Whitehead's philosophy, let me now summarize what we have found. Taking literally Whitehead's identification of objectification with data, we can now see how his thinking opens possibilities to treat data in its twenty-first-century sense—computational data-gathering—as "causal objectification," which is to say, as *data for experience* in precisely the sense Whitehead attributes to "objective actuality."[32] Like other data for experience, and in some ways more directly than other kinds of data, computational data elicits primordial feelings long before it coalesces into subjectively unified experience. More precisely still, in the case of computational data, "what is felt *subjectively* by the objectified actual entity" is not simply "transmitted *objectively* to the concrescent actualities which supersede it," but is strictly speaking *identical to them*: biometric and environmental data register *both* the objective sensibility that elicits subjective feeling *and* the subjective feeling itself. In this respect, the capacity of computational technologies to gather "visceral" data (data concerning the feeling elicited by objective sensibility) marks a massive expansion in the scope of the superjective dimension of subjectivity, the subjectivity of worldly sensibility. For in the very activity of gathering such visceral data, twenty-first-century media literally create a whole new domain of sensibility.

This capacity of computational data to be, at one and the same time, both means of access to sensibility *and* sensibility itself—or, in Whitehead's terms, both objective sensibility eliciting subjective feeling *and* subjective feeling itself—furnishes yet another concrete form of support for my central claim for access to the data of sensibility (CADS). Computational data is exemplary on this score because of its dual, simultaneous operationality as production of *and* access to data. Such dual operationality, as I have already noted, also characterizes twenty-first-century media in their specificity, as forms of media that, though continuous in many ways with earlier media, are distinct on account of their capacity to perform the revelation of the mediated character of sensibility. More precisely, the data propagation of sensibility involves a coincidence of technical access to data of sensibility and the production of new sensibility: in the case of computation, that is, the act of accessing data of sensibility is itself a form of sensibility. Thus, with every operation to access extant sensibility (the settled world), new sensibility is necessarily generated; and with this technically mediated doubling of sensibility, a model of process is set into place that can explain both how worldly sensibility is self-propagating and how its propagation necessarily involves the operation of delimited processes of superjective creativity.

Twenty-First-Century Media, or Quantitative Sensibility

To further specify the singularity of the contemporary techno-experiential paradigm, let us now explore the convergence at its core: the convergence of a certain becoming sensible of the world and the advent of third-stage, so-called ubiquitous computation. As I see it, these two processes are technogenetically coupled in the sense that the technical expansion of the scope of sensibility—the dissemination of microsensors into the environment—

allows unprecedented human access to a worldly sensibility that has re-mained latent, or at least largely inaccessible and imperceptible to humans, up to this point. At the same time, precisely on account of their technogenetic coupling, these two processes inform a fundamental shift in the function of media, or, more precisely, in the relationship of media with human experience. Because of the direct access to worldly sensibility that today's microcomputational technologies afford, we are now in a position to recognize that sensibility need no longer be channeled through higher-order modes of human experience—sense perception, consciousness, attention, awareness, and so forth—in order to have experiential impact. In this sense, the technical invention and proliferation of microsensors confirms—and crucially expands—Whitehead's insights regarding the limitations of perception. With their direct coupling to microtemporal worldly sensibilities, today's microsensors open a "wide bandwidth" contact between worldly sensibility and the host of bodily and environmental processes that constitute our dynamic embodiment.

With this development, we can speak of a veritable shift in the ecology of experience, and also, in the function of media: just as consciousness has ceded its privilege to a technically distributed sensory system, with the net result a massive expansion in the sensibility of experience, so too does media shed its human focus, its correlation with lived experience, in order to assume a far broader operational scope. To some extent, this shift in the function of media can be correlated with the advent of a new platform: unlike the media forms central to the twentieth century, especially phonography and cinematography, whose operationality was dominated by recording, storage, and transmission, today's media function as a kind of general platform for immediate, action-facilitating interconnection with and feedback from the environment. This shift directly reflects media's transformation into a ubiquitous and utterly indispensable element of daily life: in the form of today's digital devices and "smart" chips, not to mention social media and the Internet, media have achieved a *condition of transparent ubiquity* without historical precedent. While media devices continue to store and disseminate information, and to do so with more speed, efficiency, flexibility, and compactness than ever before, this function is today massively if inconspicuously overshadowed by a veritable "existential" potentiality of media: to alter the very sensible basis of our experience, or, in a more Whiteheadian vein, to impact the *total* situation in which our experience is implicated.

To conceptualize this new and expanded role of media, we need only consider the shifting economy between active and passive capacities of our digital devices and the smart chips and sensors that are increasingly populating the contemporary lifeworld. While smart phones and movement sensors, to cite two important examples, have as a "primary" function, in the former case, to allow us to make calls, send text messages, access our e-mail and the Internet, organize our schedules, and so forth, and in the latter, to register data about bodies and objects crossing their sensory thresholds, such "active" uses obscure the more powerful "passive" capacities of these technologies to register massive amounts of behavioral and environmental data without any active involvement, decision to initiate, or even awareness on our part. Critics of contemporary media have begun to take stock of this shift; for Dana Cuff and her colleagues, for example, mobile phones have a significance far in excess of their narrowly communicational functions: they "are passive sensors that can silently and continuously collect, exchange and process information."[33]

With this massive upsurge in passive sensing—to my mind, the truly revolutionary aspect of twenty-first-century media—we literally live in a new world, a world characterized by a vastly expanded and deterritorialized sensorium. For the first time in our history and (very likely) in the history of the universe, we find our long-standing and up to now well-nigh unquestionable privilege as the world's most complex sensing agents challenged, if not overthrown, by the massively replicable and ubiquitously propagating technical capacity for sensing introduced by our smart devices and technologies. Taken individually, these devices and technologies are of course vastly less complex—by many orders of magnitude—than human bodyminds; cumulatively, however, and with their capacity to operate almost entirely without interruption and across a vast range of scales, they have already begun to dwarf us in their ability to gather and generate sensory data. More importantly, their rather abrupt appearance and massive dissemination make it impossible for us to continue to overlook the deep complicity between the quantitative and the sensory; in this respect, they attest to the irreducible subjectivity of technical mediations of sensibility including the gathering of *"objective" numerical data* about our own behavior and about the world.

In the wake of this startling conclusion, we can properly appreciate the new vocation of media to mediate something other than—something more than—lived (human) experience. For it is no longer the case that media (primarily) mediate *our* senses; rather, they mediate—if "mediate" is still the proper term—sensibility itself, and they do so in the overwhelming majority of instances *prior to any engagement "we" might have through and at the level of our sense organs*. It is important that we see clearly how and why this generalized operation of sense mediation cuts across and suspends any false divide between the human and the world: the production of sub-macroscopic or sub-organismic sensibility occurs in relation to processes that belong (as components) to what, at higher levels of organization, are human "societies" in Whitehead's sense (e.g., the human body) just as much as it does in relation to processes that do not ultimately participate in such organization. In this respect, the elemental technical production of sensibility occurs prior to any meaningful (and necessarily derivative) division between human sensation and worldly sensibility.

This elemental dimension of the technical mediation of sensibility poses a difficult and unprecedented challenge: namely, how to take stock of media's impact on sensibility when this impact occurs both *within* an environmental surround that indifferently encompasses human and worldly sensibility and also, predominately, at scales that are *undetectable* to macroscopic or perceptual sensation. To access this impact, we must move beyond the limits of our object-centered *and* our body-centered models of media experience by pursuing a radically environmental approach, the first principle of which is that every sensory event implicates a "total situation" that vastly exceeds what it explicitly captures.

The point here is not so much that our object-centered and body-centered models are wrong, but that they are limited in scope and, in a crucial sense, structurally after the fact: they constitute higher-order "syntheses" of more "primordial," impersonal or prepersonal experience, syntheses that are temporally subsequent to—and to greater or lesser degrees reductive of—the elemental impact of media on sensation. What twenty-first-century media make inescapably clear (though this may, in fact, turn out to have been true of media more broadly) is that media do not only impact our experience atomistically, as our prosthetic theories would seem to suggest. On the contrary, media impact experience diffusely and by way of the causal efficacy that they wield within the domain of worldly sensibility. In this sense, media have a far greater scope of operation at the level of cosmological sensibility than they do in the form of the various perceptual mediations that our media history privileges. Indeed, this broader operation on sensibility creates the causal lineages that bring about these more narrow, perceptual mediations, and in this sense media can be said to impact our perceptual experience not simply in the form of prostheses, but by way of its more primordial mediation of the domain of sensibility itself. Even the most tightly coupled perceptual correlation between a mindbody and a media object—say, a human being watching a television program—arises out of a more primordial and diverse, multi-scaled and composite cosmo-logic of sensibility.

Superjectal Subjectivity

Let me return now to the expanded scope of superjective subjectivity that comes with computational mining of "visceral" data. If I am right that computational data marks the identity of subjective and objective aspects associated with the feeling of data, it has the effect of moving the relevant subjective element *deeper* into the domain of worldly sensibility, or, to put it another way, of rendering that subjective element more thoroughly super-jective.

In this respect, computational data-mining actualizes the reversal in priority between the subject and superject that lies at the heart of Jones's study. In concert with her interpretation, but in a way that gets at the specificity of the material processes involved, computational data-mining reveals the fundamental limitation imposed by Whitehead when he designates the "subject" half of the "subject-superject" as the pole that is at issue in the concrescence of actual entities. We can already catch a glimpse of this limitation in the definition Whitehead offers of the "subject-superject" in *Process and Reality*: "It is fundamental to the metaphysical doctrine of the philosophy of organism, that the notion of an actual entity as the unchanging subject of change is completely abandoned. An actual entity is at once the subject experiencing and the superject of its experiences. It is subject-superject, and neither half of this description can for a moment be lost sight of. The term 'subject' will be mostly employed when the actual entity is considered in respect to its own real internal constitution. But 'subject' is always to be construed as an abbreviation of 'subject-superject.'"[34]

Despite what he says here, Whitehead's injunction to treat the "subject" as a shorthand for "subject-superject" is effectively undermined by his own desire to correlate the "subject" pole of the subject-superject with the process of concrescence. More than a simple result of Whitehead's preference for the term subject in the text of *Process and Reality*, this terminological tension is the symptom of a deeper theoretical tension in Whitehead's conceptualization of the actual entity. The picture Whitehead sketches of the inseparability of subject and superject is belied by the duality of the actual entity as he himself introduces it and as both Jones and Nobo develop it more fully. Specifically, the distinction between actuality-in-attainment and attained actuality drives a logical, if not also a temporal, wedge between the subject and the superject, at least so long as the former is identified with concrescence (attainment) and the latter with objectification (the attained). On this picture, that is, an actuality must first be attained in order to be an attained actuality, must first become a subject in order to be a superject.

In order to resolve this theoretical tension, let me suggest a different understanding of the "subject-superject" that refrains from dividing it according to the two dimensions of the actual entity. Inspired by Jones, I want to suggest that it is the "subject" that is an abstraction here, or, more precisely that what Whitehead delimits as the subject is a specification of a broader and encompassing operation of the superject or, perhaps better (since less agent centered), of superjective subjectivity. What Whitehead calls the "subject" is simply one facet of a larger subjectivity. If this is the case, then the metaphysical or speculative model that describes the genesis of actualities-in-attainment does not and cannot function as a ground or foundation for the experiential power of attained actualities. On the contrary, it can only be an abstraction from the experiential exercise of superjective subjectivity, a speculative account necessary to explain how superjective subjectivity arises or why there is such subjectivity at all in the universe. This, it should be clear, is the culmination of the claim for inversion—the point at which concrescence is fundamentally refunctionalized as a component in a process originating in and generative of environmental or superjective subjectivity.

As Judith Jones has convincingly demonstrated, Whitehead does not himself fully take stock of the importance of the modification involved when actualities trade in their "subjective immediacy" for "objectivity." To do so requires breaking with the orthodoxy that identifies subjective agency exclusively with the speculative concrescence of actual entities, and extending it to their operation, as components in societies of all sorts, scales, and complexities, in the domain of experience. Rather than being reserved for the operation of the "subject" narrowly delimited, subjectivity must be extended to the entire relational field—the "total relationality"—created by the operation of superjects.

In her analysis, as we have already had occasion to appreciate, Jones rehabilitates the category of "intensity" as a form of subjective agency that correlates with the actual entity *following its objectification*, which is to say, with the superjective dimension of subjectivity and the domain of experience. Focusing on the "intensity" that ensues from the objectification of actual entities rather than the more narrow process of their "atomic" constitution, Jones develops a concept of "ecstatic individuality" which "asserts that an entity exists with the ontological status of *its* subjectivity *to* some degree in every subject in which it comes to have influence (and, to an extent, in every subject from which it originally derived)."[35] In effect, ecstatic individuality accords primary subjective agency to the superject (or better, to superjective subjectivity), understood as the broad operation of intensity across all the (attained) actual entities that it impacts or may go on to impact.[36]

To appreciate the full force of this revisionary reading, we must add to Jones's analysis a further specification of what exactly happens in the passage—of actual entities into time—that generates intensity. What happens is nothing less than a dispersal of the ontological power of the actual into the manifold of prehensions liberated from their narrow subjective unity (their subordination to the subjective aim of a given actual entity in concrescence) and set forth—as superjectal, environmental micro-agencies—into the world. In the next chapter, we will correlate this dispersal of the power of the actual with potential—with what Whitehead specifies as "real potentiality" or, as I will put it, the potentiality of the actual. In this respect, superjective subjectivity enjoys a distinct privilege that correlates with a liberation of prehensions from their exclusive contribution to a subjective unity. In this scenario, prehensions themselves must be said to undergo objectification, at the moment that the subjective force holding them together either perishes (as Whitehead, following Locke, concludes) or, as Jones's reading would have it, gets redirected to the settled world and to future concrescences and experiential events. Following their objectification, prehensions belong to what Debaise, following Whitehead, describes as the disjunctive continuity; as disjunct parts of this continuity, they constitute elemental micro-agents potentially operative in macroscale actualities, which is to say, in experiential societies of all orders of complexity.

Debaise's account of the disjunctive plurality serves to reinforce this understanding of prehensions as liberated from the subjective aims of the concrescences that brought them into being: "The first level of existence, this first dimension of being as Whitehead calls it," writes Debaise, "is that of the pure disjunction *of already existent actual entities*, which is to say, the 'disjunctive plurality.' We have seen that this latter forms the 'real potentiality' of individuation, that on the basis of which a new entity can be constituted by prehensions. It is not a question here of groupings, of assemblages, or even of totalities, but of a true disjunction, a 'being-disjunct' of entities."[37] Debaise's willingness to attribute "real potentiality" to the disjunctive plurality attests to the operation of some kind—or at least to *the necessity for* some kind—of more elementary relationality than what obtains between discrete or atomic attained actualities.

Debaise broaches such an elementary relationality when he describes the superject. What he describes, effectively, is a relationality *of the disjunctive plurality itself*:

> A thinking of the emergence of the subject from the basis of feelings is possible but only on the condition of delinking the relation of identification between "subject" and "subjectum" and of attributing to it another dimension, which does not contradict it but which limits its field of application. It is a matter of returning once again to the Latin source for the notion of the subject. Because the subject can also be thought as "*superjacio*," a word that one can translate with a series of expressions, like "to throw over," "to launch to-

ward," but also "to exceed" or "to go beyond." It is no longer a subject adequate to itself, self-sufficient, but a *tensed or stretched* subject [*sujet tendu*], in excess over its momentary identity. It is no longer identical to itself but projected beyond its factual existence. Whitehead translates it by the word "superject." It is this concept of the "superject" that can explain why a subject can exist without needing to be defined in categories of completeness, of sufficiency, and of independence. *There is subjectivity in the disjunctive plurality* to the extent that entities emerge, that they tend to a plenitude that does not define them in actuality. Thus, one could say that "feelings" are animated by virtual subjectivities that orient them toward something which, however, does not yet exist as such.[38]

With this claim, we are brought back to our above argument concerning the subjective power of the datum for experience. Following Debaise's specification, we can appreciate the crucial fact that this *subjective power has the mode of potentiality*. In this respect, Debaise's account of "subjectivity in the disjunctive plurality" differs from the account of nexus (and ultimately, of society) that Whitehead develops. For whereas the nexus, as the most minimal form of being-together of several entities, is a relation or ordering of the disjunctive plurality in terms of groupings of discrete actual entities (more precisely, attained actualities), what is at issue in the feelings that are animated by virtual subjectivities is a yet more primitive relationality. It is a relationality that occurs prior to and in independence from any concrete *relata*, a relationality of potentiality *as* potentiality. Put another way, whereas nexuses (and societies) are fully actualized relationalities (they are compositions of actualities), the subjectivity in the disjunctive plurality— what I above called superjective subjectivity—is more like a potentiality for relationality. It creates not actual relations but a field of potential relationality within which such relations can arise.

Understood in this way, superjective subjectivity introduces a different genealogy of potentiality from the genealogy Whitehead develops and, in the process, serves to raise the stature of potentiality within his philosophy. Far from deriving real potentiality from a purported "pure potentiality" that informs the universe in abstraction from its actualizations,[39] as Whitehead alleges it does, superjective subjectivity creates real potentiality through its concrete operation: potentiality is a power of and for the future that is created from, and operates within, the actual. It demarcates the radical openness of the present toward the future, or, alternatively, the excess of the actual in relation to itself. It is for this reason that superjective subjectivity compels us to ask a simple question: do actual entities following their satisfaction and entry into the world as attained actualities *continue to prehend*? And if so, what takes the place of the subjective aim that held them together during their concrescence?; in virtue of what do the prehensions constituting an actual entity continue to be bound together following attainment?

One possible answer, which could cite the authority of Whitehead's text, would be that every actuality (qua set of prehensions) itself becomes a prehension following its concrescence, and that actual entities therefore enter the world not as a network of relationalities, but as singular relations, as simple (inert) data. Another, more interesting, answer, which could cite the authority of Jones's interpretation, would be that attained actualities retain some of the subjective power they enjoyed during concrescence and it is this power that unifies their component prehensions. Yet another, in my opinion even more interesting answer, is that attained actualities lose the unity that held their prehensions together during concrescence. As a result, these liberated prehensions come to constitute more finely grained elements of the settled world that are resolutely *not* inert data waiting, in the state of passive potentiality, for revivification in new concrescences, but rather what I would call "data potentiality," by which I mean a potentiality at once more primitive and more "virtual"—but also more "powerful"—than the inert potential characteristic of discrete attained actualities on the orthodox Whiteheadian account.

Data Potentiality

This primordial operation of potentiality, data potentiality, corresponds precisely to what Debaise alludes to when he says (in the passage cited above) that "*there is subjectivity in the disjunctive plurality.*" Debaise's characterization of this potential or superjective subjectivity makes clear that it operates both prior to the emergence of any subjective unification or concrescence and in the mode of anticipation: "Feelings," Debaise notes "are animated by virtual subjectivities that orient them toward something that however *does not yet exist as such.*" On the basis of this important description, we can see that Debaise's conception of subjectivity in the disjunctive plurality denotes a primordial potentiality that is oriented toward the future, that isn't bound to any specific subject or subjective process, but that nonetheless operates wholly within the domain of the actual. As such, Debaise's characterization helps us appreciate something crucial about Whitehead's concept of "real potentiality" that will have important reverberations for other equally crucial Whiteheadian notions, including the status of eternal objects and the origin of creativity in the universe. As contrasted with "pure potentiality," a potentiality completely divorced from any actualization, real potentiality designates a potentiality that is wholly and completely relative to the actual: real potentiality is the potentiality accruing to the settled world at any given moment of its process and, as such, coincides with what I have termed superjective subjectivity. In this respect, as I shall argue at length in chapter 4, real potentiality not only constitutes a mode of sub-jective power, but it constitutes one that is markedly distinct from the more narrowly "subject-centered" power characteristic of concrescence: as the subjective power proper to attained actualities and to the superject, real po-tentiality names the potentiality of the actual, the potentiality that *belongs* to the actual but that is not relative to any given actuality-in-attainment.

To understand how this potentiality operates and to grasp its signifi-cance, we will need to return to the question of environmental power; spe-cifically, we will need to correlate Whitehead's insight into the role of the environment (or the "total situation") with the primordiality and the privi-lege his philosophy accords the objective datum and the dative phase. To put this in yet more precise terms, we will need to grasp how the *impact* of the objective datum—which we might well liken to primordial impres-sionality on a radicalized phenomenological account like that of Michel Henry[40]—provides a crucial and non-substitutable source of novelty that contributes to the creativity of the universe. If we recall how all subjective processes begin from some reaction to an objective or superjected datum— from a "feeling" or "sense-reception" *that comes before the constitution of a subject proper*—we can readily discern a correlation with a radical-ized phenomenology: at stake in both cases is the operation of "heteroaf-fection," a source of impressionality that has *not yet been* integrated into a delimited, unified and unifying, subjective process. Following through on this argument, and the homology with phenomenology, will require us to challenge the received understanding of creativity as a function unique to concrescence, and it will also validate the jettisoning of God and of eternal objects qua eternal, which on Whitehead's account remain necessary to pro-vide an impetus for the subjective aim that comes to the fore in every process of concrescence. Yet before turning to these tasks, let me briefly dwell on what precisely data potentiality—as a contemporary instantiation of real potentiality—adds to the mix here.

Because data potentiality combines the production of objective data with unprecedented possibilities for accessing that data, it allows for an excavation, or data-mining, of the settled world—which (to stick with the homology with phenomenology) is also a self-revelation or manifestation of that world—at extremely fine-grained scales. The data that constitutes the settled world today are in reality data-inscriptions of prehensions, or, more precisely, they are liberated prehensions (relationalities) that become inde-

pendently addressable through the extremely fine-grained data-gathering capacities of contemporary microcomputational sensors. What is particularly
interesting about the phenomenological structure of this manifestation qua
data-mining is its probabilistic structure: what data-mining reveals is not
the event of world manifestation but rather the potentiality for future events
of manifestation. As I put it earlier, data potentiality names the potentiality
of the actual—a potentiality already *within* the actual—that, however, is
not already relative to a particular actualization or actuality-in-attainment.

If, in the end, this probabilistic structure will prove to be common to all
events of manifestation, that is because of the function of the "total situation" in the genesis of any and every event. Here we need simply recall
Whitehead's extraordinary thought that every actual entity prehends the entirety of the settled world to which it will add itself. Having now "corrected"
or "reformed" Whitehead's orthodox account by restoring the superjective
power to attained actualities, we can readily conceive how this principle of
holism or total relationality should impact our understanding of superjectal or environmental agency. Specifically, it is in the dative phase (primal
impressionality) that the total relationality of the world is manifested as the
source of potentiality for an incipient concrescence; if the operation of that
concrescence is to prehend the total relationality, both positively and negatively, the dative phase preceding the initial conformal phase of prehension
is the moment when the potentiality manifests as potentiality, and hence as
a heteroaffective source of novelty that will, to be sure, play a role within the
concrescence to come, but that also plays a role as an autonomous environmental or superjectal agency shaping the production of the total situation
in which the concrescence will take place and will be added to the settled
world.

I shall return to this probabilistic structure below via its homology with
the structure of quantum mechanics. For the moment, let me simply make
two points about data potentiality. First, if it differs from the real potentiality operative in prior technical epochs, it does so only by degree: data potentiality gives more access to the "total relationality" informing an event,
and thus makes it more calculable than ever before, but it does not—and
cannot—give total access to that relationality. By way of its contrast with
prior configurations of real potentiality, data potentiality reveals something
crucial about Whitehead's thought of total relationality: namely, that it is a
speculative element, a regulative ideal that has acquired ontological force.
In this regard, there is perfect analogy between the speculative dimension of
data potentiality and the speculative side of actual entities: total relationality is what must be the case for experience to be what it is—it *is* the real
structure of the solidarity of the universe—but remains in principle beyond

the access of any possible experience, whether in fact (as in the first case) or in principle (as in the second). And second, precisely because it reveals the speculative foundation of total relationality, data potentiality both establishes the impossibility of any attempt to close the loop on prediction—to install a closed causal system yielding perfect predictability—and points to the double source of indeterminacy or novelty in the cosmos, namely, the compatibility of total relationality with incipient, bootstrapping selectivity that produces contrasts and intensity. Because of the ban on experiential access to the speculative, which operates here on two fronts—both metaphysically and experientially, in relation to subjective concrescence *and* to total objective relationality—the actual workings of this encounter must in every concrete instance ultimately remain a mystery.

However, as a necessarily partial excavation or mining of the objective relationality informing any given dative phase, data potentiality allows us access to a larger share of the total situation than we have ever had and, by doing so, helps us to grasp the fact that novelty or creativity is a result not simply of concrescence, as Whitehead and his commentators allege, but rather of the broader, cosmological encounter between total objective relationality and bootstrapping concrescence. As we will see below in chapter 4, the key to this operation of data potentiality is the capacity to access data of worldly sensibility that, with the expansion of computation into the environment, has become a dimension of the production of such sensibility. More precisely, today's microcomputational sensors and data-recording capacities introduce the possibility to access worldly sensibility as objective data independently of the subjective processes to which they give rise at all levels from human consciousness on down. In this corroboration of the claim for access to the data of sensibility, these forms of twenty-first-century media give us partial—which is to say, imperfectly predictive—access to the dative phase of subjective processes that are in themselves futural, yet-to-come.

Worldly Sensibility

Before returning to the environmental dimension of this probabilistic agency of data potentiality, let me explore one further corrective to Whitehead's account of creativity that it requires. In addition to reserving creativity for the process of concrescence of new actualities-in-attainment, Whitehead correlates creativity with the agency of God and the ingression of eternal objects into concrescence. The rationale for Whitehead's position here concerns the problem, already mentioned above, of accounting for the source of novelty in the initial aims of actual entities (actualities-in-attainment). Not only is God required to furnish this source—specifically, by giving a subjective direction to the conformal phase of an incipient concrescence—but the means by which God does so is through the ingression of eternal objects into the prehensions characteristic of the conformal phase and of those phases subsequent to it. Roughly equivalent to universals (or Platonic ideas, which form their model), eternal objects are timeless and purely potential elements of experience that, precisely because of these qualities, furnish a source of indetermination, and thus of novelty, to concrescences.

Resurrecting an argument made by John Dewey in his 1936 American Philosophical Association address on Whitehead's philosophy, several contemporary philosophers have begun to question both the necessity for and the coherence of this rationale. In his address, Dewey attempted to persuade Whitehead to abandon his "morphological" notion of eternal objects in favor of a "genetic-functional" interpretation. As Dewey saw it, and I would wholly concur, Whitehead's doctrine of eternal objects requires philosophically unacceptable commitments: specifically, it requires a commitment to the prior existence of eternal objects before they are actualized through ingression into concrescence, as well as a commitment to the existence of (an admittedly philosophical) God, who alone can mediate such a prior existence and process of actualization.

In his return to this argument, philosopher George Allan specifies the contribution of Dewey's counter-position. First, the agency for the mediation of (no-longer-eternal) "eternal" objects would pass from God to experience itself. Not only would qualitative determinations eschew their timelessness for an anchoring in the flux of actual occasions of experience—which is equivalent to saying, as I have said above, that they would shed their pure potentiality for a "originarily" real potentiality always anchored in the superjectal settled world—but they would come to participate in actual experience not through God's mediation but *because they are immanent to the real potentiality informing all encounters with objective data (the dative phase)*. As Allan puts it, "Experimental intelligence would replace God as the agency needed to relate actual existences and eternal objects."[41] Second, on Dewey's account, the source for creativity shifts from God and pure potentiality to the real potentiality of the settled world of objectified or superjected data: "The past that determines the fundamental conditions, the shape and content, of the world we inhabit, is also a source of possibilities that allow us to alter these conditions in novel and incrementally fundamental ways."[42] Here Allan puts his finger on that creative power of the total relationality informing any and every event that data potentiality, qua real potentiality, makes increasingly accessible to our experience.

Endorsing Allan's rehabilitation of Dewey's argument, philosophers

William Hamrick and Jan Van der Veken take the further step of correlating the resulting situation with Merleau-Ponty's conception of the flesh in terms of the ontological structures of visibility and tangibility.[43] What this correlation brings to the fore is the complex sensory texture from which novelty arises: the sensibility at issue in real potentiality, and in data potentiality specifically, is a sensibility that yields subject-directed experiences only across an *écart* and, as such, is a sensibility that operates not simply by being channeled through the subjective processes it catalyzes but also, crucially, as an irreducibly environmental or worldly sensibility.

In their account of how Whitehead's philosophy supports Merleau-Ponty's final ontology, Hamrick and Van der Veken gesture toward this conclusion without however fully appreciating its most radical consequences: "Whitehead's concept of interdependent actual entities that overlap through feelings of causal efficacy clearly underwrites Merleau-Ponty's belief that 'sensibility only makes the world appear because it is already on the side of the world' (citing Renaud Barbaras). Every actual occasion becomes on the basis of its sensibility to its past actual world that it incorporates within it. . . . In other words, there is a fundamental belongingness of each actual occasion to the world from which it springs and which it continues to create. . . . Every occasion of experience possesses the visible because it is possessed by it."[44] If Hamrick and Van der Veken fail to fully grasp the power of sensibility, it is on account of their adherence to the orthodox picture that subordinates the settled world—or worldly sensibility—to the genesis of new actual entities. Once we correct this picture, we can appreciate that sensibility exercises its power not simply via its "incorporation" into new actual entities, but as catalyst for and environmental sculptor of the concrescences that yield new actualities.

What is ultimately at stake in such a liberation of the power of sensibility is the question of how concrescence and transition correlate with one another. As we have seen, the orthodox picture views concrescence (the genesis of new actualities) as the be-all and end-all of Whitehead's metaphysics and sole source of creativity in the universe; on this picture, transition (the objectification of an actual entity and its addition to the settled world) operates simply and solely to supply inert, passive source material for future concrescences. On the corrected account, by contrast, concrescence is literally sparked into becoming by an encounter with objective data of the settled world (the dative phase), and comes into being *alongside*, and indeed *as a component in*, the ongoing sensibility of the objective world.

This dispute concerning the source for creativity in Whitehead once again introduces the claim for inversion (CIF) that has structured my reading of Whiteheadian process philosophy. Here we can see how the claim for inversion (the claim that concrescence is not the privileged operation of Whitehead's philosophy but merely a vehicle for the propagation of worldly sensibility) ultimately dissolves (or aims toward the dissolution of) the very separability and autonomy of concrescence itself. Once it gets folded into a broader account of process focused on explaining the ongoing propagation of worldly sensibility, concrescence loses its "absolutist" speculative reserve. Nothing less is at stake in discussions, sparked by Jones and developed by me above, concerning the viability of phenomenalizing Whitehead's speculative account of process. This issue receives further development in Jones's criticism of Nobo's account of the oscillation between concrescence and transition. While affirming Nobo's important effort to restore the significance of transition in Whitehead's thought, Jones argues that transition must be salvaged not as a counterpart to a separate operation of concrescence, but in a way that embeds the co-functioning of the two operations (concrescence and transition) *within a single, overarching process*:

> Nobo emphasizes that the initial phase of what Whitehead calls "mere reception" of feeling coming from diverse existents in the world of the entity, bereft of real final causality, is the scene of "transition" as the process whereby the world is objectified for the nascent occasion. This is the time of pure efficient causality, with intensive concerns of the telic demands of process coming to play only with the supercessionally later addition of aesthetically supplemental feeling by conceptual valuations, and so on. According to Nobo, the prehensions in the various stages require different understandings. The first are merely objectifications, the imposed natures of previous things in the (not-quite-present-yet) new subject. With supplementation, they acquire immediacies of feeling typical of what is commonly understood as concrescent experience. I am, however, determined to highlight the fact that Whitehead does not in any existentially important sense distinguish the "realities" felt in the one phase as opposed to the other. In other words, *the external existence felt in the prehension of mere objectification, mere reception, remains in the prehensions of those existences as clothed by the intensive considerations of subjectivity.*[45]

If I am right to understand Jones's claim here as an affirmation of a worldly sensibility that continues to exercise its power from the outside even as a concrescence undergoes its becoming, the resulting picture of process is one in which creativity cannot be limited to the activity of concrescence, in large part because concrescence itself cannot be quarantined from worldly sensibility. On this picture, every concrescence is both *caused by* and *cause of* transition: every concrescence is produced by a transition and every concrescence will go on to generate a subsequent transition (that will, in turn, go on to begin the cycle anew). The resulting oscillation, if it is one, is not an oscillation between two distinct processes, but rather between two poles of a single process. Once again, we here reach the culminating point of the claim for inversion.

I shall return to Hamrick and Van der Veken's suggestive coupling of Whitehead and Merleau-Ponty below in chapter 4 where I explore the vibratory continuum of media. For the moment, the point to bear in mind from our above discussion concerns the sensible basis of this single process of creativity. Dewey's correction of Whitehead is important because it confirms our position that creativity simply *is* the power of worldly sensibility: as rehearsed by Allan, Dewey's critique of eternal objects uncovers the fundamentally sensory nature of the power—and the creativity—of the settled, superjected world, which operates to catalyze and to accompany concrescence and, ultimately, to intensify itself by the continual addition of new superjects. Indeed, we might go so far as to say that worldly sensibility, insofar as it constitutes the concrete texture of real potentiality, itself takes the place of the pure potentiality of eternal objects and the God necessary for their ingression into experience. When we return to it below, this last claim will prove crucial for understanding how Whitehead's ontology can help us resituate media within worldly sensibility.

One particularly crucial element of this corrected picture of creativity is the role it accords the settled world as "a source of possibilities" that allow for novel change to that very world. As I have been trying to emphasize here, this picture requires that the settled world—worldly sensibility—exert its impact not solely as a passive source and by being channeled through delimited subjective processes, but as an environmental agency enveloping such processes but exceeding them in its total scope. One key consequence of this corrected account—and one that makes common cause with my conceptualization of non-perceptual sensibility—concerns temporal relationality: both because the environmental agency continues to shape the concrescence from the outside and because the concrescence itself doesn't have a duration proper to it, worldly sensibility—the superjectal power of the settled world—*must envelope concrescence within its duration.* Far from being the immediate past—the nonsensuous perception—of a somehow (magically) "present" concrescence, the settled world (worldly sensibility) is in fact *the temporal envelope of concrescence.* And its ongoing duration is, as it were, continually renewed, with a new surge in intensity, following the satisfaction of each new concrescence and its addition into the disjunctive plurality. Here we begin to get a proper picture of how concrescence belongs to a larger account of worldly sensibility, following the claim for inversion (CFI): catalyzed by objective data of sensibility, concrescences are the very means by which the world continually re-creates itself. In this sense, concrescences are less the source than the vehicle of worldly creativity: they are the means by which the extensive continuum constantly replenishes its superjective power.

Quantum Decoherence and Environmental Selection

Another crucial element of the corrected picture of creativity concerns the role of constraint exercised by the settled world, and specifically the elimination of nonviable possibilities that occur *prior to the advent of a subjective aim within a concrescence.* This exercise of constraint has everything to do with the concept and operation of real potentiality that forms the correlate of worldly sensibility, and its exploration will help to clarify why real potentiality can be said to belong wholly within the domain of the actual. Understood as an environmental agency, this exercise of constraint evinces certain marked affinities to the operation of quantum decoherence within quantum theory, and the latter in turn—as a fruitful concretization of the broader homologies linking Whitehead's organic philosophy to quantum mechanics—provides a helpful resource for conceptualizing real potentiality as environmental agency.

What the operation of quantum decoherence will help explain, in particular, is the way that Whitehead's extraordinary thought of the total implication of the universe in the operation of all actualities entails a radical decoupling of selectivity from any delimited subjective process. Selection, for decoherence as well as for Whitehead, is a radically environmental operation. In this respect, it might be useful to contrast Whitehead's vision of the "total situation"—the prehending of the entirety of worldly sensibility— with Bergson's understanding of perception as the selection by a "center of indetermination" of certain images from a universe of images.[46] The crux of this contrast boils down to the basic distinction between prehension and selection: whereas selection operates exclusively in relation to, indeed, *as the operation of,* a delimited agency, prehension includes *what it negatively rejects* as well as what it positively selects. This means that the operation of prehension *cannot be identified with the perspective and internal operations of any delimited subjective agency,* and indeed, with any *center* whatsoever. And it also means that the total agency involved in prehension, from the proto-subjective reception of the objective datum to the moment concrescence attains satisfaction, cuts across any possible subject-object division.

Prehension is primary in relation to the entities it calls forth into becoming. Like Simondon's concept of "transduction" (a relation in which the relationality is primary to the terms related), prehension primarily involves what we must call "originarily environmental" elements that only gradually acquire more specificity as they come to relate to an emergent subjective aim. As I shall suggest in my conclusion, this distinction between prehension and selectivity, between a radical environmental perspective and a (minimally) subjective one, ultimately calls on us to dispense with any philosophical gesture that would separate out a delimited "subject" from the flux of worldly sensibility. This imperative not only forbids any phenomenological commitment to a transcendent subject (no matter how minimal the transcendence in question), but it also puts into question a purportedly anti-phenomenological position, like that of Bergson, which positions subjectivity as a "diminution" or "subtraction" from the material flux of the universe of images. In both cases, what remains problematic is the privileging of a delimited subjective process as the frame of reference for the environment's relevance, when what is required is a more even balance between environmental sensibility and the delimited forms of subjective agency that emerge from it and operate within its scope.

Quantum mechanics furnishes a useful means for us to grasp exactly how such an "originarily environmental" agency might operate. Regardless of whether Whitehead directly modeled his metaphysics of actuality on quantum theory,[47] there are striking similarities between the two bodies of work that can help us appreciate the radical strangeness of the environmental perspective at issue in his philosophy. Indeed, as I see it, there simply is no better illustration of the radical environmental perspective ultimately at issue in Whitehead's work than the phenomenon of quantum decoherence: just as Whitehead stresses the exclusion, via the form of relationality he dubs negative prehension, of elements of real potentiality not directly relevant to a given concrescence, so too does quantum decoherence place emphasis on the environmental elimination of inconsistent conditions for actualization that occurs prior to actualization but that nonetheless must be held to belong wholly within the actual.[48] A consideration of the parallels at issue here will not only help to clarify the radically ahuman (which, however, is not to say inhuman) perspective of superjective becoming but will also allow us to introduce a needed clarification-correction to Whitehead's metaphysics that will form the very core of our discussion of the sensible origins of potentiality in chapter 4. This clarification-correction follows directly on the heels of the reversal to which I, following Jones's lead, have submitted the two forms of actuality in Whitehead, for if superjects hold a privilege in Whitehead's philosophy, as I have suggested they must, then potentiality must likewise hold a privilege over actuality (as the source for new actualities-in-attainment) without ceasing to be the product of—and thus part of—actuality (of past actualities having achieved attainment).

In *Quantum Mechanics and the Philosophy of Alfred North Whitehead*, Michael Epperson makes the parallels at issue here explicit in a way that manages to emphasize the crucial role of the environment to which they point:

> The superposition of this multiplicity of minimally intensive potential outcome states thus evolves, via the negative selection process of decoherence and transmutation, to become a reduced matrix of probability-valuated, mutually exclusive and exhaustive outcome states or propositional transmutations, each valuation reflective of a significant *intensity*. Thus, in both the decoherence-based interpretations of quantum mechanics and Whiteheadian metaphysics, the *intensive valuation* of the subjective forms of alternative outcome states is closely linked with the logically prior, spatiotemporally *extensive coordination* of the related data, such that the vast majority of these data are coordinated and qualified as "environmental" to the subject occasion or system of occasions.[49]

Epperson goes on to indicate how such environmental selection correlates with an operation of *quantitative* intensity that emanates from the "physical pole." With this correlation, we discover nothing less than the *mechanism* for the agency of the superject:

> qualitative intensity is in part dependent upon a *quantitative intensity* which originates in coordinate division, operative in the primary stage/physical pole. The relationship between *coordinate extension* and *quantitative intensity* in the physical pole is evinced by the relationship between (i) the *number* of actualities extensively coordinated as "environmental" to the subject system, and (ii) the process of decoherence and transmutation in the supplementary stage. For apart from a sufficient number of actualities extensively coordinated as "environmental" to the subject system, there cannot be a sufficient number of negative prehensions to drive the process of decoherence/transmutation.[50]

The reference to quantum decoherence helps to elucidate the correlation between negative selection and the objectified data that, on the orthodox Whiteheadian picture, forms the inert background for subsequent subjective concrescences of new actual entities. What decoherence shows, specifically, is that *even before such concrescences can begin*, there has to have taken place a sorting and selective elimination of a practically infinite range of incompatible possibilities ("the pure state density matrix"), of physically possible or coherent but contradictory probabilities for new actualizations. In a striking confirmation of the role we have accorded the proto-subjective or superjective reception of objective data, this *pre-subjective* or *pre-concrescent* operation of physical selection correlates with the dative phase of physical prehension that, for Jorge Nobo, precedes and produces an ensuing subjective aim. What this correlation will ultimately unearth is a coupling of real potentiality and the dative origin of actualities that fore-grounds the central role played by intensity in the "originarily environmental" operation of prehension.

In more concrete terms, decoherence helps to clarify the operation of a selection of viable potentialities that occurs prior to future actualizations (the genesis of new actual entities). Specifically, decoherence functions to reduce the "pure state density matrix" to a "reduced density matrix" that contains only the decoherent or noncontradictory probabilities (weighted possibilities) that may lead to subsequent actualizations. Insofar as it cor-relates with "real potentiality," the reduced density matrix names the pos-sibilities that are consistent with the settled world as it is and has been up to the point of the actualization in question. In the absence of such a passage to real potentiality or the reduced density matrix, "potential outcome states would . . . remain locked in a coherent superposition; the data would persist as uncoordinated bare multiplicity, each datum superposed with all others, with some aspects of the superposition mutually consistent and others mu-tually contradictory."[51]

With this account of negative selection as the preparatory selection that yields a coherent matrix of potential outcome states ("real potentiality"), decoherence foregrounds the environmental or superjective role of prehen-sions. Rather than viewing these, as Whitehead and the majority of his in-terpreters do, as attached to discrete concrescences of individual "atomic" actual entities, decoherence engages prehensions as always already environ-mental. With its focus on noncontradictory sets of probabilities (weighted possibilities), rather than discrete actual entities or quantum actualization events, decoherence thus diverges from Whitehead in reckoning the con-creteness of the actual. This divergence is important because it points to how potentiality can be inscribed into the domain of actuality. Thus, in con-trast to Whitehead's orthodox account, decoherence does not focus exclu-sively on actualities-in-attainment as the only real things and as the logical or speculative ground out of which all experience is composed, but rather *includes never-to-be-actualized potentialities as elements—indeed, as what we might call "environmental" elements—in actually occurring quantum actualizations.* These never-to-be-actualized potentialities that are nonetheless part of the actual are like negative prehensions in the sense that they are "included" through exclusion. And yet they differ in an important way from negative prehensions, for unlike these latter, which on Whitehead's account remain a function of and are entirely dependent on a concrete concrescence of an actual entity, "excluded" quantum decoherent probabilities possess a certain autonomy and are *in themselves* actual. In this sense, consideration of quantum decoherence can lend an environmental dimension to Whitehead's speculative account of the genesis of actual entities. Indeed, when Epperson concludes that "the qualitative intensity operative in the mental pole cannot evolve apart from the extensive quantitative intensity that originates in the physical pole,"[52] he manages to foreground nothing less than the irreducible environmental dimension of the physical within the operation of decoherence.

Decoherence thus furnishes a logical structure that is fully consistent with the account of superjective subjectivity I have sought to develop here. Such an account seeks to lend agency to discrete prehensions independently of the concrete concrescences in which they participate. Accordingly, it cannot simply be the case that prehensions acquire "objective" or "superjective" agency only after their "objectification," that is, once the concrescences that unified them around a concrete actual entity have terminated. The overlapping of a massive number of prehensions that is necessarily at issue in any experiential situation means that we cannot hope to purify them of their relational promiscuity, of the excess "power" they bear within themselves. And this complex situation is only made more complex when we introduce the manifold layers of societies of divergent scales, composed ultimately of gatherings of prehensions, that are involved in any experience no matter how "elementary" it may be. Ultimately, it is this excess power possessed by prehensions *in themselves*—a power not reducible to their (prior) participation in subjective concrescences—that informs the radical environmental agency of the superject.

Technically Distributed Societies

This excess power of prehensions in themselves—the power of the superject—is precisely what informs the specificity of twenty-first-century media and their potential to massively expand our sensory contact with the world. To appreciate the significance of this correlation, let us return to the issue of quantification and the role of data in this environmental superjective agency. To our above account of the deep compatibility of sensation and quantification, we can now add a reflection on the environmental agency operated by the quantified sensations produced by our digital devices—devices that, as we saw earlier, are capable of registering bodily and environmental data *as environmental to our more narrowly cognitive and affective agency.* In relation to this latter, narrow-bandwidth agency, such data may well be properly classified as "nonsensuous," following Whitehead's lead, but—and this is the crucial point—*there is no compelling reason for evaluating this data through the restricted scope of human cognitive operationality.* Indeed, in the various and often overwhelmingly complex forms of distributed agency into which we humans are today integrated or (as I prefer to say) *implicated,* this data is *explicitly not capable* of being channeled through human understanding, at least not in the operational "present" of causal efficacy.[53]

Pentland's work with the sociometer—to return to our point of departure—perfectly captures the temporal specificity of data's availability to experience. The goal of Pentland's research is simple: to use digital technologies to access, gather, and analyze what he conceives of as a behavioral form of communication—an "unconscious channel of communication between people"—that dates back to our protohuman ancestry. Because it is categorically distinct from conscious, verbal language, because it forms "a separate communication network that powerfully influences our behavior," this unconscious channel of communication explicitly does not impact conscious experience by preconditioning the communication proper to it; quite to the contrary, it directly impacts behavior as an experiential agency *wholly distinct* from sense perception and consciousness.

Precisely because of the temporal disjunction between registration of behavioral data and the scope of conscious awareness, the former—understood as the registration of data concerning causal efficacy—cannot be directly channeled through human understanding. It quite literally comes before such understanding and, as such, can impact it—prior to its eventual effect on conscious experience—in the mode of prediction. That explains why Pentland specifies that his research concerns the *futural* impact of this unconscious channel of communication: the technology of reality mining "uses sensor data to extract subtle patterns that," Pentland emphasizes, "*predict future human behavior.*"[54]

Pentland himself uses the techniques of reality mining for quite specific ends: his applications have focused on business negotiations where decisions are often acutely sensitive to timing and are made on the basis of fine nuances in informational flow. One striking outcome of his research has been to demonstrate that decisions on such issues as raises and promotions are typically made during the initial phases of interactions and are, in large part, based on the primal body language informing them. Thus, the payoff of Pentland's approach lies in its potential to lay bare how negotiations really happen, to provide "digital insight," as I put it earlier, into a process that remains phenomenologically inscrutable to humans. Given that many of the important nuances in such negotiations occur outside of awareness, executives can be coached to control and modulate their body language and timing in order to exert the maximal impact on their interlocutors in experience to come. They are coached to implement behaviors—behaviors of which they can have no direct or real-time awareness—in pursuance of a predictively likely future outcome.

In attempting to deploy this model of data sensing and access to human behavior as such, we must pinpoint and generalize the theoretical principle it instantiates: the temporal disjunction between conscious processing and unconscious behavioral expression (so-called honest signaling).[55] As Pentland explains, it is precisely because these distinct experiential modes occur at vastly different temporal scales that they can be said to constitute "really quite separate channels of communication."[56] Contextualized in relation to my concern with sub-perceptual sensibility, what Pentland's distinction underscores is nothing less than the *operational specificity* of unconscious microtemporal behavior. As he sees it, and I would wholeheartedly concur, it is not simply that microtemporal behaviors underlie and inform higher-order, conscious experience, but rather, that the microtemporal has an irreducible degree of operational autonomy: specifically, it exerts a direct impact on behavior that *does not require, and does not depend on*, a future integration into awareness.

The efficacy of the sociometer—like that of the smart phone, the Internet, and other contemporary technologies capable of "passive sensing"— emerges directly from this autonomy and the more general temporal disjunction it institutes between the two channels of experience. Because it captures data registering the subtle nuances of nonverbal signaling (and other microtemporal events of causal efficacy), the sociometer is able to record and analyze information about our evolutionarily acquired behavioral mode of interaction that is not available to our awareness, that does not take place in the time frame of conscious experience. The sociometer thus bypasses consciousness entirely in order to engage directly a domain of experience that occurs at properly imperceptible timescales. And, when coupled with a feedback interface to form a "social prosthesis," the sociometer furnishes opportunities for intervening in this imperceptible domain: specifically, it allows a "fine-grain perceptual task"—a task that occurs over milliseconds and is "impossible to do through conscious processing"—to be tweaked by the retrospective intervention of conscious attention.

Still, for all its attention to the temporal materialities at issue here, Pentland's work remains focused squarely on the retrospective or post-operational evaluation of past experience for the purpose of outcome improvement in the future. In concert with the entire Western philosophical tradition, it continues to accord a certain privilege to consciousness: conscious reflection is both the vehicle for evaluation of unconscious, temporal data and the agent that can act in the wake of what it reveals. In this respect, the sociometer functions in a manner analogous to "symbolic reference" in Whitehead's philosophy. Just as symbolic reference "is 'chiefly' to be conceived . . . in regard to the elucidation of causal efficacy by the 'intervention of percepta' that occur in presentational immediacy,"[57] the "social prosthesis" at issue in Pentland's work is constituted through the elucidation in consciousness of the data gathered by the sociometer. In focusing exclusively on how the data gathered by the sociometer can be retrospectively elucidated by consciousness and thus come to inform future behavior through consciously directed changes in embodied signaling, Pentland fails to consider the possibility that technologies such as the sociometer—technologies that open "direct," nonconscious access to our embodied causal behavior—can potentially be interfaced with human beings in "technically-distributed cognitive or perceptual systems" in which they *need not be consciously evaluated at all* in order to exert their impact.

Such a possibility—of cognitive or perceptual expansion through nonconscious *operational* interface with the causal data of one's own behavior—is particularly relevant in our contemporary moment when we are increasingly called upon to act in time frames, or at least in relation to time frames, that are not synchronous with, that are far faster than, the time of consciousness. This situation finds its well-nigh science fictional allegorization in the above discussed scenario of intelligence agents hooked up to EEG machines that directly parse their firing patterns to gather data about targets of interest in satellite images. If the human brain is fully instrumentalized in this scenario, it is precisely because it is being mined for its value as data concerning causal efficacy; not only does the data extraction take place in a time frame far more microscalar than the time of conscious awareness and of all possibilities for self-reporting, but it does so in a way that no longer includes—*that can no longer include*—such awareness and self-reporting in the cognitive loop.

This picture of consciousness having become a drag on sensibility and cognition, notwithstanding its strongly negative vibe, speaks directly to our current situation—to our ever-increasing dependence on objectal agents of sensibility; for this very reason, it furnishes us the opportunity to rethink the role of consciousness, and the economy between consciousness and sensibility, in the world of twenty-first-century media. Indeed, the above explored limitation on what our understanding can operationally encompass is precisely the point of technical distribution, what makes it useful and perhaps even necessary: technical distribution enhances our cognitive, perceptual, and sensory agency precisely because it puts us into functional cooperation with cognitive, perceptual, and sensory agents that not only follow protocols of their own, but that, most crucially, operate environmentally—independently of and autonomously from our directly experienced, conscious agency.

What today's technical sensors facilitate, then, is a revelation of the general sensibility underlying or informing all actions or compositions within the world. From this perspective, what is "environmental" and what is "subjective" in the narrow sense ultimately remain entirely relative to the designation of a perspective, with the only caveat being that all evaluations happen from some perspective or other. On this account, the operation of the technical sensors—sensors that, from the perspective of our subjectivity, form a vast and complex environmental fringe—constitute a crucial element in the rhythmic compositional dance that *is* our multi-scaled, disparate agency in the world. In participating in this dance, moreover, their operation, their sensing, is in no way "nonsensuous" (or, more precisely, is only nonsensuous from the perspective of our narrowly construed subjectivity). Rather, they, like every other "organism" in the universe, are sensuous in their operational present, and the contribution they make to larger agential compositions (societies, and specifically, technically distributed societies) is precisely the contribution of this operationally present sensibility. To narrow this sensibility to what can be perceived by some particular society or other is, I hope it is now clear, to impose unacceptable constraints on that sensibility *as well as* on the society in question: it is to impose the specific temporality of a certain society (or, more precisely, of the self-reference of that society to its own unified operationality) on the disparate, multiple, and heterogeneous temporalities that overlap with one another, that produce sensory experiential confounds by coinciding with one another, and that are necessarily at issue in the expanded, superjectal operationality of any and every society.

4 Sensibility

The philosophy of organism is the inversion of Kant's philosophy. *The Critique of Pure Reason* describes the process by which subjective data pass into the appearance of an objective world. The philosophy of organism seeks to describe how objective data provides intensity in the subjective satisfaction. For Kant, the world emerges from the subject; for the philosophy of organism, the subject emerges from the world—a "superject" rather than a "subject."

The philosophy of organism aspires to construct a critique of pure feeling, in the philosophical position in which Kant put his *Critique of Pure Reason* . . . . Thus in the organic philosophy Kant's "Transcendental Aesthetic" becomes a distorted fragment of what should have been his main topic. The datum includes its own interconnections, and the first stage of the process of feeling is the reception into the responsive conformity of feeling whereby the datum, which is mere potentiality, becomes the individualized basis for a complex unity of realization.

Feelings are the "real" components of actual entities.

Alfred North Whitehead, *Process and Reality*

The Precognitive Vocation of Twenty-First-Century Media

"With ever-expanding volumes of stored data to draw upon, and new ways of connecting people, machines and forces—distributing and sharing their functions in a larger field of human and machinic agency—relationships are uncovered among widely disparate kinds of information. Through a technologically enhanced perception, a mathematical seeing, patterns come into view that previously could not be seen by the naked eye, in ways that augment, or occlude, traditional observational expertise and human intuition."[1] With this account of the contemporary technical distribution of precognitive sensibility, media artist and theorist Jordan Crandall perfectly captures both the vastly expanded sensory field within which contemporary events occur and the fine-tuning of our access to the separate, most often microtemporal performances, both machinic and human, that contribute to their occurrence.

What is distinctive about Crandall's account, and what motivates my invocation of it here, is his readiness to associate the technical transformations that lie at the heart of twenty-first-century media—and that witness a full-scale installation of a calculative ontology of prediction—with distinct modifications in the structure of experience. He rightly discerns that technological media are in no sense simply and solely technical, but are indelibly and inseparably technical, performative, affective, experiential, and sensory. Among Crandall's various characterizations of the broad correlations between media technicity and experience, most fundamental for my purposes is his keen insight into the decoupling of effect and awareness—of causal efficacy and presentational immediacy—that characterizes the operationality of contemporary media. What accounts for the singularity of contemporary media is not simply that their data-driven operations bypass the scope of consciousness, but that they impact experience *on a much broader basis than through consciousness*. They literally seep into the texture of experience, forming a background, a peripheral "calculative ambience," that indirectly flavors any and all resulting events or phenomena:

> As tracking becomes elevated into a condition, dissolving into behavior, sensation and all manner of embodied social practices in the data-intensive, analytics-driven spaces of megacities, the "*sense* of continual access to information" that arises out of the connectivity and interoperability among all kinds of data-enhanced actors (Thrift 2008: 92–9) is not necessarily grounded in a *direct* access. It is not simply a matter of whether one has a direct connection to this data-intensive surround, since it increasingly constitutes a defining horizon against which the phenomena of the megacity are understood—a calculative ambience that imposes its distinction, categories and ways of being onto all facets of urban life—as it acts as a cognitive, ontological, and experiential supplement for the simplest forms of ordinary routine.[2]

With his appreciation for the supplementarity of twenty-first-century media's experiential impact, and for the curious logic whereby what is supplementary becomes more fundamental than what is supplements (in this case, consciousness), Crandall's analysis directly addresses the experiential paradigm at issue here. In particular, it helps us to appreciate how the data-intensive, analytics-driven media surround operative in the contemporary urban environment operates not by affording direct, *cognitive* access to information, but rather by creating a tacit atmosphere of sensibility for action and capacities for data-gathering and analysis that open possibilities for *precognitive* shaping of—and capture of information about—our actions or likely tendencies for action.

Crandall's analysis underscores the close ties linking the experiential paradigm of twenty-first-century media to an increasingly sophisticated and ubiquitous technical capacity for gathering data concerning aspects of experience that are not directly accessible to us qua individual agents, that we simply cannot experience through consciousness and perceptual awareness. In this sense, twenty-first-century media are characterized first and foremost by the capacity for capturing information that directly concerns our behavior and tendencies but to which we ourselves lack any *direct* access. This fundamental separation of data-gathering from experience forms the basis for what I shall theorize, with Crandall and others, as the *precognitive* vocation of twenty-first-century media. This vocation, in turn, stems from the tendency of twenty-first-century media to target the infrastructural or causally efficacious elements informing future behavior with the aim of reliably predicting such behavior *before it actually happens.*

The precognitive vocation of twenty-first-century media is deeply imbricated within the operation of global capital. With the advent of network capitalism, the extraction of surplus value that is a generic feature of capitalism has increasingly come to focus on the value of data, as it were, "automatically" gathered from traces left by our living activity. A broad range of theorists, including Maurizio Lazzarato, Tiziana Terranova, and Franco "Bifo" Berardi, have reflected on how forms of immaterial labor have, with the acceleration of Internet culture, transformed into free labor: the production of content that, in a closed yet infinitely expanding spiral, serves as lure for further Internet traffic, and with it the production of more value.

Post-Autonomist philosopher Matteo Pasquinelli, writing about Google's PageRank algorithm, invokes the term "network surplus value" to distinguish this shift in value production:

> If the biopolitical dimension of Google is widely debated . . . , what is missing is a bioeconomic analysis to explain how Google extracts value from our life and transforms the common intellect into network value and wealth. Besides true concerns, there is an abuse of a

Foucauldian paradigm that highlights only one side of the problem, as Google's power is not given as a metaphysical being but it is originated from its technological platform and business model. . . . The metaphor of the Panopticon must be reversed: Google is not simply an apparatus of dataveillance from above but an apparatus of value production from below. Specifically, Google produces and accumulates value through the PageRank algorithm and by rendering the collective knowledge into a proprietary scale of values—this is the core question. The political economy of Google starts from the political economy of PageRank.[3]

The crucial aspect of this example of network value is its automaticity: precisely because they contribute, because they cannot but contribute to the system of knowledge owned by Google, Internet queries using the search engine *automatically* produce surplus value. Itself an operation of twenty-first-century media, network surplus value transforms data about human behavior that is not accessible to human awareness into surplus value, which is expropriated from human users by the data industries like Google that, in the form of PageRank, have implemented technical circuits for automatizing the generation of surplus value.

The subterranean operation of such surplus value extraction explains why geographer Nigel Thrift can claim that contemporary capitalism operates first and foremost by exploiting its marginal advantage in manipulating this sub-perceptual data:

> What is new about the current conjuncture is the way in which capitalism is attempting to use the huge reservoir of non-cognitive processes, of *forethought*, for its own industrial ends in a much more open-ended way. . . . More recently, much thought has been given to understanding forethought as not just a substrate but as a vital performative element of situations, one which cannot only produce its own intelligibilities but which can be trained to produce ideas. . . . Now the intention is to read and exploit signs of invention by regarding the body as a mine of potentiality and to generate and harness unpredictable interactions as a source of value.[4]

Thrift's account of contemporary data capitalism foregrounds the temporal dimension of its operation: if capitalist institutions have succeeded in exploiting the precognitive processes of bodily life that generate "forethought," they have done so precisely because they have found ways to access these processes *in their own "operational" time frames*. Today's culture industries can tap the bodily processes leading to "foresight"—the domain of Whitehead's causal efficacy—because they are able, with the help of microcomputational sensors, to access the sensory output of these pro-cesses *independently of the normal embodied circuits* that, via some kind of emergence, yield forethought as a bodily feeling, as affective anticipation. It is as if microcomputational sensors literally wrested these processes from their natural embodied context and made them independently operable and accessible.

What *independent access* in this case affords is a capacity to manipulate "forethought" as a technical variable, and crucially, to exploit its value in time frames that are far closer to the operational time frame of the precog-nitive embodied processes than to the operational time frame of whatever cognitive output—"forethought" in its proper sense—emerges when they are processed by the body. To the extent that the time frames at issue here are smaller than those of bodily emergence, and are smaller—by an order of magnitude—than the time frames of time-consciousness, this operation is one that simply bypasses consciousness altogether, and that is literally premised upon such bypassing of consciousness.

We must, accordingly, ask what becomes of consciousness and of per-ceptual awareness in the wake of the industrial conquest of forethought. Is consciousness simply left in the dust by the technical developments facili-tating such an industrial conquest? Or must we rather find ways to rede-scribe the basic operation and function of consciousness for a new technico-experiential reality? And can we ultimately move beyond the task of tracking the temporal disjunction between data operationality and consciousness that empowers contemporary capitalist institutions in order to gain access to and deploy the troves of sub-perceptual data made available by twenty-first-century media for the end of our own experiential intensification?

Because it grasps the correlation between data-intensive media and ex-perience in its full potentiality, a theorization of twenty-first-century media like the one I have been developing here *rounds out the picture that capital-ist institutions would like to truncate*. Theorization of twenty-first-century media shows that the sway exercised by contemporary capitalist institutions is a function of their capacity to control the time of experience to exploit this time as a source for surplus value. This fact makes twenty-first-century media a crucial site for political struggle over control of time itself in our world today. To challenge the contemporary exploitation of the time of at-tention by capital, we will need to contest the temporal problematic at its core. For this reason, it is crucial to point out that contemporary capital-ist industries are able to bypass consciousness—and thus to control indi-vidual behavior—precisely (*and solely*) because of their capacity to exploit the massive acceleration in the operationality of culture caused by massive-scale data-gathering and predictive analysis. These industries benefit from the maintenance of the crucial temporal gap at the heart of experience: the gap between the operationality of media and the subsequent advent of consciousness.

We can get a sense for the temporal structure at issue here by comparing it with the microtemporal gap separating neuronal events from consciousness as neuroscientists like Benjamin Libet and Antonio Damasio understand it. In both cases, consciousness arises with a constitutive delay in relation to its causal efficacy. In the case of the brain, this delay is materialized in Libet's famous "missing half-second," the temporal gap between brain activation and awareness. In the case of twenty-first-century media, and its operation to supplement human experience, the delay is materialized outside the brain, in the temporal gap between data-gathering of the operational present of sensibility and the subsequent experience of this data by consciousness. Thus, where neuroscience questions the agency of consciousness, asking ultimately whether we have free will at all if consciousness is limited to the function of ratifying what has already been decided, twenty-first-century media effectively repress consciousness by rendering it an emergence generated through the feeding-forward of technically gathered data concerning antecedent microtemporal events.

Despite their rough functional parallelism, a crucial factor differentiates the latter, technical delay from the former, neuronal delay—namely, its radical exteriority. The information captured by microsensors is accessed and fed-forward into consciousness not as the material basis for an emergent mental state but, quite literally, *as an intrusion from the outside*. As such, it does far more than simply support emergent mental contents; indeed, it captures a far larger swathe of the causal efficacy supporting the behavior that underpins such emergent states, including much that simply cannot find its way into consciousness via any organization or assembly of neurons. In this way, the data gathered by technical inscription makes available to consciousness aspects of its own causal background that it literally has no capacity to grasp directly, via embodied pathways, including neural ones. And it does this by way of a temporal dynamics that is characterized by a fundamental futural orientation: rather than marking the essential correlation of our present experience with what is now past—or, more precisely, just-past—as it does for the orthodox phenomenology of time-consciousness as well as for Whitehead's concept of "nonsensuous perception," this technically constituted delay reorients everything to *an almost present future moment* in which present, "operational" experience becomes—or more precisely, *will have become*—available to consciousness and to further operations, including conscious reflection and deliberation and, importantly, targeted modification of embodied behavior. This is the "feed-forward" structure of twenty-first-century consciousness.

Once again, Crandall seems to grasp the technico-experiential specificity of this temporal predicament: "As performatively constituted action-densities, inferred through calculative, predictive or pro-active operations, an actor integrates and internalizes, consolidates and extends within the organizational and ontological horizon of tracking—a field that harbors a fundamentally anticipatory orientation. Actors are characterized by what they *do*—instantiation is action—and *what they do* is inflected by *what they will do*. Actuality is conditioned by *tendency*. Embroiled in a calculative, mobilizing externality, agency pushes and is pulled outward, as if seeking to become the predisposition that it courts." By grasping how behavior resonates with its own futurity, Crandall foregrounds one essential element of the experiential paradigm introduced by twenty-first-century media: the displacement of consciousness's function from direct awareness of experience as it is happening to a supervisory role that can be exerted only indirectly over future experience to come. Within the complex and heterogeneous fields of contemporary sensibility, consciousness undergoes a fundamental retooling: as its direct perception of its own causal efficacy gives way to a much expanded and radically exterior technical inscription of this same causal efficacy that can only be fed-forward into, and thus indirectly experienced by, a future moment of consciousness, consciousness comes to learn *that it lags behind its own efficacy*. What consciousness experiences as its present—the present of sense perception—is, with respect to its efficacy, always already past. That, indeed, is precisely why Whitehead calls causal efficacy "nonsensuous perception": by the time consciousness has sense perception of its sensory experience or experience of sensibility, the causal basis for that perception will have become past, will be no longer sensuously present. Yet, as I suggested above in chapter 3, perception of causal efficacy can be considered to be nonsensuous *only because and only so long as* it is forced to be experienced exclusively through and from the standpoint of consciousness, *only because and only so long as* it cannot be experienced more directly and more diffusely, through alternate, technical channels.

Everything changes, however, when we factor in the capacity of technical microsensors to capture data concerning causal efficacy. For if I am right that today's microcomputational sensors operate as sensing agents, then the data they generate about our behavior constitutes a form of worldly sensibility that marks a sensory present—*the operational present of sensibility*—

which, we can now see, is categorically distinct from the present of consciousness. In light of the newfound capacity to directly register the present of sensory efficacy, and to feed this forward into conscious experience to come, the necessity to channel causal efficacy through the presentational immediacy of consciousness—the very necessity informing Whitehead's account of symbolic reference—would seem to dissolve. And what such a dissolution makes possible, we can now fully appreciate, is nothing short of a fundamental shift in the frame of reference that determines what counts as the sensory present: by directly capturing the sensory immediacy of causal efficacy in a form that is directly presentational (and that can be fed-forward into future consciousness as an alternate, artifactual source of presentified data concerning causal efficacy), today's computational microsensors inaugurate the operation of a new level of presencing—the direct presencing of causal efficacy itself (the operational present of sensibility)—that both supplements and, in a sense, *takes over* the long-standing role and privilege consciousness has historically exercised as agent of presencing. While consciousness continues to experience its own narrow bandwidth reality through sense perception, this experience is disjoined, both temporally and operationally, from the distinct presencing of causal efficacy—from *operational* presencing—where, increasingly, behavior gets operated on and controlled, independently of any conscious access or input.

To the extent that contemporary technologies for data-gathering and analytics allow for predictive precognition of what is to come, they manage to define a microtemporal, sub-perceptual—yet still sensory—present that impacts the future independently of any input from consciousness. As a consequence of this refining of the operationality of the present, consciousness must trade in its former monopoly over presentation for a supervisory role: since its presentational immediacy always comes too late in relation to the operational present, consciousness must give up its dream of coinciding with its own production and must redirect itself to predictively shaping its future behavior in light of the insight produced by the technical registration of the causal efficacy informing it. Rather than living the operational present of sensibility as presentational immediacy (i.e., through sense perception), consciousness can only live it as a deferred or after-the-fact experience of technically gathered sensory data concerning its own efficacy: consciousness literally encounters its own operationality only once this operationality has been fed-forward, as artifactual presentification or "machinic reference," into a new present of that consciousness, a "future present" when it can be known before its belated effects come to impact consciousness directly, as an embodied causal source for symbolic reference.

Reading Organs Directly

This experiential paradigm, with its feed-forward structure, doesn't simply impact the scope and operation of consciousness, but has significant effects on the way the body can be said to "mediate" worldly sensibility. In the place of Whitehead's concept of the body as a ground where causal efficacy can be "perceived" and correlated with sense perception proper, we need to introduce a more porous and less self-referential conception of embodiment, a conception that understands the body to be a society of microsensibilities themselves directly and atomically susceptible to technical capture.

In *Society of Anticipation*, French cultural critic and science fiction writer Eric Sadin correlates such a fluid, multi-scalar embodiment with the operation of automatization; for Sadin, the key point is that technical capture of embodied microsensibilities no longer serves to facilitate action or interactivity—no longer extends the body *as an integral agency*—but rather seeks to "read organs" themselves, with the aim of inducing compliance and reducing uncertainty:

> Our present moment bears witness to an *integral automatization* that excludes all subjective appreciation or process of dialogue in favor of a mute relationship determined by the prior recording of data and their verification via "anatomo-numerical" testing. At the heart of this automatization is a "reading" of organs no longer carried out with the goal of offering a more fluid relation to data, but in order to guarantee an optimization of social regulation . . . within a milieu technically capable of carrying out a *roboticized indexing* of people and of storing in the same movement the historical background of numerous actions and antecedents.[5]

Just as it did in the case of consciousness, this direct targeting of the organs chips away at the body's privilege: no longer positioned as default mediator and integrator of worldly microsensibilities, the body has itself become increasingly dependent on technical supplements for its capacity to sense, or, more precisely, for its capacity to encounter—to *em-body*—worldly sensibility in its operational present. Again, the crux of this transformation concerns its temporal dimension; like conscious perception, bodily perception always comes too late, for by the time the body can integrate sensibility into a coherent perceptual organization, the force and living presence of sensibility will have already faded into the past. This temporal gap is precisely what gets artifactualized through the "reading of organs" performed by today's microcomputational sensors: the capacity to gather microtemporal data concerning worldly sensibility—the capacity to record "at the level of the organ"—exposes the lag of the body in relation to sensibility and positions computational sensing in the place formerly occupied by the integrated body.

It is crucial that we pinpoint the source for this transformation. For it is not so much sensibility itself but rather our capacity to operate within the domain of sensibility that has changed. Indeed, experience has always included microsensibilities of all kinds, even if, up to now, these have been largely opaque in their operation, beyond our capacities for accessing them. What computational sensing and recording introduce is the capacity—indeed the power—to engage microsensibility directly, at a more granular level than what "resolves" upward on the matrix of the integrated body and ultimately that of conscious sense perception.

If we understand this power to involve a technical contamination of bodily sensing and of worldly sensibility, as I think we must, we cannot fail to appreciate the political and ethical stakes of the transformation at issue here: by opening our embodiment to recording at the level of the organ and by making embodiment susceptible to direct microtemporal manipulation of worldly sensibility, this technical contamination risks bypassing entirely any agency we might (still) have over how sensibility gets shaped into experience. For if our bodily tendencies and susceptibilities are read independently of bodily integration, and if they become manipulable separately from and prior to such integration, then any emergent bodily integration runs the risk of being thoroughly epiphenomenal, a purely passive expression of infra-empirical manipulation that will have already taken place at a level of experience to which it lacks all access.

It is this risk that critics like Sadin and Thrift grasp so clearly. The capitalizing of precognition that they invoke constitutes a short-circuiting of bodily integration in precisely this sense: today's data industries and experience engineers target the operational present of sensibility in order to manipulate—and thus to predetermine—the future emergence of bodily and conscious experience. Their strategy is to drive a wedge between the event of sensibility and any later event of bodily or of conscious experience such that the latter, despite being a direct or "natural" emergence from the former, no longer has any power to shape or to constrain how sensibility is experienced and the ends to which it is deployed. What is thereby effectuated is a decoupling of sensibility from perception that—precisely because it opens sensibility to manipulation *independently* of bodily integration—fundamentally interrupts their "natural" continuity. With this development, we encounter a veritable threat to free will of an entirely different order than what Libet postulates: for with technical access to the operational present of sensibility, experience can be manipulated *prior* to its resolution into bodily and perceptual effect, *prior* to its being felt through embodied affectivity and consciousness.

Once again, the singularity of this threat, and particularly of its political dimension, can be discerned by way of contrast to the neuroscientific paradox of the missing half second. If this paradox can be solved, as certain philosophers have argued it can, by insisting that the mental is the relevant level of selection for neuronal events,[6] no such solution is available where technical targeting of sensibility is concerned. In this case, sensibility is captured and manipulated by a technical agency that *simply has no common ground with* and that *operates at a more primordial level than* any perceptual or mental integrations that might subsequently emerge from it. Accordingly, if technical accessibility to sensibility poses a threat to free will, it is not due to some temporal gap *within* our "natural" cognitive-perceptual system, but rather to a gap *between this* system and a sensible field *that is radically exterior to it*. With their capacity to operate directly on that *exterior* sensible field *before* it affects our cognitive-perceptual system, today's data industries are able to predetermine our responses in ways that simply bypass our agency. By exploiting the temporal specificity of twenty-first-century media—the fact that technical access takes place faster than "natural" emergence—today's capitalist institutions are able to capture sensibility, including the sensibility most intimately bound to our behavior, at a far more granular level than, and long before, we can. As a result, we are effectively deprived of the ability to shape and constrain how our sensibility becomes our experience.

This situation exposes the technicity of the operational present of sensibility, the way in which the scope of the present depends on the degree of precision of technical access. From the perspective of today's extremely fine-grained parsing of sensibility, we can appreciate just how much the "thickness" of the operational present is a fundamentally technico-historical artifact. That is why, prior to the moment when it became possible to access microsensibility *in its operational present*, the living (or sensory) present effectively encompassed a much thicker section of time than it does today: simply put, it was a function of a much cruder temporalizer, human time-consciousness. In this respect, Husserl's descriptions of the present of time-consciousness furnish proof of sorts for this historically changing artifactuality: for Husserl, the time frame of the retentional-impressional-protentional complex—the time frame of the qualitative experience of presence by consciousness—simply was the most minimal time frame for sensibility that could be accessed through the phenomenological interface.[7] Even the experiments of nineteenth-century psychophysicists, which certainly did give access to time frames beneath the thick now of Husserlian time-consciousness, could not grasp microtemporal processes *in their operational present*, but only in retrospect. And the historical fact that the philosophical legacy of these experiments was largely derailed by twentieth-century phenomenology, beginning with Husserl's *epochē* of sensation, only serves to lend support to the point being made here: for if the higher-order syntheses promoted by the phenomenologists held sway, it was on account of the need for a notion of living presence, a determination of the scope of the present *as a function of human phenomenological experience.*[8]

This situation also makes clear just how much the isolation of the operational present of worldly sensibility is a political issue calling for specific tactics on the part of critics who would seek to contest the alleged irrelevance of properly human modes of experience. First among such tactics is the exposure of the artifactuality of the operational present: far from correlating with anything "natural," "essential," or "necessary" about human experience (and indeed, about experience as such) in the world today, the narrowing of the operational present must be shown to be nothing more than the purely contingent result of a convergence of technical capacity, economic interest, and collective or social desire. In contrast to the missing half second of the neuroscientists, which in some sense does mark a delay in the "natural" relay from sensibility to perception (though see below), the disjunction of sensibility from perception that is targeted for exploitation by today's data industries is thoroughly artifactual.

Not only does this mean that it *can* be contested, it also means that it fits seamlessly within the pharmacological history of technics that I have introduced above and that concretizes why technological change is always a political issue: in the very gesture of rendering embodied humans susceptible to "integral automatization" (Sadin), today's computational data-gathering capacities open up newfound possibilities for reconstituting viable forms—or consistencies—of embodied life that are more open to and inclusive of worldly sensibility. Expressed more affirmatively, there is nothing about the data-fication of sensibility that requires it to be separated from and used against the higher-order agencies of perception. Indeed, because the separation is contingent, we can imagine—and can create—circuits that make use of the specific affordances of technical data-gathering and analysis, not solely to anticipate our tendencies and susceptibilities for purposes of manipulation and exploitation, but also to inform us about these tendencies and susceptibilities and let us act on and in virtue of them. By re-embedding the operationality of worldly sensibility within a thicker sphere of presence, such larger circuits would bring the affordances of technical data-gathering to bear on phenomenal experience in ways that could enhance our capacities to shape our future experience.

Let me now try to correlate my above account of the specificity of twenty-first-century media with the isolation of the operational present of sensibility. Extending my earlier claim (in chapter 2) that media mediate nothing other than sensation, let me now suggest that media *directly modulate worldly sensibility itself*, and by so doing shape sensation *before the emergence of bodily self-perception and consciousness*. By operating on worldly sensibility prior to any impact they may subsequently have on human sense perception, media engage directly with the causal efficacy of the world's self-perpetuation in a way that shifts the locus of presencing from perception to sensibility: on such an understanding, causal efficacy would no longer be the just-past of a present of consciousness—whether this be understood via Whitehead or via Husserl—but would assume its proper role as itself the relevant *operational* present *in relation to which* bodily perception and consciousness are still-to-come, futural emergences. In light of this situation—a situation that, to emphasize it yet again, is only made possible by our technical access to the operational present of sensibility—it should be clear that media theory must change its "object," or rather, must trade in its focus on technical objects for a concern with the sensory processes to which technics gives access. Media theory, that is, must find ways to address the operational present of sensibility, for it is directly in the space of this microtemporal present—and not in the form of subsequently emergent bodily sensations or consciousness—that media primordially shape sensibility.

What this situation requires is a *politics of sensibility* that, in contrast to the politics of memory articulated by Bernard Stiegler, focuses on the power of the microtemporal present of sensibility to shape future experience.[9] As Sadin, Thrift, and others perfectly well understand, the contemporary capitalist targeting and isolation of the operational present of sensibility exposes the powerlessness of any media theory premised on the projection of a future through past achievements of perception and consciousness. For as soon as it becomes correlated with bodily self-perception and consciousness, media can only be about the past: from the standpoint of their respective presents, bodily self-perception and consciousness will have missed any opportunity whatsoever to intervene in the operational present of sensibility. For media to address the future—and for us to have any chance of "portending" a viable future—media must be engaged at the level of its modulating of sensibility, *as causal efficacy*, where it has the power to shape emergent experience to come, including the perceptual experience characteristic of the human.

Developing the *precognitive* paradigm of twenty-first-century media sketched here thus requires two distinct, yet ultimately co-implicated, tasks. First, we must recognize and seek to understand the primordial role of media in shaping worldly sensibility, and we must differentiate this role categorically from its (still prevalent) role in recording and storing human experience as the contents of bodily and conscious life; far from a mere instrument that makes the content of bodily and conscious experience accessible to perception, media impact sensibility directly, prior to, yet in anticipation of, the emergence of such experience. And, second, we must struggle against the capitalist capture of causal efficacy by foregrounding the artifactuality of the separation of the operational present of sensibility from higher-order experience; such struggle will serve to remind us that the problem is not so much the technical accessibility to data of causal efficacy but rather the way that such accessibility can be used—and currently *is* being used   in total isolation from, and in order to bypass entirely, any and all subsequent integrations at the level of bodily perception and consciousness.

That is why we must ultimately oppose the impoverished model of today's data industries not by rejecting the basis for its operation (direct technical accessibility to data of causal efficacy), but by grasping and exploiting the pharmacological complexity of this operation: as a crucial new source of information about worldly sensibility, including information about our own behavior, the directly accessible data of causal efficacy can be integrated into larger behavioral assemblages that will help us form our higher-order behavior by modulating how media shape the sensibility from which such behavior emerges. The pattern for such integration—which stands starkly opposed to the instrumental targeting of sensibility—is precisely the operation of feed-forward where data about our behavior is "artifactually" made available to a just-to-come, future moment of consciousness *before it will have bubbled up, as it were "naturally," into consciousness.* In this way, we acquire the capacity to access sensibility literally *before we can perceive it.*

A double pharmacological imperative arises from this *precognitive* paradigm. First, we must struggle against the narrowly instrumental capture of sensibility that puts our power to shape our own experience at risk. And second, we must do this not by turning our backs on the technologies permitting such capture but *precisely by using them in the name of a resolutely technical, yet in no way instrumental, experiential integration.* We must, that is, embrace the technically accessible *precognitive* dimension of sensibility as the very ground on which to politicize media, to modulate our own becoming by intervening in how media shape sensibility, and to grasp the techno-sensible complexity involved in whatever agency we do in fact wield over the shaping our own future experience.

Beyond "Reactive Corporeity"

In his characterization of what he calls the "body interface," Eric Sadin emphasizes how our contemporary moment introduces an "anthropological turning point" in our species-constitutive relation with technology:

> Historically, the relation to the technical object has been instituted and developed on the inside of a distance that aims to make good— "from the outside"—deficiencies of the body and to amplify its physical capacities; our period marks the end of this distance, to the benefit of a ever more closed-in proximity. A displacement of the conception relative to *technē* is *de facto* called for, the latter no longer being envisaged, following the Western philosophical tradition, as a palliative and "prosthetic" production, or again, in the more informed manner described and analyzed by Leroi-Gourhan, as a relation of dynamic intermixture between *instruments* and *corporeality*. *Technē* must from now on be understood as an *enveloping* of virtualities offered to the body, which constitutes the *fundamental anchor point* for present and future technological evolutions, and which induces an *automatized* and *fluid* relation to the milieu.[10]

Sadin goes on to characterize this automatized and fluid relation as one that gives rise to an "unheard of *reactive corporeality*" rooted in the sensory fluidity between body and milieu: "The contemporary anthropotechnic condition no longer refers to a common ensemble that is nevertheless deployed in a gap (*un écart*), but to a *principle of fusion* witnessing a recent sympathy that 'mutually makes body' and that henceforth jettisons all distance for a *sensory and automatized interaction* operating on just in time fluxes, on the interior of a new *bioelectronic unity*."[11]

With this characterization, Sadin foregrounds the necessity for reconceptualizing the model of technics that has been so forcefully advanced by Bernard Stiegler, in the wake of the paleontologist André Leroi-Gourhan. What Sadin makes clear is that we no longer confront the technical object as an exterior surrogate for consciousness or some other human faculty, but rather as part of a process that is far less differentiated and in which technics (data-gathering and analysis) operates directly on the sensibility underlying—and preceding—our corporeal reactivity and, ultimately, our conscious experience. To be even more precise: the "reactive corporeity" that Sadin theorizes engages contemporary technics—data-gathering, microcomputational sensing, predictive analytics—as a *"radical* exteriority" *within* the interiority of experience. The temporal gap at the heart of reactive corporeity differs from the temporal gap involved in emergent mental experience because it marks a radical divide between a cognitive-perceptual system and an *exterior* sensible field that is nonetheless part of what informs experience. Whereas the missing half second marks a constitutive delay within a homogenous process that occurs entirely in the brain, reactive corporeity entails a far more radical *technical* distribution of experience that moves outside the brain. This shift has important consequences for our understanding of how technics "contaminates" experience: for if technical processes impact sensibility before any higher-order emergence—and long before any differentiation of consciousness and technical object—we simply cannot treat technics exclusively or primarily as an exterior surrogate for consciousness, or, more generally, as an exteriorization of life by means other than life.[12]

Yet while Sadin clearly understands how this situation gives rise to a "precognitive orientation" rooted in our direct technical accessibility to data of causal efficacy, his impoverished conception of what this access affords (the reduction of the threat of chance) not only makes common cause with the imperative driving today's data industries (the imperative to create closed data loops) but also fails to recognize any potential for our compensatory contact with worldly sensibility to yield new experiences and intensities. This situation exposes the tension between the radicality of Sadin's analysis of the precognitive orientation and his limited resources for exploring its potential. For Sadin's decision to focus on *acts* rather than *tendencies* ultimately causes him to miss the truly radical promise of a *pre-agential* experience of worldly sensibility. As our discussion of Judith Jones's *Intensity* has made clear, this is precisely what Whitehead's notion of the superject affords, once it is radicalized to overcome his bias toward concrescence. For if the causal efficacy of worldly sensibility obtains *before* there is a sensing agent—if the genesis of intensity from contrasts *is*, as Jones argues, subjectivity *without* a perduring subject—then any approach that exclusively tracks acts rather than tendencies engages at a level that is already too organized and that consequentially risks missing the promise of sensibility's power.

That is why Sadin, at the very moment when he contrasts today's datacentric model of anticipatory evolution with natural selection, simply overlooks what is most promising about today's "anthropological turn": namely, how it puts us into recursive yet open-ended contact with a vastly expanded domain of microsensation. In this sense, the precognitive orientation facilitated by our direct technical access to worldly sensibility does not so much provide an alternate model for how humans evolve as it does a much expanded domain for appreciating how the consistency of our experience involves a complex overlay of multiple levels, an "operational overlap" that we could liken to William James's notion of a "consciousness of still wider scope" where human, animal, and vegetable consciousnesses come together without losing their operational specificity.[13] In this respect, if Sadin accurately grasps the link between the "continuous quantification of gestures" and a "precognitive orientation," his continued talk about "our autonomy" (even if some of it is "delegated to our processors") and his appeal to deterministic causality make clear that his interest centers on the tracking of acts and the capacity of such tracking to predict the future rather than the, to my mind, far more important opportunities thereby opened up to tap the more open-ended and more radical potentiality of tendencies. That is why Sadin's analysis compromises its own promise: it sacrifices whatever benefit might accrue from exposing our human condition to "other modalities of existence" in favor of predetermination, of "a 'possible avoidance or bypassing of chance'" rooted in "an *anticipative and roboticized evaluation* of acts . . . that will determine the course of our individual and collective destinies."[14]

The distinction between tracking acts and tracking tendencies foregrounds the crucial issue introduced by our direct technical access to worldly sensibility: the issue of how we should understand the "precognitive" dimension. Regarding this issue, our response is clear: we must resist the strict identification of the precognitive with the predictive capacity obtained through reduction of a worldly process to a closed circuit and, instead, affirm the de jure openness of worldly sensibility. Only in this way will we be able to conceptualize the precognitive *in a fully general manner*: as the partial inherence of the future *in the present*.

Because it is Whitehead's philosophy that furnishes the resources for such a conceptualization, making good on this imperative will require us to understand his account of real potentiality as nothing less than an ontology of the probabilistic potentiality informing contemporary operations of data-mining and predictive analytics. Specifically, with his account of the inherence of the future in the present, Whitehead furnishes an understanding of data as dynamically oriented toward the future. In this way, Whitehead is able to explain the power of prediction *as a general power*, one that lies at the heart of today's predictive industries *but that also informs the pharmacological flip side of the instrumental capitalization of real potentiality*. With such an account, Whitehead helps us appreciate how human agents and collectivities can use prediction as a means to benefit from technically facilitated access to data of causal efficacy that cannot be accessed through conscious awareness and sense perception. Whitehead's perspective reminds us that prediction is much more than a means of control wielded by today's data industries and that, in its full scope, prediction furnishes a crucial resource that could potentially allow human individuals and collectivities to feed data concerning the operational present of sensibility forward into future consciousness, and thereby, to make it relevant for future-oriented modulation of experience.

In characterizing this alternate deployment of prediction as the pharmacological flip side of instrumental capitalization of real potentiality, I aim to position it as a recompense for the enhanced control over behavior afforded by today's microcomputational sensing capabilities. But I also aim to recognize its dependence on the very same technical capacities that make such recompense desirable, if not indeed necessary. In this respect, we could say that prediction focalizes the challenges faced by contemporary media theory. For with the ubiquitous dissemination of probabilistic predictive technologies in our world comes a fundamental shift in the status of sensibility: rather than being directly experienced by embodied, sensing human beings, sensibility has increasingly come to require—and indeed, to *be experienced on the basis of*—mediation via microsensors and predictive analysis.

If I am right that contemporary data industries seek to target the operational present of sensibility independently of its inclusion within larger sensory-perceptual processes, we can readily discern the threat this shift poses to the power of sensibility. For what would happen if the exploitation of the operational present of sensibility began to occur in total independence from any return to the "slower" sensory-perceptual processes characteristic of human experience? Stripped of any and all means to experience sensibility—of any and all opportunity to feed data of sensibility forward into future consciousness—we would simply lose whatever pharmacological recompense twenty-first-century media could offer by way of increased contact with worldly sensibility. Far from functioning as a scare tactic or a flight into science fiction, this scenario—whose ultimate end point positions us as simple puppets of a predictive analytical system operating in complete autonomy from the domain of our sensory and conscious experience—should serve to catalyze consciousness-raising concerning the contemporary imperative to contest corporate control over the data of sensibility made accessible by twenty-first-century media. Indeed, to combat the hyperbolically dystopian scenario just sketched, we must develop alternate ways of accessing and utilizing the data of operational sensibility such that it can be reintegrated into larger processes of sensory-perceptual life. The point, to say it yet again, is not to refuse the technification of sensibility nor to bemoan our dependence on computational microsensors for access to it, but rather to embrace both in the service of a different outcome: the broadening of human experience to encompass a greater share of the microsensible domain.

It is precisely on this point that Whitehead proves invaluable: for with his account of the future's immanence in the present, Whitehead's general ontology of potentiality shows that there is a *surplus of sensibility* underlying any and every prediction and that, to purchase reliability, predictions cannot avoid closing off such potential sensibility. What this means, to put it another way, is that contemporary computational capacities to "read organs directly" generate far more data (data of sensibility) than can be used by—and contained within—any system of predictive analytics. It is precisely on the basis of this surplus of sensibility that we can benefit from the predictive technologies driving the twenty-first-century media revolution. Reclaiming this surplus of sensibility from today's data industries can and must constitute the main "positive" task of contemporary media theory: how, we must ask, can we access this data and deploy it for open-ended experimentation with the modulation of future experience?

Exploring this possibility will require us to develop an explicitly *nonanthropomorphic, nonrepresentational*, and *non-prosthetic* account of media that situates their operation at the infra-experiential level of worldly sensibility itself. Thus situated, media become a technique for the modulation of sensibility that can be used to engineer experience in the just-to-come future. Like prediction, media modulation operates on the operational present of sensibility, but there the similarities end: for whereas prediction narrows the scope of sensibility in order to assure maximum reliability, media modulation submits future experience to the potentialities—or propensities—of worldly sensibility in a radically open-ended manner.

Because of its embrace of indeterminacy, this engineering in the operational present for the just-to-come future resonates with Nigel Thrift's conception of worlding as the process of modulating experience by shaping "active spaces." Thrift specifically contrasts active spaces to bounded spaces of technological spectacle and to the technical objects inhabiting them; unlike the latter, active spaces provide "a means of harnessing and working with process in order to produce particular propensities: this continuous activity of strategic intervention might be called world*ing*, with the emphasis on the 'ing'. . . . The intention is not . . . to create fully-formed spaces. . . . Rather it is to add mediological detail which makes these spaces resonate *in ways which would not have otherwise occurred* so that they grow in desired directions. Not the creation of discrete worlds into which participants enter, then, but a continuous process of worlding."[15] In a similar way, any media modulation rooted in technically facilitated access to sensibility would attempt to influence the future on the basis of the full sensibility of the operational present—on the basis of the entirety of its "real potentiality," and not solely through a narrow, instrumental selection of that potentiality.

Before turning to the task of articulating a non-anthropomorphic theory of media, let us dwell a bit longer on Whitehead's crucial contribution to the effort to think through the complex pharmacological recompense that emerges on the basis of technical access to the operational present of sensibility. By way of what I have been calling his general ontology of potentiality, Whitehead is able to ground the inherence of the future in the present, to clarify how the anticipated future is *felt* in the present. It is crucial that we fully appreciate just how fundamentally this grounding and clarification differ from the method of predictive analytics: rather than forecasting the likelihood of future events on the basis of present and past data, Whitehead's account foregrounds both the relative stability of the universe from moment to moment and the emergence of the future—and specifically of novelty in the future—on the basis of the real potentiality of the settled world at each moment of its becoming. If the future is felt in the present, that is precisely because the future literally is (or will be) produced from out of the real potentiality—which is equally to say, on the basis of the superjectal intensity—of the present settled world. The key point is that the connection between future and present proceeds by way of efficacy—or, better, propensity—and not of prediction. The connection is real, or, more precisely, it is *actual without being actualized*, which means, as we shall see, that Whitehead's philosophy accords a certain priority to potentiality over actuality.

With this perhaps surprising claim (given Whitehead's repeated affirmation of the priority of the actual), we come back to the operation of superjective intensity that has proved so important for our understanding of Whitehead's philosophy, and that is clearly manifest in the description of the Eighth Category in *Process and Reality*:

> (viii) *The Category of Subjective Intensity.* The subjective aim, whereby there is origination of conceptual feeling, is at intensity of feeling (∂) in the immediate subject, and (ß) in the *relevant* future. This double aim—at the *immediate* present and the *relevant* future—is less divided than appears on the surface. For the determination of the *relevant* future, and the *anticipatory* feeling respecting provision for its grade of intensity, are elements affecting the immediate complex of feeling. The greater part of morality hinges on the determination of relevance in the future. The relevant future consists of those elements in the anticipated future *which are felt with effective intensity by the present subject by reason of the real potentiality for them to be derived from itself.*[16]

To understand the full force of this claim, and specifically its promise to open a fundamentally different perspective on prediction, let us recall how

Judith Jones radicalizes Whitehead's description of intensity with her claim that the subject referenced in its final line, and the subjective aim animating it, simply *is* the agency of the contrast yielding intensity. As Jones puts it: "The agency of contrast *is* the subject, the subject *is* the agency of contrast. To be a subject is to be a provoked instance of the agency of contrast, and that is all it is."[17] We can now appreciate this claim in its full significance. For what Jones's interpretation underscores is how the real potentiality of the future is already felt *as intensity in the present*—is felt, that is, *prior to its actualization and in its full force of potentiality*: this feeling of potentiality *for the future* generates—indeed, simply *is*—the subject.

For Jones, this conclusion is the strict entailment of Whitehead's concept of the vibratory character of actuality:

> The pattern involved in an intensive contrast is . . . the feeling of the dynamic presence of the (other) individuals felt into the unity of a subject's intensity. This is the only way to understand Whitehead's repeated assertion of the vibratory character of actuality. No vibratory character has only one cycle *qua that vibratory character*—to be a vibratory character is to be an intensive imposition on all subsequent process, and, on the other end, to have emerged from the enduring vibrations of other insistent agencies of contrast. *I see no other way of understanding why provision for future intensity is included in the category respecting "subjective" concrescence.*[18]

Jones's point here is absolutely crucial: subjectivity, insofar as it *is* the intensity produced by contrasts of settled data, simply *is* a distillation of real potentiality for the future that is felt in the present, and whose feeling in the present impacts the emergence of the future, and specifically of the genesis of novelty in the future from intensity experienced in the present. As such, subjectivity cannot be restrictively located in the present, but spans the transition *from present to future*: it places the future—as real potentiality, as the force of historically achieved potentiality—in the present. Superjective subjectivity quite literally *is* the power of potentiality acting in the present on behalf of the future.

For Whitehead (and for Jones), the future *is already in the present*, not simply as a statistical likelihood, however reliable, but because each new concrescence is catalyzed into becoming by the superjectal intensity or real potentiality—the *future agency*—of the universe that will be prehended in its entirety and that it will unify during its concrescence. And, if we accept Nobo's understanding of the fundamental role played by the dative phase (explored above in chapter 3), the lure of the settled world is even more powerful; indeed, what Nobo shows is that each new concrescence actually comes into being *as a passive reaction to the data of the settled world*, replete with its real potentiality for the future, real potentiality emanating *from the future*.

How does this ontological model of potentiality bear on our efforts to adapt media theory to the situation of twenty-first-century media or, perhaps more pointedly, to the mediation of the total situation? And specifically, what significance does it have for the pharmacological reclaiming of contemporary media's ever more impressive capacities to channel and to control the inherence of the future in the present?

Recorded Future

Consider the example of Recorded Future. Recorded Future is a small, Swedish intelligence company that sells a data-analytics service for predicting future events. Initially financed by small venture capital grants from the CIA and from Google, Recorded Future has developed algorithms that make predictions about future events entirely based on publicly available information, including news articles, financial reports, blogs, RSS feeds, Facebook posts, and tweets. Recorded Future has a client base that includes banks, government agencies, and hedge funds. What it offers is a technical platform designed to monitor the likelihood of future events or, as the company's press puts it, a "new tool that allows you to visualize the future."

Two particular features of Recorded Future deserve our attention. First is its status as a "third-generation" search engine. Rather than looking at individual pages in isolation, as did first-generation engines like Lycos and AltaVista, and rather than analyzing the explicit links between web pages with the aim of promoting those with the most links, as Google has done since the introduction of its PageRank algorithm in 1998, Recorded Future examines *implicit* links. Implicit links, or what it calls "invisible links" between documents, are links that obtain not because of any direct connection between them but because they *refer to the same entities or event*. To examine implicit links, Recorded Future does not simply use metadata embedded into documents, but actually separates the content contained *in* documents from what they are *about*; Recorded Future's algorithms are able to identify in the documents themselves references to events and entities that exist outside of them, and on the basis of such identification, to create an entirely new network of affiliations that establish relations of meaning and knowledge between documents, rather than mere associations. Journalist Tom Cheshire pinpoints the significance of this capacity for external reference when he compares Recorded Future with Google: "Recorded Future *knows* who Nicolas Sarkozy is, say: that he's the president of France, he's the husband of Carla Bruni, he's 1.65m tall in his socks, he travelled to Deauville for the G8 summit in May. If you Google 'president of France,' you'll get two *Wikipedia* pages on 'president of France' then 'Nicolas Sarkozy.' Useful, but Google *doesn't know how the two*, Sarkozy and the presidency, *are actually related*; it's just searching for pages linking the terms."[19]

What is most crucial here is *what* Recorded Future does with the references it identifies, *how* it manages to construct those shadow references into a meaningful knowledge network with predictive power. To do this, Recorded Future *ranks the entities and events* identified by its algorithms. It ranks all of these entities and events based a myriad of factors, the most important of which include: the number of references to them, the credibility of the documents referring to them, and the occurrence of different entities and events within the same document. The result of this analysis is a "momentum score" that, combined with a "sentiment valuation," indexes the power of the event or entity with respect to its potential future impact. For example, as Cheshire notes, "searching big pharma in general will tell you that over the next five years, nine of the world's 15 best-selling medicines will lose patent protection"; the basis for this knowledge, which of course is only a heavily weighted prediction, is the high momentum score of the event, a score due to its being supported by thirteen news stories from twelve different sources.

To fully appreciate the substantial predictive power of Recorded Future, we must introduce a second key feature: temporal dynamics. Recorded Future includes a time and space dimension of documents in its evaluation, which allows it to score events and entities that are yet to happen *on the basis of present knowledge about them*—what, in Whitehead's terms, we would call data of the settled universe. "References to when and where an event . . . will take place" are crucial, observes Staffan Truvé, one of Recorded Future's cofounders, "since many documents actually refer to events expected to take place in the future." By using RSS feeds, Recorded Future is able to integrate publishing time as an index for this temporal analysis. Such temporal analysis affords Recorded Future the capacity to weight opinions about the likely happening and timing of future events using algorithmically processed crowdsourcing and statistical analysis of historical records of related series of such events. The result: differentially weighted predictions about the future.

At first glance, this procedure may appear to dovetail with Bernard Stiegler's account of how today's media industries support—or obstruct—"protention," a term introduced by Edmund Husserl to designate the manner in which the living present already includes a foretaste of the future. For

Stiegler, the problem of culture today is its failure to facilitate any sense for a viable future—hence his appropriation of the punk slogan "No Future"; Stiegler's wager is that this failure can be understood analytically through a transformative updating of Husserl's model of time-consciousness. According to this updating, contemporary cultural industrial products—movies, television, advertising, marketing, video games, and so on—now monopolize the production of "collective secondary memories" which, following Stiegler, provide the source for anticipations of and expectations for the future. For Stiegler, there can be no viable future because this industrially manufactured source has literally taken the place of "natural" or "lived" secondary memories, and thus of collective cultural traditions that could furnish a living source for the invention of viable futures: as a consequence, whatever we today can imagine, anticipate, or expect are mere projections of possible futures that are rooted in and emerge as permutations of past manufactured or "tertiary" memories.

How would this situation change if we were to develop a theory of protention on the basis of a media platform like Recorded Future? Whatever affinity there may be between Stiegler's conception of protention as projection on the basis of manufactured collective secondary memories and Recorded Future's weighted probabilities concerning future events, their methods are fundamentally dissimilar: for whereas Stiegler's model operates in relation to a static source of fixed possibilities, a situation reinforced by his discretization of memory and the past as tertiary—that is, recorded and inert—*contents* of experience, Recorded Future operates in terms of probabilities that are generated not primarily through a processing of the repository of past, inert data of experience, but—crucially—through the *power of present data* to lay claim on the future, or, more precisely, through the power of the future to act in the present.

By reorienting the directionality of media from past to future, Recorded Future—despite its own instrumental framework—performs an important service for the media theorist: specifically, it focuses questions concerning media's impact around their capacity to predict—and potentially, to modulate—future experience. Not only must we take advantage of this technical development in our efforts to bring media theory up-to-date with media's contemporary evolution, we must do so precisely by embracing the affordances of computational access to the domain of microsensibility, and not simply by adopting the rhetoric of futurity.

Before pursuing this crucial opportunity—which means returning to Whitehead's conception of "real potentiality"—let me explore another key point of difference between Stiegler's protention and Recorded Future's prediction. This point of difference is the complete absence from the latter of any role whatsoever for *mental* content.[20] Whereas protention via projection relies on mental content—it is literally the carrying over of past memories to the future in the form of expectations—protention via weighted prediction eschews all dependence on mental content, and with it, any narrowing of the vehicle for protention to higher-order, exclusively human operations like memory. Accordingly, in contrast to Stiegler's conception of protention as a continuity between present and just-to-come *that takes place through mental processing* (albeit collective and technically supplemented mental processing), protention as it might be modeled on the basis of Recorded Future is a function of the material, causal insistence of the future *in the present of worldly sensibility* and not, in any way, a mental projection or continuity from present to just-to-come. It is not enough to say that such "worldly" protention or protention in this more general scope—protention rooted in the power of the total present world to impact the future—doesn't depend on any mediation via mental content. For what is truly distinctive about protention is its fundamental inaccessibility to and by the mental. Accordingly, the power informing it—the power of the settled world in its totality—can only be fed-forward into a future moment of the mental life of consciousness that, by definition, *must be discontinuous with it.*

Let me note in passing that this "nonmental," datacentric model of protention goes quite a way toward resolving the impasse of phenomenological accounts of protention which founder on the vexing question of how present consciousness can portend a future content that has not yet been lived—indeed, that has not yet even been constituted—*as a content of consciousness.* The material model of protention resolves this impasse by shifting the terrain for continuity with the future from mental content to data, the vast majority of which cannot be filtered through minds or time-consciousness. If material, nonmental protention actively and repeatedly reconstitutes the continuity of present with future, it does so by wielding the power of present data to partially determine the future, and thus to include (a part of) the future within it.

To fully appreciate this power, let us put it into dialogue with Whitehead's claim that every actuality prehends the entirety of the universe as it exists at the moment of its becoming. Because it furnishes an ontological basis for conceptualizing the relation between present and future, this forceful speculative claim provides a grounding for the process of prediction *at the same time as* it provides a critical check on the scope of any and all claims to predict the future. Remember that what Whitehead means by prehension (as explored above in chapter 3) is something like grasping, and prehension can be positive, where some element of the settled world is included in an actuality's becoming, or negative, where some element is excluded, but in a mode of exclusion that *still constitutes a relation.* By saying that every actuality prehends the entirety of the universe as it exists at the moment of its becoming, Whitehead thus means something fairly straightforward: that every actuality, every new element in the universe, arises on the basis of all of what has come before. Though on the surface reminiscent of Bergson's conception of perception as selection of images by a center of indetermination within a universe of images, Whitehead's account actively eschews the operation of selection—an operation which gives pride of place to actualization of the virtual and to some privileged form of self-reference—in favor of an embrace of the total situation, and the ensuing access to the real potentiality of the total situation *as it exists in itself,* that is, prior to the selective genesis that occurs in relation to, and that ultimately yields, a new actuality. Whereas for Bergson, what is perceived is a certain actualization of the virtual universe of images, for Whitehead, what is prehended *is* potentiality, the superjective subjectivity that attaches to every element of the entire settled world and that, following the Category of Subjective Intensity from *Process and Reality,* "aims at intensity of feeling . . . in the *relevant* future."[21] In saying that every actuality prehends the entirety of the universe, Whitehead is in effect arguing not just that every actuality includes in its present feeling *its* potential to impact future actualities *but also*—and to my mind more importantly—that it feels the potentiality for the future in its present, and indeed, as part of what constitutes the causal force of the present. Its intensity simply *is* the index of the power of this potentiality.

It is the *solidarity* attributed by Whitehead to the extensive continuum that explains how potentiality implicates the future in the present: "the extensive continuum is 'real,'" he writes, "because it expresses a fact derived from the actual world and concerning the contemporary actual world. All actual entities are related according to the determinations of this continuum; and all possible actual entities in the future must exemplify these determinations in their relations with the already actual world. The reality of the future is bound up with the reality of this continuum. It is the reality of what is potential, in its character of a real component of what is actual."[22] On this account, what implicates the future in the present is ultimately nothing other than the total ensemble of causal nexuses operative at any moment in the ongoing process of the universe, or, more concretely, in any given settled state of the superjectal world: this total causal ensemble just *is* the "real potentiality" of that settled state.

Whitehead's speculative account of the solidarity of the universe, and the crucial role it accords potentiality both *of and for* the future, addresses the total causal reality of a situation that is, by definition, beyond empirical access. On this ground, we can contrast it with systems for predictive analytics, including Recorded Future, that, no matter how sophisticated their algorithms become and how much data they will be able to process, by necessity operate on delimited, closed sets of data. That is why, as I have already suggested, Whitehead's process philosophy furnishes a *general* ontology of probabilistic potentiality capable of grasping how our datacentric world works. Even though it exceeds—or rather, precisely because it exceeds—the grasp of any particular predictive system or empirical perspective, Whitehead's ontology of the "total situation" and his account of the future's inherence in the present explains what gives prediction its particular (necessarily limited) power: the implication of future potentiality as a real power in the present.

With this conclusion, we can pinpoint the accomplishment of Recorded Future and begin to explore how it might contribute to the pharmacological recompense of twenty-first-century media. For with a third-generation search engine like Recorded Future, the mining and analysis of data takes a "Whiteheadian turn" in the sense that it ceases to ground the power of prediction in a recursive analysis of past behavior,[23] and instead—taking full advantage of recently acquired technical capacities for text analysis— channels predictive power through the reference of present data to future entities and events. In this sense, we might say that Recorded Future concretizes Whitehead's understanding of how the future is felt by the present: "Actual fact," writes Whitehead, "includes in its own constitution real potentiality which is *referent beyond itself.*"[24] A Whiteheadian explanation of Recorded Future thus reveals a "positive" dimension of prediction: more than a mere extrapolation of the causal force of the present and the past to future possibility, prediction concerns the potentiality *contained in* the transition from present to future. The key point is that this potentiality, despite being imperfectly reliable as a ground for prediction, has indisputable ontological power: the very power that is at issue when Whitehead characterizes potentiality as the mode through which the future is *felt* in the present.

Of course, the scope and power of the reference involved in Recorded Future's predictive analytics and in Whitehead's ontology of potentiality are of entirely different orders of magnitude: the former is an empirical instantiation of the insistence of the future in the present; the latter, a general speculative "explanation" for the power exercised by the future in the present. This contrast in the scope and power of reference brings us back to the question of the pharmacological promise of data-mining and predictive analytics. How, we must now ask, does Whitehead's philosophy contribute to the pharmacological recompense we have sought to discover in the operation of twenty-first-century media? Or, more specifically, how does the speculative grounding of prediction in the power of potentiality help to reveal a compensatory dimension of a transformation of contemporary capitalism that seems hell-bent on simply bypassing consciousness and human agency as such?

The answer to this question has two parts. First, by furnishing a *speculative* account of the "total situation" informing the genesis of every new actuality, Whitehead's account of potentiality in effect foregrounds the *impossibility* for any empirical analytic system—no matter how computationally sophisticated and how much data it can process—to grapple with the entirety of real potentiality, or anything close to it. Rather, driven by a grandiose—and, in the end, fundamentally incoherent—desire "to organize the world . . . for analysis," systems like Recorded Future can—and no doubt will—get more reliable by including more data, but their reliability will always be purchased at the cost of inclusiveness: reliability, that is, is a function of the capacity to close off some data from the larger universe of data surrounding—and complicating—it. In this sense, Whitehead's speculative account serves as a critical check on totalizing impulses of today's data industries, a guarantee of sorts that the future, even though it can be (partially) felt in the present, can never be known or actually experienced in advance. In this way, Whitehead's ontology of potentiality exposes the surplus of sensibility that must be closed off for potentiality to become reliably predictive.

Second, by facilitating a model of technical distribution of sensibility rooted in an expansion of perception beyond consciousness and bodily self-perception, Whitehead's philosophy helps us understand how a third-generation technical platform like Recorded Future can impact human experience in potentially positive ways—ways that go beyond the narrow and largely instrumental purposes that inform governmental and corporate deployments of it. The capacity to predict future events through present reference refines a technical platform for accessing a larger quantity of data of sensibility that is relevant to human behavior but that remains inaccessible through human modes of perception; as such, it increases the amount of data that is available for the shaping of human behavior in the future.

Isn't this twofold investment in the power of potentiality the source for the appeal of the recent television drama *Person of Interest*, in the sense that it features superhero-like characters who have imperfect knowledge of the predictions of an all-knowing but fully mysterious "machine" and who must *act*—and must embrace the uncertainties of acting—if they are to prevent predicted future murders? What *Person of Interest* dramatizes is a technical distribution of agency in which a highly sophisticated computational machine accesses data of worldly sensibility and feeds it forward into human experience. Unlike its thematic precursor, Steven Spielberg's 2002

film *Minority Report* (and even more so Philip K. Dick's 1956 short story
"The Minority Report" on which it is based), *Person of Interest* contains
no possibility for an existential moment of self-recognition where one can
modify one's "precognized" fate; rather, the characters "blindly" follow the
clue furnished by the machine until they can, by acting in the near future-
oriented present, figure out how the person identified by that clue is involved
in a future murder and act to prevent its occurrence. Gone here is any hope
for a reconciliation of the knowledge afforded by data (the precog's visions
of the near future) and the knowledge afforded by experience: the "numbers" generated by the machine, which correspond to unique identities of
persons (i.e., their social security numbers), brook no interpretation. They
function simply to trigger an action-based process of search that never fails
to yield the desired goal of preventing murder.

What makes *Person of Interest* so resonant with my general claim concerning twenty-first-century media is its taken-for-granted embrace of the
"machine," or rather The Machine, as a sophisticated cognitive agent whose
workings remain absolutely inscrutable to humans—indeed, unquestionably
beyond human exploration as such. From what little we are told about the
machine, we know that it processes massive amounts of video surveillance
and cell phone data—the passive data that lies at the heart of twenty-first-
century media—in order to make incomplete but fundamentally reliable
predictions concerning the future. By depicting a co-functioning between
the machine and the characters acting on its predictions, *Person of Interest*
allegorizes the very condition I am seeking to theorize: the imperative for us
to embrace the qualified marginalization of consciousness that goes together
with—that is, as it were, the price to be paid for—any opportunity we
might have to benefit from the technical access to the operational present of
sensibility. Indeed, with its various compensatory narratives—one episode,
for example, involves the salvation of a post-9/11 war veteran whose guilt
over the death of a fellow soldier and desire to support his family has led him
to commit multiple armed robberies—*Person of Interest* could well be read
as an allegory of the pharmacological recompense of twenty-first-century
media: by depicting the use of data extracted from human activity, not as a
new source of economic value, but as the instigator of superhero-like doing-
good, the show capitalizes on the potential, and the popular desire, for cold,
quantitative—dare I say "inhuman"—data to benefit human life.

Media Modulation

What kind of media theory does the politics of sensibility I have been developing here require? To begin exploring this question, let me reiterate the

specificity of my interest in Recorded Future. I am interested in how it exemplifies what I take to be a new technical paradigm of media that is both future-directed and committed to the extraction and analysis of data of microsensibility. In this respect, Recorded Future is important less as a concrete technical platform that media theorists might literally or practically deploy than as a demonstration of the new potentials for media to open up the domain of sensibility not simply for prediction of future events but also for modulation and intensification of future behavior. What remains to be worked out is what role media might play in such modulation of sensibility.

Nigel Thrift, whom I have discussed above, furnishes one account that, due to its complexity, broad scope, and explanatory power, can serve to jump-start a discussion of the contemporary vocation of media theory. As we have seen, Thrift attempts to think media modulation in terms of propensity, where the function of media would be less that of providing stable objects for consciousness, or even stable sedimentations of memory, than that of continuously tweaking ongoing, largely precognitive tendencies in light of desired experiential outcomes. As Thrift sees it, and I would wholeheartedly concur, media modulation occurs at the level of "premediation," prior to the emergence of perceptual experience. It should come as no surprise, then, that media modulation has served the interest of those contemporary institutions of capitalism—most prominently, neuromarketing, experience design, and predictive analytics—that focus on excavating and exploiting the precognitive domain. The key question for us is how—and indeed whether—media modulation can also be enlisted in the service of experiential amelioration, of making our lived experience more intense, more interesting, more rich, and more enjoyable.

Like Sadin and Crandall, Thrift seizes on the incursions that capitalist institutions have made into the body and the precognitive dimensions of experience: thus, neuroscientific models support capital's "emphasis on more effective everyday creativity" by attempting "to mobilize the momentary processes that go to make up much of what counts as human. Persons are to be trained to 'unthinkingly' conjure up more and better things both at work and as consumers, by drawing on a certain kind of *neuro-aesthetics* which works on the myriad small periods of time that are relevant to the structures of forethought and the ways that human bodies routinely mobilize them to obtain results."[25] Thrift leaves little doubt as to who is in control of this excavation: as exemplified in strategies for design composition that mobilize "thing power" and create environments "rich enough in calculative processes to allow the neuro-aesthetic to function more forcefully," the aim of this excavation is "to produce a certain anticipatory readiness about the world, a rapid perceptual style which can move easily between interchangeable opportunities, thus adding to the sum total of intellect that can be drawn on. This is a style which is congenial to capitalism."[26]

The question this rather bleak picture raises is how any account of media that would deploy the resources of premediation for the purposes of experience modulation can manage to evade the grip of capital, of what philosopher Catherine Malabou diagnoses as the reduction of neuronal and experiential plasticity to the flexibility central to regimes of post-Fordist capitalism.[27] This issue arises forcefully in Thrift's 2008 account of how contemporary capitalism uses media to influence "hormonal swashes":

> The intent is clear—to identify susceptible populations and to render them open to suggestion. That involves a series of techniques which allow the susceptibility of populations to be described and worked upon. To begin with, contemporary information technology allows populations to be gathered up and monitored in ways heretofore impossible, for example, through emotional stance, with the result that it increasingly becomes possible to track mimetic rays. The rise of analytics premised on the mining of very large and continuously updated data sets allows "prediction competition" to become general. Then, through the internet and various mobile technologies, it becomes possible to rapidly feed information and recommendations to these populations, producing a means of trading on those susceptibilities that have been identified. Finally, it also becomes possible to enter into something like an individualized dialogue with members of these populations, so that they feedback their reactions, both producing more information on their susceptibilities, and new triggers. In extremis, they may well produce their own new and innovative variants which can themselves become the basis of new business. In other words, an era of permanent survey of populations replaces the fractured surveys of "samples."[28]

Despite its neutral tone, Thrift's diagnosis of the closed circuits of contemporary data capitalism would appear to leave little room for any more hopeful modulation: with their capacity to ensnare populations in data loops that they alone can process, today's data industries manage to hijack and to control the operation of the "precognitive," thereby wresting it from its "natural" function of priming human perceptual activity and targeting it in a hyperaccelerated time frame that simply bypasses human involvement altogether.

What this diagnosis brings to the fore is the question of the technicity involved in accessing the precognitive. And it does so not in spite of *but precisely because of* its bleakness: for if humans find themselves wholly foreclosed from this scene of precognitive sampling, the reason is—let me repeat—that they have absolutely no "natural" capacity to act within, or even to access, the microtemporal time frames involved. As diagnosed by Thrift, the operation of contemporary data capitalism unequivocally establishes that access to the precognitive requires technical mediation—and indeed, a form of technical mediation that is radically *out of sync* with the rhythms of human experience, including the affectivity associated with the neural processes that prime perception.

With this diagnosis, Thrift pinpoints precisely what media theory needs to theorize in order to understand how media operates in a world where even primordial sensibility is co-opted by industry. The broadly pharmacological perspective I have been developing here helps us appreciate the significance of Thrift's embrace of media's radical exteriority, of its operation outside of any "space of subjectivity," including the space of the brain-mind that neural imaging technologies, following in the wake of the braintime experiment, have opened up for analysis and exploitation. Specifically, it can help us see why, for Thrift, the potentiality for media to modulate sensibility must stem directly from the "extra-subjective" nature of its operationality.

Exploring the evolution of Thrift's account over the past decade will help us to get a better understanding both of the imperative for and the resistance against the feed-forward structure that I have argued characterizes human experience of twenty-first-century media. Specifically, the position at which Thrift arrives in his 2008 article on propensity perfectly illustrates the ambivalence that, I would suggest, cannot but attend any effort to embrace the pharmacological structure of twenty-first-century media. It is precisely because of such ambivalence that we find Thrift, on one hand, ready to embrace the radical demotion of human phenomenological agency made necessary by twenty-first-century media, and on the other, reticent to give up the last vestiges of this agency. As I see it, Thrift's position, notwithstanding its embrace of some of the most radical implications of contemporary technical incursions into the body, retains a misguided—because unsustainable—"faith" in phenomenological agency as well as a certain technophobia, both of which lead him in turn to adopt a misguided conceptualization of what the pharmacological recompense of twenty-first-century media precisely is or can be.

Within the terms of the 2008 article, Thrift's ambivalence centers around the possibility for "reengineering presence": "What if," he asks, "presence can be reengineered" on the basis of "an alternative realism appealing directly to sensation and perception? . . . Certainly, that is what is being attempted [in today's media industries]. Indeed, it might be seen as the construction of a *giant temporal shortcut*. For all their comparative speed, neural and genetic changes still take time to impact the body but now, courtesy of new technical practices which are driven by the logic of propensity and make appeals directly to particular biological territories, simulations of their work can come into existence all but immediately as sensations and perceptions."[29] With their capacity to operate directly on the present of sensibility, today's media industries are able to create simulations of sensations and perceptions that simply *take the place of "naturally-occurring" sensations and perceptions.* By effectively co-opting our role in generating our own experiences, this substitution manages to preserve the phenomenological appearance of experience even as it severs all ties between that appearance and its underlying causal basis in embodiment. The key question thus raised—a question that Thrift would seem to skirt more than to answer—is whether such simulated experience is indeed capable of reengineering presence, and if so, whether this would be a presence that can be experienced by human bodyminds.

Everything in Thrift's 2008 diagnosis of the industrial co-optation of sensibility suggests a negative answer to this question: what he has shown is that the simulated sensations and perceptions central to the operation of contemporary data capitalism, like our above account of the data of sensibility, take place at time frames that are faster than neural time, and that, for this very reason, simply cannot be directly lived by embodied humans. If Thrift seems reticent to accept this reality, it is, I suggest, due to a misplaced hope in "neurophenomenology" and, more precisely, to his mistaken conviction that braintime can furnish a "space of action" for embodied humans. Although it is developed most fully in Thrift's earlier work on premediation and the space of the missing half second, traces of this hope linger in Thrift's 2008 account of the "creation of neurophenomenological worlds" and the "science of 'placing'" that affords the possibility to "create something like the all-at-onceness of phenomenological worlds on a temporary basis."[30] In accord with this lingering hope, Thrift invests the changes wrought by technical incursions into neurophenomenology—changes to "the very sensory and perceptual pathways" on which people rely to experience the world—with the power to mobilize and to strengthen phenomenological experience of the world.[31] In this way, he is able to position these technical incursions as antidotes to the "the brutally instrumentalist view that underlies developments like neuromarketing."[32]

What is missing from Thrift's account is any explanation of how expanded technical agency over the operational present of sensibility can in fact benefit phenomenological modes of experience. This is just what my conception of feed-forward is intended to provide, and it does so precisely by embracing our non-phenomenologizable dependence on technics and the resulting temporal indirection or scrambling—the requisite projection into a just-to-come future—by which we are able to experience the artifactual "presentifications" afforded by technical access to data of sensibility. The contrast with feed-forward thus helps pinpoint exactly what is missing from Thrift's account: namely, an appreciation that whatever access we do have to the operational present of sensibility is mediated by—and thus dependent on—a non-phenomenologizable, thoroughly technical, and artifactual process.

More than a simple theoretical oversight, Thrift's failure to appreciate this situation is rooted, as I have already suggested, in his earlier investment in the neural space-time of the half-second delay. As he explains in an essay reprised in his 2007 collection, *Non-Representational Theory*, this neural space-time furnishes the site for the construction of a "new structure of attention."

> What was formerly invisible or imperceptible becomes constituted as visible and perceptible through a new structure of attention which is more and more likely to pay more than lip-service to those actions which go on in small spaces and times, actions which involve qualities like anticipation, improvisation and intuition, all those things which by drawing on the second-to-second resourcefulness of the body make for artful conduct. Thus, perception can no longer "be thought of in terms of immediacy, presence, punctuality" (citing Jonathan Crary) as it is both stretched and intensified, widened and condensed. . . . The result is that we now have a small space of time which is increasingly able to be sensed, the space of time which shapes the moment. Of course, once such a space is opened up it can also be operated on. . . . What is being ushered in now is a *micro-biopolitics*, a new domain carved out of the half-second delay which has become visible and so available to be worked upon through a whole series of new entities and institutions.[33]

Thrift's investment in the missing half second as a space of agency—as, precisely, "a small space of time that is . . . able to be sensed"—is premised on the notion that technicity can operate *within* phenomenological experience *as a mechanism to expand its temporal scope and sensitivity*.[34] In concert with Libet and the contemporary cultural theorists who radicalize his work, but also with the Whitehead, who restricts causal efficacy to "nonsensuous perception" (as explored in chapter 2), the 2007 Thrift depicts the technical incursion into braintime not just as an industrialization of experience but also as the revelation of a new "space of action" for embodied human beings. For this Thrift, it is as if the discovery of the neural timespace of the half-second delay opened up a space of action that is available equally to corporations and to individuals—available equally for the exploitation of attention *and* for the refining of sensory and perceptual capacities.

The governing assumption here—that technicity and phenomenality somehow operate at the same level—is precisely what must be given up if we are to understand the full consequences of twenty-first-century media's incursions into the operational present of sensibility. As I have been arguing throughout, sensibility implicates human experience from the outside: it constitutes a source for that experience that simply cannot be presentified *within* it and that must be introduced into it, through technical mediation, as a radically exterior power. In this context, we can see that Thrift's earlier position doesn't just ignore the massive imbalance in resources that allows today's data industries to atomize and hijack the operational present of sensibility (effectively wresting it from the larger circuits of embodied becoming within which it itself becomes). It also fundamentally misunderstands the meaning of the missing half second.

Contra Thrift, but also contra Massumi and others who have invoked it as an affective anticipation of perception, the missing half second simply cannot constitute a space of action in which more fine-grained sensations and perceptions can arise. This is because, not unlike the technical circuits afforded by twenty-first-century media, it is a thoroughly technical artifact that, as historian of science Henning Schmidgen has compellingly argued, results from and cannot exist or operate independently of the construction of a "cyborg assemblage" in the laboratory.[35] Far from being a faculty of (human) experience, which is how Thrift, Massumi, and others effectively treat it, the missing half second is an artifactual construction *that has no agency independently of its technical setup*—that, in short, has no "natural" agency whatsoever. Not only does this mean that the missing half second cannot exist as a self-standing agency, independently of the technical apparatus facilitating its presentification, but it also means that it cannot directly function to intensify or granulate sensing and perceiving. There simply is no direct phenomenological interface onto the operation of braintime.

The picture the 2007 Thrift paints is thus wrong, both in its thematization of the missing half second as a "space of action" and in its assessment of the neutrality of the technicity involved in its presentification. Far from first "opening up" the "small space of time . . . which shapes the moment" for apprehension in sense perception, the technical presentification of the missing half second is from its very onset an *originarily technical artifact* and one that is, as it were, originarily available to be "operated on" by the "fastest bidder," by whatever institution can access it most quickly. Although capacities for manipulating the space of the missing half second have multiplied exponentially in the wake of digital computation, the structure of its operation has remained constant since the mid-nineteenth century when the protocol of what Schmidgen calls the "braintime experiment" was initially configured. This protocol involves using technical acceleration to access psychophysiological processes imperceptible to "natural" perception in order to slow them down for subsequent perceptual apprehension.[36] What is true for these psychophysiological processes—namely, that they cannot constitute agencies independently from the technical setup that makes them accessible—is all the more true for the domain of sensibility opened up by twenty-first-century media. That is why what we learn from the longer history of the braintime experiment can help us to appreciate what is involved in the industrial co-optation of sensibility: rather than operating on the basis of a gap *within our "natural" perceptual faculty*, a gap between neural processing and subsequently emergent mental phenomena, this co-optation, as the protocol of the braintime experiment shows, operates on a gap between our "natural" perceptual faculty and the radically exterior domain of sensibility.

And it is also why Helmholtz's psychophysical research paradigm, insofar as it develops an experimental practice on the basis of the braintime experiment, constitutes a particularly crucial forerunner of the account of feed-forward I develop here. What Helmholtz puts into place as a methodology for a scientific research program premised on the dethroning of consciousness has now become an everyday reality: living with twenty-first-century media calls for a constant give and take with media flows that evade conscious presentification and that require data supplementation and an abandonment of the long-standing privilege of conscious attention and perception as the privileged or sole arbiters of experience. In short, the everyday reality I am seeking to describe in my account of twenty-first-century media is the same reality embraced by the Helmholtzian natural scientist faced with a world operating according to its own protocols: despite differences of scale, what is at stake in both cases is an embrace of a technically distributed cognitive system in which consciousness takes a backseat to the power of data and its capacity to access the microtemporal structure of worldly sensibility.[37]

We can get a clear sense for the stakes involved in the historical lineage of the braintime experiment—and in the radicalization it undergoes in its repositioning as the infrastructural pattern of experience in twenty-first-century media environments—by recalling what I have suggested above in chapter 1 concerning the contemporary perversion of the pharmacological imperative of technics. When our behavior becomes accessible as technically generated data that we ourselves cannot experience directly (which is to say, phenomenologically), the long-standing prosthetic pharmacology that characterizes media history undergoes a fundamental transformation. Put schematically, we could say that it loses its prosthetic basis since the loss of our agency over our own behavioral data is recompensed by something *that has no direct correlation with it*, namely, the affordances of social media and the Internet. By splitting the pharmacological structure of media, this transformation introduces an experiential level—the world of social media and the Internet—as a false recompense for what is really going on, namely the extraction of "data-value" in the form of user profiles. What is particularly interesting about this splitting, and what merits the characterization of a "perversion," is the way it overlays a traditional pharmacological narrative (we give up our data and are given in return the affordances of social media) on a quite different story (we give up our data and are thereby transformed into commodities, data profiles, to be sold to the highest bidder).

We can get a clearer understanding for the nuances of this transformation by comparing social media with writing. Writing, as both Derrida and Paul de Man established in their work on figures like Plato and Hegel, involves the replacement of one form of memory (interior memory, or *Erinnerung*) with another (artifactual memory, or *Gedächtnis*).[38] And despite the success of their deconstructive readings in revealing the dependence of interior memory on technical memory—which is also to say, the "originary technicity" of memory—there is a sense in which writing qua technical memory serves, or, more exactly, has always served, as a recompense, and indeed as a phenomenological recompense, for the weaknesses of natural memory. Despite its superficial similarity to the pairing of interior and exterior memory, the pharmacological relationship at work in contemporary techniques for gathering data about what happens in the missing half second—and in the braintime experiment more generally—involves the deployment of technics to access and presentify data *that is radically disjunctive with phenomenological modes of experience*. For, whereas artificial memory aids as theorized by philosophers from Plato via Hegel to Stiegler technically exteriorize memory *without changing the form of its content*, technical access to data of sensibility and to the neural processes constituting braintime operate *in lieu of* any possible phenomenological mode of experience. Twenty-first-century media operate on and with data that cannot take the form of contents of consciousness, that simply cannot be lived by consciousness. Like Etienne-Jules Marey's graphic and chronophotographic machines which must be understood to be autonomous sensing agents that *possess their own sensible domains*, and in perfect accord with the braintime experiment at the heart of Helmholtz's psychophysical research paradigm, today's cyborg assemblages that access and capture the data of sensibility do so in radical disjunction from any possible (future) presentification to perceptual consciousness. Accordingly, when this data is fed-forward into our embodied experience, as I have argued it must be if it is to be experienced by us at all, it marks and cannot but mark the intrusion of a radical exteriority into consciousness, an exteriority that cannot so much be interiorized as introjected.

This is why any attempt to grasp the technicity introduced by twenty-first-century media by way of affectivity—understood as a sub-perceptual *but nonetheless still direct* connection to sensibility—remains insufficiently radical. It remains insufficiently radical because the technical capture and feed-forward of data of sensibility *simply has and can have no direct experiential interface*. Even those affective dimensions of experience that serve to prime ensuing perceptions can neither be directly experienced, nor be made to capture the broader and more primordial interface with worldly sensibility that, as I have sought to demonstrate, *comes before the consolidation of any subjective unity capable of hosting such affectivity*. In full resonance with Whitehead's description of the dative phase, this interface generates a primordial feeling, a primal impressionality, that is *preaffective*—a feeling without a feeler.

With this clarification of the preaffective impact of technics on sensibility, we are in a position to pinpoint the significance of Thrift's 2008 account of media modulation and to gain a better understanding for why he remains unable to fully appreciate its radical consequences. First, its significance: the 2008 Thrift rightly abandons the model of an affective intensification of experience and the concomitant notion of a space of action within the missing half second in favor of a more radical localization of technicity *beneath* embodiment, including neural embodiment. It is precisely because this Thrift refrains from embedding perception in the continuity from the neuronal to consciousness and situates the industrial intervention into experiential time *"beneath" even the half-second interval* that he is able to capture what is essential about our contemporary predicament: namely, that the industrial reengineering of the present is equivalent to an industrial co-optation of sensibility. On the basis of the "giant temporal shortcut" informing the operation of today's data industries, Thrift can conclude that the reengineered present evades not just the time frame of consciousness but *also the time frame of affect and of the preperceptual affective domain*.

Yet, as I announced above, Thrift cannot bring himself to embrace the radical consequences of this conclusion: he can neither accept *that technicity is required to access primordial sensibility* nor recognize that *twenty-*

first-century media provide the means, indeed the only means, for securing such access. Thrift's lingering hope for a phenomenological interface with the reengineered present thus betrays an underlying technophobia. For if Thrift is right that the industrial co-optation of sensibility operates through a "giant temporal shortcut" that literally bypasses human processing as such, the only consequential conclusion that he could come to would be to embrace the displacement of phenomenological agency in favor of technical processing. What Thrift should have concluded is that the preaffective present or operational present of sensibility, because it can only be accessed *as a space of action in the present* through technical means, requires the (co)operation of today's data industries, or, at least, of the technical interfaces they have developed. That Thrift cannot draw such a conclusion attests in equal measure to his lingering hope in phenomenology and to his repressed, covert technophobia. The very same logic informs Thrift's failure to embrace the underlying pharmacology of this situation: he simply cannot recognize that whatever recompense might come to us from the technical access to sensibility must come through the very operations that lie at the heart of today's data capitalism. To do so would require Thrift to give up what he seems most unwilling, and indeed, unable to give up: the hope for a *direct* phenomenological interface with the reengineered, preaffective present.

It is thus perfectly understandable that Thrift doesn't envisage the possibility for an alternate, "phenomenology-implicating" engagement with the operational present of sensibility: the operation of feed-forward. Rather than seeking to restore human sensory and perceptual agency *within the present of sensibility*, as Thrift's various recipes for the creation of "neurophenomenological worlds" all do, the operation of feed-forward recognizes the radical opacity of this preconscious and preaffective domain and utilizes the technical means developed by today's data industries to access it precisely *in order to feed it forward into just-to-come future experience of embodied consciousness*. Whereas Thrift's recourse to instantaneous simulation mistakenly indulges the vain fantasy of human agency within the domain of braintime, feed-forward perfectly instantiates the "diagram" of the braintime experiment as it has been repeatedly performed in the laboratory since the 1860s: feed-forward brings very fast—and by definition, non-phenomenologizable—processes into the slower space-time interval of durationally embodied human experience.[39]

In light of the radical short-circuiting of sensory and perceptual experience that, as Thrift's analysis reveals, occurs with the contemporary industrial reengineering of the present, it is imperative that we expand our account of feed-forward. To the account I have developed thus far—an account which focuses on the feeding-forward of *actual* data of sub-perceptual, microtemporal levels of experience (data of causal efficacy or of worldly sensibility)—we must add a second, more indirect account: feed-forward as the prospectively oriented modulation of sensibility itself. With the aim of inducing particular kinds of sensory and perceptual experiences, this form of feed-forward shapes propensity in the inaccessible operational present.

On this score, there is much we can learn from Thrift. Indeed, we can find a basic blueprint for this second form of feed-forward in Thrift's understanding of how adding "mediological detail" to existing spaces might enhance their sensory potentiality or resonance. Yet in developing an account of mediological modulation, we must constantly bear in mind that we are *not* reengineering the present to expand human agency *within the space of that present*. On the contrary, we are modulating a present we *literally cannot live* in order to engineer *experience to come in the future*—a coming-present that we *can* live. Accordingly, the impact of mediological modulation *cannot be direct*—in the sense that media effects would directly impact human sensations and perceptions—but must be *indirect* and *predictively anticipatory*: such modulation intervenes at the level of worldly sensibility itself *prior to*, but *not without relation to*, whatever affective, sensory, and perceptual experience might arise from and through it. Put another way, such modulation involves designing media environments that channel preaffective sensibility in ways predictably likely to yield certain kinds of affective, sensory, and perceptual experiences. In sum: because the operational present of sensibility directly targeted by data capitalism lies outside the domain, and beyond the reach, of embodied perceptual *and* affective experience, the modulation of sensibility at issue here, including the modulation of environments for sensibility, must follow the diagram of feed-forward: such modulation must, that is, develop the potential for a mediological shaping of the domain of sensibility that would be "autonomous" from any direct connection to human affections, sensations, and perceptions, and that would embrace the technicity "essential," if not to its very mode of being, than certainly to its mode of access.

That is why nothing less is at stake here than the very status—indeed the autonomy—of media itself. For what lies at the heart of mediological modulation in the sense sketched above is an operation of media that takes place *beneath the phenomenological* (including the "neurophenomenological") and that is disjoined from any *immediate* or *direct* human impact. Exploring the potentiality for mediological modulation of sensibility will accordingly require us to develop a *non-anthropomorphic, non-phenomenological*, and *non-prosthetic* theory of media.

Mediating the Vibratory Continuum

The resources for such a non-anthropomorphic, non-phenomenological, non-prosthetic theory of media can be found in Whitehead's account of the "extensive continuum." Introduced by Whitehead to furnish a speculative explanation for the solidarity of the universe, the extensive continuum—or, more precisely, the vibratory continuum specific to our universe—provides a conceptual grounding for understanding "real potentiality" *as worldly sensibility*. For our purposes here, the most fundamental aspect of Whitehead's account of the extensive continuum is his investment in vibrations as worldly, which is to say, as wholly separate from concrescences. By establishing the independence of vibrations from the activity of concrescence, Whitehead's development of the vibratory continuum positions vibrations as the core elements of a potentiality ("real potentiality") that obtains force prior to and separately from the attainment of actualities. For this reason, as I shall now go on to argue, Whitehead's account of the vibratory continuum provides the capstone for the claim for inversion (CIF) that has structured my understanding of his process philosophy throughout this study. Indeed, Whitehead's account of the vibratory continuum furnishes an explanation for the all-important superjective power of worldly sensibility (the settled universe in Whitehead's language) that, as I have been arguing, exceeds the conceptual category of "transition" and the restricted oscillatory process informing Whitehead's account of process and creativity.

The vibratory continuum gives a concrete expression to the webs of relationality that are left in the wake of objectification (i.e., that are constituted when attained actualities reenter the settled world). Far from ratifying the attributes of inertness and passivity imposed on attained actualities by the Whiteheadian orthodoxy, recontextualizing attained actualities in relation to the vibratory continuum serves to foreground the significant subjective, or, better, *superjective* agency they possess as fundamental elements of worldly sensibility. Vibrations are the very matter of causal efficacy and, as such, are characterized by three traits—promiscuity, ubiquity, and futurity. As Jones succinctly puts it (and I shall return to this claim below), "to be a vibratory character is to be an intensive imposition on all subsequent process."[40] On this view, the ultimate "purpose" of process is nothing less than the propagation of vibrations (or sensibility), which is why Whitehead's account of the vibratory continuum marks the final stage in the inversion that reassigns concrescence the humble role of vehicle for process—or, as we can now properly appreciate, vehicle for the propagation of vibrations.

Together with this reassignation of the role of concrescence comes a shift in focus, a shift to the creativity of experiential entities (societies) that are all, ultimately, more or less complex compositions of vibrations. This shift instantiates, in yet another configuration, the claim of access to the data of sensibility (CADS) that has informed my understanding of twenty-first-century media throughout this study. Indeed, the proposal to localize media in relation to the vibratory continuum—the proposal I am here introducing as a foundation for a non-anthropomorphic, non-phenomenological, and non-prosthetic account of media—goes hand in hand with an emphasis on the creativity of access. This conjunction of localization and creativity, in turn, allows for a certain specification of my argument concerning twenty-first-century media: rather than itself introducing some new domain of experience, the system of twenty-first-century media marks the revelation of a dimension of sensibility—the operation of worldly sensibility—that has *always been there, that has always impacted our experience, but that has remained largely opaque to our understanding because inaccessible to our (human) modes of perceiving, sensing, and experiencing the world.* What is "new" about twenty-first-century media, then, is less their technical disjunction from past media than their opening of the operational present of sensibility to various forms of modulation, including most prominently (as we have just seen) capitalist ones. It is, in other words, *the very act of opening experience to an expanded domain of sensibility* that lends twenty-first-century media their power to impact human experience. To put it schematically, twenty-first-century media are characterized by two features, both of which reiterate the emphasis I have been placing on the operation of access: (1) they mark the technical revelation of (and new forms of access to) an expansive domain of worldly sensibility that lies behind and remains in excess of any delimited act of feeling, sensing, perceiving, thinking, or understanding; and (2) they catalyze a gradual shift in the economy of experience, and with it, a shift from human-addressed media to environmental or (we might now say) vibratory media, which shift however is not "determined" by media so much as it is emergent from the power of sensibility that media open up. Still more simply stated, twenty-first-century media present a situation where the very act of accessing worldly sensibility itself constitutes a transformation in the texture of experience.

In the present context, the crucial point is the localization of media in relation to the vibratory continuum: twenty-first-century media impact human experience not *"in itself"* or directly—as has been the case (at least predominately) with media up to now—but *precisely and only insofar as they open up, modulate, and channel the power of worldly sensibility itself.* Twenty-first-century media impact human experience, then, because they mediate between human modes of experience and the power of worldly sensibility, because they provide an opportunity for worldly sensibility to be brought to bear on human experience *without requiring that it first be reduced to the modes of experience characteristic of the human*. In this sense, twenty-first-century media can be thought of as a "host" for worldly sensibility, and insofar as we can position it as a "surrogate" for the human bodymind (what I have referred to above as "machinic reference"), it potentially brings the bodymind into a far more robust contact with sensibility than it can realize through its own built-in modes of feeling, sensing, perceiving, understanding, and thinking.

One of the key factors motivating my embrace of this localization of media within the vibratory continuum is a desire to avoid reducing twenty-first-century media to understandings of media that too readily and too quickly couple them to human modes of experience. Beyond this general injunction, however, my embrace of the vibrational ontology of media concerns the promise of Whitehead's process philosophy, and of his conception of the vibratory continuum more specifically, to furnish a concrete account of how media can impact human experience *by operating directly on or at the level of vibrations*. Once again, the crucial element at work here is the independence of vibrations from the activity of concrescence. At the same time as it liberates vibrations to serve as elements of a potentiality that is "prior" to the activity of attainment, this independence renders vibrations addressable for technical modulation separately from their participation in concrescences and in eternal objects that are ingressed into actualities during concrescence. When media modulate sensibility, which happens in large part simply because they open access to sensibility, they grasp and channel the power of worldly vibrations at a level "prior" to their participation in subjective unifications: they address and mediate vibrations as disparate elements of the disjunctive plurality that is worldly sensibility.

By similarly localizing media within the vibratory continuum, sound theorist Steve Goodman proffers a "non-anthropocentric ontology of ubiquitous media" that moves beyond the instrumentality of contemporary conceptualizations of media objects in order to underscore the sensory—or vibrational—power at the heart of media effects. Because of its broad convergence with the argument I am developing here—but also because of its divergence from my investment in worldly sensibility—Goodman's ontology can help us negotiate some of the difficulties involved in localizing media in relation to the vibratory continuum. Specifically, as we shall see, Goodman's allegiance to the orthodox narrative that enthrones concrescence as the site and source of creativity prevents him from making good on the promise of his localization of media in relation to the vibratory continuum. In this respect, it can serve as a lesson for how we might proceed differently.

For Goodman, what is at stake in this localization of media in relation to the vibratory continuum is the potential for media to become fully expressive:

> From cymatics [the study of how static objects are affected by vibration] to the vibratory anarchitecture practiced by artists such as Mark Bain . . . , a set of experimental practices to intensify vibration has been developed for unfolding the body onto a vibrational discontinuum that differentially traverses the media of the earth, built environment, analog and digital sound technologies, industrial oscillators, and the human body. Each actual occasion of experience that populates this discontinuum will be termed a *vibrational nexus*, drawing in an array of elements in its collective shiver. This differential ecology of vibrational effects directs us toward a nonanthropocentric ontology of ubiquitous media, a topology in which every resonant surface is potentially a host for contagious concepts, percepts, and affects. In this speculative conception of ubiquitous media, not just screens (and the networks they mask everywhere) but all matter becomes a reservoir of mediatic contagion. By approaching this topology of vibrational surfaces without constraint to merely semiotic registers that produce the "interminable compulsion" to communicate, media themselves are allowed to become fully expressive. An outline of a vibrational anarchitecture, then, diagrams a topological mediatic space that cuts across the plexus of the analog and digital, the waveform and the numeric sonic grain, implicating the continuity of the wave into the atomism of the granular.[41]

With its central notion of a *vibrational nexus*, Goodman's account takes a *cosmological* approach to media that breaks definitively with the anthropocentric pact informing (most) contemporary media theory: far from requiring media to be channeled through human faculties in order to have experiential effects, Goodman's account locates media operations and media effects at an experiential level that is both indifferent to traditional humanist divisions (human-nonhuman, animate-inanimate, etc.) *and* imperceptible to and through traditional human modes of sense perception and conscious attention.

At the heart of Goodman's ontology of vibrational force is a nonanthropocentric, cosmological conception of feeling that he discovers in Whitehead. For Goodman, Whitehead's philosophy constitutes an aesthetics of rhythm rooted in the primacy of feeling:

Whitehead's thoughts on rhythm and vibration form an aesthetic
ontology of pulses. To say that Whitehead's ontology is aesthetic
means that he posits feeling, or prehension, as a basic condition of
experience. . . . His ontology revolves around a nonanthropocentric
concept of feeling. This notion of prehension exceeds the phenomenological demarcation of the human body as the center of experience and at the same time adds a new inflection to an understanding
of the feelings . . . of such entities. To feel a thing is to be affected
by that thing. The mode of affection, or the way the "prehensor"
is changed, is the very content of what it feels. Every event in the
universe is in this sense an episode of feeling.[42]

For Goodman, Whitehead's aesthetic ontology is structured according to a
non-anthropocentric "hierarchy of categories of feeling" that encompasses
all levels of experience from the fundamental "wavelengths and vibrations"
of the subatomic physical universe to the sophisticated contrasts involving
merely possible situations characteristic of human consciousness.

The correlation of feeling with vibration is what facilitates the becoming-
cosmological of media. At the furthest extreme from the myopic imperi-
alism of human perception, Whitehead's vibrational ontology postulates
vibrations as the very root of all feelings in the universe. On this account,
feelings pertain directly to vibrations—or more precisely, to the contrasts
among vibrations that generate intensities—before they characterize properly subjective formations. When he emphasizes the excess of vibrations over
the entities in which they participate, Goodman perfectly captures this situation: "It is a concern for potential vibration and the abstract rhythmic relation of oscillation, which is key. What is prioritized here is the in-between of
oscillation, the vibration of vibration, the virtuality of the tremble. Vibrations always exceed the actual entities that emit them. Vibrating entities are
always entities out of phase with themselves. A vibratory nexus exceeds and
precedes the distinction between subject and object, constituting a mesh of
relation."[43] Beneath their phenomenological solidification into stable, per-
ceptible objects, vibrations create a field of relationality that yields the "real
potentiality" for any actualization whatsoever. Indeed, to say that vibrations
necessarily exceed the entities that actualize them is to say that vibrations
have the mode of being of potentiality. But it is also, more broadly, to assert
that potentiality is ontologically *more fundamental* than actuality.

Precisely because vibrations exceed any given actualization, the vibratory field of relationality they generate furnishes a source of superjectal potentiality within the spatiotemporal continuum. It is crucial that we grasp
this situation in its full radicality, for what it points to is an active force

or power that lies *within the settled world* but *is not proper to concrescing actualities*. This superjectal potentiality simply is the potentiality of the settled world that, as a total situation, goes into the genesis of every new actuality, and that, for this very reason, cannot itself be the product of such genesis. I call this potentiality "superjectal" precisely to indicate the radical exteriority of its operation in relation to concrescing actualities: it designates a power that belongs to vibrations *insofar as they exceed the entities* that actualize them in their own concrescences. The excess at issue here is an excess *over*, not an excess *of*: it *does not depend* on the concrescences that it catalyzes, *does not belong* to the entities resulting from such concrescences, and *is not relative* to their becoming. Far from being *the product of* particular actualizations, the vibratory continuum stands behind and supports them: it simply *is* the "real potentiality" that—in *our* spatiotemporal world—generates the vibratory contrasts that catalyze new concrescences as part of the world's continuous reproduction.

This excess proper to vibrations is crucial to what I consider to be Whitehead's fundamental contribution to a non-anthropocentric conceptualization of media. Though Whitehead himself does not address media directly, his ontology of vibration, and the fundamental correlation of vibration with feeling, allows us to locate media's operationality at the level of (or at least in relation to) the vibratory continuum itself, without requiring that it be channeled through any delimited subjective process. More simply still, Whitehead's ontology allows us to conceptualize twenty-first-century media's impact—their power to modulate the continuum—in terms of potentiality: if media shape the potentiality for the world to impact future experience, they do so *from the outside*—from the radically environmental perspective of the total situation of the settled world that, as we have seen, *precedes the genesis of any agent-centered subjective perspective*.

In his effort to develop a non-anthropocentric account of media rooted in Whitehead's vibrational ontology, Goodman would appear to seize the opportunity presented by this radically environmental operation for situating media beyond phenomenology. Nothing less seems to be at stake in his localization of media beyond perception: "If we subtract human perception, everything moves. Anything static is so only at the level of perceptibility. At the molecular or quantum level, everything is in motion, is vibrating. . . . All entities are potential media that can feel or whose vibrations can be felt by other entities."[44] By defining media in this way—in terms of potentiality for feeling or being felt—Goodman would seem to keep them open to the superjective operation of the settled world, and thus to install media directly within—indeed, as the very agency of—worldly sensibility.

And yet, Goodman cannot make good on the radicality of his definition. He cannot make good on his own radical position because of a lingering commitment to the privilege of concrescence and to the operation of "eternal objects" as the vehicle for vibrations to mediate relations. This commitment makes up one pole of what we can only describe as a fundamentally contradictory account of media: like Whitehead, Goodman holds up concrescence as the source for all actuality. Yet, directly countering this commitment is Goodman's engagement with Whitehead's vibratory ontology: specifically, Goodman invests the extensive (vibratory) continuum as a primordial source of potentiality. The result is that Goodman holds two commitments that stand at loggerheads one to the other: to the extent that the latter commitment to the vibratory continuum as source of potentiality requires an affirmation of the superjectal as the subjective modality of worldly sensibility (as Nobo and Jones both help to demonstrate), it directly impugns the coherence of the former commitment to the priority of concrescence. From my perspective, the only way to overcome this impasse is to aggressively develop the affirmation of the superjectal: we must invest in Goodman's own investment in the radical environmental agency of the superject. That is why, as I shall go on to argue, it is out of the ashes of this conflict between the two poles of Whitehead's thinking (instantiated here in Goodman's dual commitments) that a truly environmental and non-anthropocentric theory can emerge.

Signs of Goodman's ambivalence appear in the very language he uses to define media, and specifically in the phrase, "whose vibrations can be felt by other entities." For the qualification of "vibrations" with "whose" suggests that the vibrations belong to a "feeler" and are subsequently felt—as vibrations belonging to past "feelers"—by other entities functioning as "feelers" in their turn. In these constructions, all agency lies on the side of "feelers" or "prehenders," and none pertains to the vibrations themselves. Yet if the power of vibrations themselves is more primordial than the agency to which they give rise, as Jones has helped us understand, we can hazard the following functional definition of twenty-first-century media: grasped in terms of their superjectal operation, media modulate vibrations whose contrasts *in turn* produce *other* entities, and with them, new webs of relationality. This functional definition is equivalent to our earlier characterization of media as vehicles for channeling worldly sensibility toward specific experiential accomplishments. In both instances, the emphasis is on the indirect relationship between the source for creativity (worldly sensibility or vibratory continuum) and the resultant experiential events or processes: media operate as instruments that mediate sensibility for experiential achievement.

One key advantage of this definition is its sensitivity to superjective potentiality: vibrations remain *external* to the entities that feel them. Thus, even if vibrations can and do create relations between entities, their impact on the experience of such entities remains *indirect*. Grasped at the level of the vibratory continuum, media must designate something far more specific than a relation that obtains when one entity shares vibrations in common with another entity: media channel the operation of vibrations, and vibrations, together with media's modulation of them, are only *subsequently* felt by entities. Moreover, media channel vibrations for experiential accomplishments that include those experiences we typically associate with humans; in this sense, they play a much broader role than what Goodman imagines, for well beyond supporting the operation of concrescence, they mediate between the domain of sensibility and higher-order regimes of experience. In sum, entities and experiential societies alike do not feel media directly; what they feel are media *effects*, the way that media channel or modulate the vibratory continuum for specific purposes. Both entities and experiential societies can thus be said to feel media's modulation of the vibratory continuum, and it is their response to this latter, which catalyzes their feeling, that bootstraps them into becoming.

By correlating media with the channeling of sensibility, this definition helpfully specifies the scope of media's operationality: media operate on real potential prior to any actualization, and indeed, as I said above, they potentialize real potentiality in the sense that they bring the latter to bear on specific forms of experiential achievement. This correlation with potentiality underscores the error that is involved when media are identified—as they are on Goodman's account—with the activity of concrescence. Simply put, media cannot be identified with concrescence because such identification contradicts the vibratory continuum's status as real potentiality. To the extent that they operate in and through the vibratory continuum, media impact *the potentiality of vibrations themselves*. They thus modulate a field of potentiality that can only be environmental in relation to any future concrescence, as well as to any experiential society they may inform.

That is why Goodman's effort to place media in the vibratory continuum, and to accord mediatically inflected vibrations a priority over actualities, founders. This effort, despite its general congruence with the account I have sought to develop here, is simply incompatible with Goodman's overriding insistence that concrescences of actual entities produce the continuum:

> Whitehead's notion of the extensive continuum undoes the split between space and time. It expresses a general scheme of relatedness between actual entities in the actual world. More than that, Whitehead insists that the extensive continuum is, above all, a potential for actual relatedness. The continuum gives potential, while

the actual is atomic or quantic by nature. The continuum is not pregiven but exists only in the spatiotemporal gaps between actual occasions. *Rather than an underlying continual invariant, each actual entity produces the continuum for itself from the angle of its own occurrence. Only in this way is the continuum the means by which occasions are united in one common world.*[45]

Everything comes down to how we understand Goodman's phrase, "a potential for actual relatedness." On the one hand, the invocation of potential here would seem to indicate an awareness of—and an effort to capitalize on—the status of the vibratory continuum as the font of real potentiality for the genesis of new actualities. Yet, if that is the case, what can it mean to claim, as Goodman goes on to do, that each actual entity produces the continuum for itself?

Let us explore this question—and the problem it poses for Goodman's argument—by looking to an alternate view of how the vibratory continuum relates to actualities. In his complex and innovative work on extension in Whitehead's speculative ontology, philosopher Jorge Nobo argues that the extensive continuum weaves together a meshwork of real potentiality—a meshwork rooted in the superjective power of attained actualities—and thereby provides the basis for the thinking of solidarity that anchors Whitehead's ontology. Nobo's work will be useful here on account of its radical claim that the real potentiality created by worldly vibrations is more primordial than the production of actualities: understood in relation to our earlier exploration of the key and grounding role played by the dative phase, we can now see that it is the vibrational continuum itself that furnishes the objective datum for concrescences, and hence for the production of new webs of superjectal relationalities that, as I have sought to emphasize (following my claim for inversion), are the true agents of process in our contemporary world. In this respect, Nobo's account furnishes a mechanism for appreciating how media impact experience by way of their flavoring of real potentiality for the future: if twenty-first-century media produce data, and if their production of data has become increasingly central to the operation of contemporary society and the worldly sensibility involved therein, we can conclude that media now play a predominant role in supporting the ongoing production of real potentiality itself. Both in the form of actual data objectified and reentered into the settled universe and, equally importantly, in the form of data about this objectified data of sensibility (which in turn becomes objectified data), media have a pervasive, yet diffuse and indirect, impact on the production of actualizations at all scales—from new concrescences to the evolution of complex societies.

With this argument concerning media's flavoring of real potentiality for the future, we are once again returned to the key claim for access to the data of sensibility (CADS) that has structured my argument about twenty-first-century media. The double data-structure just predicated of media should recall my earlier discussion of the second-order oscillation that computation introduces as a third form of process distinct from both microscopic processes of concrescence and transition and higher-order processes of perception and symbolic reference. Where we earlier saw how this third form of process folded the speculative back on itself, in a way that relativized it to relationalities operating within experience, what we learn in the current context is how the double data-structure of media—the fact that the act of accessing worldly sensibility *is itself* a new sensible instantly and automatically added to worldly sensibility—provides a concrete structure for the data propagation of sensibility *as potentiality*. As such, this double data-structure helps to clarify the ontological and temporal status of twenty-first-century media, or, more precisely, to flesh out precisely what is at stake in the question of access that, for me, is the crucial operation of twenty-first-century media. In the figure of "data sensing"—the act of accessing sensibility that *is itself* the production of a new sensible—we encounter the perfect expression of the "indirection" of twenty-first-century media: twenty-first-century media come to bear on human experience as the simple result of the activity of accessing worldly sensibility. And it is, moreover, potential in its mode of being, or, more precisely, in relation to any events that may be constructed out of it: thus, the sheer activity of accessing worldly sensibility doesn't directly or necessarily wield any impact on any given human experience; it simply furnishes an expanded sensibility, which is to say, a source of potentiality, that could lead to concrete effects at the level of human experience.

By forging an indirect link between human modes of experience and the data of sensibility, the very act of accessing this latter can be said to constitute the "content" of twenty-first-century media: rather than introducing new prostheses for human capacities, or registering, storing, and transmitting experience beyond its lived parameters, twenty-first-century media are quite literally composed of the act of mediating the domain of worldly sensibility for human modes of experience. And again, let me emphasize the independence of this mediation from those modes: like Étienne-Jules Marey's graphic and chronophotographic machines, which (as we have seen) enjoy a sensory domain all their own, the processes of twenty-first-century media aim not to translate sensibility into the framework of these human modes of experience, but to introject into human experience data of sensibility that could never be lived by humans and that, in some sense, remain marked by their radical exteriority. It is for this reason that I have sought to show precisely how twenty-first-century media mark a shift from human-addressed to environmental media: without in any way simply abandoning the operation of media in their more traditional forms (and indeed media continue to function as prostheses or as registration, storage and transmission systems), the system of twenty-first-century media—or, more exactly, the expanded access to sensibility afforded by twenty-first-century media—is currently in the process of gradually excavating the diffuse operation of sensibility and emancipating its power (or causal efficacy) from the sensory, perceptual, and cognitive acts which it has long supported (and through which it has long been channeled, and, in effect, operationally restricted). With twenty-first-century media, we can address sensibility itself independently of its correlation with human modes of experience, and it is this address itself, or rather the production of new sensibilities it yields, that constitutes the content—and the promise—of twenty-first-century media.

Now that we have grasped how data propagates sensibility *as potentiality*, let us return to Nobo's claim that the extensive (or vibratory) continuum generates a meshwork of real potentiality that holds a priority over any actualities that will come to be attained on its basis. As Nobo sees it, Whitehead's account of the extensive continuum—an account Nobo recognizes to be fraught with inconsistencies—forms an absolutely crucial element of his process philosophy. Indeed, as Nobo sees it, Whitehead's account of extension in terms of a continuum furnishes nothing less than a *metaphysical* guarantee for the solidarity of actual entities: "The intelligibility and logical consistency of the solidarity thesis," argues Nobo, "presupposes positing the existence of an eternal continuum of extension whose metaphysical function is to ground the mutual transcendence, and the mutual immanence, of any two actual entities."[46] As we discover from Nobo's effort to bring coherence to Whitehead's position on extension, the tricky issue this metaphysical guarantee raises is how to correlate what Whitehead calls the "eternal continuum of extension"—a continuum that abstracts from all "additional conditions proper only to the cosmic epoch of electrons, protons, molecules, and star systems" and that does not even "include the relations of metrical geometry"[47]—with the "extensive continuum" underpinning our world. How do these two operations of extension relate to one another, and which one can be said to be foundational?

In his effort to clarify this situation, Nobo begins by aligning "mere extension" with "pure potentiality," and "spatio-temporalized extension" with "limited, or conditioned, [i.e., real] potentiality." In this way, Nobo manages to invert the apparent hierarchy underpinning Whitehead's ontology of extension: rather than beginning from the purely metaphysical continuum,

Nobo insists on the necessity to subordinate this purely metaphysical notion of extension to extension as the basis for experience. As Nobo sees it, this inversion is crucial to the coherence of Whitehead's scheme: because it only comes into effect through being instantiated in some vibratory configuration of our world, the metaphysical guarantee for the solidarity of the universe is not a transcendental condition for the vibratory continuum, but is, on the contrary and paradoxically, itself *a part of the extensive continuum*. Because of the Whiteheadian principle that each new actuality "has to arise from the actual world as much as from pure potentiality,"[48] Nobo feels justified in claiming that "pure potentiality is an abstraction from real potentiality; for the latter is always impure, that is, always conditioned by attained actuality."[49]

Nobo's decision to privilege real potentiality and the extensive continuum helps us cut through the confusion created by the following, often-cited and often-misunderstood passage from *Process and Reality* where Whitehead seeks to clarify how mere extension (the eternal continuum) correlates with the extensive continuum. Far from clarifying matters, however, Whitehead's analysis only seems to increase confusion. Specifically, Whitehead appears to identify the extensive continuum *both* with the purely metaphysical eternal continuum *and* with the continuum underpinning *our* world:

> The real potentialities relative to all standpoints are coordinated as diverse determinations of one extensive continuum. This extensive continuum is one relational complex in which all potential objectifications find their niche. It underlies the whole world, past, present, and future. Considered in its full generality, apart from the additional conditions proper only to the cosmic epoch of electrons, protons, molecules, and star-systems, the properties of this continuum are very few and do not include the relationships of metrical geometry. An extensive continuum is a complex of entities united by the various allied relationships of whole to part, and of overlapping so as to possess common parts, and of contact, and of other relationships derived from these primary relationships. . . . This extensive continuum expresses the solidarity of all possible standpoints throughout the whole process of the world. *It is not a fact prior to the world; it is the first determination of order—that is, of real potentiality—arising out of the general character of the world.* In its full generality beyond the present epoch, it does not involve shapes, dimensions, or measurability; these are additional determinations of real potentiality arising from our cosmic epoch.[50]

As I propose to understand it, following Nobo, this difficult passage asserts nothing less than the primacy of the extensive continuum in its fullest sense, namely as the continuum of *our* spatiotemporal world in all of its richness: only in its constitutive fullness can the extensive continuum fulfill the crucial function of expressing "the solidarity of all possible standpoints throughout the whole process of the world." From the standpoint of this entailment, the notion of mere extension (the eternal continuum) constitutes what amounts to a metaphysical guarantee of solidarity that, as I suggested above, is *derived* by abstraction *from* this full concept of the continuum.

In his commentary on this passage, Nobo clarifies the primacy of the extensive continuum by contrasting it both with the eternal continuum and with what he terms "a continuum of actualized extension." As careful analysis of the above passage shows, "mere extension" (the eternal continuum), far from being a source for the extensive continuum, is rather an abstraction from it and one that is, in some crucial sense, fully included in it. "It should be evident," states Nobo, "that by 'extensive continuum' we are to understand . . . not the Receptacle or mere extension as such, but either the spatio-temporal continuum peculiar to our world or, in general, the standpoint of any actual entity belonging to our cosmic epoch."[51] In both phrasings, the extensive continuum must be categorically differentiated—as the source for real potentiality—from any continuum of actualized extension. Thus Nobo continues: "Many a commentator of Whitehead has cited these or similar passages in support of the contentions that the extensive continuum is manufactured, bit by bit, by actual entities and that, therefore, it has the ontological status of a derivative abstraction from actuality. I have been defending the opposite theses, namely, that the extensive continuum is ontologically prior to the actual entities that come to be in it and that only a continuum of actualized extension can be considered as a derivative abstraction from actuality."[52]

Goodman, of course, fits Nobo's characterization to a tee: not only does he predicate his interpretation on a claim that the extensive continuum is *produced incrementally by* actual entities, but in so doing he simply levels the crucial distinction on which Nobo here insists, the distinction of the extensive continuum from any continuum of actualized extension. Once Goodman decides to channel the vibratory continuum through the concrescence of actual entities, he does the opposite to what Nobo urges: he treats the vibratory continuum as a fully actualized one. As I pointed out above, what is most striking about this decision is how it compromises the very power that Goodman seeks to attribute to vibrations: by rendering vibrations nothing more than the derivative product of actuality, of a continuum of actualized extension, Goodman compromises their real potentiality, the power they wield beyond, in excess over, and in some sense prior to, the becoming of concrescing actualities. With this conclusion, we can see exactly why Goodman's conflicting commitments render his position incoherent: channeling vibrations through concrescence deprives them—and the extensive, vibratory continuum they would continually produce—of the power to impact experience from the superjectal outside.

Nobo's bold conclusion that "the extensive continuum is ontologically prior to the actual entities that come to be in it" perfectly clarifies how real potentiality informs the genesis of new actualities: as the power of the settled world at a given moment in the ongoing genesis of the universe, the vibratory continuum is precisely what yields, via contrasts that express the real potentiality of the universe, data whose superjective subjectivity catalyzes new actualities as well as experiential entities at all scales. Whatever promise the vibratory continuum holds for rethinking media beyond anthropomorphism must accordingly stem from its capacity to host the heterogeneity of the superjectal outside. Because it accounts for the solidarity of actualities in a way that does not depend on their actualization via concrescence, the vibratory continuum furnishes a "ground" where media can operate "prior" to their capture by narrowly subjective processes, where, in short, media can express their superjectal power, their capacity to channel the force of worldly sensibility.

Vibratory Sensibility

To grasp how media operate within and through the vibratory continuum, and thus in indirect relation to human experience, we will need to introduce yet another dimension of the argument for the priority of real potentiality over actualities, and for the vibratory continuum as an expression of this priority. This dimension is the role played by eternal objects in Whitehead's account of concrescence but also in recent efforts, like Goodman's, to explore the correlation of media and the vibratory continuum on the basis of this account. To anticipate our trajectory here, we will counter this orthodox account by demonstrating why we must repudiate eternal objects *as eternal*. We must repudiate their eternal status for the same reason that we must repudiate the priority accorded actuality on the orthodox picture: *both accounts make the error of privileging the actualized continuum over the vibratory or extensive continuum.* Indeed, we can go so far as to say that the liberation of the real potentiality of the vibratory continuum depends directly on—and perhaps amounts to—a liberation *from its channeling through eternal objects.* Or, to put it otherwise, that the localization of real potentiality directly in the vibratory continuum accordingly furnishes a model for potentiality that conflicts with—and can take the place of—the orthodox account of real potentiality as a determination of the pure potentiality of eternal objects.

Because of its lingering commitment to precisely this element of Whiteheadian orthodoxy, Goodman's account once again founders precisely where it should triumph. In a word, Goodman finds himself compelled to subordinate vibratory contrast to the ingression of eternal objects:

> Whitehead's extensive continuum points to vibratory potentials jelling a multiplicity of space-times: here there is a resonance of actual occasions, which are able to enter into one another by selecting potentials or eternal objects. It is in such a potential coalescence of one region with another that an affective encounter between distinct actual entities occurs. The vibratory resonance between actual occasions in their own regions of space-time occurs through the rhythmic potential of eternal objects, which enables the participation of one entity in another. This rhythmic potential exceeds the actual occasion into which it ingresses.[53]

Rather than viewing the extensive continuum as generating vibratory contrasts that *precede and indeed catalyze* actualizations, along with any ingression of eternal objects into them, Goodman renders such contrasts—and whatever excess they may possess—both subordinate and relative to concrescing actualities.

This interpretation is anathema to the aim of my argument here: to situate media within—or, perhaps more precisely, at the level of—the vibratory continuum. In accord with this aim, we will need to repudiate the entirety of Whitehead's received account of real potentiality as a determination of the pure potentiality of eternal objects; like the reduction of the vibratory continuum just explored, this account subordinates real potentiality to the production of actuality (the actualization of eternal objects). By repudiating the canonical Whiteheadian account, we clear the ground for the development of a more radical account that situates potentiality wholly *within our world* and accords it a primacy as the source for actuality. Indeed, drawing on Nobo's key understanding of the extensive continuum as ontologically prior to the actual entities that come to be in it, we can simply dispense with the category of "pure potentiality" altogether and transform "eternal" objects into temporal, experiential ones that, like actual entities, find their objective source in the domain of vibratory potentiality.

No more the product of the ingression of eternal objects than of the actualization of the continuum, real potentiality is nothing other than the potentiality of the vibratory continuum itself. In this sense, the demotion of eternal objects I am here proposing parallels the demotion of concrescence central to Nobo's, Jones's, and my own understanding of Whitehead: just as concrescence loses its separateness and its exclusive status and becomes one element in a larger process culminating in repeated additions to the ongoing universe that increase the potentiality of the settled world, so too must eternal objects shed their purity and their status as "eternal" in order to become, as John Dewey thought they must, temporal elements that emerge "within the flux of experience in response to the resourcefulness of experience."[54]

On this modified account, which picks up on my earlier criticism of eternal objects in chapter 3, real potentiality turns out to be much more than simply the achievement of the ingression of eternal objects into actual entities (both in itself and as productive of future actualities). Real potentiality becomes the potentiality not of eternal objects exclusively, but of the entirety of the settled world out of which (no longer eternal) "eternal" objects are produced and which includes them. As I suggested above, this means that worldly sensibility, insofar as it constitutes the concrete texture of the settled world, takes the place of the pure potentiality of eternal objects (together with the God necessary to ensure their ingression into experience) as the source for potentiality. What remains to be understood, and what I shall focus on here, is precisely how worldly sensibility can support the potentiality of the settled world and how it might matter for our understanding of media.

Once again, the crucial point at issue concerns the operation of access, and in particular how access to the domain of sensibility (the vibratory continuum) *in itself* constitutes the power of twenty-first-century media and accounts for their potential to impact human experience. The power of twenty-first-century media is a power of potentiality, and the potentiality in question is the "real potentiality" of the actual world, the potentiality of worldly sensibility or vibratory intensity. What we can now add to our previous discussions of the claim of access to the data of sensibility (CADS) is a specification concerning the precise role twenty-first-century media play in potentializing worldly sensibility for human experience: as the vehicle of access to the data of sensibility, twenty-first-century media operate as brokers for the potentiality of sensibility. By gathering data from the operational present of sensibility and feeding it forward into a future operation of consciousness, twenty-first-century media make the surplus of sensibility into a potentiality for human experience, a power that can (but that doesn't have to) modify how we experience. In playing the role of "host" for worldly sensibility, twenty-first-century media thus frame sensibility in a way that makes it the "real potentiality" for experiences of all kinds, not least of which is the belated experience of consciousness I am calling feed-forward.

If the crucial point here is that twenty-first-century media operate at the level of the vibratory continuum—of the vibrations whose contrast generates the real potentiality of the settled world—it is important that we emphasize their role as mediator. As I put it above, twenty-first-century media mediate worldly sensibility itself, meaning that they operate to channel the power of sensibility (vibratory intensity) toward experiential creations of all sorts. In this sense, we can understand twenty-first-century media as an operation for tapping into the power of sensibility (the power of real potentiality) that dispenses with eternal objects entirely in favor of the power of superjective subjectivity. Recalling our earlier discussion of the fold of the speculative, we can appreciate that this operation is resolutely empirical, in the sense that it takes place within the domain of superjective relationalities constituting the settled world, even as it nonetheless remains speculative in relation to specifically human modes of sensing, perceiving, and thinking. With respect to our interpretation of Whitehead, we might say then that mediation simply replaces eternal objects, and in the process displaces the distinction of pure and real potentiality in favor of a doubling of real potentiality that allows us to claim (as I have just claimed) that twenty-first-century media potentialize sensibility (which is to say, that they potentialize real potentiality itself). The force of this displacement hinges on the capacity of worldly sensibility to furnish an alternate account of real potentiality that lets us dispense with Whitehead's eternal objects. Thus, what remains for us to explain is how vibrations directly generate real potentiality without implicating eternal objects and how the superjective existence of attained actualities can be directly "taken into account" (as Nobo puts it) by worldly processes (societies at all scales) without being channeled through concrescences.

With his distinction between "position" and "definiteness" of actual entities, Nobo provides just such an account. By reserving "position" to designate the metaphysical essence of actual entities, Nobo discovers a way to divorce the problem of explaining the solidarity of the universe from the doctrine of eternal objects that has traditionally been used to explain it.[55] As a result, Nobo is able to give a concrete account of exactly what happens when eternal objects are demoted—stripped of both their purity and their eternal status. More importantly still, he is able to unpack the "categoreal" nature of real potentiality, the way in which the attained world imposes its pervasive forms on the world in attainment, exercising an agency on the latter that can only come from the superjectal outside.

In his effort to unveil a metaphysical guarantee for the solidarity of the

universe that inheres within the experiential solidarity of the extensive (spatiotemporal) continuum, Nobo identifies "properties" that "must belong to
extension prior to actualization." These properties, crucially, are *ontologically more fundamental than eternal objects*:

> Actual entities are related to one another according to the deter-
> minations of the extensive continuum; but this is only to say that
> their becoming atomizes the continuum and thereby makes actual
> the solidarity *that was antecedently merely potential*. The extensive
> continuum, then, is to be understood as *imposing on the actualities
> that atomize it* the necessity that they function in, or be components
> of, one another. The sense in which actual entities are mutually im-
> manent accounts for, indeed is nothing else than, their solidarity
> or connexity. But we must not forget that, in a different though re-
> lated sense, actual entities are also mutually transcendent and that
> without their reciprocal transcendence there is no accounting for
> their discreteness and their individuality. Consequently, what we are
> now searching for are those properties of pure extension that will
> explain not just mere immanence but the *mutual immanence of ac-
> tual entities having non-overlapping extensive standpoints*. We are
> searching, in effect, for those properties of extension that account
> for mutual transcendence as well as for mutual immanence, that
> account, in short, for the solidarity of discrete occasions. And these
> properties *must belong to extension prior to actualization* because
> according to Whitehead the discrete actualities that atomize exten-
> sion are realizing a solidarity of standpoints that was antecedently
> potential.[56]

These properties are the unique "position" of every actual entity and its
modal presence in all other actual entities. Every actuality is, as Nobo explains, the "coordinate reality of all of its locations," meaning that it is
transcendentally implicated in every other actual entity. Nobo traces these
properties to "the *separative*, the *prehensive*, and the *modal* characters of
space-time" that Whitehead develops in *Science and the Modern World*: "By
reason of the separative, modal, and prehensive properties of the extensive
continuum, the unique immanent location of a subject-superject and the
many transcendent locations of its objectifications are all coordinated into
the one manifold reality of a single actuality."[57]

This argument has important consequences for the status of eternal objects that resonate with my above, Dewey-inspired criticism. Not only does
it obviate any need to appeal to eternal objects in order to explain solidar-

ity, but it grounds an account of solidarity in terms of every actuality's real potential for relationality. As Nobo explains, this account is far more capacious than the orthodox appeal to eternal objects:

> The whole point of the doctrine of position, then, is that an actual entity "has a status among other actual entities *not expressible wholly in terms of contrasts between eternal objects*" (citing *Process and Reality*, 229). The complete contrast of eternal objects ingressed in an actual occasion constitutes the determinate definiteness of that occasion. This definiteness is *part* of the occasion's essence, but it cannot be the *whole* of its essence. Accordingly, the occasion's definiteness is termed its *abstract essence*, whereas its complete determinateness is termed its *real essence* (citing *Process and Reality*, 60). . . . From this it follows that the uniqueness of an occasion's real essence—the uniqueness of its determinate constitution—is a function of its position and not of its definiteness.[58]

Nobo's point here is that eternal objects cannot explain solidarity precisely because they cannot capture the transcendent operation of every actual entity in all other actual entities: simply put, they fail to grasp the superjectal subjectivity of every actuality qua attained actuality. Moreover, by introducing the crucial distinction between position and definiteness, Nobo's account paints a very concrete picture of what happens as eternal objects become temporal: effectively stripped of their role as "pure potentials" for all actuality, eternal objects are able to take on a more specific function as determinants of the definiteness (the "how") of concrescence.

By transferring the burden of explaining solidarity from eternal objects as determinants of definiteness to the unique position of actualities, Nobo, like Jones, gives sway to the superjectal operation of actualities within other actualities as the source for creativity: "Considered in themselves," he writes, "the functionings of eternal objects in an actual entity will only give us the definiteness, or abstract essence, of that actuality. Therefore, it is the functionings, or objectifications, of all the other actualities in the said actuality which account for the latter's unique determinateness and self-identity. Accordingly, an actuality's position—its unique, nonshareable, determinateness—is a function of the objectifications within itself of the other actualities in its correlative universe."[59] On this account, there is solidarity of the universe and of every actuality with all other actualities *precisely* and *only* because of the superjectal operation of attained actualities *outside* of their own subjective geneses.

That is why the real potentiality of the vibratory continuum is a "categoreal" feature of the actualities of our world: by way of the superjectal subjectivity that yields position and solidarity, the attained world *imposes* its pervasive forms on all future attainment. For this reason, space and time, understood as the basic forms of the vibratory continuum, must be said to characterize the structure of extensiveness *prior to any atomization of the continuum*:

> Our world . . . is to be construed as resulting from the incoming of certain forms into the real potentiality provided by the extensive continuum. . . . Physical space and physical time are two such incoming forms. They are eternal objects of the objective species which have become, through social reproduction, pervasive features of the actualities of our world. Furthermore, it is because of their pervasiveness in the relevant supersessional past that their continued reproduction in the relevant supersessional future is, for all practical purposes, guaranteed. In other words, *the world as attained imposes its own pervasive forms on the world as in attainment.* In this manner, spatio-temporality, though not a true metaphysical category, becomes, nonetheless, a "categoreal" feature of the actualities of our world. It thus comes about that the actualities of our cosmic epoch are not merely extended; they are spatio-temporally extended. And this is *not* to say . . . that they are extended *in* space-time; rather, it is to say that their extensiveness is spatio-temporally structured; for, as I have explained, *extension is ontologically prior to, as well as a logical presupposition of, the spatio-temporal structure that it gains by reason of the world's component actualities.*[60]

With this conclusion, we have further proof that the vibratory continuum exercises agency independently of the actualities that come to be in it: the power of the vibratory continuum simply *is* the source of the data that catalyzes all attainment and, as such, the very basis for the solidarity of the universe.

We can now return to our discussion of the vibratory continuum and its promise to facilitate a becoming-cosmological of media. Having introduced the crucial distinction between position and definiteness and the way it deepens the agency of superjectal subjectivity, we are now in a position to appreciate more fully the fundamental limitation of Goodman's argument: because he retains the canonical account of potentiality in terms of eternal objects, Goodman *simply has no way to value the potentiality of the spatiotemporal (vibratory) continuum* other than through its atomization by actual entities that ingress eternal objects. He is therefore unable to make good on his own move to align media with a vibratory continuum that operates beneath any continuum of actualized extension. This is why, in complete antithesis to Nobo, Goodman must in the end credit the atomization of the continuum *as the very source for its potential*: "The actual entity breaks up its continuum realizing the *eternal object*, or particular potential that it selects. This breaking up, atomization or quantization, forces the eternal object into the space-time of the actual occasion; in other words, as the pure potential of the eternal object ingresses into actuality, it forces the becoming of actuality, and at the same time, pure potential becomes real potential."[61] We can now fully appreciate that, on Goodman's reading, real potentiality belongs exclusively—*and can only belong*—to the space-time that is actualized by actual entities, to an actualized continuum of actuality, rather than to the vibratory continuum itself. And with this conclusion, we can fully grasp the limitation of Goodman's account: so long as he insists on the primacy of actuality as the source for the atomization of the continuum, Goodman cannot avoid jettisoning the very element—the potentiality of the vibratory continuum—that could in fact support a non-anthropocentric and radically environmental account of media.

What we must take away from this critical analysis of Goodman's position is an appreciation for how much more is and must be at stake in a "nonanthropocentric ontology of ubiquitous media" than just a conversion of pure into real potentiality via a "vibratory tension between contrasting *occasions*." What is and must be at stake is the direct operation of *intensities* that are generated from contrasts *within the vibratory continuum itself*, or, in other words, from the operation of the superjective subjectivity of attained actualities operating as an environmental force. As we have already had occasion to observe, such intensities need not be channeled through subjective becomings, but operate first and foremost to qualify the extensive continuum as *real potentiality*: as the concrete potentiality for relationality resulting from the immanence and transcendence of every actuality. We might even say that the intensities generated within the vibratory continuum are what makes the metaphysical continuum ("mere extension") into an *empirical basis for the solidarity of the universe*: by defining concrete webs of potential relationality, these intensities literally render the continuum experientiable! The qualification of the extensive continuum by intensity is, in this sense, equivalent to a *making-sensible of the continuum*: for us and for all the beings in our universe, the extensive continuum is a "real potentiality" *within actuality* whose power—the power of intensity—is vibrational or sensory in nature.[62]

The emphasis Nobo places on the superjectal operation of vibrations as they impose themselves on all future attainment aligns with his emphasis (explored in chapter 3) on the objective datum as the "nonsubjective" agent (the "dative phase") through which the real potentiality of the settled world can give rise to new actualities. Indeed, as Nobo concludes, the dative phase simply *is* the real potentiality for the settled world to generate novelty. We can thus begin to see how it is the world itself—the "objective" or "dative" potentiality of the settled world—that exercises itself causally *outside of* and *independently from* the subjective operation of concrescence generative of new actualities. As Nobo explains, this operation is crucial to understanding the creativity Whitehead attributes to the universe:

> Attained actualities can function as efficient causes of a new occasion *only if their superjective existence is taken into account by the macroscopic process begetting the dative phase of the new occasion* . . . . This taking into account of the universe by the transcendent creativity *is not to be understood as belonging to, or as being part of, the new occasion's own subjective experience.* For the occasion's subjective experience *presupposes the existence of the occasion's dative phase*, and the dative phase itself presupposes, and results from, the transcendent creativity's taking into account of a newly completed state of the universe. Therefore, the notion of *taking into account* must be construed as . . . an essential aspect of the universe's extenso-creative or existential matrix—the aspect whereby each transcendent, or individualizing, manifestation of the universe's creativeness is determined, limited, and enabled by the state of the universe relative to that manifestation. . . . The point is that the Receptacle, the Creativity, the Ultimate—or whatever else we may wish to call it—must be able to take into account, or envisage, the existence of every new disjunctive plurality of completely attained creatures before it can create, relative to each new disjunction, the dative phase of a new creature. The dative phase thus created, since it is a finite extensive region containing within itself the objectification of the plurality in question, is the *real potentiality* for that plurality of attained creatures to be synthesized into the constitution and subjective experience of a novel creature.[63]

As an account of the environmental agency of the world, Nobo's characterization of the "taking into account of the universe" helps us situate the worldly or environmental operation of media, their tendency to impact the vibrational continuum directly. The crux of such environmental agency is the fact that worldly vibrations—together with the operation of media within and through them—remain *external* to the entities that feel them.

Thus, in stark contrast to Goodman's definition of media as the *feeling of* vibrations, *by and in* concrescing entities, the environmental agency of media guarantees vibrations a certain *autonomy*: as instruments for channeling the superjective force of the vibrational continuum, media only indirectly impact macrolevel experience, including human experience. Together with the vibrational power they channel, media can thus be said to take part in an environmental agency that remains autonomous from any subsequent, higher-order experience.

As I have been arguing throughout my study, this kind of environmental agency is central to the operation of twenty-first-century media: unlike nineteenth- and twentieth-century forms of recording which offered humans the capacity to experience the same events multiple times (Stiegler) or which formed the basis for complex disjunctions of machine and human (Kittler), twenty-first-century media typically afford no direct correlation to human perceptual experience whatsoever. The operation of computational microsensors, ubiquitous computing environments, and data-gathering and predictive analysis all share a common pattern: they all modulate worldly sensibility directly, prior to any processing by and indeed any correlation to higher-order human modes of experience. And if they do impact human experience, they do so only indirectly, by impacting the vibrational continuum of worldly sensibility in ways that remain imperceptible, and that are only sensed through means other than the macro-senses (sense organs) and at scales beneath what characterizes ordinary human experience as we know it, or have known it, up to now.

In her unpacking of what she calls the "intensive achievement" on the part of the settled universe, Judith Jones correlates the vibratory character of the universe with the worldly or environmental power of superjects. As Jones sees it, vibrations are by definition external to the actualities they impact. They are in excess over concrescing actualities and operate prior to their genesis. That is why it makes no sense at all to speak of a vibration that terminates in the concrescence of an actuality:

> Both individuality of concrescent process and "sameness" of enduring character refer to intensive achievement. Intensive achievement is the formed agency of contrastive feeling. It is my suspicion that the denial that a subject is "the same" in its objectifications *stems from a conception of agency as something that belongs to the unitary subject of concrescence.* The agency of contrast *is* the subject, the subject *is* the agency of contrast. To be a subject is to be a provoked instance of the agency of contrast, and that is all it is. Thus, wherever the contrasts achieved by an individual are reiterated in

another individual, the original individual *is* there in the agentive
sense. The pattern involved in an intense contrast is more than a
mere arrangement of eternal objects. It is the feeling of the dynamic
presence of the (other) individuals felt into the unity of a subject's
intensity. This is the only way to understand Whitehead's repeated
assertion of the vibratory character of actuality. No vibratory character has only one cycle *qua that vibratory character—to be a vibratory character is to be an intensive imposition on all subsequent
process, and, on the other end, to have emerged from the enduring
vibrations of other insistent agencies of contrast.* I see no other way
of understanding why provision for future intensity is included in
the category respecting "subjective" concrescence.[64]

Intensity simply *is* the process through which worldly vibrations generate
superjective force by means of contrast. On this understanding, vibrations
should be thought of neither as belonging to subjects, nor as being ingressed
into subjects in the form of eternal objects. Rather, as Jones puts it, vibrations constitute *"an intensive imposition on all subsequent process"*: they
operate by constraining, but also by enabling, the genesis of contrasts in the
future. Only by conceptualizing vibrations in this way can we avoid the error
of construing the power involved in the vibratory throbs constitutive of experience as a power pertaining exclusively or primarily to the subjective aim
driving concrescence, and properly view its operation—its generation of
contrasts—*as what gives rise to subjects*, understood here (following Jones)
as nothing more nor less than the agencies of contrast.

Grasped as a supplement to Nobo's notion of the "taking into account
of the universe," Jones's development of the environmental agency of superjects locates the source for the creativity of novelty squarely in the experiential domain of the settled world. In this sense, Jones's conception
of intensity expresses the payoff of the claim for inversion (CIF) that has
guided my reading of Whitehead: what we learn from her contribution is
that concrescences are not simply instruments for the operation of process,
but that they are, *like everything else in the world*, generated on the basis
of the power of intensity produced by vibratory contrasts. Indeed, given
what Jones has to say about the "vibratory character" of actuality—and
specifically, about how it captures the force of the mutual transcendence of
attained actualities—we could go so far as to claim creativity to be a function of the vibratory continuum itself, where the continuum is understood,
not, with Goodman, as an "achronological nexus outside the split between
space and time," but rather as the most basic, most minimal periodicity of
our spatiotemporally determinate, causally efficacious world.[65] On Jones's

account, intensities are achievements of the vibratory continuum that, if they express the solidarity of the latter, do so not by instantiating some abstract metaphysical schema, but by way of their concrete, empirical activity: "In a vibratory cosmos," Jones concludes, "intensities must come to be."[66] To this, we might add that their coming to be simply *is* the becoming of the vibratory cosmos.

Insofar as it explicates the vibratory continuum as worldly sensibility—as the real potentiality for intensive achievement—Jones's theorization of intensity furnishes a basis for conceptualizing the agency of the vibratory continuum both as a materialized and causally efficacious real potentiality and as an agency not relative to any particular actuality-in-attainment. In line with Nobo's understanding of the extensive continuum as ontologically more fundamental than any actual entities that come to be in it—and yet as fully empirical—the vibratory continuum of intensity captures the seething, heterogeneous, and multi-scalar power of a concrete world—the worldly sensibility—always already at play at any particular moment of actualization. The point, as Jones makes clear, is not to ratify "the relentlessness of perishing that marks a boundary between existents," but rather to affirm "the persistent vibratory achievement of intensive feeling that marks the interpenetration of individuals in a non-idealistic and nonmonistic sense."[67] Insofar as intensity precedes any distinction between subject and superject, it expresses an agency of real potentiality that cannot be relativized to a particular individual perspective; as the power of the vibratory continuum (the agency of vibratory contrasts), intensity explains how—indeed it simply *is* how—worldly sensibility comes to wield subjective force, or, more precisely, how it comes to exercise its superjective subjectivity. And because it operates at a level that precedes the self-reference, no matter how inchoate, constitutive of subjective concrescence, intensity can help align the vibratory continuum, and can itself be aligned, with a radically environmental perspective. Following such a radicalizing alignment, the vibratory continuum of intensity can be seen to be an "existential matrix," to borrow Nobo's term, that is "*sensitive* . . . to its own successive states of actual and potential determinateness," but that is not and cannot be "relative to some actual entity" or other.[68] It is a generalized field of sensibility without which, to paraphrase Whitehead, there would be nothing, nothing, pure nothing.

Let us finally return to the becoming-cosmological of media. As we have anticipated, the above analysis of the vibratory continuum facilitates a localization of media outside of the narrowly subjective processes that emerge, indirectly, from it. Shedding its former role as surrogate for the perceptual flux of experience, media comes to mediate a level of sensibility—what I have been calling worldly sensibility—whose operation is ontologically more fundamental than the sensory qualities produced by the ingression of eternal objects into concrescing actualities. Because of their capacity to record and process data of sensibility, twenty-first-century media give us access to a domain of experience, and indeed to a domain of our own experience, that has long been inaccessible: through their direct modulation of the vibratory continuum, they mediate the worldly sensibility (potentialize the real potentiality) out of which our experience emerges; and by capturing sensibility as data, they give us a means to feed sensibility forward into our future conscious experience.

We can now fully appreciate why Whitehead's conception of the vibratory continuum is so fruitful for our task of developing a non-anthropocentric account of media. Vibrations are both antecedent and transcendent in relation to the specific concrescences of actual entities that would seek, even if only punctually or atomically, to contain them. Whatever promise vibrations might hold to support a non-anthropocentric, non-prosthetic, and radically environmental theory of media is bound up with their status as independent from concrescence, which is to say, as a more primordial element or unit of process than what comes to the fore in Whitehead's orthodox account. It is only on account of their radical excess *over* any concrescing actualities they may inform that vibrations may be said to constitute a field of real potentiality—a texture of worldly sensibility—whose efficacy is more primordial as well as broader in scope than any unitary subjective aim. And it is only on account of this excess that media can assume their own proper primordiality, as instruments to channel the power of worldly sensibility, to potentialize the world's real potentiality in ways that bring it into nonconscious, environmental contact with human modes of experience.

Conclusion: Implication

The oneness of the universe, and the oneness of each element in the universe, repeat themselves to the crack of doom in the creative advance from creature to creature, each creature including in itself the whole of history and exemplifying the self-identity of things and their mutual diversities.

Alfred North Whitehead, *Process and Reality*

In his recent, prizewinning critical performance piece, *Gatherings* (2011), media artist Jordan Crandall implicates the subjectivity of his performance within larger, specifically technical, environmental confounds—what he characterizes as "diffuse, 'animated' surrounds" that offer "cognitive and ontological supplements to human agency."[1] In the artist's description, *Gatherings* "is a performative study of the nature of the event and the new forms of awareness, cognition, and material agency that are emerging in data-intensive environments. It is about how things come together as matters worthy of attention: how actors assemble, relate, and affiliate in entities and phenomenal occurrences that are more than the sum of their parts."[2] To concretize the argument for the expansion of perception that I have been developing in this study, I shall now explore how Crandall's performance foregrounds the transformation of subjectivity within contemporary media networks.

I propose to interrogate Crandall's performance as indicative of a certain tension between the dispersal of experience elicited by twenty-first-century media and the ongoing—and perhaps never more pressing—necessity for a return of and to human-centered attention. As I have stressed all along, my conceptualization of the *feed-forward* of data into consciousness lies at the very center of my interest in exploring the notion of experience in the light of twenty-first-century media. Indeed, it constitutes the core of my conviction that (human) experience remains crucial in the face of its apparent marginalization by the networked regimes of twenty-first-century media. For if the dispersal of experience produced by contemporary media marginalizes not simply the operation but the very role and relevance of consciousness, and if at times my focus has centered on analyzing such marginalization for its own sake, my aim throughout has been to discern and to develop what I take to be the "upside" for consciousness—and for humans—within the networked regimes of twenty-first-century media. That is why I have insisted on developing a theoretical account of consciousness's reconfiguration capable of laying the ground for practical developments that directly engage the expanded access to sensibility afforded consciousness by the structure of feed-forward.

By focusing on Crandall's *Gatherings* as exemplary of the way in which human bodyminds encounter and make use of the various kinds of information-rich, media-saturated environments within which we now typically live and act, I thus hope to thematize in a particularly clear and compelling manner the centrality of the operation of consciousness under the new conditions installed by twenty-first-century media. For, more than a simple inventory or diagnosis of media change, what Crandall's performance brings to the fore is the imperative for human subjectivity to undergo a transformation that aligns it with—or as I shall prefer to say, that *implicates it within*—the vibratory sensibility of an ever-increasingly technified world. Crandall's performance will accordingly be evaluated for its success in responding to the experiential challenges posed by our becoming implicated within the complex ecologies of twenty-first-century media. How, I shall ask, does Crandall's performance engage the situation of consciousness coming to awareness—acquiring "presentational immediacy"—well after the occurrence of the events that cause, or, more precisely that will go on to cause, such awareness? By performatively enacting the human bodymind's implication into mediated circuits of sensibility, Crandall's work discovers—indeed, *inaugurates*—new modes of "acting" in which the *propensity* of the situation as a whole holds sway over any delimited agency that may operate, already fully constituted, within it, including the agency of a human subject understood as a minimally transcendent or otherwise separable constituting force.

What Crandall's work thereby makes salient is how the *propensity* of the total situation that has been the focus of my analysis in this book impacts our subjective experience. More precisely, Crandall's work exemplifies and performatively elicits how such propensity breaks fundamentally with the core phenomenological commitment to the principle of subjective transcendence: the subjectivity it extracts from the propensity of the total situation is not a subjectivity that withdraws from the world, but one that *expresses* the creativity of the total situation understood exclusively in and for itself, as a distinct and self-contained moment in the ongoing becoming of the universe. This subjectivity, which may be "anchored" in a human bodymind, does not however *belong to* that bodymind. Indeed, far from constituting the interiority of a transcendental subject, this subjectivity is radically distributed across the host of circuits that connect the bodymind to the environment as a whole, or, more precisely, that broker its implication within the greater environment.

Human bodyminds do, however, enjoy some privilege as the locus of the subjective expression of the propensity of a total situation. As I have sought to suggest at every turn in the argument developed above, human bodyminds are always implicated within—and always acquire their agency from—experiential situations that exceed their perceptual grasp. This implication generates a perspective that, though only one perspective among myriad others, nonetheless remains special for us: without being the sole or dominant agents of situations that exceed the scope of our survey, we nevertheless experience such situations, and their excess over our modes of apprehending them, from our point of view and in relation to our interests. Our implication within larger situational ecologies thus goes hand in hand with a newfound capacity to appreciate such implication, a capacity that, as I have underscored here, is facilitated by the technical feeding-forward of environmental information into just-to-come apprehensions of consciousness.

This compatibility of implication with a new, technically mediated form of appearance [*Erscheinung*] suggests a potential trajectory for rethinking the role of phenomenology in the context of twenty-first-century media. For, when they feed data of sensibility forward into futural consciousness, today's microcomputational sensors and predictive analytic systems introduce technical mediation into the very heart of phenomenal appearance and, in so doing, call into question the "autonomy" of the transcendental subject of (orthodox) phenomenology. In accordance with my aim to explore the predicament of human beings in the new experiential environments created by twenty-first-century media, I want to conclude my theorization of the feed-forward structure of twenty-first-century consciousness by sketching out a phenomenology of implication. Rooted in Crandall's performative embrace of the propensity of the mediated lifeworld, such a phenomenology contrasts explicitly with the phenomenology of constitution still central to much contemporary work in phenomenology: where the latter looks to consciousness to *constitute* phenomena, a phenomenology of implication looks instead to the world—to the worlding of the world (to "de-presencing")—as the source for the total situation within which appearances arise and can be made manifest to consciousness.

Engaging Crandall's *Gatherings* from this theoretical perspective, I shall focus on how his performative self-implication into twenty-first-century media circuits undercuts the distance of intentionality—the minimal self-transcendence—that allows the subject to *constitute* the phenomena of its experience. Taken as a contribution to a phenomenology of implication, Crandall's performance exemplifies how the world can manifest directly in and through the activity of human bodyminds, without requiring any form of subjective transcendence, including the distance of intentionality. Human activity materializes in *Gatherings* as a part of the propensity of the greater total situation; and the way in which the human bodymind can indeed *host* the manifestation of the world is precisely by implicating itself—or rather, by letting itself be implicated—within this propensity.

On this understanding, any appearance of worldly sensibility as a "content of consciousness"—as a element *constituted by* the activity of a separated and self-contained consciousness—is, at best, a derivative phenomenon, and one that, as we have seen, has become increasingly superfluous in the environments of twenty-first-century media. Or, to put it more simply, we could say (again) that the inaugural dream of phenomenology—to constitute consciousness at the moment of its self-present happening—has run its course: confronted with the networks of twenty-first-century media, constituted consciousness has been forced to relinquish any operational role it may have in creating sensible presencing. In the worst-case scenario, it relinquishes this role to the marketing campaigns of contemporary data and cultural industries which do everything they can to bypass the domain of consciousness. And in the best-case scenario—the theorization of feed-forward at the heart of my argument here—consciousness relinquishes its operationality to the feeding-forward of technically gathered data of sensibility into future or just-to-come awareness that comes to consciousness directly from the environmental outside, "contaminating" its "intimacy" with artifactually produced contents that not only haven't been lived, but *cannot ever be lived by consciousness.*[3]

Gathering as Implication

Crandall's performance begins with the artist adopting the persona of a familiar figure, a man sitting at a café watching people pass by; reminiscent of that icon of modernity, Poe's "man of the crowd," this figure is almost immediately displaced as the artist quickly swaps it out for that of an "observational expert sitting at the interfaces of an intelligence agency, interpreting movements on images, maps, and screens."[4] No more than a third of the way into the performance, this figure is displaced in turn, as the specialized eye of the observational expert finds it agency surpassed by "the vast reservoirs of datasets" that yield their "patterns" only to a "calculative seeing."

Enacting these discrete stages in the displacement of human seeing by machine vision, the performance features Crandall narrating the transformations of human agency and subjectivity—of his own agency and subjectivity—as various screen-based images and videos as well as environmental sounds materialize the agency of the environment and bring it to bear on his experience. The three main sections of the performance describe three stages in the advent of a hybrid agency composed of human elements implicated within larger technical circuits. As we witness the assimilation of the artist's subjective point of view into a broader environmental perspective, we participate in the gradual displacement of "the centrality of the human agent in the process of tracking": within the broader environmental picture materialized by technical tracking, human agency enjoys no de jure privilege and can lay claim to no transcendence or mastery.

As we might expect from our earlier consideration of Crandall's theoretical writing in chapter 4, *Gatherings* pays careful attention to the ways in which the technification of the urban environment has modified the modes in which humans act, perceive, and sense. More specifically, and most crucially, it directly engages the operation of sensibility at the level of the total environment. Indeed, Crandall's performative exploration of and experimentation with contemporary media makes common cause with the main argument of my study; he too accepts, indeed welcomes, the transformation wrought by twenty-first-century media, and he takes as the very basis for his practice some of the concrete ways in which today's microsensors and datamining capabilities catalyze a wholesale revolution in the economy between narrowly subjective sensation and worldly sensibility.

In *Gatherings*, Crandall approaches this general transformative potential of twenty-first-century media through a specific lens—that of contemporary technologies of tracking; such technologies, he explains, undergird the experience of movement common to all levels of phenomena and operative *beneath* perception proper:

> I explore the constitution of agency and event in terms of a very specific historical context: a contemporary environmental space driven by the techniques of tracking. Ascending with the rise of compu-

tation in mid-century wartime, . . . tracking as a science of movement optimization . . . has shaped a very specific kind of practiced
timespace. It has shaped an urban environment where movement is
understood as strategically calculable: a world where all entities are
regarded as transported with some degree of predictive regularity.
All urban phenomena are categorized, standardized, and rendered
interoperable within the analytical architectures and procedures of
this strategic, calculative mobilization. It constitutes a defining organizational horizon for the movements of the world—a sensory,
cognitive, and calculative ambience against which the phenomena
of urban life are understood.[5]

Gatherings focuses on how tracking, with its contemporary reliance on
"algorithmic procedures" and "automated systems," now operates within
complex "distributed network environments" where its functionality is supplemented and augmented by microsensors and location-aware technologies
that are typically embedded into mobile devices, automobiles, buildings,
and urban spaces. In Crandall's theoretical vision, but also in his performative practice, this expanded functionality of tracking technologies, and of
the "interoperability" of movements that it facilitates, induces crucial modifications not simply in how humans experience their lived environments,
but also, and most strikingly, in how environments themselves directly
contribute—*as sensors*—to the genesis of experiences. As Crandall puts it,
"Environments become able *to directly sense* phenomena and respond to
what they apprehend, in ways that complicate distinctions between body
and space, as well as between human, artifact, and computer."[6]

Consider the striking way in which Crandall's piece manages to move beyond simply thematizing this new situation in order directly to implicate the
very agency of the human subject within the technological shift it chronicles.
In contrast to theoretical writing, his own not excepted, Crandall's *Gatherings* is able to *express* the impact of this shift literally—*as* the progressive modification undergone by the artist (and, by extension, the spectator)
across the duration of the performance. *Gatherings* advances a subtle, indeed subterranean, "argument" that the impact of the "interoperationality"
of twenty-first-century media *can be accessed only via a logic of expression*,
which is equally to say, only through and by means of the subject's implication within its broader environmental logic.

To understand why, we need only consider Crandall's rejection of the
media theoretical figure of the "interface" in favor of what I would propose
to call "implication." As he sees it, the figure of the interface only serves to
reinforce long-standing philosophical divides—between subject and object,

human and world—that themselves stand in the way of a fuller theorization of what is at stake in twenty-first-century media. That is why *Gatherings* approaches the new sensing capacities of the technologized environment not "in terms of formed and distinct objects or subjects" but "in terms of their complexes of practices" which, moreover, it understands "as involving affective transmission and absorption"—elements that break down the separation between human and world—far more than "reflective distance."[7]

In the place of the "interface," which can only impose distance, Crandall proposes the "program." More than simply algorithmic, the program is "a guiding principle of structural inclination" that is equally technical, social, and practical. Every program, claims Crandall, "is sensitive to the patterns, rhythms, and affects of its surrounding environment—speeds, material constitutions, and regulations; flows for pedestrians, vehicles, information, utilities, and goods. It meshes with the very scene it contemplates, amid the ebb and flow of movement, in the midst of the fugitive and the common. Everywhere at home, it is a fluid regulating agency that registers the world, yet remains hidden from it: a mechanism of awareness, as vast as the streets themselves, whose flickering presence it both gathers, reflects, and incorporates."[8] The program thus furnishes an alternative principle of organization—of *gathering*—that differs fundamentally from the figure of the subject. As developed in Crandall's performance, the concept of the program underscores the retreat from any internal, subject-constituted process of unification; thus, programs are said to operate at multiple levels: as the code underlying the technical script of the performance; as the gravitational center around which materials, themselves already burgeoning with "inherent awareness," gather; as the principle for opening onto and accommodating "more structures of life," and thus more potentiality; as the organizing principle for a "diffuse, 'animated' surround [that] offers a cognitive and ontological supplement to human agency."[9]

The program is the operation by which affiliations are forged across technical, affective, symbolic, and rhythmic dimensions of experience. It is what facilitates the production—in Crandall's performance specifically, but also in general—of *gatherings* understood as continuously and incrementally *renewed*, distinctly *horizontal* and *anticipatory* compositions. Gatherings implicate distinct elements, including humans, into their immanent and future-directed inclination, and for this reason must be considered expressions of worldly metamorphosis rather than products of subjective synthesis.

Because they generate worldly sensibility as I have sought to theorize it here, gatherings anchor an account of human implication within larger worldly confounds where the human element remains one among many. Such an account contrasts in significant ways with phenomenological positions that introduce a transcendental subject as the—allegedly necessary—recipient of the world's manifestation. At once theoretical and performative, Crandall's notion of gathering furnishes nothing less than an account of how the technically facilitated self-sensing of the world, despite positioning the human as one agency among (a multiplicity of) others, nevertheless implicates the human in a special way: as the "observer" of what Merleau-Ponty would call the reversibility of the flesh (or, as I would prefer to say, of worldly sensibility).

In one description of how such implication occurs, Crandall draws attention to the way the interoperationality of today's media environments compel human agents to attune their activity to the "inclinations" of larger compositions: "In order to endure, I must continually 'update,' extend, maintain and be maintained in continuing moves. I must affiliate, cultivate my modulation in gatherings that can carry me forth. As I do so, I must negotiate adherence to the demands for movement and attendance that these affiliations seek. I must push forth and be pulled forth through gatherings and adjust myself to the prevailing terms of their movement-constitution, their structural inclination."[10] Taken in its full radicality, Crandall's notion of attunement would require him to put the "I" in parentheses, since it—the "I"—emerges precisely and always transitorily from out of the process of gathering. In this it makes common cause with the conceptualization of affective attunement proposed by child psychoanalyst Daniel Stern:[11] for Crandall no less than for Stern, what is at issue is precisely a process of attuning—or *gathering*—that occurs prior to and beneath the level of any self-referential, substantial subject or "I."

Like the experience of subjectivity as understood by Whitehead (and in particular by Whitehead as read through Judith Jones's *Intensity*), the "I" of Crandall's performance is itself a composition, a *gathering*, of a host of agencies that act on one another (thereby generating intensity) and that, as superjective potentiality, are in excess over their own proper subjective power: actors, Crandall tells us at the end of Section 1, "solicit one another, act upon one another, recruit one another, harness and channel one another's transmissions. They are agency of one another. Concentrated and networked. Analytical and active. Objective and immersive. They band and disband, accumulate and release. They extend and consolidate. They attune . . . to the sensory, rhythmic and atmospheric exchanges that compose them." With this explanation, and particularly with his claim that gatherings are "*agency of one another*," Crandall taps directly into the power of the Whiteheadian superject: by hosting superjectal relations, gatherings facilitate the interoperability—the interagency—of the world's worlding.

Implicated within this interagential relationality, actors find their power

to act in the potentiality of the relational field itself: "Actors," notes Crandall, "are less constituted in movement, however directed or distracted"
than "in a teeming, vibratory instantaneity. They are excessive, 'beyond
themselves'—impersonal, . . . rendered public and precarious, not at the
center, not primary or alone."[12] Mobilizing the very same vibratory power
that animates the extensive continuum and real potentiality, Crandall's performative gatherings enact a *phenomenology of implication* that is equally
an ontology of potentiality. Operationalized by programs which are as much
technical as social, as much rhythmic as affective, gatherings always implicate more than what can be calculated and tracked. That is why, at the heart
of Crandall's practice, and at the culmination of his performance, programs
are explicitly identified with potentiality. "The challenge" faced by the phenomenology of implication is how "to meet an external agency without
preconceptions, without filtering it through a scaffold of preferences, clas-
sifications, or rules-based requirements. Without reducing it to an object."
To meet this challenge requires Crandall—and us in turn—to move beyond
resistance: we must ride the wave catalyzed by the program not to close it
in on itself, but to open out onto the world's potentiality. What is required,
Crandall reiterates, "is not a resistance to program but *the amplification of
its potential*—the extension of program to allow for *the accommodation of
more structures of life*." In his conjuncture of implication with potentiality,
program with gathering, Crandall thus positions the interoperationality of
contemporary tracking technologies—standing in for twenty-first-century
media as a whole—as a critical, productive, and no longer avoidable mediation of potentiality.

   In a move that cuts through whatever lingering opposition continues to
inform my above juxtaposition of Whiteheadian potentiality and the probabilistic models of predictive analytics, Crandall positions tracking itself—
tracking as a technical mediation of activity—as a crucial means of generating experiential excess. Where I focused on the disparity between the
closed models of predictive analytics and an open ontology of potentiality,
Crandall introduces the possibility to view tracking as an ontological potentiality *in its own right*, and one that is in itself *in excess over its own instrumental functioning*: "The approach is not resistant so much as extensive
and excessive—not a resistance to tracking so much as *an exceeding of it, a
washing over it*. It involves the creation of flexible databases—scaffolds on
which categories are crafted and make sense—that are as rich ontologically
as the social and natural worlds they map." With this ontologizing of tracking, we come back to the expressive dimension of *Gatherings* alluded to
above, though in an expanded frame that speaks to the specificity of the *aesthetic* dimension of twenty-first-century media. What is productive about

Crandall's performance—its channeling of tracking through its impact on Crandall's own bodily agency—is here extended to the impact of tracking as such. Thus, when Crandall's performance expresses the experiential impact of twenty-first-century media as the displacement his own agency undergoes following its implication into machinic arrangements of sensibility, so too does it position the impact of tracking in the aesthetic register. More specifically, by amplifying tracking well in excess of what could be captured by any human perceiver, Crandall manages to unveil a dimension of tracking's operationality that can be accessed *neither* instrumentally *nor* theoretically, but can only be experienced performatively. Accordingly, it is only through practice—and indeed only through a practice dedicated to keeping open the relational potential of technics—that the aesthetic dimension of tracking, its excess over its instrumental function, can be accessed at all.

Appearance as Sensibility, or the World Is Self-Sensing

With its conjunction of implication and potentiality, Crandall's performance helps specify how the transformation of human subjectivity explored here—its becoming implicated within and as part of the propensity of a total situation—finds its source in the potentiality generated by twenty-first-century media's direct modulation of sensibility. To the extent that potentiality constitutes the mode in which the settled world—what I have been calling worldly sensibility—expresses its power to create future worlds, the conjunction of implication with potentiality calls for a conception of subjectivity as *the power of potentiality*. We have already seen how this conception requires a modification of Whitehead's philosophy that brings the superject to the fore: in its role as subjective power of potentiality, the superject expresses the creativity of worldly sensibility, or, more precisely, the propensity of its total situation.

My invocation of the late work of Merleau-Ponty at the end of chapter 4 was aimed precisely at fleshing out this superjectal creativity of worldly sensibility and specifically at understanding how its propensity encompasses subjectivity, including human subjectivity, as part of its potentiality. There we saw how worldly sensibility, once it is conceptualized on the basis of Merleau-Ponty's final ontology, is revealed to be consubstantial with the continually growing real potentiality of the universe. As an alternative to Whitehead's overtly Platonizing account of eternal objects, such an account of worldly sensibility not only avoids privileging concrescence (or any delimited subjective operationality), but manages to integrate it as one element in a broader and continuous intensification of the settled world's potentiality. On this picture, far from forming a separate process primarily responsible for the universe's creativity, concrescence (or any operation of subjective actualization) assumes a more modest role as part of a larger operation of ongoing sensibility—as one element in a larger propensity—that is only *as a whole* generative of creativity.

What remains to be theorized is how this liberation of the propensity of the total situation yields a notion of subjectivity as implication that breaks with the phenomenological commitment to subjective transcendence, no matter how minimal. In this respect, it is significant that the integrated operation of worldly sensibility I have sought to develop in this study manages to rebut a crucial recent criticism that has been raised against Merleau-Ponty's final ontology, and that would by extension apply to any post-phenomenological ontology whose aim is to dissolve subject-object dualism and extend subjectivity beyond higher-order phenomenological beings.

By critically interrogating contemporary French philosopher Renaud Barbaras's recent criticism of Merleau-Ponty's final ontology, I hope to make clear that there is a crucial subjective dimension to the experience of consciousness within the environments created by twenty-first-century media, but also—and this is the key point—that this subjective dimension *substitutes for* the orthodox phenomenological subject and indeed for any figure of the subject understood as transcendent in relation to the world. With twenty-first-century media, we are able to see clearly what has perhaps always been the case: namely, that our subjectivity is due not to some purported "autonomy" of our interior experience but to our implication in dispersed and heterogeneous circuits that modulate the total situation we always find ourselves within and that—by way of their tensions and "metastability"—make up its propensity, its power to create the future.

In his 2008 essay "The Three Meanings of the Flesh: On an Impasse in the Ontology of Merleau-Ponty," Barbaras raises doubts about the adequacy of Merleau-Ponty's monism of the flesh to overcome the persistent dualism of his earlier phenomenology of perception. Recognizing the allure of this monism, Barbaras compares it to the work of a magician: "Just as the rabbit that reappears in the hat of the spectator is not, in reality, the same as the one that disappeared in the prestidigitator's scarf, it is not certain that this inversion of the circuit of phenomenality gives us a point of arrival that coincides with the point of departure." With this in mind, Barbaras is able to clarify what he calls his "malaise":

> In other words, in making the flesh, as visibility, the subject of phenomenality, do we give ourselves the means to account for the subject from which we started? By the intermediary of its own flesh,

the subject is dissolved into a world that thereby becomes Visible. It is in this sense that one can speak of a flesh of the world. But can we make the inverse journey and account for vision beginning from the Visible? Can we climb back up from the flesh of the world to the flesh as *mine*? In Merleau-Ponty's terms, how can the relation of the visible to itself move through me and constitute me in seeing? We have passed from an ontic concept to an ontological one, but can this latter integrate that to which it has opened access?[13]

At the heart of Barbaras's objection here is a conviction that Merleau-Ponty's overriding desire to ontologize phenomenology conflicts with the very imperative of his final philosophy to account for the appearance of the flesh of the world. For Barbaras, there simply is no way to get from the ontological continuity of body and world to the experience of a subject in and to which this ontological continuity—the flesh—would appear.

Barbaras's further elucidation of this conflict makes clear the target of his criticism: what he ultimately objects to is the very notion *that the world could be self-sensing*, that the "Visible" could self-assemble in a way that would produce vision. As Barbaras will conclude (in righteous and, as I shall explain below, overly literal defense of Merleau-Ponty's claim that "the flesh of the world is not self sensing like my flesh"),[14] the subject is the very condition for the sensing of the world, which has no other means to become sensed: "The subject," insists Barbaras, "is not a *moment* or a degree of concentration of visibility but simply its *condition*."[15] Merleau-Ponty's effort to ontologize phenomenology thus comes at the expense of what is, for Barbaras, the very kernel of phenomenology: intentionality, or the irreducible, minimally transcendental distance between sensing and sensed.

Returning to his "impression of malaise," Barbaras can now pinpoint its provenance. This malaise

> stems fundamentally from the fact that Merleau-Ponty advances a univocal concept of the flesh, to which the fundamental distinction of the sensing and the sensed, which is to say, ultimately, the intentional distance, must be able to be traced back. In effect, the ontological generalization of the carnal reversibility leads inexorably to a transformation of one of these terms. My flesh manifests a yoking together of sensing and sensed, which is to say that my body is always and throughout present to itself. But this relation cannot be transposed *willy nilly* to what is exterior to the body [*à l'extériorité*] *because it makes no sense to say that the world senses itself*, is present to itself as is my flesh.[16]

On Barbaras's account, the body and the subject simply can never coincide. They designate what he considers to be distinct and to some extent non-correlated operations: on one side, the immanent, ontic body senses itself; on the other, the transcendental, ontological subject receives the appearance of the world.

This noncoincidence of body and subject explains why, for Barbaras, Merleau-Ponty's ontological transposition "gives rise to a reformulation":

> The flesh of the world signifies that being is everywhere and always on the side of phenomenality and that a being that would be foreign to phenomenality makes no more sense than a body that would be foreign to its sensibility, incapable of sensing itself. It is thus the subject of sensing or of appearing that disappears as the cost of the ontological transposition. In other terms, the descent of subjectivity in the world by the body corresponds to an ascent of the world toward phenomenality, but *never toward subjectivity*. The two inverse movements do not coincide; the point of departure of the one (the subject of sensing) cannot be the point of arrival of the other because one simply cannot understand how an appearing that is immanent to the world can give rise to its own subject, how visibility can give birth to vision.[17]

The final result of Merleau-Ponty's ontologization of phenomenology can only be an "inconsistent concept": a "doubling" of the flesh into two fleshes—flesh of the world and sensing flesh—that simply cannot be brought together.

My conjunction of the final Merleau-Ponty with a de-Platonized Whitehead lets us question precisely what remains unquestionable for Barbaras: the impossibility for the world to sense itself. Barbaras's entire account literally stands or falls with this purportedly unquestionable impossibility: indeed, it is precisely what justifies his phenomenological commitment to the transcendental subject—his insistence that the world can only manifest itself *to a transcendental subject*. What Whitehead brings to the table is an account of subjectivity—and thus a source of self-sensing, of generalized sensibility—that does not have to be possessed by a subject separate from or transcendent to the world. Subjectivity, for Whitehead, is generated from out of the world's worlding, from the intensities produced by its vibratory tensions. On this score, Whitehead's thinking helps us appreciate the radicality of Merleau-Ponty's final ontology, and in particular, helps us to see precisely how it manages to overcome the subject-object split that attaches to any commitment of transcendence.

Indeed, by excavating how worldly sensibility continuously gives rise to novelty, and thereby to its own renewal, Whitehead's account of process lends a certain concreteness to Merleau-Ponty's notion of the *écart* and to the "dehiscence" between sensing and sensed that it informs. Specifically, Whitehead's insight into the potentiality—the power—of the settled world opens up a source for subjectivity that would no longer need to be a function of a narrow subjective unification. That is why Whitehead is able to encompass subjective unification within a broader model of process: his account can explain how actualities-in-attainment are catalyzed by the real potentiality of attained actualities (or superjects) in order to be added, or to add themselves, to this potentiality in an unending cosmic dance. Once again, we see how Whitehead's technical account of concrescence, far from forming the cornerstone of his speculative empiricism, is simply one element in a larger account of process: the ongoing production of ever new actualities and relationalities.

In their own rendition of this same conjunction, philosophers Hamrick and Van der Veken turn their back on this broader model of process in order to stress, as countless commentators have done before them, the synthesizing capacity of concrescence: "Whitehead's concept of concrescence," they suggest, "offers Merleau-Ponty . . . a way to disentangle the concept of synthesis from that of constitution, and to keep the idea of synthesis at the same time as the reversibility of the flesh. This is possible because the synthesis of an actual occasion, the formation of its prehensive unity, is the *sentant*-half of the reversibility relationship, but which already includes the *sensible within* it."[18] How we understand this passage hinges entirely on how we understand the word "within" that here qualifies the correlation of *sensible* and *sentant*. If we take "within" to qualify the "synthesis of an actual occasion," as Hamrick and Van der Veken do, then the reversibility of *sensible* and *sentant* can only be a function of concrescence; on this account, reversibility cannot serve to expand the scope of subjectivity in any consequential way. If, however, we take "within" to qualify reversibility itself, as I would propose, then the coupling of *sentant* and *sensible* can no longer designate the product of some operation of a subject narrowly defined; rather, reversibility would take on its proper and expansive role as the very subjective texture of the world as such, as worldly sensibility.

By attributing reversibility *to the operation of concrescence*, Hamrick and Van der Veken effectively compromise the promise of their juxtaposition of Whitehead and Merleau-Ponty. This is because their attribution simply reinstalls the orthodox valuation placed by Whitehead and the vast majority of his commentators on concrescence as sole source for subjective agency. On such a valuation, as we have seen, the settled world—the domain in which reversibility operates—is and can only be relegated to the status of pure passivity, of mere *sensible* that can only await a *sentant* for its (re)activation. Whether this agency be conceptualized as a concrescing actuality or a phenomenological subject proper, the resultant privileging of synthesis removes the agency *for* worldly sensibility *from* worldly sensibility in order to ascribe it to some mysterious, metaphysical operation.

With their appeal to concrescence, Hamrick and Van der Veken fatally compromise their own more general goal of developing a "radically new conception of subjectivity." For whereas concrescence provides these philosophers with a means to sneak synthesis in the back door, the crux of their new conception of subjectivity, as they themselves make clear, centers on the displacement of synthesis in favor of metamorphosis that animates Merleau-Ponty's final work. The fruit of Merleau-Ponty's effort to dispense definitively with Husserl's concept of constituting consciousness, this displacement is intended to yield "a contact with being across its modulations or its reliefs," a contact that *would not be mediated* by any subjective synthesis. As should be clear by now, such a radically new conception requires a subjectivity without a transcendental subject—a radically democratic, if still differentiated, distribution of subjectivity to all elements of worldly sensibility.

Conceptualized in relation to Whitehead's larger account of process, where both concrescences and superjects wield subjective power, Merleau-Ponty's account of the *écart* and the reversibility between sensing and the sensible furnishes precisely such a conception of subjectivity without subject: specifically, it accords subjectivity, that is, the power of sensing, to every entity in the world. Merleau-Ponty's reversibility thereby liberates superjectal subjectivity and situates it as the power of worldly sensibility. On his account, not only would every actual occasion become "on the basis of its sensibility to its past actual world that it incorporates within it," as Hamrick and Van der Veken point out, but it would become *because of the power of the sensibility of all past actualities now operating as superjects and acting, as it were, within it.* Such an account makes the power of superjectal subjectivity autonomous from and broader than its operation within concrescence: this power designates nothing less than the capacity for the world to sense itself, to be a primordial domain of sensibility from which all else springs. As the "wielder" of the real potentiality informing the superjective subjectivity of all things, the settled world must be understood to enjoy a sensory relation to itself: it is a primary texture of sensibility whose potentiality is incessantly "realized" by the superjective intensity of its elements

In preserving the distance between sensing and sensed (though, importantly, not as a distance of intentionality), Merleau-Ponty's conception of the *écart* parallels Whitehead's distinction of concrescence and superject: in both cases, a structure of oscillation or reversibility is crucial for the power of sensibility. And in both cases, what fills in the space of the *écart* is temporalization, conceptualized not as a product of constitution (as on Husserl's account of time-consciousness) but as a power of worldly metamorphosis. Rather than requiring some transcendence of a subject over the world, the temporalization that informs this reversibility is resolutely a worldly temporalization: the power of worldly sensibility to act through its own agency and to enhance its own potentiality. Conceptualized in this way, temporalization *is* "de-presencing" [*Entgegenwärtigung*] (following Fink's development of the term), which I have elsewhere positioned as a worldly temporalization underlying and giving rise to the retentions and protentions that structure phenomenal experience.[19] Yet, where Fink's theorization remains abstract, Merleau-Ponty's perspective adds a much-needed concreteness: as a specification of how worldly sensibility self-proliferates, reversibility encompasses a plethora of degrees of sensitivity that inform subjective processes of vastly differing force.

In this respect, reversibility qualifies the above-cited Working Note in which Merleau-Ponty specifies that the flesh of the world "is not self-sensing *like my flesh*." Far from marking an either-or relation (being self-sensing or not), as Barbaras maintains it does,[20] this claim might better be read as an opening onto a continuum of differentiation, a plethora of modes of self-sensing, only one of which is that of the human body ("my flesh"). When he says that the flesh of the world is not self-sensing *like my flesh*, Merleau-Ponty does not mean that the world is not self-sensing. What he *does* mean is that the flesh of the world *is* self-sensing *in a different way than my flesh*, or, more precisely, that it is self-sensing *in a host of ways all of which differ from that of my flesh*.

We can thus conclude, with Hamrick and Van der Veken, that the world is not univocally or indifferently self-sensing, but also, contra Barbaras—and this is the fundamental point—that it *is* self-sensing: "There are various degrees and modalities of reversibility depending on the degree of sentience possible. A 'univocal sense of flesh' would mean one kind of flesh with many modalities. . . . With regard to Merleau-Ponty's monism some entities, such as the pen, are clearly not sentient in the ways that we are. Others—such as the experiences of higher life forms—are very like our fleshly reversibilities. And there is a vast array of lower life forms with various degrees of sentience and, therefore, reversibilities."[21] As the fundamental operation of temporalization, sensible reversibility informs every actuality in the universe, from the most minuscule speck of dust to the greatest achievements of collective consciousness. At every level and scale of being, this reversibility yields a subjectivity *without* any subject, a superjectal subjectivity *prior to* and *necessary for* the emergence of any higher-order subject, including the transcendental subject of (orthodox) phenomenology.

As a specification of superjectal subjectivity, reversibility opens onto a sensibility produced by the causal efficacy of the world itself in all its variety. That is why reversibility makes up the general texture of worldly sensibility. Reversibility characterizes the human relation with the flesh of the world *in the same way* as it does any other relation—as concrete productions of worldly temporalization, of sensibility's self-proliferation. That is why, its special status and its distinct perceptual capacities notwithstanding, the human bodymind is rooted in worldly sensibility just as is every other entity in the universe. If the human bodymind has unique capacities to experience reversibility directly (to perceive the causal efficacy underlying presentational immediacy or the "withness of the body"), this perceptual reversibility is in turn rooted in a deeper and more general reversibility involving the worldly sensibility (the vectors of causal efficacy) informing this very "withness."

In the convergence of Whitehead's non-perceptual sensation with the phenomenological concept of worldly sensibility, we thus acquire what is needed to treat sensations as elements of the world, even when they are experienced (or "lived") by perceivers (or consciousnesses). This convergence allows us to generalize subjectivity to *any entity that is capable of reversibility*—to any entity that is produced from other (or hetero) sensibility and that generates further worldly sensibility on the basis of its own operation.

This transformation—of other sensibility into worldly sensibility—gives the formal recipe for conceptualizing how the proliferation of objective sensation accompanying the advent of mobile media and ubiquitous computing is able to generate an intensification of our properly *human* sensibility *that is at the same time* an expansion of the domain of *worldly* sensibility from which it arises. With the unprecedented capacities of our digital devices and sensors to gather information about behavior and about the environment, we literally acquire new and alien "organs" (which must not be confused with prostheses of *our* human sense organs) for excavating extraperceptual dimensions of experience—our own as well as that of other entities. By experimenting with the potential for the sensibility of twenty-first-century media networks to catalyze new forms of human experience, Crandall's *Gatherings* foregrounds the *exteriority* of these new and alien organs in relation to the human body: displacing his own agency as the privileged (or exclusive) channel for media to enter experience, Crandall implicates his sensibility within the circuits and flows created by the ubiquitous media surrounding him precisely in order to open new possibilities for experience. Specifically, his self-implication allows this media environment to express its potentiality directly, as primary elements in the very gatherings in which Crandall himself is implicated and, importantly, to which he can bear witness.

With this clarification, we arrive at a solution to—or rather a dissolution of—the problem posed by Barbaras. Far from requiring a subject that transcends the appearing of the world and that would have the burden of giving subjectivity to it, Crandall's bearing witness entails nothing more than a "going-along-with" the gathering of potentialities. The subjective perspective his witnessing introduces is simply one perspective among others, and, as such, it remains partial and immanent to the gathering within which it emerges. If this perspective enjoys a privilege, it is one that differs in kind from the privilege Barbaras claims for the transcendent subject of phenomenological manifestation: for whereas the latter privilege sets the subject off from the world that manifests itself through it, the privilege claimed by Crandall's performance positions the subject—or rather the coalescence of superjective subjectivity that occurs around every human-implicating event of gathering—as fully immanent to the world and as directly emergent from the total situation of any given gathering. To put it more simply, we could say that the privilege claimed by Crandall's performance is wholly relative: it marks the specifically human experience of a process—gathering—that can neither be reduced to this experience nor fully grasped from its perspective.

Far from being a mere accident of its particular configuration, the partiality of the witnessing at issue in Crandall's piece is an endemic aspect of the experience of any gathering whatsoever. And what his performance underscores so effectively—here in marked contrast to most contemporary theorizations of computational networks and sensor technologies—is how the specifically *human* experience of gatherings remains central. By repositioning the human witness as an emergent phenomenon that is fully immanent to the world from which it emerges, Crandall's performance manages to capture *both* the particular "marginalization" of the human subject that occurs as human bodyminds are implicated within twenty-first-century media networks *and* the continued, if repositioned, "centrality" of human witnessing that alone can make this implication, and the greater expansion of environmental agency it betokens, meaningful for *human experience*.

I have been arguing throughout this study that the transformation of human experience within twenty-first-century media networks must not be viewed as a purely negative development. If it is a reality that we must live with, one that we must adapt to, such adaptation need not take the form of a purely passive acquiescence. Rather, as I have sought to emphasize with my concept of feed-forward, the transformation of experience wrought by twenty-first-century media furnishes an unprecedented opportunity for us to reconceptualize our agency, to implicate our agency within the larger total situation of environmental gathering. And this can lead, as I suggested in my introduction, to a fundamental reconceptualization of the human that embraces the marginalization of consciousness and the environmentality of process as catalysts for new modes of collective becoming on the far side of the human-inhuman divide. We must, let me reiterate, embrace this opportunity: for what we lose in the way of perceptual access and cognitive mastery over experience is recompensed by what we gain in the way of participation within larger environmental gatherings. Following our re-embedding within the multi-scalar complexity of an always flowing, massively technified world, we come to enjoy an expanded sensory contact with worldly sensibility that affords us new potentialities for experiencing ourselves and the world—and for understanding how we experience ourselves and the world. Such possibilities are, needless to say, simply not available through our historically privileged modes of perception and conscious access.

Let me underscore, however, that this potentiality for recompense will be actualized only if we struggle against the myriad contemporary entities and institutions that seek to capitalize on the technical revelation of sensibility in ways that bypass our agency entirely. We must fight to appropriate the fruits of our expanded sensory contact with worldly sensibility for non-instrumental purposes—for making our lives better. Such struggle requires concrete appropriations of the operations of twenty-first-century media as well as a recognition of the generality of sensibility beyond any human-world division. If we have any hope of bringing our newly acquired alien or exterior organs to bear on the way we experience and the way we theorize our experience, we will need to make sensibility once again central to our being-in-the-world. But crucially, and in contrast to any narrowly phenomenological framing of sensibility, we must embrace the technical dimension of sensibility in its entirety. For, it is only on the basis of and through our primitive and preperceptual sensible contact with the world—a contact that in today's world *can only be* mediated by twenty-first-century media—that the world can appear to us. Far from being a product of some minimal transcendental distance, some transcendence generative of subjectivity, the world's appearance is the strict correlate of our immanence within its sensible texture. Or, as Merleau-Ponty believes, "sensibility only makes the world appear because it is already on the side of the world."[22]

Adapting it to our media-saturated world, we can inflect this principle with a recognition of the centrality of technics in the sensory circuits linking humans to the world. Technical media only make sensibility appear *because they themselves are already on the side of and are already immanent to sen-*

sibility. As autonomous supplements that operate in place of our limited perceptual faculties, technical media are resolutely *of the world*: they are responsible for our contemporary implication within worldly sensibility, for our primordial sensible contact with the world, and for any resultant complexifications of the human as a form of process.

Notes

PREFACE

1. Alfred North Whitehead, *Science and the Modern World* (New York: Free Press, 1967), 144.

2. Whitehead, *Science and the Modern World*, 150–51, emphases added.

3. Whitehead, *Science and the Modern World*, 151, emphasis added.

INTRODUCTION

1. Alexander Galloway and Eugene Thacker, *The Exploit: A Theory of Networks* (Minneapolis: University of Minnesota Press, 2007), 157.

2. First introduced into media studies via Jacques Derrida's reading of the "pharmakon"—to designate a poison that is also its own antidote, i.e., writing—and substantially developed in Bernard Stiegler's philosophy of media technics, pharmacology conceptualizes the way that media, from the invention of writing on, simultaneously diminish and supplement sensory, perceptual, and expressive capacities of humans.

3. I am thinking, of course, of Husserl's distinction between perception and sensation generally and his characterization of sensation as the nonintentional material on which perception, and intentionality, is erected. See, for example, the Fifth Logical Investigations, in Husserl, *Logical Investigations*, vol. 2, tr. J. N. Findlay (New York: Routledge, 2001). It is Deleuze who stages the encounter between Bergson and Husserl, for example, in *Cinema 1*, chapter 4, where he writes: "Two very different authors were to

undertake this task [of overcoming the duality of image and movement, consciousness and thing] at about the same time: Bergson and Husserl. Each had his own war cry: all consciousness is consciousness *of* something (Husserl), or more strongly, all consciousness *is* something (Bergson)" (*Cinema 1: The Movement-Image*, tr. H. Tomlinson and B. Habberjam [Minneapolis: University of Minnesota Press, 1986], 56). For his characterization of Bergson, Deleuze is of course referring to *Matter and Memory*. In the case of Raymond Ruyer, a less well-known French philosopher, the distinction is even stronger since Ruyer works with both concepts, distinguishing what he calls "primary consciousness" (or "absolute survey") from "secondary consciousness." See Ruyer, *Neo-Finalism*, tr. A. Edlebi (Minneapolis: University of Minnesota Press, 2014, includes an introduction by me). Related critiques of intentionality can be found in the projects of Emmanuel Levinas and Michel Henry, among others.

4. Alfred North Whitehead, *Process and Reality: An Essay in Cosmology*, Corrected Edition, ed. D. Griffin and D. Sherburne (New York: The Free Press, 1978), 228.

5. Whitehead, *Process and Reality*, 160.

6. Whitehead, *Process and Reality*, 160.

7. Galloway and Thacker, *Exploit*, 132.

8. Galloway and Thacker, *Exploit*, 124.

9. Whitehead, *Process and Reality*, 15.

10. I thank Patrick Lemieux for this suggestion.

11. The examples enumerated here are those of Jane Bennett. See *Vibrant Matter: a Political Ecology of Things* (Durham, NC: Duke University Press, 2010).

12. Luciana Parisi, "Technoecologies of Sensation," in *Deleuze/Guattari and Ecology*, ed. B. Herzogenrath (Basingstoke, UK: Palgrave Macmillan, 2009), 189.

13. Steven Shaviro, *Without Criteria: Kant, Whitehead, Deleuze, and Aesthetics* (Cambridge, MA: MIT Press, 2009), xiii.

14. Alfred North Whitehead, *Adventures of Ideas* (New York: Free Press, 1933), 181.

15. Marshall McLuhan, *Understanding Media: The Extensions of Man* (New York: Gingko Press, 2003).

16. See H. U. Gumbrecht and K. L Pfeiffer, eds., *The Materialities of Communication*, (Stanford, CA: Stanford University Press, 1994).

CHAPTER ONE

1. Bernard Stiegler, *La technique et le temps, II: La déorientation* (Paris: Galilée, 1998), 276.

2. Gilles Deleuze, *The Fold: Leibniz and the Baroque*, tr. T. Conley (Minneapolis: University of Minnesota Press, 1993), 19.

3. Deleuze, *Fold*, 19–20.

4. An important exception here—and one that makes the history of media more complex and more interesting—is analog sound-recording technology which, as Kittler has pointed out in the most forceful terms (but which is common to much of the literature on the history of audition and sound recording), inscribes sonic phenomena well beyond the range of human hearing. For a development of Kittler's work on Fourier transformations, see Mark B. N. Hansen, "Symbolizing

Time: Kittler and 21st Century Media," in *Kittler Now*, ed. S. Sale (Stanford, CA: Stanford University Press, forthcoming). These sub-perceptual sonic phenomena lie at the basis of contemporary microsonic sound production which effectively deploy digital granular synthesis to bring the microsonic into the realm of human hearing. See Curtis Roads, *Microsounds* (Cambridge, MA: MIT Press, 2001).

5. See D. N. Rodowick, *The Virtual Life of Film* (Cambridge, MA: Harvard University Press, 2007).

6. I discuss Rodowick's arguments in a more critical register elsewhere; see Mark B. N. Hansen, "New Media," in *Critical Terms for Media Studies,* ed. M. Hansen and W. J. T. Mitchell (Chicago: University of Chicago, 2010).

7. Wolfgang Ernst, "Cultural Archive versus Technomathematical Storage," in *The Archive in Motion: New Conceptions of the Archive in Contemporary Thought and New Media Practices*, ed. E. Rossaak (Oslo: Novus Press, 2010), 58.

8. Ernst, "Cultural Archive," 58.

9. Ernst, "Cultural Archive," 67–68.

10. Ernst, "Cultural Archive," 58.

11. Ernst, "Cultural Archive," 59–60, emphasis added.

12. There is a deep resonance between my position in this book and Ernst's project to bring the microtemporalities of media technologies into the purview of contemporary media theory. Since my full appreciation for Ernst's project post-dates my conceptualization of the argument of *Feed-Forward*, I cannot do justice to that deep resonance here. However, I can say, in harmony with Ernst's own vision of a "trans-Atlantic crossing" of media theory—an encounter of German media science and American media phenomenology, as he puts it—that I view my own project as an effort to excavate the experiential implications of the very shift in media materiality that forms the basis of Ernst's work. Like Ernst, I view the operational perspective of media machines to be crucial, and like him I focus on how the operation of machines as measurement devices is able to tap into domains of operationality, what I call sensibility, that are not directly accessible on human modes of perception. Where Ernst maintains that the signal processing, which cannot be observed by human perceivers (and which falls out of the scope of sense perception), can be observed by time-critical media, I hold that the sensibility as such that falls out of the scene of human perception, is everywhere at issue in the operation of twenty-first-century media. In this sense, *Feed-Forward* can be under-stood as a proleptic engagement—a response avant la lettre—to the friendly and in my opinion very fruitful provocation of Ernst's call for further work to construct a transatlantic alliance within the field of media theory. My current project, *Logics of Futurity*, will include a more protracted engagement with Ernst and, specifically, will seek to expand the scope of media, in accord with his understanding of media as time-critical measuring machines, so as to include the role of instruments in sci-ence, and specifically in quantum physics.

13. See Hansen, "New Media."

14. I thank Luciana Parisi for pointing out the limitation of my earlier concep-tualization of bodily enframing. See Parisi, "Technoecologies," 189.

15. *Wikipedia*, s.v. "Perception," http://en.wikipedia.org/wiki/Perception.

16. See my discussion of this legacy in "The Primacy of Sensation," in *Theory Aside*, ed. J. Potts and D. Stout (Durham, NC: Duke University Press, 2014).

17. See, for example, Edmund Husserl, *Ideas: General Introduction to Pure Phenomenology* (New York: Routledge, 2010); Martin Heidegger, *Being and Time*, tr. J. Stambaugh (Albany: SUNY Press, 2010); Maurice Merleau-Ponty, *The Primacy of Perception: And Other Essays on Phenomenological Psychology, the Philosophy of Art, History, and Politics* (Evanston, IL: Northwestern University Press, 1964).

18. I explore this legacy at greater length in my chapter, "Ubiquitous Sensation: Toward an Atmospheric, Collective, and Microtemporal Model of Media," in *Throughout: Art and Culture Emerging with Ubiquitous Computing*, ed. U. Ekman (Cambridge, MA: MIT Press, 2012), 63–88.

19. On this point, Whitehead's work can be compared with the ecological psychology of J. J. Gibson, who argues that perception involves a "direct pickup" of information from the ambient environment. See Gibson, *The Ecological Approach to Visual Perception* (New York: Psychology Press, 1986), chapter 14.

20. I explore the notion of "radical exteriority" in relation to technology in my *Embodying Technesis: Technology Beyond Writing* (Ann Arbor: University of Michigan Press, 2000), chapter 3.

21. Joel Snyder, "Visualization and Visibility," in *Picturing Science, Producing Art*, ed. C. Jones and P. Galison (New York: Routledge, 1998), 379–80, emphasis added.

22. Snyder, "Visualization and Visibility," 381, emphasis added.

23. Whitehead, *Process and Reality*, 15.

24. Sandy Pentland, *Honest Signals: How They Shape Our World* (Cambridge, MA: MIT Press, 2008), 98.

25. Nigel Thrift, "Pass It On: Towards a Political Economy of Propensity," *Emotion, Space and Society* 1 (2008): 83–96.

26. Fulda 2000, cited in Oscar Gandy Jr., "Datamining, Surveillance and Discrimination in the Post-9/11 Environment," in *The New Politics of Surveillance and Visibility*, ed. K. Haggerty and R. Ericson (Toronto: University of Toronto Press, 2006), 369–70.

27. Patočka's phenomenology manages to do this despite a twofold restriction that, to my mind, compromises the power of his attempt to reform phenomenology: a restriction, on one hand, of the materiality of worldly temporalizing to the activity of manifestation and, on the other, of the destination of worldly manifestation to human subjects. These restrictions will require correction.

28. Gilbert Simondon, *L'individuation à la lumière des notions de forme et d'information* (Paris: Editions Jérôme Millon, 2005).

29. For an overview of recent work in neuroeconomics, see P. Glimcher et al., eds., *Neuroeconomics: Decision Making and the Brain* (New York: Academic Press, 2008). For a skeptical position, see Joseph Dumit, *Picturing Personhood: Brain Scans and Biomedical Identity* (Princeton, NJ: Princeton University Press, 2003).

30. Friedrich Kittler, introduction to *Gramophone, Film, Typewriter*, tr. G. Winthrop-Young and M. Wutz (Stanford, CA: Stanford University Press, 1999).

31. And it should be pointed out that Kittler's account of digital convergence and autonomy is more than counterbalanced by his archaeology of technics in relation to nineteenth-century psychophysics and the resistance of the body to disci-

pline, as well as by his investment in education, from the Enlightenment system of compulsory education to his calls for students of cultural studies to learn computer programming languages as part of their cultural literacy. This situation lends some weight to the suggestion that Kittler's contentious claims regarding the digital may in fact be contentious for the sake of being contentious—provocations designed to spur his readers (and his students) to acquire literacy, and hence competence, in the language of technics and instrumental domination.

32. See Derrida's responses to Stiegler's claims concerning realtime media in *Echographies of Television: Filmed Interviews*, tr. J. Bajorek (New York: Polity Press, 2002).

33. Richard Wolin, for example, insists on the temporal dysynchrony separating technical capitalism from democratic aims:

> The mass of the population is periodically doused with the rhetoric of democracy and assured that it lives in a democratic society and that democracy is the condition to which all progressive-minded societies should aspire. Yet that democracy is not meant to realise the demos but to constrain and neutralize it by the arts of electoral engineering and opinion management. It is, necessarily, regressive. Democracy is embalmed in public rhetoric precisely in order to memorialize its loss of substance. Substantive democracy—equalizing, participatory, commonalizing—is antithetical to everything that a high reward meritocratic society stands for. At the same moment that advanced societies have identified their progressive character with perpetual technological innovation they have defined themselves through policies that are regressive in many of their effects. Democracy is where these effects are registered. By virtually every important official norm—efficiency, incentives to unequal rewards, hierarchical principles of authority, expertise—it appears anachronistic, dysynchronous. The crux of the problem is that high-technology, globalized capitalism is radically incongruent with democracy. (Wolin 2000, 20, cited in Nigel Thrift, *Non-Representational Theory: Space, Politics, Affect* (New York: Routledge, 2007), 3)

The temporal dimension of this conflict is made even more prominent by William Connolly, *Neuropolitics: Thinking, Culture, Speed* (Minneapolis: University of Minnesota Press, 2002), especially chapter 6. Connolly juxtaposes his portrayal of the rift in time to Wolin's presentation of acceleration:

> Uneven pace across zones helps to reveal more poignantly what has always been in operation, a rift between past and future that helps to constitute the essence of time and to enter into the constitution of politics itself. It now becomes possible to come to terms with this condition in a more affirmative way. . . . Perhaps the best way to proceed is to strive to modulate the fastest and most dangerous military and corporate processes while interven-

ing politically within accelerated processes of communication, travel, population flows, and cultural intersection to support a more generous ethos of pluralism. . . . The challenge is how to support the positive connections among democracy, uneven zones of tempo, and the rift in time without legitimating a pace of life so fast that the promise of democracy becomes translated into fascist becoming machines. (147)

34. Vilém Flusser, *Into the Universe of Technical Images* (Minneapolis: University of Minnesota Press, 2011), 74.

35. On this point, Flusser's media history dovetails nicely with Simondon's pinpointing of the Industrial Revolution as a moment of reversal in the relationship of human beings and machines. See Gilbert Simondon, *De mode d'existence des objets techniques* (Paris: Aubier, 2001).

36. Vilém Flusser, *Towards a Philosophy of Photography* (London: Reaktion Books, 2000), 71.

37. Ian Ayres, *Supercrunchers: Why Thinking-By-Numbers Is the New Way to Be Smart* (New York: Bantam, 2008).

38. Thrift, *Non-Representational Theory*, 92.

39. Semir Zeki, "A Theory of Microconsciousness," in *The Blackwell Companion to Consciousness*, ed. S. Schneider and M. Velman (New York: Wiley-Blackwell, 2007).

40. Flusser, *Towards a Philosophy of Photography*, 53, 57.

41. We must, however, diverge from Flusser on the political content of this rethinking and specifically from his claim that it necessitates some neo-modernist program for reclaiming what is new in the apparatus. Despite his rejection of "humanistic criticism" for its refusal to embrace "the terrible fact of this unintentional right and uncontrollable functionality of apparatuses," Flusser's own political program—a politics of freedom rooted in the reappropriation of chance from the apparatus—seems to me to retain traces of this humanist position:

The task of the philosophy of photography is to question photographers about freedom, to probe their practice in the pursuit of freedom. This was the intention of the foregoing study, and in the course of it a few answers have come to light. First, one can outwit the camera's rigidity. Second, one can smuggle human intentions into its program that are not predicted by it. Third, one can force the camera to create the unpredictable, the improbable, the informative. Fourth, one can show contempt for the camera and its creations and turn one's interest away from the thing in general in order to concentrate on information. In short: Freedom is the strategy of making chance and necessity subordinate to human intention. Freedom is playing against the camera.(Flusser, *Towards a Philosophy of Photography*, 74, 80)

42. I develop this criticism in detail in my article "Technics beyond the Temporal Object," *New Formations* 77 (2012): 44–62.

43. See Hansen, "Ubiquitous Sensation" for a fuller development of this phenomenological (Husserlian) legacy.

CHAPTER TWO

1. Judith A. Jones, *Intensity: An Essay on Whiteheadian Ontology* (Nashville:
Vanderbilt University Press, 1998).

2. I say "certain presentness" to mark the confounding fact that concrescence
happens prior to the advent of time or outside of temporalization. I return to this
problem below.

3. "The conditions of order, whereby fully determinate subjects of adequate
intensity emerge where they are needed and constitute the world of which we
are aware . . . , impose themselves on the observer as well as on the entities so
ordered. . . . One might object that this reduces metaphysics to a sort of sophisticated phenomenology that attempts to describe how reality must be, given how we
experience it. . . . It is unlikely that Whitehead would be troubled by this notion:
he never denied the ultimately experiential origins and endpoints for metaphysical
explanation" (Jones, *Intensity*, 49). I discuss this passage below.

4. A more complete enumeration of the recent attention to Whitehead would
have to give a crucial place to the work of Isabelle Stengers, as well as to Debaise
and Bruno Latour.

5. The specificity of the speculative pervades Stengers's encyclopedic study of
Whitehead, *Thinking with Whitehead: A Free and Wild Creation of Concepts*, tr.
M. Chase (Cambridge, MA: Harvard University Press, 2011).

6. Actually, the situation is somewhat more complicated, since Whitehead himself seems to make such an identification in the text that French readers seemed to
rely on, namely *The Concept of Nature* (1920). In this sense, Debaise's indictment is
actually an indictment of readers' neglect of *Process and Reality*. See Debaise, *Un empiricisme spéculatif: Lecture de* Procès et réalité *de Whitehead* (Paris: Vrin, 2006), 106:

> Numerous are the commentators, particularly in France, who
> are primarily interested in *The Concept of Nature* and who find
> in *Process and Reality* the prolongation and the metaphysical
> generalization of the problems which are posed in the earlier text.
> From this moment, they recur, more or less implicitly, to the dif-
> ference central to *The Concept of Nature* [ontological dualism]
> along with the terms from out of which it was constructed [objects
> and events], and apply it willy nilly to *Process and Reality*. Once
> this separation has been introduced, one can certainly try to
> analyze their implications and their relations at the level of con-
> crete existence; it remains the case, however, that it creates a true
> incoherence in relation to the speculative schema, and above all an
> obstacle for a thinking of individuation as the production of new
> beings that is extremely difficult to overcome.

7. Debaise, *Un empiricisme spéculatif*, 75.
8. Shaviro, *Without Criteria*, 29.

9. Whitehead, *Process and Reality*, 214.

10. Jorge Luis Nobo, *Whitehead's Metaphysics of Extension and Solidarity* (Albany: SUNY Press, 1986), 19.

11. Nobo, *Whitehead's Metaphysics*, 19.

12. While this reading might appear to leave us with a vicious chicken-and-egg problematic—since attained actualities precondition the genesis of actualities-in-attainment which themselves produce attained actualities—it only becomes a problem if we fail to factor in the particular disjunction between the experiential and the speculative that informs Whitehead's metaphysics. We must remember that the speculative account of the genesis of actual entities, as Didier Debaise makes clear, has the purpose of explaining how things must be in order for experience to be what it is; on that score, there is nothing that forbids a scenario in which the geneses of the speculative entities constituting actuality are themselves catalyzed by experiential events.

13. Jones, *Intensity*, 49. She goes on to regret the missed opportunity at issue here: "In this sense it is unfortunate that he never fully entered into conversation with much of post-Kantian critical philosophy and with the continental thought to which it gave rise" (49).

14. Parisi, "Technoecologies," 189.

15. Parisi, "Technoecologies," 193.

16. Actual entities, in Whitehead's very specific definition of them, are the basic existents of the universe; as "drops of experience" that arise, grow, and perish, they form the "atomic" or "epochal" units of becoming that, although not directly experientiable, constitute the basis for all higher-order compositions (what Whitehead calls "societies").

17. In a related and still technical use of the term, Whitehead also occasionally refers to the unification of the concrescence around a subjective aim as a "prehension."

18. Debaise would seem to concur when he emphasizes the "technical precision" of the term: "The definition of 'prehension' as appropriation and integration in the individual of a new actual entity gives a precision to the term "actual entity.". . . Prehension is the activity constitutive of actual entities; they are nothing other than centers of prehension" (Debaise, *Un empiricisme spéculatif*, 71). To move directly and seamlessly from prehensions to events (bearing in mind that events are experiential entities) is thus to conflate the speculative and the experiential.

19. Indeed, as we shall see, the production of intensity is the source for new concrescences.

20. Whitehead, *Process and Reality* 27.

21. Jones, *Intensity*, xii.

22. Jones, *Intensity*, xii. With this distinction between "the actual process of temporalization" and a more abstract analytical differentiation of the present from future and past, Jones's development converges with Fink's crucial distinction between "de-presencing" [*Entgegenwärtigung*] and the analysis of time-consciousness (retention and protention).

23. Jones, *Intensity*, 3.

24. Jones, *Intensity*, 21.

25. Jones, *Intensity*, 21.

26. Whitehead, *Process and Reality*, 83, cited in Jones, *Intensity*, 20–21.

27. Jones, *Intensity*, 45, emphasis added. Jones cites Whitehead in support: "The deterministic efficient causation is the inflow of the actual world in its own proper character of its own feelings, with their own intensive strength, felt and re-enacted by the novel concrescent subject" (*Process and Reality*, 245, Jones, *Intensity*, 45).

28. Jones, *Intensity*, 45.

29. This point provides the basis for a certain functional distinction in Whitehead between animals and nonanimate beings: like humans, though in less complex ways, animals (or at least some animals) have the capacity to perceive the causal infrastructure of their bodily activity. Nonanimate beings do not, even if they, like animals and humans, and every other entity in the universe, participate in and are materialized by and through lineages of causal efficacy (that lack any perceptual dimension). On the issue of Whitehead's account of the living, see Didier Debaise, "Life and Orders—A Speculative Approach to Life," in *Chromatikon: Annales de la philosophie en procès/Yearbook of Philosophy in Process*, 3 (2007): 57–68.

30. Indeed, as if to underscore the correlation of actual entities at the speculative level with *different levels of experience*, Whitehead distinguishes "four grades of actual occasions, grades which are not to be sharply distinguished from each other. First, and lowest, there are the actual occasions in so-called 'empty space'; secondly, there are the actual occasions which are moments in the life-histories of enduring non-living objects, such as electrons or other primitive organisms; thirdly, there are the actual occasions which are moments in the life-histories of enduring living objects; fourthly, there are the actual occasions which are moments in the life-histories of enduring objects with conscious knowledge" (Whitehead, *Process and Reality*, 177).

31. Alfred North Whitehead, *Symbolism* (New York: Fordham University Press, 1985), 63, cited in Jones, 153.

32. Jones, *Intensity*, 153.

33. Erin Manning explores the notion of "preacceleration" in her book, *Relationscapes* (Cambridge, MA: MIT Press, 2009); for a more in-depth development of my criticism here, see Mark B. N. Hansen, "Digital Technics beyond the 'Last Machine': Thinking Digital Media with Hollis Frampton," in *Between Stillness and Motion: Film, Photography, Algorithms*, ed. E. Rossaak (Amsterdam: Amsterdam University Press, 2011).

34. Parisi, "Technoecologies," 193.

35. Whitehead, *Adventures of Ideas*, 180–81.

36. Debaise, *Un empiricisme spéculatif*, 133–34.

37. The distinction between existence and experience, as it has been applied to Whitehead by philosopher critics from Leclerc to Debaise, furnishes another, closely related means to grasp the fundamental correlation linking experiential heterogenesis and speculative withdrawal. On this distinction, the speculative actual entity accounts for the being of what is, independently of the modalities of its existence, including (most fundamentally) experiential modalities. Both Leclerc and Debaise help us appreciate the value of this distinction. Debaise clarifies exactly

what is distinguished in the distinction: "The concept of actual entity aims to give an account of existence itself, and not of the modalities of existence, such as perceived or imagined existence" (Debaise, *Un empiricisme spéculatif*, 48); and Leclerc underscores the primary metaphysical function at its heart: "The term 'actual entity,' in its primary sense, signifies the general metaphysical category of 'that which is'" (Ivor Leclerc, *Whitehead's Metaphysics: an Introductory Exposition* [London: Allen and Unwin, 1958], 54). For both of these critics, the metaphysical singularity of the actual entity would appear to go hand in hand with a certain experiential diversity, a potential experiential diversity, even if their stress remains firmly on the metaphysical payoff.

    38. Whitehead, *Process and Reality*, cited in Debaise, *Un empiricisme spéculatif*, 36.

    39. For example, Debaise situates the composition of experience as the fundamental goal of *Process and Reality*:

> It is experience which must become, in the course of this reading, an evidence. Far from being an initial moment, an origin from which the system could unfold as the amplification of first impulsions it would receive from experience, it is experience itself that becomes the object of construction. The success of this construction is dependent on two conditions that are at the origin of what we will call a "speculative empiricism": the preservation of the coherence of ideas and the production of an evidence concerning experience. It is a radical empiricism because it has the ambition to elucidate immediate experience in the plurality of its aspects. But when the concept of experience is displaced and shifts from the origin to the endpoint of the elucidation, it is as if empiricism was transformed in a form of speculative, abstract and conceptual thought. The concept of experience thus becomes indissociable from a philosophical form which is the principal object of our reading. (Debaise, *Un empiricisme spéculatif*, 20–21)

For her part, Jones, as we have already seen, finds nothing troubling in the notion that metaphysics in Whitehead is "a sort of sophisticated phenomenology that attempts to describe how reality must be, given how we experience it"; indeed, she goes so far as to claim Whitehead's tacit assent to this for "he never denied the ultimately experiential origins and endpoints for metaphysical explanation" (Jones, *Intensity*, 49).

    40. Debaise, *Un empiricisme spéculatif*, 134–35.

    41. Debaise, *Un empiricisme spéculatif*, 137.

    42. Debaise, *Un empiricisme spéculatif*, 136.

    43. As I see it, the paradoxical disjunction between Debaise's account of the disjunctive plurality and his privileging of speculative actual entities instances a larger ambivalence on his part concerning the "doubled" status of actual entities. In this respect, he does appear to recognize the distinction of actualities-in-attainment and attained actualities, though without naming it as such: "The concept of actual entity is taken here in what appear to be two distinct senses: it

is deployed to describe existences that compose the disjunctive plurality as well as the entity in the process of individuation. In more Bergsonian terms, we could say that the actual entity seems to apply at once to 'already created reality' and 'reality in the process of creation'" (Debaise, *Un empiricisme spéculatif*, 76). However, in marked contrast to both Jones and Nobo, Debaise immediately discounts the significance of this recognition and affirms the ontological monism central to White-head's thought: "There would indeed be a contradiction if the concept of actual entity were to be identified with one single phase, if it was without becoming. This is why, to avoid needing to specify each time at what moment of existence we are situated, Whitehead introduces a technical distinction. Relative to individuation, one will call 'objects' those entities that are already in existence—the ones that compose the disjunctive plurality—and one will call the new entities 'subjects.' Let us not misunderstand what is at issue here: the distinction is purely functional. In any given relation of individuation, certain entities are called 'objects' and others, 'subjects'; but in the two cases, it is certainly a question of actual entities, and of actual entities that have the same status and forms of existence" (Debaise, *Un empiricisme spéculatif*, 77). Suffice it to say that I find this explanation paradoxical, to the extent that it ignores the crucial difference between the two "sides" of the actual entity—the fact that, in "perishing" as a subjective concrescence (a becoming of continuity) and in becoming objectified and entering the disjunctive plurality, the actual entity enters into time and becomes temporalized.

44. Whitehead, *Process and Reality*, 89, cited in Jones, *Intensity*, 107, emphasis added.

45. Jones, *Intensity*, 107–8, emphasis added.

46. Jones, *Intensity*, 108, emphasis added.

47. See, for example, Shaviro, *Without Criteria*, 28–29:

> To avoid the anthropomorphic—or at least cognitive and rationalistic—connotations of words like "mentality" and "perception," Whitehead uses the term *prehension* for the act by which one actual occasion takes up and responds to another. Clear and distinct human sense perception as it is conceived in the classical philosophical tradition from Descartes to the positivists of the twentieth century, is one sort of prehension. But it is far from the only one. Our lives are filled with experiences of "non-sensuous perception": from our awareness of the immediate past to the feelings we have of "the *'withness' of the body*.". . . The earth prehends the sun that gives it energy; the stone prehends the earth to which it falls. Cleopatra's Needle prehends its material surroundings; and I prehend, among other things, the Needle. A new entity comes into being by prehending other entities; every event *is* the prehension of other events.

48. Shaviro, *Without Criteria*, 18–19.

49. Shaviro even appears to recognize this problem, though with a gesture of repudiation that indicates, at least to me, a failure to grasp the stakes of the speculative ban. After citing a passage from Deleuze that serves as the model for his own

litany of prehensions, he observes: "However, regarding Deleuze's summary, as well as my own," the following precaution is in order: ". . . as Didier Debaise notes, all these examples refer to what Whitehead calls *societies*, rather than—*as would be more proper*—to actual entities themselves" (Shaviro, *Without Criteria*, 29, note 11, citing Debaise, *Un empiricisme spéculatif*, 73–75, emphasis added). The cited passage from Deleuze's *The Fold* is the following: "Everything prehends its antecedents and its concomitants and, by degrees, prehends a world. The eye is a prehension of light. Living beings prehend water, soil, carbon, and salts. At a given moment the pyramid prehends Napoleon's soldiers (forty centuries are contemplating us) and inversely" (Deleuze, *Fold*, 78). Not only does Shaviro refuse to embrace Debaise's caution concerning the need to distinguish what characterizes the speculative domain (prehensions) from what characterizes the experiential domain (societies), but he actually implies that the examples in both his and Deleuze's texts would be more "properly" correlated with actual entities that with societies. This interpretation, as I put it above, runs roughshod over the carefully conceptualized (if not always carefully expressed) distinctions that lie at the heart of Whitehead's speculative empiricism. And it also effectively eliminates any compelling rationale for beginning from societies in the effort not simply to develop a neutral account of experience but specifically to unpack the productive affinities between Whitehead's thought and twenty-first-century media.

50. Shaviro, *Without Criteria*, 23, emphasis added.

51. Given this conflation, it is easy to understand why Shaviro can reduce a society to the status of a mere set of actual entities united by purely external factors. While implicit in the passage cited above (where he characterizes events— "applying to a nexus or a society"—as "an extensive set, or a temporal series, of such occasions"), this reduction becomes altogether explicit when he seeks to clarify—again by way of an apparent but false gesture of recognition—the role of societies in the composition of events. After first claiming that, for Whitehead, "events do not 'happen to' things" but rather that "events *are* the only things," Shaviro specifies—as if in recognition of the distinction between events and the real things (actual entities)—that "the things *to which* events happen are not actual entities or occasions, but societies and enduring objects"; as soon as he says this, however, he effectively retracts it: "At the same time, these societies and enduring objects are themselves composed of *nothing more than a set of actual occasions*, together with the 'historical routes' (*Process and Reality*, 63) or 'routes of inheritance' (180) that link them together" (Shaviro, *Without Criteria*, 25, note 7). It is only because Shaviro (mistakenly) views actual entities as experiential entities that societies can be reduced to this subsidiary or epiphenomenal role of mere aggregates.

52. For example, Shaviro: "Every event or entity has what he [Whitehead] calls both 'mental' and 'physical' poles, and both a 'private' and a 'public' dimension. In the vast interconnections of the universe, everything both perceives and is perceived. Weird as this may sound, it is a necessary consequence of Whitehead's pursuit of univocity, or of what Manuel De Landa (2006) calls a *flat ontology*: one in which entities on different scales, and of different levels of reflexivity and complexity, are all treated in the same manner" (*Without Criteria*, 27–28).

53. The irreducibility of the experiential basis for societies—and the primacy

of (experiential) intensity that goes with it—can perhaps best be grasped in the limit case example, discussed above, of a society composed of a single actual entity. Despite what Whitehead appears to say, or at least what Shaviro appears to hear, *even in the case of a society or event with only one member* (one actual occasion), there would still be a distinction between that actual occasion as the speculative basis that explains the existence of the event and the same actual occasion as what is experienced in the event. Whereas the former occurs once and for all, remaining as Whitehead says "where it is and what it is," the latter endures and, in enduring, undergoes a continuous development of intensity. If a single actual occasion is the limiting type of an event with only one member, as Whitehead states, that is precisely because it underscores the distinction between the speculative status of that actual entity and its operation as a minimal experiential nexus or event. When Shaviro glosses this passage to mean that "an event may be just one particular occasion, *a single incident of becoming*," he undermines the key Whiteheadian distinction (one that he elsewhere endorses) between the continuity of becoming and the becoming of continuity. What this distinction stipulates is simply that there is a difference in kind between the becoming of an actual entity at the speculative level of its concrescence and the becoming that constitutes the temporality of experience. In order for an actual entity to operate as an event, it must instantiate becoming in the second sense, which means that it must be taken as an attained actuality, and not as an actuality-in-concrescence. And if we want to claim that a single attained actuality constitutes the limit case of an event, we can do so provided we appreciate that it *will have always already become part of the temporal domain of experience.*

54. Microsounds are sonic objects that lie beneath the threshold of [human] perception and can only be made perceivable by aggregation; they are, however, and this is an important point given my use of Whitehead here, *fully real* despite their individual imperceptibility. See Curtis Roads, *Microsound* (Cambridge, MA: MIT Press, 2004).

CHAPTER THREE

1. These works are the focus, respectively, of chapters 6 and 7 of my *New Philosophy for New Media* (Cambridge, MA: MIT Press, 2004).

2. Pentland and his collaborators have developed the "sociometer" in order to gain access to what Pentland conceives as a fully autonomous bodily channel of gestural communication, which, except for its alleged autonomy, is largely akin to Whiteheadian perception in the mode of causal efficacy. The sociometer is a badge-size wearable computational device that records various sorts of data; in its current version (as of 2008, the publication date of his book *Honest Signals*), the main measurement features of the sociometer include:

   — "Capturing face-to-face interactions using an infrared sensor to determine how much time users spend talking face-to-face"
   — "Performing speech feature analysis to measure nonlinguistic social signals and identify the social context"
   — "Recognizing common daily activities by measuring body movement" using an accelerometer

— "Performing indoor tracking and user localization" using a
GPS device
— "Communicating with cell phones and computers in order to
send and receive information from different users as well as
process data"
— "Measuring the physical proximity to other people." (Alex
["Sandy"] Pentland, *Honest Signals*, 102)

3. One crucial part of my general argument will focus on the term "experience"
itself: we must expand the scope of the term so it does not exclusively designate
higher-order subjective experience, *Erlebnis* and *Erfahrung*, lived experience and
qualitative experience, but—in the wake of Whitehead and James—the incipient
agency that is characteristic of all actualities, and indeed of *both* their "subjective"
and "objective" perspectives.

4. Ultimately, I will assert the identity of experience with temporalization,
where the latter is understood not (originally) as a higher-order synthesis along the
lines of Husserlian time-consciousness, but rather as an indivisible sensory event
(what Fink calls "de-presencing" [*Entgegenwärtigung*]). See Eugen Fink, *Studien
zur Phänomenologie, 1930–1939* (The Hague: Nijoff, 1966), 36ff.

5. I introduce this specification to distinguish the resonance at issue here—a
resonance that is, in effect, mediated by computational sensors and technical data-
gathering and analysis—from the "internal resonance" Gilbert Simondon proposes
to characterize living individuation from nonliving individuation and to index the
complexity of such living individuation.

6. This relativizing or phenomenologizing of the speculative goes hand-in-hand
with its absolute status in Whitehead's metaphysics. That is to say, the operation
of relative speculative-empirical "economies" in the phenomenological domain is
possible only because of an in-principle speculative reserve, the fact that the total
structure of the world, the total account of the way the world must be in order for experience to be what it is, remains outside of the domain of experience, something that
simply cannot be given in experience. This compatibility of a total speculative reserve
and a relative empirical operation of speculation has its roots in Whitehead's integration of mathematical logic with logics of experience (what he calls the "formal-
mathematical" and the "genetic-functional," respectively [see Whitehead's response
to John Dewey, "Remarks," *Philosophical Review* 46, no. 2 (March 1937): 178–86]).

7. James develops the concept of the fringe in *Principles of Psychology*, volume 1 (New York: Dover, 2007 [1890]), 258ff.

8. J. J. Gibson, *The Ecological Approach to Visual Perception* (New York:
Psychology Press, 1986).

9. Jerry Kang and Dana Cuff, "Pervasive Computing: Embedding the Public
Sphere," *Washington and Lee Law Review* 62, no. 1 (Winter 2005): 93–146: accessed via ProQuest, p. 6 (of 26).

10. Whitehead, *Process and Reality*, 86.

11. Whitehead, *Process and Reality*, 87.

12. Whitehead, *Process and Reality*, 173.

13. From the perspective of my argument here, the sharing of a "common
ground" becomes a limitation on the operation of symbolic reference, insofar as it

ties it to the performance of human perception. "The first principle, explanatory of symbolic reference, is that for such reference a 'common ground' is required. By this necessity for a 'common ground' it is meant that there must be components in experience which are directly recognized as *identical* in each of the pure perceptive modes" (*Process and Reality*, 168, emphasis added). When datasense displaces perception in performing symbolic reference, the latter involves an indirect correlation between human perception and the technical presentification of causal efficacy.

14. Steven Meyer, "Introduction" to Whitehead Now, *Configurations* 13, no.1 (Winter 2005): 1–33.

15. Whitehead, *Process and Reality*, 173.

16. Whitehead, *Process and Reality*, 172.

17. Whitehead, *Process and Reality*, 168.

18. Whitehead, *Process and Reality*, 47.

19. Jones, *Intensity*, 45.

20. Whitehead, *Process and Reality*, 159.

21. Whitehead, *Process and Reality*, 159, emphasis added.

22. Whitehead, *Process and Reality*, 157.

23. Whitehead, *Process and Reality*, 155.

24. Whitehead, *Process and Reality*, 113.

25. Whitehead, *Process and Reality*, 114.

26. Whitehead, *Process and Reality*, 141.

27. Whitehead, *Process and Reality*, 141.

28. Whitehead, *Process and Reality*, 166.

29. Whitehead, *Process and Reality*, 167.

30. Whitehead, *Process and Reality*, 167.

31. Whitehead, *Process and Reality*, 160.

32. Whitehead contrasts "causal objectification" with "presentational objectification": in causal objectification, "what is felt *subjectively* by the objectified actual entity is transmitted *objectively* to the concrescent actualities which supersede it" (Whitehead, *Process and Reality*, 58).

33. Cuff et al., cited in Jordan Crandall, "The Geospatialization of Calculative Operations," *Theory, Culture and Society* 27, no. 6 (November 2010): 79.

34. Whitehead, *Process and Reality*, 29.

35. Jones, *Intensity*, xii.

36. On this understanding, the superject is more than the mere inclusion of past actual entities (and eternal objects) as contents of a new concrescing actual entity; specifically, it is permeated by the lingering agency—the intensity—of the past actual entities it includes. Jones's elucidation of this privilege of the superject focuses on the continued subjective aspect of actual entities (in the narrow sense of their genesis) following their objectification: "It is my thesis," Jones announces at the very outset of her study,

> that the functioning of an existent in another existent must be ascribed to the internal account *of the first existent*, as much as it is to be ascribed to the present self-constitution of an entity in concrescence. The fully determinate feeling characterizing the "satisfaction" of any occasion includes elements whose sources lie

> in *other* entities that to some significant extent retain their charac-
> ter as determinate unities of feeling *in themselves* even as they are
> objectified in a present concrescence. The objective functioning of
> one thing in another, in other words, never completely loses the
> subjective, agentive quality of feeling that first brought it into be-
> ing. (Jones, *Intensity*, 3)

37. Debaise, *Un empiricisme spéculatif*, 137, emphasis added.

38. Debaise, *Un empiricisme spéculatif*, 85, emphasis added.

39. "Thus we have always to consider two meanings of potentiality: (a) the 'general' [or 'pure'] potentiality, which is the bundle of possibilities, mutually consistent or alternative, provided by the multiplicity of eternal objects, and (b) the 'real' potentiality, which is conditioned by the data provided by the actual world. General potentiality is absolute, and real potentiality is relative to some actual entity, taken as a standpoint whereby the actual world is defined" (*Process and Reality*, 65).

40. See Michel Henry, "Hyletic and Material Phenomenology," in *Material Phenomenology*, tr. S. Davidson (New York: Fordham University Press, 2008).

41. George Allan, "A Functionalist Reinterpretation of Whitehead's Metaphysics," *Review of Metaphysics* 62 (December 2008): 327–54, here 328.

42. Allan, "A Functionalist Reinterpretation of Whitehead's Metaphysics," 346.

43. William S. Hamrick and Jan Van der Veken, *Nature and Logos: A Whiteheadian Key to Merleau-Ponty's Fundamental Thought* (Albany: SUNY Press, 2011), 217–18.

44. Hamrick and Van der Veken, *Nature and Logos*, 202.

45. Jones, *Intensity*, 66, emphasis added.

46. Bergson's figure of the body as a center of indetermination in a universe of images forms the central philosophical concept of my exploration of new media art in *New Philosophy for New Media*.

47. Critics differ on this issue, though there is a general consensus that White-head was at least broadly familiar with the quantum theory of the 1920s and that his philosophy was an attempt to provide a metaphysics for the latest scientific work at the time. On this question, see Michael Epperson, *Quantum Mechanics and the Philosophy of Alfred North Whitehead* (New York: Fordham University Press, 2004).

48. Decoherence is a feature of quantum physics that allows for a certain reconciliation of quantum physics with classical physics. Specifically, decoherence stresses the necessity to eliminate coherent but contradictory possible outcomes and to conceptualize future actualization in terms of probabilities calculated on the "reduced matrix" thus achieved. One major benefit of decoherence is to provide a coherent resolution of the problem of quantum nonlocality (the coupling of nonlocal events); it is able to resolve nonlocality without resort to any violation of Einsteinian relativity (of the constancy of the speed of light) because it operates on a physical-causal matrix that implicates one-directional temporality and that discovers the connection between nonlocal events in this physical-causal matrix. *Wikipedia* defines decoherence as "how quantum systems interact with their environments to exhibit probabilistically additive behavior. Quantum decoherence

gives the *appearance* of wave function collapse (the reduction of the physical possibilities into a single possibility as seen by an observer) and justifies the framework
and intuition of classical physics as an acceptable approximation: decoherence
is the mechanism by which the classical limit emerges out of a quantum starting
point and it determines the location of the quantum-classical boundary. Decoherence occurs when a system interacts with its environment in a thermodynamically
irreversible way. This prevents different elements in the quantum superposition of
the system+environment's wavefunction from interfering with each other" (http://
en.wikipedia.org/wiki/Quantum_decoherence, accessed March 9, 2010).

49. Epperson, *Quantum Mechanics*, 168.

50. Epperson, *Quantum Mechanics*, 168–99.

51. Epperson, *Quantum Mechanics*, 169.

52. Epperson, *Quantum Mechanics*, 169.

53. This is not to say that we cannot understand this data at all, only that we
cannot understand it *at the moment of its sensory liveness or presence.* In other
words, here is a vast difference between this kind of coincidence of our understanding of data and its present operation, which I am arguing is impossible, and our
understanding of data after its operation and once it has been fed back, or rather
fed-forward, into our cognitive experience.

54. Sandy Petland, "The Next Net: Reality Mining for Honest Signals," lecture at MIT, April 29, 2010, http://www.gbcacm.org/seminars/evening/2010/next
-net-reality-mining-honest-signals.html, emphasis added. See also the website for
the "MIT Human Dynamics Laboratory," http://hd.media.mit.edu/, accessed
May 6, 2011.

55. The concept of "honest signaling" gives the title for Pentland's book, *Honest Signals: How They Shape Our World.*

56. Pentland, *Honest Signals*, 30.

57. Jones, *Intensity*, 152, citing Whitehead.

CHAPTER FOUR

1. Jordan Crandall, "Geospatialization of Calculative Operations: Tracking,
Sensing, and Megacities," *Theory, Culture and Society* 27 (November 2010): 68–
90, here, 75.

2. Crandall, "Geospatialization," 87.

3. Matteo Pasquinelli, "Google's PageRank Algorithm: A Diagram of the
Cognitive Capitalism and the Rentier of the Common Intellect," available at http://
matteopasquinelli.com/docs/Pasquinelli_PageRank.pdf, accessed, January 15,
2014.

4. Thrift, *Non-Representational Theory*, 36–37.

5. Éric Sadin, *La société de l'anticipation* (Paris: Éditions inculte, 2011), 43–44.

6. For example, Walter Sinnott-Armstrong, "Lessons from Libet," in *Conscious
Will and Responsibility*, ed. W. Sinnott-Armstrong and L. Nadel (New York: Ox-
ford University Press, 2010).

7. Incidentally, this is also why Stiegler's resurrection of Husserl's model for
contemporary media culture misses what is most central: Stiegler doesn't grapple
with the shift in scope, the extreme narrowing, of the operational present that is

centrally at stake in twenty-first-century media. For a further development of this argument, see my essay, "Technics Beyond the Temporal Object," *New Formations*, 2013.

8. On this issue, see my chapter, "The Primacy of Sensation," in *Theory Aside*.

9. Stiegler develops his notion of the politics of memory in his series *Technics and Time* of which three volumes to date have appeared.

10. Sadin, *La société de l'anticipation*, 13.

11. Sadin, *La société de l'anticipation*, 34.

12. In *Technics and Time, 1: The Fault of Epimetheus*, Stiegler explores the evolutionary role of technics via the figure of "epiphylogenesis," or the exteriorization of life by means other than life. Epiphylogenesis constitutes a form of non-genetic, techno-cultural evolution.

13. William James, *A Pluralistic Universe* (Cambridge, MA: Harvard University Press, 1977), 72.

14. Sadin, *La société de l'anticipation*, 30.

15. Thrift, "Pass It On," 93, emphasis added.

16. Whitehead, *Process and Reality*, 27, last emphasis added.

17. Jones, *Intensity*, 130.

18. Jones, *Intensity*, 131, emphasis added.

19. Tom Cheshire, "The News Forecast: Can You Predict the Future by Mining Millions of Web Pages for Data?," *Wired UK*, November 10, 2011, available at http://:www.wired.co.uk/magazine/archive/2011/12/features/the-news-forecast, emphases added, accessed March 14, 2012.

20. In the present context, I use the term "mental" in its received philosophical meaning, to designate a domain that corresponds to the activity of minds. Mental content here is equivalent to the Husserlian *noema*, that is, a content of consciousness. This sense of the mental must be kept separate from Whitehead's regrounding of the mental as the correlate of the physical in his explanation of the operation of prehension: for Whitehead—and here he stands in total opposition to the philosophical tradition—every occasion, no matter how primitive, has both a physical and a mental aspect.

21. Whitehead, *Process and Reality*, 27.

22. Whitehead, *Process and Reality*, 66.

23. In his analysis of data-mining, Oscar Gandy Jr. expresses its constitutive past-orientedness clearly and succinctly: "The application of data-mining techniques for predictive purposes uses data gathered in the past in order to generate descriptions about events that may occur in the future." ("Data Mining, Surveillance, and Discrimination in the Post-9/11 Environment," in *The New Politics of Surveillance and Visibility*, ed. K. Haggerty and R. Ericson [Toronto: University of Toronto Press, 2007]), 169–70.

24. Whitehead, *Process and Reality*, 72, emphasis added.

25. Nigel Thrift, *Non-Representational Theory: Space, Politics, Affect* (London: Routledge, 2007), 37.

26. Thrift, *Non-Representational Theory*, 37–38.

27. Catherine Malabou, *What We Should Do with Our Brain*, tr. S. Rand (New York: Fordham University Press, 2004).

28. Thrift, "Pass It On," 91.

29. Thrift, "Pass It On," 95, emphasis added.

30. Thrift, "Pass It On," 92.

31. Thrift, "Pass It On," 92.

32. Thrift, "Pass It On," 92.

33. Thrift, *Non-Representational Theory*, 186–87.

34. Indeed, despite a series of gestures toward the technical infrastructure of this new structure of attention—Thrift invokes the "growth of new forms of calculation in sensory registers " and the "advent of a whole series of technologies, small spaces and times, upon which affect thrives and out of which it is often constituted"—he fails even to mention the conflict between phenomenological experience and the technical mining and analysis of sensory and perceptual data that comes to the fore in his 2008 article.

35. Henning Schmidgen, "Lecture in the Mellon Sawyer Seminar on Phenomenology between Mind and Media," Duke University, April 19, 2012, audiofile available at http://phenomenologymindsmedia.wordpress.com/. See also Schmidgen, "The Donders Machine: Matter, Signs, and Time in a Physiological Experiment, ca. 1865," *Configurations* 13 (2005): 211–56.

36. Schmidgen, "Lecture."

37. The media theoretical expert on Helmholtz is, without any doubt, Henning Schmidgen. See his recent and forthcoming studies: *Die Helmholtz-Kurven: Auf der Spur der verlorenen Zeit* (Berlin: Merve, 2009), translation from Fordham University Press (*The Helmholtz-Curves: Tracing Lost Time*, tr. N. Schott), forthcoming, 2014, and especially, *Hirn und Zeit: Die Geschichte eines Experiments, 1800–1950* (Berlin: Matthes und Seitz, 2014). See also the earlier, but also very interesting work of Timothy Lenoir: for instance, "Helmholtz and the Materialities of Communication," *OSIRIS* 9 (1994): 185–207; "Operationalizing Kant: Manifolds, Models, and Mathematics in Helmholtz's Theories of Perception," in *The Kantian Legacy in Nineteenth-Century Science*, ed. M. Friedman and A. Nordmann (Cambridge, MA: MIT Press, 2006); and "The Politics of Vision: Optics, Painting, and Ideology in Germany, 1845–95," in Lenoir, *Instituting Science: The Cultural Production of Scientific Disciplines* (Stanford, CA: Stanford University Press, 1997).

38. See my *Embodying Technesis: Technology beyond Writing*, chapters 3 and 4, for a discussion of these concepts of memory.

39. Schmidgen, "Lecture."

40. Jones, *Intensity*, 131.

41. Steve Goodman, *Sonic Warfare: Sound, Affect, and the Ecology of Fear* (Cambridge, MA: MIT Press, 2010), 79.

42. Goodman, *Sonic Warfare*, 95.

43. Goodman, *Sonic Warfare*, 82.

44. Goodman, *Sonic Warfare*, 83.

45. Goodman, *Sonic Warfare*, 97, emphasis added. Considered closely, Goodman's account of Whitehead in this passage seems to combine elements of two different and almost certainly incompatible interpretations. On the one hand, there is the argument, akin to the position of William Christian, that actual entities atomize (and thereby *produce*) the continuum by selecting specific eternal objects, and that this atomization is what renders the pure potential of mere extension the

real potential of the extensive continuum. ("The continuum is not pregiven but exists only in the spatiotemporal gaps between actual occasions. Rather than an underlying continual invariant, each actual entity produces the continuum for itself from the angle of its own occurrence.") On the other hand, there is the metaphysically bolder claim, or rather suggestion, akin to Nobo's position, that the extensive continuum furnishes a general scheme of relatedness in which actual entities can come to be. ("Whitehead's notion of the extensive continuum undoes the split between space and time. It expresses a general scheme of relatedness between actual entities in the actual world. More than that, Whitehead insists that the extensive continuum is, above all, a potential for actual relatedness.")

46. Nobo, *Whitehead's Metaphysics*, 205.

47. Whitehead, *Process and Reality*, 66.

48. Whitehead, *Process and Reality*, 80, cited in Nobo, *Whitehead's Metaphysics*, 218.

49. Nobo, *Whitehead's Metaphysics*, 218.

50. Whitehead, *Process and Reality*, 66, emphasis added.

51. Nobo, *Whitehead's Metaphysics*, 218.

52. "These or similar passages" refers to the passage just cited from Whitehead as well as the passage immediately following: "This extensive continuum is 'real' because it expresses a fact derived from the actual world and concerning the contemporary actual world" (*Process and Reality*, 66, cited in Nobo, *Whitehead's Metaphysics*, 218). Nobo, *Whitehead's Metaphysics*, 218.

53. Goodman, *Sonic Warfare*, 98.

54. Hamrick and Van der Veken, *Nature and Logos*, 217.

55. On this orthodox account, exemplified by William Christian, eternal objects are required so that the subjective forms of feeling that are repeated in new concrescences can be repeated in the consequent actual entity: "In this way," suggests Christian, "Whitehead's theory of influence requires the existence of entities which can be multiply located, as actual occasions cannot. Their function, as he puts it, is relational. Further, since there are no *a priori* restrictions on the influence one actual occasion may have on another, any such entity must be such that it *might*, abstractly speaking, be realized in *any* instance of transition. Such entities therefore must be timeless in their mode of existence and indeterminate as to their physical realization. That is to say they must be pure potentials" (William Christian, *An Interpretation of Whitehead's Metaphysics* (New Haven, CT: Yale University Press, 1967), 217. What Christian's position boils down to—and here it can stand for a host of similar interpretations—is that actual entities participate in other actual entities through the prehension of eternal objects; and the error of this position, from the standpoint of the perspective I have been developing here, is precisely that it constrains the operation of prehension, and thus the role of the ingression of actual entities in prehension, to actual entities *qua* concrescing agents.

56. Nobo, *Whitehead's Metaphysics*, 220, emphasis added.

57. Nobo, *Whitehead's Metaphysics*, 270.

58. Nobo, *Whitehead's Metaphysics*, 272, first emphasis added.

59. Nobo, *Whitehead's Metaphysics*, 273.

60. Nobo, *Whitehead's Metaphysics*, 217, emphasis added.

61. Goodman, *Sonic Warfare*, 97.

62. In this respect, there seems to be a fallacy at the heart of Goodman's claim that because "rhythm proper cannot be perceived purely through the five senses," it is "crucially transsensory or even nonsensuous." This fallacy, which we might call the "fallacy of misplaced sensation," occurs when Goodman (here following Whitehead and those interpreters who embrace causal efficacy as nonsensuous perception, e.g., Manning, Massumi, and Shaviro) recurs to the very definition of sensation (sense perception) that Whitehead's expanded conception of perception would seem to discredit. If sense perception (presentational immediacy) involves a reduction of perception (causal efficacy), it stands to reason that it also involves a reduction of sensation itself; otherwise put, once we abandon the correlation of sensation with the five senses and with sense organs, sensation is liberated to function as a general medium of worldliness, a point made in quite different but equally crucial ways by Merleau-Ponty's later work and by the ecological psychology of James Gibson. In sum, and as I put it earlier, causal efficacy is only nonsensuous *from the standpoint of the perceptual or concrescing subject*; from the standpoint of the vibratory continuum, by contrast, all contrastive agency, all intensity, is irreducibly sensuous.

63. Nobo, *Whitehead's Metaphysics*, 309, first emphases added.

64. Judith Jones, *Intensity*, 130–31, emphasis added. See also Jones, 112: "The occurrence of transcendence of one entity by another is simultaneous with the completion of the entity superceded. This is the essence of 'vibratory' existence, to which I have given the label 'ecstatic' so as to be expressive of the ontological unity of all of the 'vibrations' referable to the intensity of 'an' actuality."

65. Such an understanding resonates with Whitehead's own stated desire to conform his philosophy of the organism to the latest discoveries of science. Thus, when he explores the vibratory basis of the physical world, his point is both to criticize any "materialist concept" that postulates some minimal substance as "ultimate actual entity" and also to flesh out his own conception of the real potentiality of the spatiotemporal, that is, vibratory continuum:

> The atom is only explicable as a society with activities involving rhythms with their definite periods. Again the concept has shifted its application: protons and electrons were conceived as materialistic electric charges whose activities could be construed as locomotive adventures. We are now approaching the limits of any reasonable certainty in our scientific knowledge; but again there is evidence that the concept may be mistaken. The mysterious quanta of energy have made their appearance, derived, as it would seem, from the recesses of protons, or of electrons. Still worse for the concept, these quanta seem to dissolve into the vibrations of light. Also the material of the stars seems to be wasting itself in the production of the vibrations. Further, the quanta of energy are associated by a simple law with the periodic rhythms which we detect in the molecules. Thus the quanta are, themselves, in their own nature, somehow vibratory; but they emanate from the

protons and electrons. Thus there is every reason to believe that rhythmic periods cannot be dissociated from the protonic and electronic entities. (Whitehead, *Process and Reality*, 78–79)

66. Jones, *Intensity*, 148.

67. Jones, *Intensity*, 84.

68. Nobo, *Whitehead's Metaphysics*, 308; Whitehead, *Process and Reality*, 65. Nobo likens his understanding of the sensitivity of the matrix to what Whitehead called *envisagement* or taking-into-account:

> Attained actualities can function as efficient causes of a new occasion only if their superjective existence is taken into account by the macroscopic process begetting the dative phase of the new occasion. More generally, the universe as a whole—including its eternal objects and its extensiveness, as well as its actualities—can be involved in the becoming of a new occasion only if it is taken into account by the transcendent creative activity begetting the new occasions dative phase. In other words, the transition from newly settled universe to newly emergent occasion presupposes that an individualizing manifestation of the eternal creativity is not to be understood as belonging to, or as being part of, the new occasion's own subjective experience. For the occasion's subjective experience presupposes the existence of the occasion's dative phase, and the dative phase itself presupposes, and results from, the transcendent creativity's taking into account of a newly completed state of the universe. Therefore, the notion of *taking into account* must be construed as signifying an essential aspect of the universe's extenso-creative or existential matrix—the aspect whereby each transcendent, or individualizing, manifestation of the universe's creativeness is determined, limited, and enabled by the state of the universe relative to that manifestation. (308)

CONCLUSION

1. Jordan Crandall, "Performance Interface for *Gatherings/Gatherings* Player," download available at http://jordancrandall.com/gatherings/index.html. *Gatherings* was awarded the 2011 Vilém Flusser Theory Award for outstanding theory- and research-based digital arts practice, by the Transmediale Festival in collaboration with the Vilém Flusser Archive at the University of the Arts, Berlin.

2. Jordan Crandall, "Summary of *Gatherings*," available at http://jordancrandall .com/gatherings/index.html.

3. In this sense, the feed-forward structure of consciousness introduces a radicalization of Stiegler's understanding of tertiary retention as technical memories that are not lived by consciousness. What is, in Stiegler, a limitation due to consciousness's finitude—the fact that it can only live a small amount of content— becomes here a limitation of capacity: human consciousness can *never* live the

contents or data of sensibility because these latter occur at levels of experience to which consciousness has no direct access.

4. Crandall, "Summary."

5. Crandall, "Summary."

6. Crandall, "Summary."

7. Crandall, "Summary."

8. Crandall, "Performance Interface," Section 1.5.

9. Crandall, "Performance Interface," Sections 2.4, 3.1, 2.4.

10. Crandall, "Performance Interface," Section 1.8.

11. See Daniel Stern, *The Interpersonal World of the Infant* (New York: Basic Books, 2000), especially the chapter on the affective self.

12. Crandall, "Performance Interface," Section 1.7.

13. Renaud Barbaras, "Les trois sens de la chair: Sur une impasse de l'ontologie de Merleau-Ponty," *Chiasmi International* 10 (2008): 19–32, here 23.

14. Maurice Merleau-Ponty, *The Visible and the Invisible*, cited in Barbaras, "Les trois sens de la chair," 27.

15. Barbaras, "Les trois sens de la chair," 27. Incidentally, Barbaras raises the very same objection against Jan Patočka's asubjective phenomenology of movement: just as Merleau-Ponty's desire to develop an ontological monism of the flesh leads him to abandon phenomenology, so too does Patočka's desire for an cosmological monism of movement lead him to compromise the singularity of *Dasein*. Despite whatever advances Patočka makes in relation to Merleau-Ponty, as least as Barbaras sees it, he too abandons phenomenology in the end:

> But in characterizing *Dasein* by a movement in which the essence of all worldly movement becomes apparent, does not Patočka engage phenomenology on a path toward cosmological monism in which the singularity of *Dasein*'s mode of being (and consequently the very possibility of correlation) would be lost? . . . Everything occurs as if, in clarifying *Dasein*'s mode of being, in justifying fully its difference in relation to the *Vorhandenheit*, Patočka found himself forced to restore an ontological continuity on another level, a level discovered by means of the analysis of movement of a cosmology. Determining *Dasein*'s ultimate sense of being as movement of realization compromises its unicity at the very moment in which *its singularity* is fully revealed, as if a rigorous determination of the subject of the manifestation's sense of being had as its counterpart a questioning of the tear inherent in the correlation—as if, therefore, we abandoned phenomenology at the very moment in which we succeeded in establishing its possibility. (Renaud Barbaras, *Desire and Distance: Introduction to a Phenomenology of Perception*, tr. P. B. Milan [Stanford, CA: Stanford University Press, 2006], 149–50)

16. Barbaras, "Les trois sens de la chair," 26, emphasis added.

17. Barbaras, "Les trois sens de la chair," 26–27.

18. Hamrick and Van der Veken, *Nature and Logos*, 200, emphasis modified.

19. See Hansen, "Ubiquitous Sensation," 63–88.

20. Barbaras, "Les trois sens de la chair," 26.

21. Hamrick and Van der Veken, *Nature and Logos*, 189.

22. In Barbaras's paraphrase, Barbaras, "Les trois sens de la chair," 21.

Index

absolute constituting time-consciousness, 65, 79. *See also* time-consciousness

actual entity, Whitehead's definition of, 92; experiential power of, 110; speculative withdrawal of, 122, 123; two-sidedness of, 92, 93, 163, 280, 281

actualities-in-attainment, 13, 85, 86, 90, 91–94, 96, 97, 99, 100, 107, 108, 110, 113, 124, 129, 130, 143, 163, 164 168–70, 176–78, 225, 249, 264, 278, 280, 283

actuality, 28, 30, 62; subordinate to potentiality, 229; vibratory character of, 205, 248

Adventures of Ideas (Whitehead), 19, 115, 117, 121

affect, 79, 289

affective anticipation, 189, 258

affectivity, 20, 95, 195, 222

affirmative character of Whitehead criticism, 21

Allan, George, 171

Alta Vista, 206

analog sound-recording technology, 272

anarchival recording, real-time operation of, 42

anarchive, 41

ancestral, 15

anthropocentrism, 12

antihumanism, 16, 18

apparatus, 75, 77, 78

appearance, autonomy of, 67

appetition, 108, 109

archive, 41, 42

artificial memory, 71

asubjective phenomenology, 96; asubjective phenomenology of experience, 118; asubjective phenomenology of manifestation, 67, 68; asubjective phenomenology of movement, 293; asubjective phenomenology of sensibility, 111

atmospheric media, 3

atomization of the continuum, 289

attained actualities, 13, 62, 70, 84–87, 90, 92–95, 96, 99–101, 108, 109, 112, 113,